Crafting h[...] spells!

Casebook confessions of the Rogue Hypnotist!

By the Rogue Hypnotist.

Disclaimer: the Rogue Hypnotist accepts no legal liability for the use or misuse of the information contained in this book. People who are not qualified professionals use the information at their own risk. This book is intended for entertainment and educational purposes only. Only the hypnosis scripts, deepeners etc. contained within are for your personal or public use copyright free. They may not be resold.

Note: British English spelling and punctuation is used throughout. What appears as 'bad grammar' is often hypnotic language. Some of the very long scripts in the kindle version have been compressed in formatting style but not in content to make this book affordable for all.

Also available on Amazon in the Rogue Hypnotist series:

'*How to hypnotise anyone!*' *(Amazon.com and Amazon.co.uk no 1 bestseller in hypnosis titles. For over a year!)*

'*Mastering hypnotic language!*' *(Amazon.com and Amazon.co.uk no 2 bestseller in hypnosis titles.)*

'*Powerful hypnosis!*' *(Highest rating Amazon.com no 3 and Amazon.co.uk no 2 and Amazon.de no 1 bestseller in hypnosis titles.)*

'*Forbidden hypnotic secrets!*' *(Highest rating Amazon.com no 1 and Amazon.co.uk no 1 bestseller in hypnosis titles.)*

'*Wizards of trance!*' *(Highest rating Amazon.com no 1 and Amazon.co.uk no 1 bestseller in hypnosis titles.)*

'*Escaping cultural hypnosis!*' *(Highest rating Amazon.com no 1 and Amazon.co.uk no 1 bestseller in hypnosis titles.)*

CONTENTS

ACKNOWLEDGMENTS

I would like to sincerely thank Amazon and Create Space for allowing the 'Rogue Hypnotist project' to become a reality.

A welcome warning to the curious...

This book, like my others, is for those who want to be more than an 'average' hypnotist. Why would you aim for mediocrity? What you do with the information is down to your integrity, intelligence, adaptability and imagination. A rich tapestry of the applications of hypnotic suggestion follows. For those who like to think beyond the obvious: enter here...

The 'therapy establishment' (so-called), the quacks and gurus don't like my books. Some of the things I write about are controversial. The general public internationally like them very much. The second rate therapists etc. don't like my highly successful books because they can't cure people in an hour of anything! I can. I have. What I teach threatens their position: the fact that you are reading this means some part of you is rebelling against the b*llsh*it. That's a good place to start. If you read my books you will not be in Kansas anymore Toto! They say, 'You can't handle the truth!' I say you can...

By the way my books are written to be accessible to <u>everyone,</u> not just hypno-nerds, professional hypnotists and

hypnotherapists etc. *I am aiming to popularise hypnosis as an interesting topic for the general public. I make no apologies for doing so.* <u>*Hypnosis needs to lose its fake aura of mystery fast! That will come through a simple understanding of what is not at all complicated.*</u>

- As a hypnotist/enthusiast etc. do you want to learn what is real and works?

- Do you want to CURE people fast or let them linger in unnecessary suffering because it makes you more money?

- Would you rather learn what fits your existing beliefs because you feel comfortably incompetent there?

- This book isn't just about hypnotherapy, oh no: you are going to learn things about applications of hypnosis and persuasion that you simply will not find anywhere else. *What's more, I'm practically giving it all away for nothing.* We may put some con men and women out of business. I'll live with that side effect.

- You have been conditioned to think in a linear fashion. That is a problem. Things that appear disconnected are connected you know...Are you capable of putting it all together? Really?

Why you should read my sixth book in the Rogue Hypnotist series!

By some total fluke that was completely unintentional I have written not 1, 2 or 3, 4, 5 6 but 7 bestselling, internationally bestselling books on NLP (my own twist on the few bits of it that work) and hypnosis. They top the charts on Amazon worldwide. *This was a complete accident.* My first book, 'How to hypnotise anyone' has been a bestseller for over 12 months at time of publishing the paperback version of this title. I am a top NLP and hypnosis expert from the UK who remains incognito! I am giving away my knowledge for a bargain price. These 7 books contain more practical knowledge on hypnosis than any other course I ever attended in order to become a qualified professional – read them and you will have a large base of field work tested knowledge that you can use as you see fit. Oh by the way I use lots of humour which makes the read more enjoyable and helps you learn easier!

IN this book you are getting the equivalent of at least 6 books in one! And note that this book IS part of a series but does stand alone, like all the rest do.

The biggest reason why you should read this book is that it is already spawning a whole host of rip off artists and sad sack competitors creating fake accounts to attack me! That to me is the greatest, funniest compliment – if you're being plagiarised and annoying the half-witted second raters, you must be doing something right!

All hypnotist's need a BIG tool kit...if you'll pardon my French!

I have a readership base which clearly likes what I have to offer and it seems to be only growing. This is quite humbling really. Many people have left me very kind reviews on Amazon and Goodreads for which I am incredibly grateful. The feedback is often helpful. It is now time to teach those who want to know how to use hypnosis for good.

Once you've entranced folks you need to know how to use just the right 'spells' to cure them: if cure is what they seek. In tone and content this book is similar though more advanced and in depth to my 3rd book, 'Powerful hypnosis' and adds some useful info to similar topics raised in parts of book 4, 'Forbidden hypnotic secrets' and book 5, 'Wizards of trance'. Shall we?

Introduction: casebook studies of real hypnosis and hypnotherapy in action.

All hypnotists need a 'spellbook' to be successful. A spellbook is the toolkit that allows any hypnotist to get results. This book teaches you which 'spells' work!

This latest book in the Rogue Hypnotist series is seemingly about specifically how to do 'hypnotherapy' and how to create pleasure states in anyone, which pretty much amounts to the same thing – it's actually about my own system of creating suggestions and interventions etc. which I call **'Directly-Indirect Hypnosis (DIH)'.** In part it is taken from actual interactions with clients in a hypnotherapeutic practice. No confidentiality will be violated – all names and personnel details have been changed to protect the innocent; including mine! It will tell you how to run a hypnotherapeutic practice if you don't already know. It will provide you with 'transcripts' of how I help people 'self-cure' themselves of a great many psychological health problems. It will be thorough, comprehensive and contain full scripts and successful 'patterns of change' templates. My promise to you is that at the conclusion of this book you will have...

1. A full understanding of what a hypnotist/therapist does.

2. A greater understanding of how the human mind works and responds to 'therapy'.

3. An ability to use this knowledge to help others if you so choose.

But there's more! I wrote this because new clients are always asking,

'What are you going to do?'

This book will amply explain that, with apples on top. Hypnosis is a fascinating subject. Although hypnosis and NLP are now used in many areas of public life: politics, education, 'recreational hypnosis' (erotic hypnosis), 'seduction', sales and marketing, its finest and 'noblest' application will always be as a drug free cure for a wide range of health problems.

This book will provide you with details about what you can expect from your clients. After all, who becomes a hypnotherapy client? Crazy people! Right? Wrong. They are 'ordinary' people just like you.

As I am the Rogue Hypnotist this isn't going to be a dull, dry academic affair that is so badly written and dehumanised that only an individual with a masochistic streak will sit through a reading on pain of exam failure. Oh no – this is a hypnotist's casebook with the juicy bits left in. **There is no such thing as a standardised hypnosis cure-all formula.** People are not statistics. Hypnosis treats the unique individual who sits at the other side of the 'therapy room' like no other. A hypnotist uses words. Just words. But in order to do so, like all wizards, like all magicians, he or she needs a spell-book. Words must be said in a certain way, in a certain order, certain 'rituals' must be followed. What follows is a hypnotist's spellbook.

But we are covering more here than just 'therapy' whatever that means. What else will you find? What hypno-spells will you learn to cast?

- I will provide full scripts and explanations of how to do 'blissnosis' in a variety of pleasure inducing ways. Most of your clients are going to be bloody miserable — my spells will cheer them up.

- You will learn by osmosis how to create **directly indirect** suggestions.

- I will also teach you the 'cold reading formula' that will enable you to convince anyone that you have 'psychic powers'. I'll teach you how to create cold reading 'probes' by basing your questions on missing human needs.

- The instant hypnosis level 2, 8 step formula will be revealed for use in stage hypnosis, hypno-tricks and hypnotherapy.

- How to gain cross-cultural rapport by using direct and indirect communication styles at will.

- I'll show you how easy it is to induce hypnosis using the 'utilisation' principle alone.

- We will examine various diverse uses of 'authoritarian hypnosis'. I will explain what authoritarian hypnosis is and why it is at best clumsy.

- I will expose 'erotic hypnosis' and what it is. I will include a few spells to spice things up hypnotically if you so choose with a person who might appreciate such things. *I will also point out its potential dangers – no one else will.*

- I will expose 'hypnosis' in religion. Or at least start to in more depth.

- I will give you more ways of using **SSC – 'Subconscious Symbology Communications'.** These can be used to treat lots of unwanted feelings states, elicit good ones and carry out low-level trauma removal, e.g. what we call 'phobias'.

- I'll give you some tips of how to turn your hypno-skills into hard cash!

- I provide 10+ proven tricks to fend off unwanted persuasion.

- I will teach you how to make anyone 'hypnotically happy'. Sound like a good deal?

- We will be examining two more 'Trance Wizards' that I couldn't fit into my last book - Dr. George Estabrooks and Dr. Ernset Dichter.

- You will learn how to create 'hypnotic robots'. And much more.

- Like to help a sportsman or woman enhance mental toughness and enter the zone? Read on Padwan.

Ready to peek into my private grimoire my young padawans? Then let's begin...

Case studies part 1: principles of hypnotic success.

How do you get hypnosis clients?

You did the courses, paid the fees, attended the lectures, bought those home study courses and got those silly pieces of paper called certificates! You sit there waiting for hypnosis clients and...no bugger/bum phones. You sweat, panic – where did I go wrong? I know all this stuff and...

Take a chill pill.

To interact with any human you must communicate to them that you exist! You must get their attention. How are you going to do that? Obviously you need to advertise. The best form of advertising is? No-budget word of mouth. When you get word of mouth advertising up and running your client base will hugely increase. In fact in my experience I can pinpoint this to one summer, when I was babysitting my niece and nephew. We were out in a park on a beautiful sunny day and my mobile phone/cell phone would not stop ringing. I had eight clients in one day booked! That was more than my first year of practice combined! But how do you get to the word of mouth stage?

You think it's by putting ads/commercials in the paper right? Wrong! Wrong big time with knobs on top! Local newspapers are money pits. They drink your money away like a vampire thirsting for blood. Look at it this way: local newspaper advertising does work if you are 'somebody', if you are a local celebrity or an international one then that form of advertising will work – you are known, your prestige will sell you. If you are just a common all garden hypnotist who isn't known from Adam, you must start from the bottom up and build. What was the best method I found (at least at first) to build a client base from? Direct marketing. Or in normal lingo – junk mail. Get your walking boots on boys and girls! Or get someone to deliver masses of leaflets/flyers (US) for you. For some reason an advertising leaflet landing on someone's doorstep attracts clients like nothing else. **Remember you are starting to 'hypnotise' someone at your first point of contact with them.** You sales flyer should be simple:

- It should avoid marketing gimmicks.

- It should list a wide variety of the specific problems you can solve.

- It should indirectly reveal your attitude and personality.

- It should point out your qualifications somewhere: in small print.

- It should clearly state the price of a session and your 'unique selling point'.

Other marketing methods are:

Street hypnosis marketing: Perform displays of your hypnosis powers in your local shopping mall etc. Don't do serious therapy, just hypno-tricks, street hypnosis, nail biting cures: this will appeal to the more extravert 'showman' type hypno-bums! Introverts interested in 'serious therapy' won't go this way and that's fine. I didn't use this method but some do and they are very successful. **A powerful testimonial of your hypnotic abilities is a public demonstration of them;** it also says, 'I am so confident in my hypnotic powers that I can approach random strangers, whack them into trance fast and 'cure' them, stick their hand to a lamppost etc.' If you go this way make sure you have plenty of your business cards handy. People love 'street magic' and that kind of thing. EVERYONE is curious about hypnosis whether they think it's a scam or not. Use that curiosity in your favour. Look, people's lives are humdrum and dull. That's the system. You're giving them some free entertainment as they go about their shopping etc. will put a smile on their face; they'll remember you and because you gave them a freebie they will most likely want to return the favour (influence pattern of reciprocity – see book 5, 'Wizards of trance'.) You might stick someone's hands together and they tell all their smoker friends about you. You then start building a word of mouth advertising base that sells you at zero cost. If you want to be a famous hypnotist this is a good way to start.

Why I don't ask for doctor's referrals but you can.

Let me just come right out and say it: *I have no respect for the medical profession whatsoever.* I think they are the leech quacks of our day. I have never asked local doctors to refer clients to me. Hypnotherapy and drug treatments are polar opposites. Doctors are not at the top of some imaginary hierarchy of healing: I don't need my success rate validated by a quack. You can do it if you like, it will get you clients if you hit it off with a particular doctor BUT expect to be treated as though you are low down on the totem pole; you know, the way they treat nurses etc. Ask yourself this: how many doctors have you known CURE anything? Precisely. I have seen too many clients diagnosed with 'depression' who were just stressed to have any time for such arrogant, pompous buffoons.

Internet marketing: Now it isn't enough to have a good looking website and most people's are lousy, you must deftly and briefly display to any potential customer that...

A. You are qualified.

B. You know what you are doing.

C. Most importantly *you must 'sell' your theory of mind and therapy AND yourself as a unique individual* to attract customers.

Finding your unique selling point.

As with all marketing it can help to have a unique selling point (USP). This is simply what makes you stand out from 'Joe Bloggs' as they say in England. So why are you different and for that matter better than other hypnotists? Are you cheaper? Quicker? Smellier? I mean honestly think about it, why should some random suffering person come to see you? What do you have to offer that the long line of other hypnotists don't?

My unique selling point was and is that I can pretty much guarantee a 'cure' in 1, 1 hour session 99.9% of the time with basic problems; even when all I knew how to treat was stopping smoking, weight loss, confidence boosting and phobia removal. I can actually treat some people in just 15 minutes but this is so bold a claim to make that most people, especially in England simply won't believe you. I was asked by a sales representative from the company that took over Yellow Pages in the UK, preposterously called 'Hibu', what my USP was. I simply replied,

'I can cure people in one hour.'

'That's a bold claim!' he responded somewhat taken aback.

'I know,' I replied. I was just stating a humdrum fact actually.

Take note: just because I can help people so fast doesn't make things all milk and honey. I am so effective that in order to get new clients I must constantly find ways to attract new customers. You might not want to adopt my UPS – there are many people willing to pay for a 4 session weight loss cure when only 1 is required. You have to earn a living. The main task for the hypnotic based business is: how do I make money ethically? Often there are other ways other than just meeting real people. You can use the Internet to – sell online hypnosis products. Next, how to design a good hypno-website...

Hypno-website musts.

- Make it look **highly professional and stylish.**

- **Steal ideas** from other hypnotist's websites. Change them so much they become original.

- Have a great, short **brand name.**

- Have a **great logo** that symbolises your hypno-company.

- Litter it with **testimonials.**

- Have a **welcome section** in which you tell your prospective clients in as brief as possible a way, what you do and who you are.

- Tell them briefly and in no uncertain terms **what problems you can help them solve** with hypnosis.

- **Display your knowledge of hypnosis and the mind** subtly to create client confidence in you.

- Have **stylish artwork** that appeals predominately to women (the ladies will make up the bulk of your clients) but avoid crappy 'motivational' stock images etc. *Find images that symbolise problems.*

- You need at least 4 sections: 1. **Home -** greet and let them know what you know and do. 2. **About -** who you are – qualifications, training, therapy philosophy etc. etc. Don't put up a full C.V – stay on message. 3. **Map -** so they can find you – decide whether to add your home address or not; personal safety is paramount. Note: some online safety/consumer watchdog websites warn people to avoid businesses with no listed address. 4. **Contact -** Phone number, email etc.

- Make sure your website can be **accessed on multiple technological platforms** – iPhones, PCs you name it. My brother is the best CGI animator in the world – he designed mine.

- On the contact page tell them exactly **how much you want to be paid.** Do you take cheques etc.? I only take cash.

- The website should be designed to **lead the person to the contact page.**

- Keep it **simple, clean and uncluttered.**

Now, let's talk about...

Selling online hypnosis products: THE best way to make money as a hypnotist, the most lucrative, the one path that could make you a millionaire hypnotist is to sell products online. You can sell books, self-help CDs, downloadable mp3s, DVD training courses etc. You will need to find an online identity and persona that connects with a potential audience. You may choose to specialise in a particular 'genre', say getting rid of phobias or you may choose to cast a wider net. But to get to this stage you need experience. You need real world clients to test your weird and whacky methodologies upon. And during that process you must get regular and repeated results for clients. Again...

IF YOU WANT TO BE A MILLIONAIRE HYPNOTIST GO THIS ROUTE! The Internet is in its 'Wild West' phase: grab your patch of land!

Other ways of attracting interest that have worked: You can become famous. This will guarantee you a client base without question.

I never wanted to become a famous hypnotist, some really do and that's fine – you will make a bundle of loot that way. You will need an 'image' – at best this will be you simply being you. Few people become famous imitators. Again we are getting back to the unique selling point. This used to be called charm, charisma, talent.

You can go onto local radio shows and talk about your business to the host. You can use a stage hypnosis show to get crowds in and advertise your hypnotherapy business. Make sure you have products available for them to buy at the show. **NOTE: if you can _demonstrate competence_ in front of a camera, on a stage or other media outlet you will reach a big or bigger audience than would otherwise be possible.** Even local newspapers are potential publicity avenues. They are such dull little affairs that the hacks who write for them are dying for some razzmatazz. If you are a male hypnotist you can hire a cute woman, say a busty professional model and hypnotise her to do various things – act like a zombie etc. This will get you attention. I am afraid what gets attention is not necessarily the most ethical thing. But people are people and human nature does not change.

Other people go a more 'respectable' route and tout themselves as great and wise healers. You could pretend to invent a new system of 'psychotherapy' and sell it: that has been done countless times. You can send a letter to local doctors and get referrals. I knew one top NLP practitioner in the UK who is friends with Richard Bandler – he fuels his busy practice by running training courses in NLP specifically aimed at doctors and others working in the British NHS (National Health Service). Clearly he is going to be the first person the quacks think of when sending patients for help.

You can just build up a successful business over time. It takes hard work, a terrible first year that must be survived and then something happens. You start getting phone calls. Flyer drops can take 2 years to get results. You will get clients who have sat on your advert, nervously twiddling their thumbs for the right moment to call you. The best clients are what I call **'super-connectors'**. A super-connector is so happy with what you did for them that they tell everybody about you. I had one woman who no joke must have gotten me over 50 clients simply by referring people to me because I changed her life for the better. Gratitude is your best seller by far. Sometimes an ad will tap into a gaggle of smokers or weight loss clients.

This section is really for the hopeful hypnotist: the person just qualified or thinking of entering the profession one way or another. ***To attract customers ask: what do people NEED?*** And then give it to them. Quite simple. In an upcoming section I will give an example of a Rogue Hypnotist casebook study. It is an edited interview transcript with a lady who wanted to stop using weed, marijuana, cannabis – DOPE!

Fees – how much do you charge real world clients?

Charge what you are worth. When you start out and have zero experience you MIGHT have to lower your fees to attract customers. It's up to you. Just to get a flow of cash. However at some point you are doing this to make money. You are not a charity. Nothing in life is free: don't kid yourself if you live in the UK that the NHS is free. It is an incredibly expensive insurance scheme that does not pay out when you need it most. You cannot choose what type of treatment you receive on it.

I now charge £80/$134.99 to my clients per session. Most other hypnotherapists charge between £120/$202.49 and a whopping £300/$506.22 a session. A hypnotist deserves to earn a good living. If you are penniless you won't be able to help anyone. It is funny but caring people often undervalue what they do and don't want to 'rip people off'. Ask yourself with all the work you do –

'What am I genuinely worth?'

In the UK a plumber can routinely charge £90/$151.87 for fixing a small tap washer! Not bad if you can get it. A professional hypnotherapist can cure people – not manage symptoms, not 'treat' but cure. Why should you give that away for peanuts? There is a saying which isn't true but, 'If you pay peanuts you get monkeys.' When people pay a reasonable sum for help it raises their motivation to heal. It should cost enough so you can live well, get a good reputation and also state to the world, 'I am damn good at this. If you want my help you have to pay for it.' Ultimately how much you charge is down to you. Americans not being so indoctrinated with 'socialism' as everyone is in Britain will not find the idea of having some business savvy as a bad thing. The more you know about how to run a business, any business the better!

As a hypnotherapist you should expect to be earning a good 'middle class' income. For God's sake you are a trained mental health care professional. Shrinks and psycho-anal-cysts charge a fortune and can't cure anyone of anything. Getting a fat wad of cash for what you've done feels good let's be honest. Be caring but don't be a mug/pushover. A genuinely 'nice' person is a rare gem. No matter how most start off, most end up a lot nastier than when they first came into this world. Just because someone has a 'mental health problem' does not mean they have any sense of common decency or honour – in my experience a heck of a lot of people don't; especially as you move up the social food chain. ***Remember a cynical fact of life: people are more than willing to use your***

kindness against you. Especially wealthy people. An illuminating example is when I raised my fees. Only one person complained and felt hard done by. He was the richest client I had – a multimillionaire several times over. Need I say more?

The 'fee formula' is: charge people what you are worth!

With all fees you find with experience there is a 'sweet spot'.

The wealthy and fees.

Be wary about setting your fees too low. I'll tell you why: you will attract wealthy people. Know why? Here's a hidden secret of the rich: **rich people want everything for nothing.** What's more, they often get it. The rich are so well-connected and their patronage so favourably prestigious that they will get a great deal of stuff and services in life for FREE! They often do not pay in restaurants or for high fashion because the providers would rather get the advertising from the rich person's name being associated with them. If you price low and then at a later stage up your prices, the ones who complain will be your richest clients, trust me. The reason they have so much money is that they are so f**king tight/stingy. When dealing with wealthy clients think Scrooge and you won't go far wrong. In fact their ungenerous natures are often part and parcel of why they have mental health problems; unfortunately for them they never have any insight into this truth.

Why does confusion work really?

There is some kind of unnecessary mystique about 'confusion' and why it works. Confusion is hypnotic because it creates absorption: that's it! If you are confused you are temporarily trying to understand something – this absorbs your attention. Confusion linguistic, physical or otherwise works for that reason alone. Remember from my other books (if you've read them) that anything that absorbs the attention is potentially hypnotic. **All language which creates internal or external absorption is trance language. Hypnotic trance creates an artificial state of agreement.** More of this in the next book.

A new induction.

Just in case you haven't yet read my other bookies...

Quick formula for reading a hypnosis script:

- Embedded commands are highlighted. Say them with a downward command tonality. You can lean in toward a person as you emphasise that line or you can point at a person etc.

- Use a relaxing, soothing tone of voice: your tone affects the brain's neurology.

- Take your time: use a slower rhythm than normal speech.

- Squeeze the meaning from the words – say 'relaxing' as if it is!

- For full details see books 1 and 2 in my series.

I have crafted an entirely new induction for this book. It is a Progressive Muscle Relaxation variant; feel free to use as you wish: it will work with all the interventions in this book. I call it...

The stress and tension reduction induction.

Step 1: Induce hypnosis and relaxation.

'Close your eyes and just focus on your breathing...That's it...Draw all your attention to the process of breathing...Notice how you are sitting...The feeling of the socks on your feet etc....The support of that cushion...Sounds of birds outside singing and tweeting... (cars outside if it's a town.) _The sound of that plane soaring off on some relaxing destination, no doubt far away...Just pay attention to some different things, now. It can be nice to **go off on a journey** can it not...Where does your attention naturally wish to **introspect** to, **inside...now... (?)** 1. Can you visualise a fruit?_

(Note for hypnotist: with each of the next 3 tasks allow processing time – 5 secs or so. Do not say the numbers out loud!)

That's it...2. Can you imagine an appropriate noise? Ok...3. Can you smell a nice smell, inside? Lovely...4. Can you feel something soothing? Good...There is no right way for you to **experience a beautiful trance...**And so, *we will **relax each part of your body** to help you **become absorbed in hypnosis, now...**a little at a time...and each time I say the word 'relaxed,' you will automatically become ten times more 'relaxed' than you already were...each time I do...So now **focus on the feelings** in your toes and feet...Just allow all the muscles and fibres in your toes and feet to **become very deeply relaxed.** It's not hard to picture inside what that would look like...if you had X ray vision...for all those tiny muscles and tissues to **relax and soften...**to **become fascinated by the process of loosening and relaxing profoundly...**allowing yourself to **get that kind of feeling** you have when you find a way to **take it easy** after a busy day...A wave of comfort spreads so that you...**just release unwanted tension, NOW** and **feel that massaging all through you...**That's right...Imagine that this comforting, soothing process is continuing to flow pleasantly...Up and up it goes...easing away that tension you had in your lower legs...allowing you to **be deeply, restfully, cosily relaxed...**Thoughts and images may drift in and out in passing...and that's just fine...*

Wondering how that gorgeous feeling of comfort is continuing...flowing upwards...over your knees...into your hard working thighs...which can simply **remain still and calm here...***Remaining tension is unnecessary...as they* **become more deeply and hypnotically relaxed...***Notice any sensations in that place...How whatever they are allows you to* **just sink** *down limply, loose, so relaxed. Mysteriously that comfort knows how to flow upwards and ease its way at its own pace...into your torso...effortlessly flowing into your hips, tummy, lower back...letting that soothing...knowing:* **deep tranquillity, spreads...***bit by bit progressively through that body...Here and there and eventually everywhere...Your body is becoming serenely relaxed...and your mind follows suit...Your growing relaxation...that sense of it...gradually develops, changes and...flows upwards into your chest...into your upper back...Your shoulders* **letting go more...***with each out breath...***deeply...blissfully...relaxed...calm ...***Breathing away any tension you had in that spinal column...that works so hard in supporting you...giving you confident* *posture...And merely allow, merely observe that lovely sense of comfort and relaxation...As it massages its way into, throughout your neck area...Inside and out...It's not difficult to picture that...what that would look like? As all the sinews and fibres and muscles there simply...**softly, comfortably relax and recover...** The relaxing process is ongoing and deepens this state further. Soothing the neck area so nicely...It flows up the top of your head...**going deeper and deeper feeling better...**Bathing your head with wave after wave of restful comfort and soothing relaxation...Scalp...Forehead...Around the eyes and nose...The place where you speak...* (Inner and outer voice) *Your whole face soothed...Deeply, utterly, relaxed...**Tension fades away...**And you feel, really feel totally relaxed...No need to question...* (Implication? 'Conscious mind 'Shhh' now!') *The flow continues on its journey as you go off on yours...down those arms...Might feel heavier or lighter or something else nice...Hands feeling relaxation...Those fingers and their tips...**letting go of all the past stress and strain that you can only TRY to hold***

onto... Allowing that body that's always working in the best way it knows how to **rest, becoming totally...relaxed all over, now.**

This is a time for healing...Who wants anything like this? Who needs anything like this? Who anticipates anything at all but a pleasant changing process? You have now become so deeply relaxed, have you not? That **your far deeper mind has become very sensitive and receptive to what I say...**so that everything that I do say (this implies the stuff I said during our 'pre-talk' etc.) can leave a positive, deep and lasting impression there. I don't know how it remains there...Thankfully 'it' does...Certain ideas, notions that will always be for your benefit. **Every thought, feeling, belief and behaviour that I tell you of...you can experience...you will experience precisely as I tell you in your own way in your own best interests, now....**In this place and state you **feel calmer, more assured and secure** than you have in a long time and it feels good to have that sense of things, does it not?

Step 2: Relaxation symbology deepener

Using that movie generator in your mind...just visualise a relaxing place outside in nature...Notice somewhere there...there is an entrance way through an opening...in something...there somewhere...Go through that opening and **calmly** stroll into the most charming, natural oasis...Whatever the word, 'oasis' means to you...just the sight of it fills your with a sense of peace...This is your private inner sanctum...Notice the sights...colours...shapes and things vividly...It all seems so real...Any soothing sounds of nature. And just locate a location that seems just right for lying down and resting...As you lie down, you look up at that perfect sky...and you notice something relaxing heading you way...It is your symbol of **deep relaxation and hypnosis, now...**It's yours alone...It's special...Just the sight of it approaching gently...makes you **feel filled with peaceful sensations...**And as you wonder about this wondrous thing...it starts to **drift down** toward you somehow...floating down like a feather or leaf perhaps...on a pleasant breeze...And amazingly, delightfully it reaches you and **absorbs you completely,** somehow...I don't know how, you do...softly...gently...It massages your body and brain and mind and soul...**soothing and invigorating...**with a super subtle compassionate vitality and zeal that impresses you deeply...**you feel incredibly, irresistibly calm...**You feel great safety and a life-affirming energy rekindled within you...All past negativity is smoothed...away in your symbolic balm of deep, profound relaxation beyond anything you thought was possible...that relaxing symbol from your deep unconscious mind has formed a haven around you, within you...mind and body from unpleasant outside burdens of any kind...Quite invisible and it can, does and will remain where, when it need be available to you. It moves, is absorbed by your mind and body and simply eradicates former troubles and concerns...you thought you had...What feelings do you feel in response to this hypnotic reality? You **go deeper and deeper into hypnotic trance, feeling blissful...**You have a perfect feeling of peace and clarity of mind...beyond black and white thinking...Beyond the illusions of past silly fears and shrinking sized worries...Beyond old *responses to people, places, emotions and things that did once trouble...Able to handle things more than just a little, perhaps more easily than ever before when you return to waking consciousness...Knowing you can always come back here to* **recharge this deep profound relaxation and peace after a good night's sleep, every night...***And that's a nice thing to know isn't it? At just the right level your learnings and understanding made here...will remain with you. Now...'*

(Proceed as you wish Padawan.)

The 8 step formula for almost instant inductions.

Some people like more stage hypnosis style inductions, even during therapy work. I designed this section with you in mind.

I am going to teach you a tried and tested formula that lies behind about 90-95% of all stage hypnosis and so-called instant inductions. It is easy to learn, repeatable, adaptable and tremendously effective. If you follow the steps with total conviction that it will work and practise by hypnotising your chair or family members and friends etc. you will have an incredibly powerful way of creating almost instant trance by knocking out consciousness fast. This may help with overly-analytical clients or in naughtinosis with women who want the illusion of being 'dominated'.

First the formula then examples ok?

The almost instant induction formula pattern.

1.   **Set a psuedo 'authoritarian' framework:** like a sergeant in the Army make sure it is clear that you expect

'commands', instructions etc. to be followed without question. Now 'authoritarianism' in hypnosis is an illusion. *Real authoritarianism is based on fear of punishment.* You have no way to punish your client other than not helping them etc. Make a mental note: **_you never dominate anyone, you create the illusion that they should 'submit'._**

2.   **Tell them to adjust themselves physically somehow.** This is the so-called 'compliance test'. In my experience with clients people usually smile as you do this because they know the process is about to begin. Think of it as 'benevolent bullying' (it's not bullying, bullying is EVIL. I was bullied at school so I know what it's like). Think that your hypnotee is a naughty child and now has to buck up their ideas: firm but fair.

3.   **Explain that all responses from now on are to be subconscious ones.** No help is needed from the conscious mind. The client must simply let things happen and do nothing.

4.   **Hold or manipulate a part of their body.** This creates a fixation on the body which is inherently hypnotic. It also starts to narrow their focus of attention. It is also

mildly shocking, strange and confusing to be 'manhandled' by a stranger (in therapy ask their permission to touch!). If you know someone it will still be odd when you touch them in this context with a hypnotic intent.

5. **Tell them that whatever happens will be pleasurable.** This motivates them to cooperate consciously and unconsciously. People generally don't resist healthy pleasures. You appeal to the fun, adventurous part.

6. **Tell them to focus on something but physically indicate that they should focus on something else.** So what you say must contradict what you do. This induces confusion. At the moment of confusion they become absorbed with attempting to work out what you're doing and more importantly - what *they* should be doing next. You have created a momentary opening to the subconscious; consciousness must be slapped offline fast!

7. **Command them to sleep!**

8. **Do something physically/nonverbally to symbolically suggest they're entering**

instant hypnotic sleep. See scripts below.

Example 1 rapid stage hypnosis inductions: look at my wrong eye script!

(The following is just an example of what you could do. I suggest you make up your own. What I have outlined above needs to be assumed. It is the theory. The script is the practise. Make it short, direct, competent and to the point.)

'Just do as I say... **(Set authoritarian framework in 1 simple phrase.)**

Sit back, sit up straight etc. **(Issue direct commands for physical adjustment.)**

*All you have to do is **do precisely what I instruct.***

Don't try to assist in any way, shape or form,

Allow whatever will happen to just happen. **(Consciousness butt out!)**

I promise it'll be fun. **(The pleasure promise.)**

I'm going to take that hand and **(lift up one of their hands – this is 'the moment of**

touching'...)

turn this/that palm toward your face...
(strange physical readjustment continues...)

*And I want you to **focus** on my left/right eye, testicle, elbow, zit...* **(Single point of focus! Point to the opposite eye etc. you asked them to verbally stare at. They will look totally confused. Look for the 'look of utter confusion' as their 'pattern of expectation' is interrupted.)**

SLEEP!' **(Direct command for instant hypnosis given at the same time as you confidently yet carefully throw the arm of the hand you are holding down – this is a non-verbal 'deepener' suggestion.** It may slightly tip the person forward knocking their reality orientation out. Now they are your hypno-bitch. Give them an instant deepening suggestion, also brief and to the point.)

Go deeper and deeper and even deeper. That's right!'

I suggest you do a formal deepener or two and then: play time!

Example 2 rapid stage hypnosis: Shocking elbow fractionation script.

(This one uses a variation of the 8 step formula. The order can be played with: the principle remains the same.)

'All I desire you to do is to **(command framework set via presupposition...)**

focus all your attention *on my finger tip.* **(Point of focus sought;** hold this about a foot/12 inches away from their face.)

When I say apples/close/the number 1 - you close your eyes... (brief, simple instructions given; choose 1 option for the 'when I say' trigger – what you say isn't important. It is the structure that counts...)

When I say pears/open/the number 2 - you open them...And you will find that when you close your eyes **it becomes progressively harder to open them** *when I tell you to. Each time you close 'em* **it's harder to open 'em.** *They just increasingly yearn to stay shut...almost as if* **it's their only growing wish...** (A simple 'in a moment pattern' instruction is given, see book 1 and 2 for explanation.)

Apples/Close/1 (Say simply and directly. Pick one option buster!)

Pears/Open/2

Apples/Close/1

Pears/Open/2

Apples/Close/1

Pears/Open/2 (You are setting up a dull predictable pattern. This lulls them into a false sense of security. Soon you will use their sense of expectation against them - known as shock and surprise!)

Apples/Close/1

Pears/Open/2... (At this point just before the eyes open, point your elbow, teddy, cock, boob near to their face instead of your finger. As they open them and look confused fling down your bent arm spreading out your fingers near their face/eyes **– *it must be close enough to induce mild shock!***
NOTE: don't whack them in the face. Knocking them unconscious doesn't count!)

SLEEP! (Command them! Watch for eyelid flutter.)

Go all the way down...

deeper and deeper etc.!'

Simple and easy but needs practise to look flawless. Go practise and do not be afraid to fail. Swimming instructors in my country used (sometimes) to just throw kids into swimming pools if they were too timid, although in practise this can create water phobia; the best thing to do is just get in there and get your hands dirty! *Faint heart never won fair lady!*

De-dopefy me please!

Throughout this book there are transcripts of interviews with 'clients': they are highly altered composites. Poetic license has been used to create what you might call teaching 'factions' – I never violate client confidentiality but I had to show how 'real' hypnotherapy interviews are actually constructed and what you can expect to experience; especially for young and beginner hypnotherapists who may have squeaky clean views of what genuinely occurs when helping people. 'There is nowt (nothing) as queer as folk,' runs the old saying – that's the understatement of the millennia! The atmosphere and 'feel' of all the interviews is 100% genuine.

Cannabis is given far too easy a rap by the mainstream media. It is a nasty little drug that insidiously wheedles itself into a person's life and takes it over. Some people become so addicted that they end up living in a 'cannabis fog' for a decade or more. They literally do not know who they are because everything has been perceived through the dirty cloud for as long as they can remember. Which as cannabis users know ain't that long! The following is a questionnaire I use for 'addicts' and the addict's response. It will highlight the realities of drug abuse, how it really affects lives and why druggies use it at all. I will also make comments on the process etc. as it unfolds. To those of you who have imaginary views of what 'therapy' is or isn't prepare to enter reality now!

Interview with marijuana user: 'Skinny L'.

'Skinny L' is the pseudonym I have given this lady who was using drugs to stay sane. I have changed details where I see fit to protect her identity. However the thrust of what follows is 100% genuine. It will also reveal to the more astute reader the familial and social crisis that creates such unhealthy and self-destructive behaviour.

First let me describe how this lady came to be my client. It almost always begins with a phone call. Her nervous voice gave away how she was feeling. She had come off of marijuana all by herself after reading a book on how to stop using 'puff'. She had been clean for 24 hours and was feeling very anxious as a result. She told me that the effects were psychological and not physical withdrawal. She described herself as tearful, sweaty and highly anxious with moments of 'depression'. When asked to rate her anxiety level on the SUD scale (standard units of distress) she replied 8 out of 10. 10 being the worst the anxiety could be. She was unable to go to work or function as a result of 'going cold turkey' – I offered her an appointment that evening. Although I had an idea what to do, I couldn't be 100% sure till I met her in person. She said her aim was to maintain her decision to stay off drugs and to 'feel better' about doing so. When I suggested she might have come off the drug too quickly and perhaps a gradual period of coming off it would be better, she insisted she would NEVER touch weed again. She was clearly brave and motivated despite the turmoil she was going through. She was scared at the prospect of hypnotherapy and asked me,

'What are you going to do?'

To cut a long story short and cut to the chase I told her I was going to 'negotiate with her subconscious', to ask it to do something else to help fulfil the 'positive intention' of what using puff did for her. I also said I could make her feel better and deal with 'withdrawal'. She was smoking 6 large joints before and after work. We clearly had a window of leverage – she could control herself when she needed to be 'responsible' enough to hold down her job. She said that she still smoked nicotine cigarettes and had no desire to quit them too less it 'push her over the edge'. She said that,

'Mental health problems do exist, no matter what you said on your website.'

I said I know they do but what the medical profession calls 'mental illness' is based on a drug model of 'symptom management'. I cure things. Also the average client has no idea what is meant specifically by the term 'mental illness' – you could write a book on that alone! To her there was a clear and agreed upon definition. In fact there is not. All mental health problems develop as a result of a stimulus or challenge that evokes a response. These responses to 'stressors' are either successful, less successful or ultimately self-destructive. Most people don't know this.

After the appointment was booked she texted my mobile/cell phone and then phoned me for my address, even though I had given it to her.

This was pure nerves. I noted however that her voice was much calmer than in our first conversation. She was also assuring herself that I was not a physical or psychological threat to her. This assessment of her state was confirmed to me when she turned up with her boyfriend. Many female clients, whether habitual stoners who have been rendered excessively 'paranoid' by their drug of choice, bring friends or relatives to assure personal safety – this is quite normal and to be expected. From her point of view she is meeting a 'strange man' at his house, not a doctor's surgery with lots of other people milling around. She is potentially isolated and vulnerable. Also her subconscious does trust me – it has made that decision but her conscious mind is so out of touch with it that anxiety results.

A very skinny lady, clearly not eating well and dressed in the usual uniform of leggings and tracksuit top plus hair scraped back into a harsh ponytail of the post Thatcher-Blair English 'underclass' known as 'chavs' turns up at my gate with a stocky looking boyfriend. She is hugging herself and clearly nervous. As I greet her at the door she smiles nervously and her boyfriend also now quite nervous at seeing me (I was a power lifter and bodybuilder) says he'll be back to pick her up later. I feel uncomfortable, not nervous but this woman is giving off what can only be described as a 'weird vibe'. I invite her in and she is shown to my living room, I offer her a seat on the sofa by the window...

I always ask first,

'How are things at the moment? Are you stressed, happy? Are things going well?'

She sits opposite me on the other side of the room. She is hunched over. Almost bent. She looks as if she has very little energy.

'I am constantly stressed. I work in sales. It's target based. You get paid by commission only. I am a happy person if I am making money.'

Ok let's stop and analyse this. What have we discovered? By her own admission she is 'stressed' – she works in a job which only fulfils her most basic needs of survival. It is so insecure a job that if she doesn't 'hit targets' she starves. Already we are building up a more accurate view of her reality. When asked,

'Do you like your job?'

'I like making money. I am money motivated,' she answers.

Again, she is restating it clearly – only my basic need for money is being met. In this system we all need money or we end up in a cardboard box. Does it also tell us that she is 'good with people'? That she has talent as a 'saleswoman'? That she likes to take risks? Possible yes. We may infer such. We must enquire further. It's not all doom and gloom however.

'What's your living situation? You have children and a partner yes?'

She confirms she has two young children. One is almost a teenager and the other half that age. She admits she is not a very good mum. She comes home from work. Dumps the kids in front of the TV and smokes weed all evening. Now we see how the drug use is affecting her family life. A happy family? We can't answer yes. But she's come to see me.

She feels guilt and shame at her actions, she wants to change – there is hope! A 'do-gooder liberal' (authoritarian control freak) would steal her children and leave them open to rape or worse in a 'care home'. I am not going to let that happen.

She is not epileptic. I ask,

'Are you taking medication for 'this' or for anxiety, depression etc.?'

'No. I was on anti-depressants.' (Because of drugs – one drug for another. Mmmmm? At least the 'doctor's drugs' make him money; UK doctors get drug company kickbacks for replacing one drug addiction for another). She says the doctor gave her them to 'improve her mood'. She pauses and says, 'He probably just wanted to get me out of there.' (Clients know full well the shoddy 'service' they receive from the NHS. They have been trained from birth to view doctors as infallible popes and the NHS – which is simply compulsory socialist drug dealing as a new religion. The 'British' have no faith in anything but the 'NHS'. Like all golden calf deities it has a tendency to be a jealous God and to not answer prayers!)

Next I ask,

'So what are your goals today? What do you want to have specifically accomplished by the time you leave?'

This is not psychoanalysis. I do very brief 'therapy'. I want goals. Targets we can reach that are 'measurable'. She will know *experientially* whether we have been successful or not. She is used to 'meeting targets' after all. Accomplishing targets = 'reward'. She replies,

'I want to 100% never go back to marijuana. And I'll have more money.'

She admits that her drug habit is costing her and her family £130/$220.93 (conversation rate at time of writing) a week!

I ask,

'Is it your friend?'

She sighs, 'It's my *best** friend!' she admits as is common, even with smokers, that she feels as if she is grieving for a recently dead relative, 'It's a habit every day.'

(*You should hear the intensity of feeling that

goes into the word 'best'!)

I continue, 'So when did this all start? How old were you when you started using weed?' (We use euphemisms/indirect communication so as not to appear 'judgemental' and to appear 'understanding' – the real question under this polite veneer is, 'How long have you been getting stoned?' I am looking for potential triggering 'trauma'. I don't find any.)

'I started taking it when I was (late teens). I am now (late 20's). I don't remember why I started it just happened.'

This again is common. Often there is NO trauma. Drug use is widespread and believed a 'normal part of growing up'. It is. In a society that is falling apart.

'How many joints do you smoke?'

'6 a day. Big ones.'

'How many do you enjoy?'

'I haven't enjoyed one in 5 years. But that is me. That's who I am.'

This is typical – the drugs don't work anymore. Law of diminishing returns. Also she links the drug to herself at an <u>identity</u> level. It is not something she does to cope, it is 'who she is'. Of course this is not in any way true but a common perception of drug users.

'What does the drug do for you?'

'Everything! It keeps me calm, it makes me feel good. It's how I get to sleep. It helps me with stress at work. It does everything for me. But really it hasn't. It's just fucked everything up!' she remembers and adds, 'Oh I do it when I watch TV too! I do it all together...'

The drug is linked/associated to many daily rituals and coping mechanisms. It has generalised throughout the system. The question is why? We haven't got there yet. She is holding back.

'On a scale of 0-10, how high would you rate your honest motivation to **stop using drugs*** ?' (*Never miss a chance to throw out an embed!)

'9. 1% is that I enjoy getting stoned.'

(On the phone the client had admitted her 'enough is enough' moment had been reached. These were her words. She claimed that as she had been on the drug over 10 years at time of interview, she couldn't remember if she was depressed or anxious beforehand. This turned out to be a lie as you will see.)

If someone loves using a drug because it 'obliterates' reality for a while, it is being used as a self-medicating substance. Some 'thing' is being sought escape from. Usually feelings as we shall see. But what feelings?

'Ok can you tell me why you want to stop? What are the reasons? I know it's kind of a dumb question but...'

'My children and money.'

BINGO! The right answer! She feels bad and wants to move away from that bad feeling and become a 'good mum'. We are on the right track. Phew! She admits her oldest daughter is being taught about drugs at school and recognises that, 'Mummy does that.' As I have said if 'social services' find out they may legally kidnap the children. The daughter is clearly smart enough to keep her mouth shut or remain 'stum' (Old English 'quiet' - pronounced 'shtum' the Yiddish variant) as they say in England.

'What things have you done to try to overcome this problem? Did anything work for any length of time?'

'I read a book,' she replies. She reaches into her handbag and tosses it across my carpet. I wonder why she does it this way!? There is no need to tell you what it was. It was blandly typical of its useless genre. I had not read it. I don't have to; I know how to help people stop using drugs painlessly. Clients are taught that they must 'understand' a problem first. No, often you need to know *HOW* to change fast. You could become a total expert on the 'science' of addiction and still be well and truly hooked!

'What do you enjoy about your life?'

'Nuffin,' she says as she shrugs her shoulders without energy to do so. She is painfully thin, like a broken scarecrow. There is anorexia here obviously. Or was. Now and again as she answers questions she fights back tears.

'In what situations are you most happy secure and confident now?' I ask. She is not revealing much. She talks in short, fed up, staccato bursts. But I relax as I am building up a picture of her. It's not so bad as she thinks. The tumultuous anxiety has amplified the 'severity' of her problem in her mind. This is solvable.

(There then followed an indication of her 'relationship' with her partner. She informed me that he drank too much, too often and that because she abused weed so much he used this against her if she complained. He also frequently reprimanded her for not being a good mother. Like most drug users she had kept her habit secret for a great length of time: it is actually easy to do so. I have had coke users boast about this ability. They say stuff like, 'I could fool you if I wanted to.' Once her family discovered her habit she claimed she had been treated as 'scum' ever since.)

I then carried on with,

'What achievements are you most proud of? Can be anything? (I had just been told the last 10 years were a fog so...) It can be from before you were using drugs. Even as a youngster etc.?'

She simply replied,

'I struggle to go back to before. I've been like this all my adult life. I don't know what I'm like without weed. I haven't discovered who I am.'

The roots of this problem obviously ran deeper than she had let on. We are getting close to what caused this mess, although the more experienced will probably already know.

'So what strengths have you got that will help you overcome this?'

Blank stare greets this question. Pause.

'I don't know.'

When you get this kind of response you are dealing with a sense of 'shattered self-worth'. Conveniently I next asked,

'If you could rate your self-worth from 0-10. 10 being, you know you feel pretty good about yourself, like yourself that kind of thing and 0 = utter worthlessness, you know, you hate yourself, what would it be?'

'Don't know. 3.'

I joke this is 1 less than the national average for most of the women clients I see. She half laughs. A toughie! I tell her that if her self-worth is low we will have to do 'stuff' to raise it. I say,

'You can't push a boulder uphill if you don't believe you deserve to do it?'

Even I know this doesn't make sense...but it sort of does???! I tell her,

'Look I know you can do this because you don't do weed when you work. That shows there is some control there. We can build on that. You need to take that ability and associate it to other times when you need it. That's what the hypnotherapy will help you do. She said she had no cravings in the 24 hours in which she had bravely 'jumped without a life jacket'. The reason she was so anxious was that she didn't have faith in her ability to cope without drugs. It had smogged her entire adult life. At first I thought work stress might be maintaining the problem. It wasn't that. It was a bit but not at the core. The problem was she had almost zero self-worth. I had to deal with this or fail. It's actually easy to do. Her boosted self-worth would give her confidence that she deserved to succeed; it would help her make much better choices in the future. People who hate themselves punish themselves. They are 'bad' after all.

She went on,

'I was the quiet one. I was ok with that. I had my daughter at 16 and it felt rubbish.'

I next asked,

'What relaxes you?'

'I associate it all with that,' (the drug) she sighed. Later on she said, '...in the bath.'

In response to,

'Do you exercise?' a seemingly innocuous question. I got...

'I jumped off a balcony after a row with my boyfriend and damaged my ankle/foot.'

Do you see how the questions merely provoke responses? The response the client wants to give in her own time as she builds trust with you. I also gave her my usual 'exercise controls stress' spiel which I outline in book 3,

'Powerful hypnosis' so I won't repeat it here. Due to her injury she thought she might enjoy swimming. I had to find out about this. So why did she jump?

'Dunno. I was stoned at the time. I am messed up ain't I?' she said, actually looking for reassurance she wasn't. Of course she was cuckoo! Loco! Nuts! But I couldn't say that. And it wasn't really true. She WAS fucked up, now she was on the path to healing. I said,

'Look, just because you did this doesn't make you 'mentally ill'; people with poor educational backgrounds tend to take everything at face value, especially words. She was worried that coming off the drug would lead to more, 'mentally ill things'. I assured her this was not so and that her behaviour was understandable in context. I had to start to reassure her of her worth at this point,

'Look you shouldn't be so hard on yourself. Are you as bad as Hitler?' this made her laugh a bit, 'No exactly. No one is perfect, I'm not. Loads of people down this street are probably on drugs, the difference is you are doing something about it.'

This made her smile. *Telling clients everyone else is secretly fucked up eases their fear of madness.* This lady was not evil or mad. She had no self-worth. Next to none of her needs were being met, as you will soon see. Lacking good feelings naturally existing on the inside, not knowing how to get them - she turned to marijuana. It gave her a fake boost. It was hollow. It needed constant drug taking just to stay in place.

I almost forgot to mention she said she was 'sectioned' in an anorexia clinic. To be sectioned in the UK means that the local health authority (they used to be called 'services'. Lenin said they'd become 'authorities') forcibly locks you up in a 'looney bin' or psychiatric department. This woman thinks this will throw me. Oh no, she must be so screwed up she can't be helped! WRONG! I ask,

'Are you anorexic now?' (I can cure that too.)

'No!' she says a little affronted. She is a stick insect. I have her now...

'So you mean you got over that all by yourself which is much worse than this?' she nods and smiles, knowing where this is going, 'Then this stuff today will be easy (a walk in the park etc.)!'

Whatever they have overcome and try to use as a sign of weakness you reframe into a strength and proof of their very real power to overcome. Humans are not weak: they are super tough. Women have enormous capacities for physical and mental toughness that they little compliment themselves upon, consciously. I say,

'You are just going up another level in the process of maturing. You are nearly there...'

Next,

'Do you have any intuitive sense of what has to change within yourself in order for you to get the change you want?'

'The majority of the change is made.'

'You just want it stabilised and want to feel calm, yes?' I asked.

'Only there is that 0.1 of me that still wants to do it...' she admitted.

'Yeah I know, we can deal with that in the

hypnosis part,' I reassured her.

'Is there any reason you shouldn't change? Do you have warring parts?'

'No. I just want to be a <u>normal person.</u>' Note this: her 'trance words' for good health are the nominalised phrase 'normal person' whoever the f**k he is!!! I didn't but you could feed this back to her with suggestions that include this phrase, e.g. – '...you are a normal person again etc.'

I noticed she was hugging herself. It is mid spring and colder when the clouds blow over the spring sun.

'Are you cold?' I ask.

'I'm always cold,' she said.

Here I learn something. Long-term drug use (well weed) stops healthy circulation or she lacks emotional warmth on the inside. I didn't press,

'I can shut the windows?'

It wasn't that she assured me. Sad isn't it. A little tragedy. Not important to you. Just someone you pass on a street neither knowing or hating but...

'So what's stopped you from getting this sort of help till now?'

'They say (who are 'they'? 'They' know everything!) you have to be at your lowest to change. I've reached the enough is enough point.'

I think, 'The only way is up then,' but don't say this out loud.

Nearly done...

'Have you ever reached a point where you thought I have to make changes and go off on a better path in life? You don't have to tell me what it was...'

'Once before.' She said after nodding and a pause, 'With an ex-partner. He was abusive and...'

This is always the pattern with these types of women. At some point their core 'inner strength' has enough of being someone's punch bag. We attract those we feel we deserve I'm afraid. That's reality.

I could tell you how she told me about feeling

like the 'black sheep' of the family. How her sisters were married but she wasn't. How...but you get the idea. I told her about hypnosis etc. Again, see book 3, 'Powerful hypnosis' for the low down on how this works. She had no more questions. You know when you've asked all the right stuff because they go on an internal search as you ask,

'Anything I haven't covered? Anything I need to know?' (Speak now or forever hold your peace!)

And they can't think of anything else. We are ready. What had I discovered? What was the problem matrix and solution? See book 3 again for explanations.

- **Problem matrix** = low self-worth, inability to cope with stress, marijuana addiction.

- **Solution matrix** = boost self-worth. This is the support structure of all the following modules and needs to be carried out first. Second, a 'beat marijuana addiction' module. This involves hypnotic dissociation from times when she would have used and association into future imagined times when she does other stuff that is healthier etc. Next, I negotiate with all the 'parts' responsible for the 'addiction'. Finally I nail it all home with a brief but punchy 'mock-authoritarian' or as I call it 'directly indirect' series of 'commands' to become a non-smoker in all circumstances. We are done. She is cured.

But before I did this I had to find out if any or to what extent her universal human needs were being met or not. The answers did not surprise me. The 13 or so questions that help me discover the reality of her current life and how satisfying it is follow. Note what the answers tell us about human nature in general. **Our system is so artificial and anti-human that we don't even know (often) what being human is.** We have NEEDS like a cat or dog has you know. Are drugs human cat nip? Hmmm?! Let's move on swiftly...

Universal human needs questionnaire.

(If I am not satisfied that a client's life is satisfying and so by its 'nature' the person before me is missing certain essential human prerequisites for good physical or mental

health I ask the following set of questions.
Skinny L's responses are given.)

'Ok,' I continue, '(Client's name) I need to ask
you some more questions about your needs
as a person. Everyone has them. If they are
not fulfilled that can cause background anxiety
and stress. The subconscious can start to
make you worry about them so that they get
fulfilled. If you still don't take action the
subconscious will make you ruminate/obsess
about them. If these needs still aren't met – if
you don't take the hint - you can be in danger
of developing an anxiety disorder which at its
worst is depression. Can you rate them from
0-10? 10 means that need is being satisfied,
taken care of etc. 0 means no part of that
need is being met. If you think that need is
not important, and for some people the things
I'll say aren't particularly important just let me
know. Everyone's different.'

'Ok,' she smiles.

'First one: are you eating properly and
exercising?'

'Not at all,' she looks glum.

'So that's zero?'

'Yep.'

'Do you feel that you are isolated from the wider world? Do you feel cut off from others?' I ask.

'I do feel separated. I live in a cloud of smoke,' she says. (Notice her unconscious has supplied a metaphor/symbol that represents her problem. She is not consciously aware of this fact. It is communicating to me alone. It hopes I am listening. I don't push for a numerical rating.)

'If you need it can you get time on your own to **relax** and think your own thoughts?' (This is the need for privacy we all have. This is massively under threat in the modern world.)

'Yeah I can.'

'So that's a 10?'

'Yeah.'

'Good.' One hit, two misses.

'Are you accomplishing goals in life that make you **feel good about yourself?**'

'Yeah.' (I assume a 10.)

'Are you totally accepted for who you are by one person? At least one?'

She thinks about it. (She is going on a transderivational search – aka 'remembering!' to access the info.)

'No. Zero,' she says with a sad smile. (This may or may not be true. People with low self-esteem think they are worthless and see the world through that prism. This may only let me know what she 'perceives' not her reality. The main thing is she doesn't accept herself.)

'Is your life secure? Humans have a need to feel secure. Is your work life secure? Home? That sort of thing?' I ask.

'No,' she laughs. I mark down yet another zero. No wonder this lady threw herself off a balcony!

'Do you feel you get enough positive attention from people in your life?'

By now you can guess the rating.

'What about from you? Do you help others or give positive attention to enough other people? When we do stuff for others it makes us feel good.' (Doing work in which you focus on others and helping them was an old therapy for depression. Now Doctors just zombify people with drugs.)

'Do you have a good best friend? Someone you get on really well with and trust?' I ask.

'Yeah. 10...but she smokes weed too. A lot of it with me,' she looks concerned.

'Ok, do you think that you are capable of thinking for yourself when you're around her? What I mean is if she does drugs do you feel you *have* to do them too? Most people can think for themselves (this isn't actually true but I'm being diplomatic) in some situations but do you think...say you see this person again, by the way I'm not suggesting you cut her out of your life, but when you are with her can you deal with her doing drugs when you aren't? Or do you need help with that?'

'No. It's more her that's like that,' she says and I believe her.

'Do you feel enough of an emotional connection to other people?'

'What do you mean? Like the world??'

'No. Just enough people so it makes you feel good.'

'Uuuum? 5,' she says. That's not too bad. I carry on...

'Do you feel that the roles in life you play like mum, girlfriend, employee, whatever are respected and recognised by others?'

'As a mum,' she replies. Her kids obviously like her.

'Do you feel that you have talents or that you have proficiencies and skills in at least one area of life?'

After a pause,

'I could be a better mum,' she says despondently. She is riddled with guilt. Guilt can be a very good and motivating thing.

'Look, you aren't a bad person. This drug is powerful. You haven't been getting your needs met. The way you have acted is normal. It's a normal response to stress. It's not the best response but you know that and are here,' I try to keep her chin up at least till

I zap this sh*t out of her in a moment.

'Do you feel (notice I am asking for feeling responses, unconscious ones therefore) that you are sufficiently challenged by life? Is it too boring? Are you overloaded? Is there too much stress? Do you think you're living your life with meaning and purpose?'

She asks me,

'What do you mean by purpose?' (WOW! I take it as a big no!)

'Well, what gets you out of bed in the morning? What are your passions? Are they being fulfilled? Do you know what you want to do with your life?' (These are all admittedly quite 'deep' 'philosophical' questions in their way. Especially this one. But how can you ultimately be happy if your life is not being lived with purpose? The opposite is - by accident, aimless, meandering, merely existing. Deep joy comes from having a life's purpose that is unique to YOU.)

'Well I get up for my kids but they are not my passion,' she says.

'Ok you have got quite a few needs there that

aren't being met at all. This alone, just one need not being met is enough to create background stress and you have several not being met. See (her name) this is why you've been doing weed. It was making you feel good with all this stress going on,' I tell her.

'I am a mess aren't I?' she asks again.

'Nope. I have seen worse,' not much worse but...sometimes you lie to build in a foundation of strength afterward. This has been her drug ridden reality for over a decade – no wonder she is a pot head. When any of these needs are rated under 3 that = STRESS! I hypnotise her and sort all this sh*tty mess out. Goals achieved. End of session. It is EASY when you know how. This book is going to teach you more of the 'how'. These are your spells. All questions lead her to a point of having **exhausted problem identification and identifying desired goals and solutions.** They reach a point when you've squeezed all the details you need out of 'em. That's when they are ready to go. Everything needed is wrapped up neatly. Then you zap 'em!

The way to zap an 'addict' (a self-medicating

anxious/low self-worth person) is a four step process in my experience. If you want to be 100% successful that is.

1. **Induce hypnosis.**

2. **Ericksonian module to dissociate person from 'habit state' and associate them into imagined times of acting healthily and differently.**

3. **Negotiate with all 'parts' involved in 'addiction process'. Sometimes just this part is required.**

4. **Usually the above is enough. If you feel you want to 'bombard' the subconscious into submission as a final coup de grace (death blow). Use a short and very 'authoritarian'/directly indirect series of direct commands as a hypnotic summation. Almost as though drawing a line under the problem.**

I have found this to be 100% effective if no further life stressors arise.

A short note on self-esteem and trauma.

Recent studies have revealed something that does not surprise me in the slightest. Let's imagine you have two people. One has 'low self-worth' another feels very good about themselves. Ok, now both undergo a 'trauma'. The researchers have found that the individual with very good self-worth is far less likely to develop post-traumatic stress. It is almost as though the self-worth shields people from extreme stressors other things being equal. In my professional experience almost all of my clients with low regard have experienced trauma of one kind or another. This trauma is 'simply' the trauma of being raised by parents who hate them. I once had a client whose friend had learnt a smattering of NLP b*lls%!t. This client had been systematically beaten with a belt by his father as a child and locked in small chests. His mother had never said anything nice to him. And I mean never. This would-be NLPer had asked him,

'Hey do you think your parents deliberately tried to screw you up?' (Typical hippy, liberal, wishy-washy halfwit question). This implies they didn't. **OF COURSE THEY F***ING**

DID! Does anyone think treating a child like this is 'loving'? If you do, there really is NO hope for you at all. Please leave the healing profession immediately. My client believed that they didn't mean to harm him. When he kept repeating this to me I would not reply but just nodded my head with a blank face. It is not always best to challenge client's delusions and inability to face reality. Sometimes the delusions people live by keeps them in a kind of 'sanity'.

Directly indirect removal of marijuana addiction script.

NOTE: the extensive therapy scripts in this book were crafted by me, RH. I am giving you full permission to use them as you see fit for personal or client therapeutic use. They are very powerful.

(I had great successes with my style of authoritarian hypnosis which for brevities sake from now on will only be referred to as directly indirect and addictions, about 97-98% of clients benefitting to point of cure. But a 2-3% failure rate was not good enough for me. I outline my addiction beating treatments which gave me a 100% success rate in the

next book but one. Keep your eyes peeled –
you'll want it! By the way if you can use the
word 'marijuana' during hypnosis as opposed
to cannabis; it sounds weird and foreign to
English speaker's ears and is more loaded
with negative connotations. The reasons for
this apparently go back to Randolph's Hearst's
desire to prevent hemp paper use. The
underlying protocol for my form of
authoritarian hypnosis can be found in book 4,
'Forbidden hypnotic secrets'. I have included
embeds to offer you added punch and choice
but I never used any while doing directly
indirect hypnosis. Deep hypnosis is assumed
before the following. Be direct, purposeful but
never bullying or domineering - **you tell the
subconscious what to do *vaguely*, you
directionalise it but leave it free to
generate its own solutions.** I am quite
brief and to the point, so I speak quite quickly
but always intelligibly and never rush. Some
of my clients are surprised at how quickly I
can speak if I have to. I RAM IT IN!!! What
follows is more 'enhanced' than the original.)

Step 1: pace ongoing reality.

'I am now speaking directly to the subconscious part or parts responsible for this old pattern of behaviour this person wants to **change to be and feel normal again.** *Firstly let me really thank you for all you've done to look after them and protect them. I fully acknowledge your positive intent in doing what you did back then. You had generated the perceived need to do x (smoke marijuana) for a whole host of very good intents and motivations in response to certain challenges and you did it very well indeed. But the time for that old behaviour is now past. It's time to* **stop x** *(stop smoking marijuana). You know that this is not right for this person in any way, shape or form in any area of this person's life. And I know that you know this too.*

Step 2: directly indirect change.

It is far better for them to **be x** *(drug of choice)* **free,** *a non (-smoker/user etc.), now. Because their identity has changed, because they are not an ex (smoker etc.)* **there are zero cravings or withdrawal** *at all. They don't obsess about x. Because people who are*

totally free of x *don't do that.*

This person may be around people who do use x. That's fine. Just as this person has made a choice so have they. What others chose to do is simply their business. This person isn't bothered by what other people chose to do at all. They can think for themselves. They go their own way and have no desire to 'fit in' to make others comfortable. They are ***focusing on good health and longevity*** *from now on. You just don't have an urge to do what you did. Old triggers are inoperative. They have zero power now because that is the reality of people who are* ***free of x.*** *There are no unpleasant cravings, no problem whatsoever. Even the very idea of doing x in any way, shape or form seems childish, unbelievable, silly and downright ludicrous*. As this is a fact* ***you have no desire to do it.***

(*Note for hypnotist: I often include suggestions that the unwanted behaviour/s is silly or a bit weird because when you think about it, it often is. You might call these **absurdity suggestions**.)

Your reality has experientially altered for the

*better. In ways that **focus you on health and long life.** You focus on long-term gain not short term pseudo-satisfactions that never lasted anyway. If you have a need that requires satisfaction get it satisfied naturally and **use your creativity** to find ways to do that unconsciously on a daily basis. Keep the intent of doing x but find new ways of satisfying that intent. It's that simple. All parts of you will help maintain this new set of decisions and behaviours for their own unconscious reasons. Your rebel part can help. Your stubborn part can help by altering what you will do and won't do for the better. Your inner strength and leadership part supplies all the strength needed to **keep you on track permanently.** You've somehow crossed a line in your life toward fresh/clean air/living and a clean bill of health, efficient working lungs/body/mind etc. and what's more you know it and want it very deeply, now. No sensory stimulants of the past associated to behaviour x affect you anymore. You are indifferent to them. No problem, irrelevant. If someone asks you if you'd like some x or to do x, just let them know in a kind and confident way in your own words* *that you don't do that, you don't want that, anymore.*

*There is an abundance of **good feelings within you.** Good relationships, good self-worth, good food and exercise, fresh air, achieving deeply desired goals, daily pleasures all allow you to feel good naturally and more. You have deep reservoirs of **calmness and relaxation within** which you can connect to. Re-access them, now. The reality is that old, unwanted behaviour is dangerous and counterproductive. The old reality is outside of the new, better healthier patterns of living. Of processing information. Of **dealing better with the ups and downs of life.** Your thought patterns can and do change. Your motivation and willpower is boosted. Your ability to focus and concentrate is reconnected to as you find better things to become absorbed in. Your lifestyle choices, associations to certain things are changed; some are done away with for good. Those old things can't happen in this healthier reality* to someone like you. **You are free** at last and it feels amazing! **Feel pride and joy every time you continue on this new path!** It's easy and lasts forever. What benefits do you* *notice first?*

(* **'Reality suggestions'** are powerful –
their old reality held them locked in misery.
Suggest 'new realities'.)

*You have more resources to succeed than you
consciously know.* **You are determined,
responsible and persistent.** *You* **stop
doing/using x** *and that's that. Not because I
tell you to but for a whole host of reasons that
are your own. You are now* **a happier,
healthier person** *with a higher level of
functioning and a clean bill of health. A line
has been crossed, now*. New perceptions
that help are made. Things alter. Time
changes things. You make all the needed
change and more now, unconsciously. Change
only in the ways that are purely advantageous
and safeguard you from certain types of
unwholesome risk at all times. Your reality
had changed. The past ways are unattractive
and repulsive to you. You can laugh at what
once was. Feel good about these positive
changes. Access anything at all you need to
create this change at all deep levels of your
mind, now...*

(***Crossing a line symbolism** of any kind is

powerful with addicts.)

You **feel calm** and experience no sense of grief. Drug x was not ever your friend, he was a clever con man and you know it deeply. Instead of satisfying genuine healthy urges he stopped you getting them met. Those habits are gone, gone for good. Good, worthy people with many people that love and appreciate them don't require that stuff anymore. You are a strong-minded person who knows that all their other than conscious processes with regards to this goal are now fully marshalled and mono-motivated to allow you to **achieve this wonderful goal now.** Your life is correspondingly enhanced in ways you can't wait to discover.

Future rehearsal.

Imagine being in a situation that confirms: **this has worked...**That's it. **You are** (drug x) **free and you know it.** You care about your mind and body, what you put into it and what you don't. You no longer treat yourself as a dumping ground for poisonous chemicals. You know honestly that the old ways were nonsensical. Your body knows how to detoxify and it does, now. You are a person who looks *after their body in sensible ways. You have many ways of achieving such things, powerfully. You are a healthy person; trust yourself, each and both of you, unconsciously, now. Finalise and tidy up any changes that are required while I'm quiet for a few seconds...........Fantastic!* **These changes are locked in** *and occur automatically, effortlessly! You are doing brilliantly!'*

If you use this approach I advise you throw I my coping with withdrawal module that I invented from book 3, 'Powerful hypnosis'. Nowadays I use something like this as a summation; after all other interventions are completed. Sometimes not at all. You can do this; add to it, you can shorten it. Up to you. NOTE: on its own I have found zero success with this approach and cocaine use.

What did I do?

- **Acknowledge the subconscious**/unconscious is in charge.

- **Thank it** for creating the problem: after all it was a coping mechanism. To an extent, that 'worked'.

- Give suggestions that **change their perceived identity** from druggie to a healthy non-smoker etc. Do not say an 'ex-marijuana' user because exes can always get back together!

- Tell them directly **how to respond** to old triggers differently. Coach them; let them know how a non-drug user would act.

- Make sure **all parts are on board** and that they are doing it to **please themselves** not others.

- Get their own **creativity to generate alternative ways of getting needs met** and so experience true satisfaction. _When needs are met - all addictions vanish._

- Give suggestions that **positive feelings and 'changes'** occur due to the change. This is hypnotic operant conditioning. Internal states reward for achievement.

- **Focus/directionalise the mind on success** patterns and templates.

- Tell them that **the old ways were not as good as the new,** even that they were a bit silly.

- Give various **ego-boosting** suggestions to assist - 'You are strong-minded etc.'

- Give them the **expectation that the subconscious will help.** This tells them it will all happen automatically without any effort.

- **Future rehearse** a life without drugs through visualisation.

- ***You are basically building in the hypnotic reality of a drug free person and stabilising it.***

You can use a similar template for nail biting etc. Now you broadly speaking know the principles you can make up your own. You don't need my words at all. This isn't the only method of getting someone to stop taking a drug. The ways are endless. I'll show you more in a later book as promised. Again: I have found the best way to kill an addiction is to negotiate with parts and dissociate someone from addictive states and associate them into 'healthy choice states'.

Advanced utilisation skills: explanations and methods.

Most hypnosis teachers bang on about 'utilisation' – at the basic levels this is taught as 'pacing and leading', 'truisms' etc. I am now going to show you, in great detail, how you can hypnotise anyone using utilisation alone, so it requires no thought on your part. This was one of the American psychiatrist Dr. Milton Erickson's greatest contributions to modern hypnotic practise. Let's unravel the utilisation formula. This in many ways is the ultimate 'conversational hypnosis' – it doesn't look like hypnosis BUT it feels like it! Oh yeah baby!

The 'intellectual' trance.

Erickson was greeted by a weird client who wanted to be hypnotised 'intellectually', without 'mysticism'. The patient said he wanted a method that did not use suggestions but that **questioned him about his own thinking and feeling with regards to reality.** In other words absolute facts regarding the nature of ongoing reality and experience were to be acknowledged and not denied in any way. The man was tense and nervous, trembling in fact – he wanted this reality acknowledged in 'trance induction'. He was also sitting on a chair which was in front of a desk – he wanted this reality acknowledged too. His present reality was that he was so 'distracted' that he noticed 'everything' around him! No wonder he was tense! You could just say, 'What are you not, not noticing?' that would start to f*ck with him nicely, but...Erickson told the man to explain these 'ideas and understandings' fully so that he could comprehend fully but he asked for permission to interrupt to seek further 'clarity' of what was desired.

Erickson pointed out his desk and all the stuff on it. He suggested the man start noticing that first...The following is my version of what could be applied to any client.

'Of all the things here that are grabbing and fighting for your attention, can you describe what distracts you on my x (desk/bookshelf etc.)?'

You are covertly suggesting that they focus on a limited number of potentially competing stimuli. You are narrowing their focus of attention. It doesn't

appear that way because your client has no idea what real hypnosis is. In effect you are saying – 'Look at all the shit here!' This presupposes nowhere else.

At this stage the idea is to <u>hijack their attention and focus it where you, the hypnotist want.</u> Be sneaky, and wery, wery quiet – we're hunting wabbits!

Let's say your client starts pointing out various objects in your room: your anal lube, your subscription to penthouse lying on the floor, that rudely disturbed pack of tissues! Anyway you get the idea...As they go on and on, you start subtly pointing out other things they've missed. Focus on external tangible realities at first. I had a client say he didn't think hypnosis existed (boring managerial type – no imagination, used to people taking his moronic opinions seriously, you get the idea); he said it wasn't 'tangible'. 5 minutes later he was tangibly snoring like a pig.

'Do you notice the remote control?

The TV?

The picture of the bird on the wall?

The patterns on the carpet?

Its colour?

Your left foot? (First subtle directing to the body. Fractionate in and out quick.)

The reddish curtains?

Your arm on the arm of that chair?

The way your eyes focus in differing ways as you look at various things at varying distances?

Book titles on my shelf that make you think, 'I'd like to read that!' (I have some wery interwesting bookies on my shelves believe me! All hypnotists should! Not too freaky just enough to make them think your are knowledgeable and a bit odd, this starts to play with their reality orientation – think a wizard's chamber but not so creepy and it has comfy chairs!)

The tense nature of a part of that body?

A distracting noise?

Troubling thoughts? (NOW! GO! GO! GO! You start directing them internally – external to internal, gradually. Give them just enough time to pay attention and process, then move on taking advantage of 'rolling consciousness'.)

Worrying thoughts? (They are having them – use now: change later!)

The weight of that hand, that foot, those problems?

How much do you suppose the sofa weighs? (A mental task that requires introspection, they are being overloaded.)

My CD collection?

Your ongoing experience? (Introducing some weird vague sh*t gradually)

The process of living?

The reality of changes that people make?

Of certain problems one may have?

Or imagine one has?

Certain physical and emotional processes that have/had bothered you?

The potential relief of relaxation?

The need to pay genuine attention to one's needs? (All clients are failing to get needs met otherwise they wouldn't be clients.)

Or the remote control?

Or the sofa/couch supporting you?

Of things becoming somewhat samey? (Indirect suggestion for monotony.)

The cosiness of becoming remote from this place? (By the way, say all these as commands not questions, falling tone please!)

A pleasant weariness and how that develops...

That unchanging nature of certain things out here...

A remote control is just that (in other words nothing to fear – relax! The remote control is repeatedly mentioned = boring = trance!)

The boredom of the window?

The need we all have to rest...

The pleasant sensation of shutting one's eyes... (Leading and pacing all in one go.)

How we relax as we take a deep breath...

The reality of learning best by osmosis...

The reality and ability to use the intelligence of your unconscious wisdom?

The reality that you are already feeling more comfort, are you not? Etc.'

Formula – 1. External realities focus: sound, sights, touch, taste etc. are focused on – _gradually_ (take your time). 2. Focus is directed to 'inner' subjective, experiential concerns. These are processes of internal experience – images, thoughts – even if stressful, feelings – even if at first unpleasant, psychological needs, wishes, daydreams about 'possibilities' etc.

This is really a waking hypnosis version of the 'Betty Erickson' induction outlined in book 1, 'How to hypnotise anyone'. If you just point out facts to people, how can they possibly know they are being hypnotised? You are just deliberately focusing their attention. Outwardly at first and then inwardly. As you can see you can even fractionate between the two – rapidly deepening. If a car goes by acknowledge it and say, 'People go on journeys...' FACT - they do!

From this go onto PMR (progressive muscle relaxation), deepeners and Bob's your uncle – that sucker is under baby! Dancing with the pixies!

NOTE: when people are stressed and panicky they become hyper-aware, the brain is frantically pattern matching for danger! This is exhausting. Use this pattern 'against' them. Pace it, activate it and the CHANGE it. Geddit! Easy-peasy-lemon-squeasy.

Another 7 step formula would be:

- **Bland statements about the environment.**

- **Bland statements about the objects in it.**

- **Bland statement about the clothing of the subject.**

- **Bland statements about the body and its processes.**

- **Bland statements about physical sensations.**

- **Bland statements about <u>feelings</u>.**

- **Bland statements about <u>mental processes.</u>**

- **Deepener.**

Think bland! The blander the better! The weirder and more 'NLPesque' the language, the more you sound like a freak and freak people out. Keep it simple. Some folks love to say 'complex' (actually convoluted!) is best. Bullshit. Hypnotising is easy. It's what you do with someone once they are under and how swiftly you heal that separates the men from the adolescent boys. Let's repeat this so it goes in...

How to hypnotise a compulsive, anxious talker without any words.

Milton Erickson was such a great hypnotist that he didn't even need words to hypnotise someone so thorough was his understanding of what 'hypnosis' really is. Let's imagine a client enters your office etc. They are so anxious and unhappy that they keep talking about all the objects in your room. For some reason they seem to have a **need** to do so.

Perhaps so as to not face up to the issues at hand; as little children do by changing subjects. If someone has a need to comment on everything, then that is what you use to zap the t*ts off em! If they keep commenting on various items you simply pace and lead this non-verbally. Instead of letting them set the agenda of what will be noticed – you hijack this propensity.

So let's imagine this person notices your pen and describes it, the money jar, the Selloptape. The patterns on the wallpaper etc. Then you say,

'You forgot to mention the money jar... (Or just point to it.)

(Let them notice and comment and move on just before they complete their sentence – pattern interrupt.)

You didn't even notice my nice new bookshelf... (Or just point to it and wait for the reaction.)

- Open and close your appointment diary.

- Wipe your glasses.

- Move that hole puncher to the other side of your desk etc.

(The talkative client may be commenting on your every move. BINGO! You are re-directionalising their thought and attention and thereby narrowing it gradually but quite swiftly so they follow your lead.)

- On my writing desk I have a door knob which comes from an old wardrobe. I could hold it up and offer that for comment.

- What about my old nail file?

- I have the complete works of Shakespeare with a brown tea stain on the pages. I could leaf through it. Or point out a play title. At first do this quickly. Keep using the human psychological reality of 'rolling consciousness' to your advantage (explained in 'Wizards of Trance'). At some stage the client will be mesmerised by what you are doing and quieten down in expectation of what the heck you'll do next!

- I might show them my small pen torch next and shine it in their eyes for fun. **_NOW COMES THE SHIFT POINT._** You then start doing what they did. You start making comments on the objects.

'This is an interesting hand mirror. My wife left it here etc.,' you might say. Continue in this vein and the person will start paying more avid attention. They'll start to shut up and listen. Erickson had to do this for a whopping 40 minutes! Yikes! The person will start to take the lead from you as to what to do next. Keep showing them things and making brief comments, perhaps throwing in some hypno-language as you do. Look out for when the person starts to become still and their eyes stare without blinking - they just look 'zonked' for want of a better word. Then offer them this command,

'That's it. Just close your eyes...and now, from memory, recall everything you have seen in order or not and name it to yourself in your own mind...do this until you develop a state of deep hypnotic sleep.'

(By doing this you get them to go inside and repeat their compulsion from memory.

Memory is an unconscious mechanism. You have activated it. You have made them 'go inside'.)

You could assist by saying stuff like,

'My wooden clock...and go deeper...

Did you remember my pot of pens and go even deeper still...

Deeper into trance with the recollection of the waste basket...'

Do this until their physiology indicates deep trance is achieved. ***Whatever bizarre behaviour you are offered, do it back to them to get trance and then get them to do it internally ensuring hypnosis is achieved.*** Seems complicated but is actually very simple. So what did we do?

- **Observe how client does behave. Not how you wish they did.**

- **Whatever they do, you do back to them 'hijacking their pattern' of 'resistance'. You are matching their state effectively.**

- **Use the hijacked pattern to narrow their focus of attention until such time as physiological trance occurs.**

- **Give a serious of tasks that need completion...don't always let the completion occur. This activates a 'need for completion template' unconsciously. Vainly seeking the satisfaction of completion they'll follow your lead.**

- **Remember words aren't needed and can be kept minimal if required.**

- **When the moment of hypnotic surrender is reached, suggest they close their eyes and carry on from memory or imagination the behaviour they have been engaged in. This is almost like the childhood game (age regression?) of copying everything someone says. _REMEMBER: activating memory and imagination are the twin paths to conversational trance._**

The key principle in any success in life, in successfully hypnotising anyone is _**PERSISTENCE! NEVER GIVE UP!**_ Be relentless till success occurs.

Using their own words against them.

This is actually simple. You can use it with 'resistant' clients and/or those who have never experienced a formal trance (that they are aware of!).

1. Create an atmosphere of total free expression – you could say, 'Just feel free to tell me whatever you want.'

2. Ask the client to speak about what they imagine trance is like.

3. Whatever they say, even if they say trance does not exist etc. you use it against them to hypnotise them. Let's take an imaginary client to amply illustrate this procedure.

4. Use a hypnotic tone on embeds; if you use them – they aren't needed.

Me – 'So what's the problem you've been having with regards to (pause) ***you're going into hypnosis*** ? **Now,** just tell me whatever comes to mind spontaneously.

Client – 'Well I just can't see what trance is. I can't imagine what it is?'

Me – 'You just really can't **see or visualise what trance is** ?'

Client – 'That's it! I can't. Can you tell me what it is?'

Me – 'That a good question! What is it when you **experience hypnosis** ?'

Client – 'Well I imagine it's a state of mind? I suppose so...'

Me – 'That's a good start; you **imagine** it's a specific psychological state. **You suppose** that's what it is?'

Client – 'I just don't know?'

Me – 'That's right. You really don't know, nor do you need to know to **experience that**...'

Client – 'I haven't a clue! I do not know!'

Me – 'You just do not? **You might wonder** or think you know but...'

Client – 'What should I think about it? It's outside of my experience...'

Me – 'That's true it is outside of your normal experience...but what might you think, would you **think**? What things might you **sense**? Most importantly what might you **feel in that state of mind**?'

Client – 'I have no idea. Do I go to sleep or feel sleepy? Is that it?'

Me – 'Good question. Is that it? Are ideas needed there even? Some **feel tired, relaxing, sleepier and sleepier...'**

Client – 'I'm really puzzled by it all...'

Me – 'When we are puzzled we unravel riddles to solve problems do we not? **You wonder**, think, **ponder**, and **feel things** about it...**now**...'

Client – 'I feel different...'

Me – 'You do...and what do you feel? **Feel that**...'

Client – 'I feel like I have tunnel vision. My eyes are blurred somewhat...'

Me – 'That happens...you do **get tunnel vision...**eyes might seem blurring, tired, closing perhaps...'

Client – 'They're...shutting...'

Me – 'They want to *close*...breathing is shifting...you sigh...or yawn...more relaxation spreading easily...breathing more comfortably...breathing without effort...nothing doing here...how much sleepier do you feel? No need to reply...can do in your mind...finding own ways to *go all the way down*...deeper and deeper...you're feeling so much better...are you not? Ever been so *comfortable you* just wanted to listen and learn? When you got a warm feeling that didn't require any talk? You don't have to sleep soundly to *enter deep trance, now*...but you could. Some *sleep soundly*...but you needn't...learning deeply...and not knowing how is the point...wasn't it? Your breathing breathes you all by yourself and that gives you a certain sense of *security...inside* that can and does take you to where and when not you wish to go beyond...etc.'

You can do it without embeds just using trance themes etc. Twist what they say into presuppositions of trance. ***Remember the golden rule: what if everything is the start of trance?***

After getting someone like this under, set up a powerful post-hypnotic command to get immediate hypnosis on cue so you don't need to go through this sort of crap again!

No one feels forced to do anything. Just repeat a few ideas...certain trance ideas that they offer but didn't know they did. It doesn't even seem like hypnosis because it isn't. It's just talking. What if hypnosis IS just talking?

Talking of reinductions...

Utilising reinductions for hypnosis.

You have a good hypnotee, they go under easy-peasy. Say...

'Can you recall the physical environment of the last good trance you experienced?'

They say yes etc.

'Can you tell me...as we sit here...your recollections of that place...of that trance situation?'

Or

'Could you recall and describe that hypnotic setting?'

Blah!

'Can you tell me as best as you are able the suggestions that person gave you in order?'

Or

'Can you get the gist back of what happened chronologically?'

Blah...they might trance out here.

'Who is there...where are you? Or where are you not?'

Underlying hypnotic principle? Memory!!! – from book 1, recalling anything = trance. Find ways to revivify desired states.

If all the above fails that's fine because they didn't have a clue you were trying to re-hypnotise them! You just move on – it was just some random questions. Watch for trance signs as feedback to move on with the process – watch them!

As said, this is trance by revivification. Get them to describe a state in full sensory based detail and it will be revivified – this goes for all states,

emotional ones too.

That'll do pig. That'll do...for now!

Saying NO to persuasion tips!

I really can't stand anybody trying to persuade me of anything. It just p*sses me off and insults my intelligence. People who seek to persuade do not like hard, cold facts! It is their kryptonite. There follow 10 tricks with which to swiftly demoralise any would-be persuader. They are easy to follow and very practical. Of course there are more but these are amongst my favourites...

1: The broken record technique.

So how do you do this? What is it? *When anyone repeats their request to you, simply repeat your words of refusal over and over and over again like a broken record.**

(For the youngsters out there this refers to vinyl LPs that were scratched. The record player's 'arm' would 'snag' on the scratch and repeat a phrase or piece of music over and over and over!)

Intention/objective of the technique: to get the persuader to GIVE UP and GO AWAY/STOP BADGERING YOU.

This is easy to learn: essentially you are

embedding a phrase into the listener's unconscious, examples follow:

*'I did listen I **disagree strongly...**uhum, it's important to you from your current perspective but I **disagree strongly**...That's tough...it presently has meaning for you but I **disagree strongly** etc.'*

Can you guess what phrase we embedded?

*'I know that you would like that but it would be painful for me. **I am not going to do that.** Yes I think you would enjoy that...I'm sure that true. It turns me off. **I am not going to do that.** Drop it...I bet you would and that's a shame. **I am not going to do that.** There are sites on the Internet you can visit if you are that way inclined etc.'*

You can pick a theme: too expensive, cruel, inhumane and keep repeating a phrase around that core idea/meme. Think slogans!

Persuaders are often semi-robotic and not really thinking at all. Often sales people are paid by the results they get. They may be highly motivated to jabber on and on until you cave in. Some people see the world in such black and white ways that they cannot listen to reason. Some people see any refutation or lack of acceptance as a sign that their 'strategy' isn't working but that the 'message' is essentially sound. Sound can be weaponised – it can be used for or against something.

Why does this work?

Essentially repetition triggers the pattern-matching function of the human brain. You are swiftly reprogramming their assumptions. You are saying: 'I am a brick wall. An unassailable obstacle and that crap won't work with me.' It is a strange thing but persistence one way or another does produce change. People put interactions into discrete time packages, unconsciously. If you overextend them past their unconscious time limit they cave in. Goals are time limited. At some point almost everyone gives in. Almost everyone.

The formula is: deny a shyster even an inch of gratification!

2: The sound of silence.

How to do it? This is the easiest and by far the most effective. The good old 'silent treatment'. Effectively it says: what you have to say is so offensive/stupid/beneath me that I can't be bothered to respond. Keep your face blank: think top poker player!

Why does it work?

Because you are not communicating anything directly. It causes the persuader to search for meaning in what you are doing or not doing. People can't stand ambiguity. It causes their mind to speculate. This raises their anxiety levels. No response = no feedback = they cannot know if their goal is achieved. It is the disdain of the snob. It is the ignoring of the inconsequential. Still, silent, impassive, powerful. Think king and jester. It shakes people's self-worth. You won't even acknowledge their existence. This only fails with 'the social rapist'. I will discuss him or her later perhaps and how to handle them. We have all encountered them and they need to be put back in place fast.

The formula is: you are so low status

that I will not deign to communicate with you at all!

3: The best form of defence is? ATTACK!

This is an old adage but how do you do it effectively?

1. Get mad! Get angry! Pump yourself up! This is what US 'shock jocks' do and they have massive audiences.

2. Attack the opponent verbally in every way conceivable to man – personally, generically, attack their level of intelligence, call them arrogant, out of touch, pompous etc.

3. Target arguments aggressively: it's ridiculous, crazy, incompetent, shouldn't be taken seriously, outside area of 'expertise' etc.

4. Question the morality and clumsiness of the technique being used to sway you.

5. If you are very clever you can use a biting form of sarcasm which is relatively subtle and treats the opponent like a moron. Added with a great sense of wit this can devastate an opponent.

Why does it work?

When you attack someone verbally you are knocking them off balance. The person may be some smug salesman or woman (female sales reps are in my experience more subtle in their approaches using guilt etc.) who feels they are armed to the teeth with a repertoire of techniques. They are not expecting hostility from a target. When you verbally attack someone you activate their fight or flight responses unless they have been trained otherwise – policeman, prison guards, soldiers often do have training in such techniques. For example in Vietnam the US troops were trained that when ambushed you do not flee but aggressively counterattack immediately thus out-ambushing the enemy. When people's stress levels are raised they cannot think rationally – it is literally impossible. Stress makes us make stupid decisions.

Pros and cons.

The Celts and Germans were capable of experiencing massive 'berserker rage' responses when attacked by varying civilisations. This was and is known as the 'furore barbaricas' (barbarian fury!) to the

Romans. Rage and anger can give you massive power with which to repel an attack. It is a form of blitzkrieg. However if prolonged it is draining, also if you are aggressive and someone else responds aggressively which they may, you may end up in a fight and then in a court: always use this trick wisely and in a controlled fashion. You can use anger but don't let it overwhelm you: control it. Unless a furious barbarian is needed of course!

The formula is: better put the opponent on the back foot rather than the other way around.

4. Grabbing the moral high ground.

In war a well-known maxim is 'he who has the high ground has the advantage'; which is why aerial warfare is so effective. With that in mind...

If used honestly this is THE most powerful technique of all outside of a full military response. Why does this work? Even arse/assholes like to be thought of as 'good people'; most people do seem to have a strong sense of right and wrong even if they are acting immorally - they know that what they are doing isn't right and if exposed, wider 'public opinion' would condemn them.

The Christians who were massively persecuted and fed to lions as entertainment by the Romans actually converted the masses by utilising their persecution to show their moral superiority. When fed to animals the Christians passively accepted their fate knowing that soon they would be with God. This equanimity in the face of death had the opposite effect than intended by the Roman nobles: the pagan mob was so touched by the bravery of the Christians who had (up till that time) harmed no one that they wanted to know more about this new religion from the Syriac provinces of the Empire. Rome unwittingly unleashed the agent of its own destruction.

So how do you do this without offering to become a martyr? Although don't discount that as a strategy: it is very powerful. How do we grab the moral high ground in reality? Let's say that an authority figure suggests you do something even *slightly* immoral, how would you respond? You could attack them personally and ask how they could even suggest such a thing – in some circumstances that's best but it could backfire. You could lose a job etc. What you do is you simply say, 'No.'

The person knows what they asked you is morally wrong. You know. Don't argue. Don't justify yourself as that weakens you. Just say, 'No.' This little big word is very powerful. I'll give an example from my own life.

I was once acting in a play in London. The director told me to grope an actress's tits. It was not written in the play. He had added it, like most directors he imagined himself a genius who could improve on what Shakespeare wrote. This is how it happened. First he asked the actress if it was o.k. if I grope her. She looked at me as if sussing up as to whether I was a perv or not.

'Ok,' she said. She didn't want to do it but felt social pressure to do what the director said.

'I'm not doing that,' I simply said. The actress looked stunned and delighted. The director looked at me and said,

'You will do it.'

'No I won't,' I said. And that was that. He never had the balls to ask me again. It was just dropped. However during a performance when I had to grab this actress my hands did slip one night and accidentally slide up over her tits. She turned around and smiled at me!!! I suppose that's actresses for you. Very small bee-sting tits too!

- NOTE: when you take the moral high ground you are really playing a trump card. It sends a powerful message to others. Morals and values include not being abusive, not molesting others in any way, not being selfish, not setting out to exploit or deliberately cause pain. If you point out the immorality of a suggestion the person who suggested it will often back down. The social pressure of exposure of their immorality is enormous. You can simply imply immorality by saying, 'No.'

If misused this can be a low form of emotional blackmail and is best avoided. If you overuse ANY tactic you will extinguish its effectiveness which is the real moral of the boy who cried wolf. Some perverse people try to use certain words as verbal cattle prods feigning a high ground position which is in reality merely a form of tyrannical social control. Tyrants often step forward claiming they are acting from a position of preserving 'morality' when the exact opposite is the case. We can find a good metaphor for this in Christianity whereby the devil is said to appear as an angel of light so as to better deceive Man.

Pros and cons.

This will only work if – you <u>are</u> moral and not a secret hypocrite and the other <u>is</u> in the wrong and knows it. An immoral person will be terrified to argue their immorality openly with you.

The formula is: people with no morals have no place seeking to influence those who do!

5. We tried it already!

This seems so simple as to almost not be a technique. But when it is used truthfully or otherwise it is remarkably effective. You basically say, 'I tried that already it didn't work.' A salesperson etc. will have a very hard time carrying on with their spiel when you point this out. They actually can't continue without sounding desperate or stupid.

Why does it work?

What you are in effect doing is **stealing the authority position.** The salesman pretends/plays the game of being an 'expert' on x. They aren't, they're just shysters. When you say, 'We did that already,' you are saying – 'We know from real world experience that this don't work mister; we are the experts not you.' You have primary evidence of the stupidity, incompetence, madness of the proposed idea etc. This makes your position superior. It is a strong negotiating position.

Socialism in all its guises is a great example of something that has been tried so often and failed miserably so often as to not even warrant rational discussion: however socialism is a political religion and its cult members are not interested in reality which they fantasise they can recreate to their own design. I will write more about this in 'Escaping cultural hypnosis' my next book – I will expose how Stalin tried to create a human-ape hybrid slave army. That's real socialism for you.

The formula is: imply stupidity and incompetence.

6. The menyana strategy: procrastinating them into giving up.

It's so God damn hot in Spain that the Spanish are known for saying, 'Menyana!' 'Tomorrow!' in response to any proposal. This is the complete antithesis of 'our' Anglo-Saxon 'now culture' that it works brilliantly at demoralising the would-be persuasive.

What you are saying without saying it is,

'You are an idiot. I have no intention of buying diddly-squat from you. I am going to keep putting you off till you get the message.'

This is a technique much beloved by teenage girls to potential dates. So as to avoid physical or emotional conflict, women are experts at indirect communication.

- You can make up any excuse you want to delay. Your favourite canary died and you have to deal with it.

- You can rank that decision low on your priority list. I just have more important things to do. I'll get back to you babe.

Why this works?

This is an indirect form of operant conditioning. Why do it? If you simply say no, the persuader may come back with more stupid sh*t later. You want to break their spirit so they don't EVER bother you again. At some point the penny drops for them. It is a form of moral sadism.

The formula is: *don't do today what you won't do tomorrow!*

7. Hidden agendas and conspiracies!

The implication is that deception is taking place: the persuader is trying to take you for a ride - as is often the case! How do we do it?

J'accuse!

Simply state that you feel, think, believe, have evidence that the opponent has a 'hidden agenda' and is being deliberately deceptive. Blow this out of all proportions and so easily dismiss everything they say as merely being a further thread in a tapestry of lies.

- Assert that the persuader is attempting to 'control' you for some nefarious reason or intent.

- Let them know in no uncertain terms that you see through their game.

- State that you have proof to back up your assertions.

- Gather supporters to back up your cause and give yourself weight of numbers.

Design a 'conspiracy theory' that explains 'the truth'.

Why does this work?

Persuaders are persuading for selfish reasons. With this in mind it is wise to question any persuader's stated motives: this is certainly so when they claim they are doing what they are doing for some 'altruistic cause' with no thought of personal gain. Riiiight!

- Children, lovers and those in business etc. often use this tactic. Where power battles are ongoing, this strategy can be used.

- It is true that most people seek various forms of gain through persuasion to achieve power over others.

To do this simply ask:

Why is this person really trying to persuade me of x?

What's in it for them?

The formula is: act 'paranoid' and accuse the person of being secretly immoral.

8. Break rapport!

Most second rate persuaders have been trained in NLP 'rapport', 'yes sets', 'pacing and leading', 'matching and mirroring' and all that B-S that a child should be able to see through. How do you counteract it? It can work on some people. You start off knowing that **the persuader is trying to artificially create an 'agreement frame'** – this is their intent. You simply counter this with a **'perpetual disagreement frame'.**

- If they try to pace your emotions, change your state.

- If they try to copy your body language alter it.

- Find fault in all they say. Find niggling points to argue about.

- If they make a statement question it, and then question the next one etc.

- If they make truisms say, 'That's just a generalisation.'

- If they seek to extract info from you by asking personal or open-ended questions say little, be brusque, 'That's none of your business/not relevant to this discussion etc.'

If you have ever seen a clever child in a contradictory mood, you'll know exactly what I'm talking about. All the parents are nodding now!

Why does this work?

Persuasion is by definition seeking agreement. That is not possible in an 'environment' of mistrust. The other person will give up from exhaustion. All human behaviour is motivated by reward. If not even a slither of reward is given at any point their motivation is quickly extinguished. Use the fact that most people do not persist, are lazy, inflexible and time conscious against them. They will give up if they think you are a waste of their time. There are other fish to fry!

The formula is: I am not like you! We have nothing in common.

9. I am an expert you are not.

In all human interactions, right or wrong, perceived 'hierarchy' is important. In any interaction 99.9% of people are unconsciously asking themselves, 'Am I higher up the 'pecking order' than this person?'

Say you are confronted by an 'expert', how do you undermine them? You **outbid them or you state that their expertise is theoretical but not practical.** In other words you are not swayed by ivory tower experts.

- If they quote qualifications you quote yours. Frame them in such a way as to 'outbid' the opponent. 'Qualification x is fine if you've been in an institution all your life protected from real life concerns etc; however in my *experience* etc...' I have met several people with degrees in psychology, even Master's degrees etc. who have never word-cured a single person of depression.

- Ask them what they have done with those qualifications: after all, those who can't teach? I once had a teacher who taught business to high school kids who had never run a successful business! Yikes!

- People are conditioned to be impressed by 'academics' – they are the new priests of our time. If someone yaps on and on about their academic achievements as opposed to real life ones – you know, like actually doing things – rather than just writing essays, you have a big clue as to their value system. This insight can be used against them. They value superficiality, book knowledge and perceived social prestige over depth, experience and getting your hands dirty in the risks of reality. Everyone is great in a C.V – till you see them at work!

Why this works?

Since ancient times artisans, workmen etc. have been seen as slaves. Real nobility lay in not working but in living off of the labour of others. This is the root of what we call 'snobbery'. ***However in real life which is an exceedingly practical and results driven affair, the public is interested not in what you know, or think you know but in what you've done.*** Successful practise beats fancy theory all the time.

Variation on a theme.

The nuclear option with this sort of 'persuader' which should be saved for real a-holes is simply to say, without looking at your opponent, 'Why are you speaking to me. I don't even care that you exist.' Say this calmly, matter of factly. They will be dumbstruck. Most people have a deep unconscious desire through external validation that their existence is important. If you deny them this, they are totally gobsmacked. As I say, save for real dickheads. You'll thank me for this one, trust me! You are effectively trivialising them and what they say.

The formula is: artfully belittle a bighead!

10. Pre-emptive strikes!

If someone has a set of attack strategies and you know what they'll be, why wait for the first onslaught of persuasion? Get in first and undermine them! How?

- Assert dominance immediately in no uncertain terms as the interaction begins.

- Make the topic they wish to cover off limits for discussion.

- Tell them the topic they want to discuss is irrelevant.

- 'I've heard this all before. All you are doing is x, y, z!' (Nobody likes being exposed – I once had an argument with a man about rising gold prices. Everything he said I simply turned into an analysis of his feeble attack strategy, pointing out its childishness and ineffectiveness to listeners.)

- Say you are about to interact with someone who believes, supports cause x.

Could be anything. Before they say anything produce visual 'proof' that y is the case.

Why this works?

All persuaders are in a certain state of mind that helps facilitate persuasion. They have a battle plan. Most people are uncreative and inflexible, lacking all spontaneity of response by adulthood which is entirely knocked out of them; especially in work place/professional settings. This trick works as an effective 'pattern interrupt' – before they even have time to start operations they are uncovered and besieged. This is very disconcerting indeed.

The formula is: steal their thunder!

11. Your bonus tip - Interrupt their flow!

Folks it don't matter how you interrupt the persuader's flow, just do it! For persuasion to work you need flow: it is essential. Disagree, question, cough, ask to go to the toilet or just go, smoke a cigarette or pretend you need to and pop outside, pretend Barak Obama just walked past the window and point too! Sales people etc. often seek to apply psychological pressure on would-be suckers. If you break the flow of their verbal diarrhoea etc. you will be able to gather your thoughts and disrupt theirs.

Why this works?

Most people are robotic; in fact studies have shown that a whopping 90% of what most people do is totally predictable. Persuaders have received training in specific procedures 'do x then y and z etc.'; when you break up their flow they cannot stick to the plan. Most people are not flexible: they rarely have a plan 'b' let alone a 'c' or 'd'. When you know this fact you can pretty much disrupt anyone. It causes them anxiety, stress – they cannot maintain external focus as they go into negative mini trance states and worry. In addition persuasion often uses overload and fixation which require unbroken flow to work. As does hypnosis.

Formula: using any means available break up the pattern of the communication and disrupt the planned agenda.

What do these things intend to do?

Destabilise and demoralise the would-be persuader.

These ten plus tricks have several points in common which you can use to screw up any unwanted persuasion...

- Interrupt the opponent's comfortable habitual patterns.

- Seeks disagreement.

- Upset the opponent emotionally.

- Takes control of the interaction immediately.

- They are active and not passive.

- They question their assumed right to be doing what they are doing.

- The main underlying aim of any such tactic is simple – *raise your opponent's stress levels so they can't think straight. You are intentionally activating a fight or flight response.* The exact opposite of most hypnotic states.

In closing...

Of course there are more – you could play the blame game, but the most powerful persuasive tool is the truth! Didn't someone rather influential once say,

`...the truth shall set you free,' ?

All persuasion is based on 'perception management' – kick that in the nuts with the truth.

Success secrets of the psychopath! Yay!

Only in 'modern' times. Would you like to be successful? Heck yeah! Would you like to be as successful as only a psychopath can be? What the f**k!??

Functional or 'good' psychopaths?

Ever heard of Andy Mc Nab? Mr. Mc Nab wrote a famous book in the 1990's in Britain. He was ex S.A.S (Special Air Service) – one of the toughest Special Forces in the world. The book details his exploits in the 1st Iraq War. Turns out that Mr. Mc Nab has 'come out' at time of writing as a psychopath. In fact he's rather proud of the fact – he claims it's 'the secret of my success'! He has co-written a new book 'Two- faced' about being a successful psychopath. By the way Andy was decorated for his erm, efforts (?) during the first Gulf War by the British army. It gets better. Andy tells us how his 'good psychopath' traits have made him a 'success' in the army and 'business'. He wants to teach you how to get in touch with your 'inner psychopath'; a 'doctor' helped him. A certain doctor Kevin Hutton. It gets better!

Andy tells us he came from a 'broken home' (boo-f**ckin' hoo, pass the hankies!), he tells us that bad psychos just can't control themselves whereas 'good' ones can. He never contemplates 'failure' in any venture – he's a good psychopath, a winner! To be a goody-two-shoes psycho, cuddly Andy recommends you have certain 'winning attitudes' –

- Complete ruthlessness – to fire 'dead weight' etc.

- To feel calm and relaxed in a chaotic environment. He tells us of a hedge fund manager who boasts of having just such traits! Super!

- He tells us of a neurosurgeon who is proud of his emotionless nature. He tells us the good doctor boasts of having zero compassion for those he operates on. He is a machine, reborn when cutting and drilling into people's skulls with his wide paraphernalia of surgical equipment! Joy!

- Cuddly psycho Andy says the best way to spot a...well someone like him is to show them films of torture, death, road accidents etc. things that would turn most folk a wee bit queasy! Not psychopaths – they're winners!

- Andy has a small and non-working amygdala – it means he has no concept of danger or real fear: he sees life as a 'video game'.

- During fights Andy sees everything in slow mo' – with no emotion just a void of 'clear thinking' – what must I do next?

- Cuddly Andy says that the key principle to his success is, 'Do it now!' The live in the now principle taught by many 'therapists' as the key to happiness and it is a key trait of all good and bad psychopaths. Psychos like Andy never procrastinate! Heck no! This is why he is a 'winner' and you a loser!

Andy gives three golden rules to psycho level success and he's going to share class – oh my!

1. **Visualise what you are going to do before you do!** He tells how the S.A.S taught him how to programme himself for his role by

visualising the steps involved in a 'kill room'. 'Lob in grenade...scan area...quick, abrupt bursts of gunfire...clear space...continue etc.,' Just like the Terminator in the films of the same name. It gets better!

2. **Focus on the future!** Or as I call it and I hope Andy won't mind – f*ck the consequences! Andy doesn't think about all the pain and suffering he causes – he focuses laser like on his goal. He sees the job done and how good he feels! You could too. Er...if you have no conscience.

3. **Downsize your time!** Don't wait for the perfect time and place to start discovering your inner psycho – just be flexible and deal with whatever situation you are in and make the best of it, adding your own psycho twist of course. Psychopaths utilise the situation at hand!

Get that girl or promotion: cuddly Andy, the very good psychopath shows you how! Available from all good bookstores and lunatic asylums today! Or should that be now???!

The Western world is stark raving mad and getting worse. You wonder why therapists have clients? Self-help from psychos! Dating tips from rapists next? We will delve into pathological cultural hypnosis in the next book; I will disclose the utilitarian/functional beliefs of psychopaths. See book 4, 'Forbidden hypnotic secrets' for more info on psychopaths.

The Rogue Hypnotist's case study numero duo (2!) – the case of the man who needed a nappy/diaper*.

(*Note: a nappy is the UK term for the US term diaper.)

Some years back I received a call from a very old gentleman (and he was a 'gentleman': a rare thing in these times). I shall simply call him 'Nappy Man'. You see Nappy Man could not control his bladder after he stood up. Although he was over 80 years of age he insisted that the problem was not physical but psychological. I accepted his analysis. He did tell me that his pee problem had started after he had contracted a 'urinary infection' whilst on holiday in the US. He was an interesting fellow, as the following interview will reveal. As this is such a strange thing for any therapist to encounter I have also included the entire hypnosis session that I used for Nappy Man.

Part 1: the client interview with nappy man.

The purpose of the hypnotic interview is to discover:

- Who this person is. Or who they pretend to be. You always meet the 'agent' then the real person. The agent is the socially acceptable 'front alter' emitted to social reality.

- To find out what the problem really is and what really caused it. This helps you to...

- Design an individualised solution.

Remember: the way people respond to the challenges of their life is the thing that lands them in hot water or to a certain extent 'sets them free' – you are stimulating/creating ways that can help them meet the challenges of life in 'better ways'. These better ways must ultimately come from the client. You merely set them in the right direction. It's like rewinding an old Swiss clock that broke down. Once it's rewound again it should be perfectly able to function without you. Life is not a 'box of chocolates', for most people: the social system, which is totally artificial in almost all ways conceivable, makes just living a tough, hard struggle. Often for survival. Most folk are one pay cheque away from penury and a cardboard box. This sword of Damocles hangs seemingly intangibly but is very genuinely present in the subconscious of 99.9% of 'civilised' humanity. We don't hunt animals anymore. We 'hunt' bits of paper and circular metal disks called 'money'.

Let's take a look at the interview. The following is taken from notes taken at the time on my standardised questionnaire form. The interview took place several years ago and so is, in part, reconstructed from memory. Nappy Man described his complaint in these terms, 'Bladder weakness. Urge incontinence when standing.' Urge incontinence is an unpleasant 'condition' whereby you can't control when you pee! It could happen any time. It mainly 'affects' babies and the elderly.

'In general how are things going at the moment?' I ask.

'Very good. I am writing a book on the nature of mind. I believe it is the operative force in the world. I am also a member of the Society for*... (a paranormal investigation group that shall remain nameless). Uhum, yes,' he replied.

(*RH note: This is a quote on the society's

website, 'I shall not commit the fashionable stupidity of regarding everything I cannot explain as a fraud,' C.G. Jung.)

'That sounds interesting. I'd like to read your book when you finish it,' I say.

'You would? Oh really (he is genuinely surprised). I'm still researching it...Yes, uhum,' he says.

'Ok so are you retired or still working X (his name)?'

'I am retired. I was an accountant. I was good at maths (math) and my mother said I needed a stable job. So I became an accountant. I specialised in Commercial Law. And I am well-pensioned and studying the 'nature of mind'. Yes, uhum,' he tells me before joking, 'I like retirement and still have my faculties so, yes, uhum.'

So we are dealing with a man whose life is coming to a close; at least his final bow as you might say. He has lived as a successful middle class English gent. His face is almost skeletal and his full head of hair dyed jet black. He wears a navy blue suit jacket and white shirt. Being 'smart' is clearly important to him. A suit, even of a casual nature communicates something: especially in a retired person. He wears pale beige slacks. _Note his trousers._ His entire outfit looks two of three sizes too big for him. Age or illness is emaciating him. He gives off an almost priestly air. Something pervades from him, a feeling, a sadness somehow. I feel he is deeply lonely. I ask,

'So what's your living situation?'

'Sorry what do you mean?' he queries.

'Are you married, live alone? That sort of thing.'

'Ah! I live on my own,' he says.

'Do you suffer from epilepsy?'

'No.'

'Are you taking any medication for a psychological problem? What about this problem (urinary one)?'

'No. I am not taking antibiotics for the problem.' (No doctor to 'worry' about me interfering with his patient.)

'Ok, can we clarify – what are the specific problems and what are the exact results you desire?' I ask.

'Well I want to control my bladder when standing up,' he admits simply.

'So when did these problems start? Is there an event or situation that you feel started them?'

'Well it is largely habitual. There is a trigger. I call it 'doorkey syndrome' (at first I thought he said 'Dawkey Syndrome', I thought it was a known medical condition!) – whenever I go out and suddenly the urge to urinate takes me I can make it home and hold it until I reach my front door and get my key out. I can sit on a bus for ages...I dribble when standing. I go 7 to 8 times a night and am never fully emptied in one go. If I rush to the loo I leak before I reach the door, usually in my car,' he tells me, 'It started 12 years ago when I was on holiday in America.'

(Notice how long he has put up with this sh*t!? Clients endure problems like troopers. It takes them AGES to try to get things sorted out. If you ever need help – get is quick, as soon as the problem arises.)

'What are the positive benefits of making this change?' I ask.

'I can get rid of my urine bottle. I have an incontinence sheath and an incontinence advisor. I can sleep better too; uhum yes...' he says. He is clearly embarrassed. Poor old f*cker. Imagine having to put up with that sort of crap day in, day out. He reminds me of a listless bag of bones with no muscles, like a puppet with its strings cut.

'What have you done to overcome this so far and (if anything) how successful were they?' I ask.

'I saw the American doctors at first about the infected bladder. I had a prostrate operation and I took antibiotics.' (He tells me that somehow they can't 'kill' the infection: it is still ongoing and worsens the problem but is not the sole cause.)

Question 11...

'What future evidence will let you know you've succeeded today?' (This makes results measurable. His conscious mind will be able to evaluate proof.)

'I can stop urinating when standing. I can hold it now for only half an hour. Half an hour and I need to go, then I hold it a further half hour and on and on,' he says, 'I want a _full bladder and to continue in a strong flow till fully empty._' (In the original i.v. - I underline in a yellow luminous pen, the highlighted section above. I used to do that if something stood out as important to me. I don't now. It just sort of goes in.)

'What do you enjoy about your life now? Are there any situations in which you are already confident/happy/secure/content? What achievements are you most proud of?' (His answers are surprising!)

'I do accountancy work for the (protestant religious sect). I don't watch TV (that is a spectacular achievement in this day and age – this man is or was a 'doer': he engages with life and does not passively observe). I enjoy walking,' he tells me then, 'Six months after my operation in America my problem started.'

'What are your strengths as a person?'

'I am not a worrier. I can be amusing. I am able to make the most of a situation and am reasonably fit. Or was. I walked 2 miles every day before the operation.' (Likes routines/rigidity? Don't know...)

By Nappy Man's answers we note what? That he has good self-esteem. We can eliminate this as a component part of his problem. Any self-worth 'issues' are due only to being embarrassed in public. This is quite a rational response to pissing yourself.

The self-worth 0-10 question is asked.

'I am a lucky person. I feel the 'mind' (my quotation marks – what he means by mind is defined shortly) guides life and self. I am critical with small mistakes,' he replies. (He means professionally – being an accountant you would expect that, detail being important.)

'What specific things do you do to relax?'

'I enjoy learning about computers at the moment. I am busy doing things for the (Christian sect) and that relaxes me,' he tells me. (I have no idea if he is member of the religious sect he's told me about. It's none of my business and irrelevant to his problem – never be nosey for the sake of it.)

'Do you exercise?'

'I walk at night (because of pee problem?). I like walking up a steep hill. (Where he lives is very hilly. I went to school in that area.) I do hip exercises twice a day (he is about to undergo a hip operation. His walking is doddery. He has a cane. He appears like a 'Thunderbirds" character with a few strings cut when walking); I also do public speeches on various topics (apparently this is exercise to him?!).'

He also tells me that he had 6 holidays a year when he first retired but now only has 4. He's right, he is a lucky bastard!

'Do you have any intuitive sense of what has to change within yourself so that I can help you, or rather, what will need to occur *during the process* for you to make the changes required?' I ask convolutedly.

'It's a habitual behaviour of the bladder.' (He says something about 'doing his prostrate' later – I can't remember what this was all about. I am not a court stenographer.)

He is basically saying, 'This problem is an unconscious psychological habit. I have no conscious idea why it is here.' In the next session I hold with him you will discover WHY he is so anxious to present this idea, true though it may be.

'Can you think of a suitable metaphor that represents the desired change? An image or symbol of change from one thing to another?' I ask. Hypnotherapy is in many ways quite a ritualised, repetitious process. It never seems boring though. The people interest me. Even the sh*ts. I will include a session with a sh*t later.

He thinks, 'I feel lucky and well-guided (by God?) as a person. I fear being 'an old man in a nursing home.'

He wants independence. This is the value he seeks. The problem stops him having it. His human need for control and influence is not being met. This is stressful and leaves him feeling 'old', frail and vulnerable. He fears interfering others who would 'know what is best for him'. Plenty of those bastards about! In response to being asked if there is any reason he shouldn't change – he says no. I ask what stops him from changing on his own. He says,

'The willpower to persist and concentrate.'

He is concerned the lack of these will stop him from getting what he wants from hypnosis. This is because his model of 'hypnosis' is currently insufficient. I am about to rectify this.

'Have you ever made a similar change?'

'No.'

As I thought, this man has led a safe and 'civilised' accountant's life that pleased his mother. He has faced little real challenge. He is sensible. Too sensible in a way. He has it seems to me failed to live a life with sufficient risk. This is my own assessment. He is highly intelligent and very well informed. At some point towards the end of the quiz, in response to something I ask that is totally unrelated he blurts out...

'No. I've never been married or had children.'

O-kay. I didn't ask. His hearing is bad. I have been speaking as though he is on the other side of a busy road throughout. Why did he mishear this? A latent thought pops into my mind: this old man is a virgin. I don't even think he's kissed a girl or fondled her breasts in the back of a car. He's 'pure'. He has missed out by choice. I wonder whether this penis related problem is somehow symbolic of something. Of what I have no idea. I don't really need to know. I don't think I do anyway.

'Is there any part of you that doesn't want change?' I ask.

'It makes me urinate at inconvenient moments. I am worried I won't be able to concentrate on the hypnosis,' he says sweating profusely, red-faced etc. Why this physiological change? Well quite simply, at some point during this conversation this old codger pisses himself in my living room. As I talk to him a growing and darkening patch of piss stains the clean pair of beige, old man slacks he is wearing. I pretend not to notice, watching perversely with my peripheral vision. He knows I know he has pissed himself in my living room. Some strange piss-vulnerability bond passes between us. There is a look on his face that says help and sorry all at once but being English we discuss it not! I feel both sorry for the poor old bugger and pissed-off that he was pissed on my nice sofa (US – couch) and I will have to fucking clean it! After all I am the Rogue Hypnotist!

Thank God he is my last client of the day. Feeling vaguely traumatised and violated by this unexpected turn of (turn off) events I ask,

'What do you know about hypnosis? (Piss Man!)'

'The mind is a force. A major force.'

I ask what he means by 'mind'. He eloquently replies,

'Mind is the faculty that expresses itself in thought.'

He means the soul. Regarding hypnosis I tell him it's like being interested in something. What interests you?

'The company of others interest me. I am interested in other people. I am interested in history and where we are. This economic mess we are in isn't really anything the Government can do anything about. The bankers caused it,' he says.

'I know.' This man is no dope. He tells me he is hypnotised by the BBC programme hosted by David Attenborough, generally believed to be a nice old man and grandfatherly figure to the nation. Actually Attenborough believes too many people inhabit the earth and some will have to be culled off. Not him presumably. Nappy Man also watches the news twice a day. Well that made up shit would hypnotise anyone. I get his permission to hypnotise him; I have pre-planned the whole thing and written out his session and I leave it here for you my hypno-padawans...

Nappy man's stop pissing on my lovely sofa/couch script!

(This directly indirect form of hypnosis shows how I worked about 2 years into running my practise. It superficially appears 'authoritarian' but in many ways it's quiet indirect. One woman described my method as being like having your subconscious told off! My success rate was about 98% at that stage. With the addition of my latter Ericksonian approaches my success rate reached 100%. If you are a NLP purist or serious 'therapist', the following with conflict with your brainwashing – that's a good thing! What follows was the script for the follow up session. You see – nappy man lied to me! Yes clients do. His infection was still ongoing but he decided I was better off not knowing in case I refused to treat him. I advised he use Ali-C, a garlic-based natural antibiotic to treat the infection as the doctors' approaches had failed repeatedly.

I saw Nappy Man at a local train station about a year later. He was walking around comfortably with a big smile on his face, unaware of my presence. He had no piss patch! In the original there were no embeds; I also had a 'scatter gun' approach then. I fired out a load of suggestions and hoped they hit home. Now my work is more methodical and I created the idea of the 'problem matrix' to attack each component part of a client's problem matrix one bit at a time...)

Step 1: Acknowledge subconscious efforts + begin redirectionalising mind (Pace and lead).

'Up until now you had been creating certain

problems for (client's name)...*Certain unpleasant, unhelpful, embarrassing problems – what his conscious mind calls 'door key syndrome.' And you know what this is unconsciously, you know the justification/s, the purpose for that old behaviour, those old associations in the past and you did that so well. I would really like to thank you for the progress from the last session but we want even more and we want it to be* **more long lasting,** *more durable, just a part of his behaviour, just a new habit that was an old habit, old but renewed habits can reassert themselves now. It is often* **just a matter of timing with these things,** *because the door key syndrome is no longer what is a good, healthy or an adequate response for this man...That's what needs to change now, we are really only talking about* **a delay factor** *of seconds. Is it too much to ask to just -* **delay the urge to urinate** *– for just a few seconds more (?)...Maybe even twenty seconds, twenty five or thirty...just enough,* **just enough delay,** *just enough time to reach the toilet and urinate in the way he always used to and can again, and you can, can you not?*

*Those old ways aren't what is good for him anymore; those responses had caused him to feel embarrassed, lacking control. Grown men like to **be in control** when they urinate, they like to control the flow, learning to control our bladder and bowels is one of the first things we do learn, as a child. **Things must change** to help him **be more comfortable** emotionally, physically and in his communications with others. As a child we learnt our abc's and those symbols seemed so strange at first but bit by bit we learned what an A was and how to draw a B, because all words are just symbols, hieroglyphs if you like and then as we **absorb the meaning of the words,** we began to write short sentences, learning from teacher how to **do things that at first seemed hard until they became automatic processes, now...***

Step 2: Immune system boost module (activating unconscious mechanisms).

And you the subconscious mind control, really control so many processes on a person's behalf – your control the immune system's response to fight off infection...from the 1970's some American doctors started using visualisation to **boost the immune system...***they would ask clients or as they call them patients to* **imagine that the infection was some sort of baddy from the movies,** *or more like a baddy and his henchman, and the white blood cells that* **fight infection unconsciously** *were represented as heroes. And one boy liked the film Star Wars and saw the infection, the problem, as the baddies' spaceships and saw the goodies as the goodies' spaceships, it would all depend on the person but as* **he imagined the immune system winning that fight to beat off infection, now,** *because that is what the unconscious processes do and have done and will do throughout our lives...Others like to get people to* **imagine a control room** *in their mind...this control room is the part of the mind that runs the immune system...this system uses the most advanced methods known...they would imagine a control panel with dials that read...'Immune system booster'. They would see on the screen a representation of their body and just next to it a button under which read...immune system booster. They pushed this button and a colour* *that represented that boost would flood through the entire representation of that body boosting the immune system and just by taking some time; say two or three times a day at most, maybe just once to* **imagine this process vividly** *some people found they got much fewer colds; that would be an interesting thing to experience would it not?*

Step 3: Time distortion processes activated.

And your mind controls how you perceive time...we all have times when our **perception of the passing of time changes...***we can experience time as passing very fast when we are excited and fearful; and physiologically fear and excitement are the same more or less and it is just our perception of whether* **the experience is good** *or bad, and sometimes when we are fearful and embarrassed - it is really being fearful of others opinions from time to time,* **in the past,** *yet when we were fearful back then we may feel the urge to go to the toilet, because fear and past fearful expectations in the past did lead things to leak when what we want is just a delay.* **Putting things off for just the right time.** *And then we have times*

169

*where time passes so slowly...when we were bored at school or some other activity, maybe shopping with mum/mom as a young boy...and time passed by so slowly, time is relative to the observer...And although we could argue whether the time that exists is space-time if there is such a thing, one thing we can know is that until the 14th century there was no modern conception of time or time keeping, people noticed the changes in animal life or vegetation cycles, the seasons...but in the 14th century, so I read, in Europe, the priest would call his parishioners to church **at a certain time, a certain special pace to engage in certain activities.***

*And time really is solar time, that is time is spatial and represents the position of the sun in the sky, the whole system of time is, in recorded history, traced back to Babylon and they must have got it from someone else too...but the passing of time just used to occur...**the subconscious can alter the perception of time according to the changing circumstances that we find ourselves in**...time can change appropriately, and when we give ourselves more time and* *realise that there really is **much more time left to put off certain things whilst we focus on others**...We have many urges that we don't act on because it would be inappropriate and we have all experienced that kind of control...but time is more than just spatial clock time, we can take our time to know, really know that the subconscious mind controls your sense of time passing. If someone said I'll give you one million pounds/dollars to **hold that urge to urinate till you are through that door and standing in front of the toilet,** that's right, could you – **do it** right? But as I was saying, what if, and it can from now on, your subconscious mind can allow you to **experience time passing differently,** you can experience time passing more slowly, so you have much more time to get things done, at just the right time, just the right place, just the right amount of delay...And slow time can occur when we are enjoying ourselves, when we laugh and experience fascination at the wonders of this world...when we are in pleasant company and the subconscious knows how to do this...like the long day of childhood before we became the slave of clock* *time...get up at this time, eat at this time, work for this length of time, as though a human was an automated machine, rather than a living thing with* **natural rhythms that must be listened to***...so as you have more subjective time, now, to do many things, experiencing this time so pleasantly slowly now, you will have much more time to* **get certain things just right***, because as they say, do they not, time is everything and you can unconsciously make adjustments that help at this opportune time, haven't you?*

Step 4: Persuasion of the reality of psycho-physiological change through hypnosis.

...Because the subconscious mind is very, very powerful and this is known. Experiments were performed in which just using hypnosis in the 1930's and 40's at Yale University - willing subjects allowed themselves to block out incoming stimuli; now I won't go into detail...but the implications were that **massive psycho-physiological change was and does occur with many people,** *the mind and body are one, not separate, a simple example that I will tell you about is* **hypnosis to control** *pain. The mind has*

*mechanisms to **switch off certain pathways, certain gateways** if you will, so not all messages get through or if they do they are more pleasant, tolerant, altered beneficially in some way...During this session your breathing rate has changed, your muscle tonus has altered, your heart rate is **much more relaxed,** your pulse is therefore slower and your blood pressure has improved, this is standard...So as **these changes can be observed** the question is to what degree can your unconscious mind now **make all the psycho-physiological changes that are required** to get you what you want and the other mind knows just how, because it knows more than the other mind...only progress and learning, **change is possible** here: here your life and things re-associate, even dis-associate, now...changing for the better...nothing stays the same, except our sense of self, no matter what mattered once, our core remains the same...and you can feel very confident knowing **these learnings are being made...***

Step 5: Multiple layered metaphors addressed to the subconscious.

*You do need keys to open doors but the trick is to only open the door at just the right time and **the key is timing, timing is the key.** Doors open only when they are meant to and not before and that old association that you had to reaching the door and turning the key and having the urge to urinate won't happen in quite the same way, at all, now, you will find that using the power of your unconscious or subconscious mind you can **take your time and get to a toilet** and then relieve yourself and **feel more confident in life** and in your ability to do so, now. Just about holding those muscles tight just a bit longer, so easy, we all have a lifetime in which we took the time to learn so many differing ways of using our muscles to our own purposes, the muscles of the digestive system don't need the conscious mind – they know what to do – at first you fell over when you learnt to walk but sooner than you knew it, you had those **abilities pass over to unconscious habit,** something you just did. Practise makes perfect until it passes over to **mastery in many differing areas** – you have a lifetime* *of unconscious learnings that you can re-access to **solve a problem unconsciously.***

*That's it. Now, that day when **this business is cleared up** is your business, no one else's business, it could happen today, it might happen in a few days' time but sooner or later **there will be noticeable change, right now,** because although the subconscious mind can change certain things, I know that it also likes things to stay the same, in fact it is known that the subconscious would have like everything to have been the same since anyone were born...but the world does change, people change, for some reason and many times they don't know why - some shifting, changing patterns, behaviours, certain better responses do occur and there may be setbacks on the way but all problems are either solvable or not, now, some things can be changed and I always say to any client who comes to me with help in achieving any goal they have wisely set for themselves...if you are doing something that doesn't work **do something different...consciously, unconsciously, now...***

The extent of the old problem is just

something that couldn't and wouldn't happen as it once did because as you build on progress - only **more progress** *is possible for you, each and both of you, now...Let's return to the ocean you visited last time. It is beautiful there...there are rock pools perfectly contained within the rocks...in which there is a small body of water...the perfect home for water. The tide's rhythms we know are controlled by the moon, it is interesting how* **nature has its own control mechanisms built in,** *the moon's gravity affects the water, the moon acts as* **the master controller above** *the oceans and tide pools of various bodies of water. It contains them well within the ocean beaches, allows tide pools to remain in their natural basins, the moon controls the tides and tide pools there, the moon does this for the oceans and* **your mind can control things precisely for you.** *As the moon high above controls, your deeper mind controls your natural rhythms for you, whether you are asleep, awake or standing, old associations can and do change, now, you can allow the deeper mind to* **regain control of your bladder** *when standing, when reaching your door, you will* *be calm and relaxed, confident* in control, no fear, no worry, no wetness, you are dry and you reach the toilet and then urinate – those old associations are broken, by making the right changes, doing this *you experience the confidence of dryness and feeling very good.* You have learnt greater control here by the ocean of deep tranquillity within, greater control of mind and body, things becoming easier with practise; it's pleasant and easy now.

You can and will *control your bladder when standing* or when you reach your door. You learn how good it is to *empty your bladder completely at just the right time* – you have just the right time. You control the flow of urine through your penis. You can learn to enjoy the feeling of urine flowing through your penis but only at the right time. *The gates work perfectly.* You enjoy this natural ability, you can practise stopping every time you pee. Every time you do this you are knowing, really knowing that you are the boss of your bladder. A wonderful feeling of pride only remains. Happy and dry during the day, when standing and this is so. Whenever you stand or reach your door, you will find you are *in control, now and in your future. That's right.*

<u>Step 6: Total unconscious acceptance.</u>

(Use this stage to give a 'list blitz' of helpful suggestions.)

Finalise, alter, modify this man's perception of time, immune system functioning, appropriate bodily responses, access to his real potentials and abilities, allowing his actual power to **succeed** *- to manifest in his life, his resourcefulness to be available whenever he needs it, alertness and relaxation, reorganisations, re-associations, new associations, feelings, thinking, values, attitudes and beliefs, creativity, priorities, problem solving abilities, habituate what you know needs to be changed to* **get this man exactly what he wants here today,** *whatever else you know needs to be rectified and fine-tuned as quickly as possible in the next few seconds...The other doesn't need to know how...All changes are inviolable, protective, enjoyable and harmless...at all times...* **Make all the necessary changes that you know this man needs to succeed** *in the way they truly desire, right* now. You can access your own associative matrix to uncover useful responses that can be structured into new, healthier behaviour patterns, now.

You accept this totally now...Just acknowledge to yourself that **these changes have been made.** Great you are doing brilliantly subconscious mind!

Step 7: Future pace/mental rehearsal/associate into new abilities etc.

Dissociate - observe.

Imagine now that you reach your front door...see it as a movie over there, watching yourself...You look so calm, so much more in control...the old associations have been broken...if you can **hold it to the door and beyond easily** there is no reason why you cannot **hold it just a few seconds more,** maybe even a minute more...you are on your territory and can **feel so calm and confident, a sense of control returned.** See yourself reach the door...open it. Still in control. You enter the house or wherever you are...**no problem whatsoever**...You see that you are dry and smiling, even laughing to *yourself at how easy this was...See yourself going towards a toilet and still you are dry and there is no leakage, just control...Now see yourself reach the toilet, open the door and there are no nerves, no sweat, just calm, dryness, ah! The relief as you pleasantly relieve yourself. **<u>You</u> have succeeded.***

<u>*Associate – experience/participate.*</u>

*Now when **you are happy** with what has occurred, float into that you in the movie and start it again from the beginning, experiencing it through your own eyes, ears, feelings, changes - and **go through that whole process feeling dry,** feeling good...confident, calm and happy, no feelings of guilt, shame, worry or embarrassment. The **old associations have gone completely** replaced by dryness, control, more time to get where you need to go, that's right and then see through those confident eyes, hear through those confident in control ears, that confident bladder control, just a wee bit longer will do. You relieve yourself successfully into the toilet. That's it. Now you can take this act as a sign and a signal that **you can control the urge to urinate.***

When you mentally rehearse things like this, you actually activate the same neural networks as if you were doing it...Maybe for the next few weeks, perhaps once a day you could go through this same process, reinforcing the neural networks, locking in the changes more and more, the more you do it. The old problem has gone or at least improved, we will accept improvement, now.

Step 8: Future pace for summation of generalised ego-boosting suggestions.

(This bit is for wrapping up and saying some more, nice, helpful sh*t to the subconscious.)

Dissociate.

See yourself going about your business in some confirming situation of your success...That person who he really is, is a good-hearted individual, you have a fully deserved sense of self-worth; a loving, caring person and those qualities are returned to him. He is fully in control again. That man is self-confident, happier than previously. He is a highly intelligent man, a man of tremendous value, unique and still much to offer...important just for being him, nothing to

*prove...that is a man who reaches his door,
any door, opens it and holds the urge to
urinate until he reaches his toilet, he simply
has total, rock solid belief in his wholehearted
success. All your other than conscious
processes are working on your behalf
powerfully 24/7! Day or night etc.*

Associate.

*Float into that man who is you. Your
experience verifies all I have said. You are a
man who has regained mastery and full
independence easily. A man with calmness,
confidence and a sense of timely relief
returned, now and still much to offer, much to
do...everyone decent deserves to think well of
themselves, nothing to prove...you are a man
who reaches his door, any door, opens it and
holds the urge to urinate until he reaches his
toilet, perceptions of time changing, in trance,
in life at just the right time, just the right
place to relieve yourself – your total, rock
solid belief and self-assurance in your
wholehearted success is in place and all your
other than conscious processes are working
on your behalf powerfully 24/7! As a result*
you are confident and happier *once more.*

And that's a nice thing to know, really know, is it not?'

(Add in exduction of preference. You could simplify the above. But this is a teaching manual and not a proof-reading class. There are far too many things that I have done above than can be reasonably broken down in 1 book; you'll have to read my other ones for an explanation of the component parts. Better yet: analyse it and THINK!)

Basic formula:

(Be simple, direct and TELL the subconscious in no uncertain terms <u>what</u> to do and if necessary <u>how</u> to do it! BUT do it vaguely!!!)

1. Pace and lead subconscious.

2. Activate subconscious mechanisms.

3. Use metaphor to bypass conscious resistance.

4. Future pace specific change.

5. Future pace generalised change.

6. Exduction.

Case study part 2: The hypnotic structure of pleasure.

My genuine justification in writing this part of your book is that EVERYONE IS SO GOD DAMNED MISERABLE!!! Hypnosis can *start* to change that. Prepare to make people hypnotically very happy…and then some. **However please note: the purpose of hypnosis is not to hypnotise someone into being a 'happy zombie' who is stupidly happy in intolerable circumstances. This was the desire of the World Controller in Huxley's Brave New World: a dystopia where a bottle-hatched residue of mankind had come to love their slavery.**

This section is a first interlude in the main feature. If you want to know how to 'cure' using hypnosis or just how to use hypnosis for fun, you must know how to generate hypnotic pleasure. It's easy. This bit of your book will teach you *'the hypnotic structure of all pleasure'* – how might that knowledge be helpful for any hypnotist, hypnotherapist or anyone who just happened to be interested in the possibilities? Hmmmm. I didn't coin the term but in 'hypnosis circles', if such a thing exists, this is known as 'blissnosis'. This part of the book will teach anyone how to be a blissnotist...I have quite a few tools from my tool box to show you. After having read this jam-packed zone you will be 100% guaranteed to be able to create - at will - extremely pleasurable states of mind and body using hypnosis alone because...***WORDS CHANGE FEELINGS and in hypnosis they do so with sugar on top!*** With that in mind...

Feeling a pleasant emotion on command.

Let's just dive right in shall we? With blissnosis simplicity is often the key. What if you could make someone feel amazing on cue, very quickly without formal trance? You can! Therapists can ask questions like...

'When did you last feel at least okay?'

'Can you tell me about a time you had a great day?'

These are simple ways to steer a brain back onto the path of happiness. What I call 'directionalising'.

Or you can do this...

Feel pleasure on command.

(Hypnosis is not needed but it will amplify results)

'Can you recall a time you felt absolutely wonderful?

Feeling a pleasant emotion that you'd like to experience more of...

See what you saw...

Hear what you heard...

Feel how good it felt!

That's it!

Step into that fantastic time as if it's happening now!

See what you saw!

Hear what you heard!

Feel how amazingly good that feels!

Make the colours stronger, brighter, more Technicolor!

Make the scene 3D, panoramic...

Immerse yourself joyously in that time...

Notice how you breathed then...

Turn the sounds up using surround sound stereo!

Breathe that way now!

Focus in on that wonderful feeling...

Get a sense of exactly where it starts!

Where does it go next?

Imagine that you can take control of that feeling!

Take that feeling and amplify it now...

in just the right way...

Maybe they whirl or spiral faster?

Maybe they radiate more intensely? (I use 'they' instead of 'it' because it's odd and more hypnotic.)

Maybe they cascade in wave after wave of delight?

I don't know – you do!

Without effort!

Let these awesome feelings get stronger and stronger and stronger...

Amplify them to a peak now!

Imagine a time you could use these incredible feelings!

Amplify these feelings in your own unique way...

Intensifying these wonderful states of mind and body...

as you imagine what you'll be doing over the next few weeks or so...

don't be too surprised as you find yourself feeling fantastic...

for no particular reason, now.'

(This is level one, beginner's stuff. Let's go up a level.)

The peak of ultimate bliss script!

This is one of the best scripts there is for curing a lifelong miserable so and so of his self-pity and moaning. It is the happiness reconnector par excellence. Without further ado prepare to make someone VERY happy. This is true blissnosis.

The peak of ultimate bliss script!

(Deep hypnosis assumed)

'Imagine it is a beautiful summer's day...you are somewhere in the open air...the countryside...lush green fields and trees thrive around you...the air is fresh and clean...there is a certain atmosphere...you know the one that perfect days have...when everything just seems to go right? You feel so clear-headed...so glad to be alive...so totally serene...This place is naturally calming...nature has that effect...on all people...Hear the soothing sounds of nature...notice the feel of the ground beneath your feet...any fragrances that drift through the air...And then you suddenly notice a hill...it's not a very tall one...but neither is it small...it is climbable...you feel a natural desire

to climb to the peak of that hill...the crest of that hill...to its peak...where you will enjoy all that new perspective, that high point has to offer...BUT...I need to let you know a secret which you may have already intuitively been aware of...this is no ordinary hill...oh no...This hill symbolically represents your peak of ultimate bliss...

(Symbols tend to be common in a culture and even throughout mankind, wherever he is found. You don't have to use a hill and you can allow the client to select a 'thing' that can be climbed that represents bliss for them.)

*At the top of that peak you will **discover your vast capacity for boundless joy!** Only pure perfect joy awaits you there...A state of ultimate bliss that lies deep within you...It has always been there...and somehow you know this is true...Soon...in a moment you will head toward that hill...On my count of 5-0...**going far deeper into hypnosis and trance** with each descending number...maximising your unconscious response to these delightful suggestions...As I reach 0 you reach the base of that hill...and begin your ascent to the peaks of your bliss!*

*You will soon **reach the highest peaks of bliss...**and just knowing that makes **you feel happy...**Ok, ready? Start toward that hill of bliss, that peak of all your **joy!** 5...4...closer and closer...3...you can run and sprint if you want...2...maybe you fly there at super-fast speed...use the power of your imagination...Out there, there are limits...in here there are incredible possibilities! 1...so very close now...Perhaps you **feel an excited surge of anticipation** of the joy you will own and experience soon? 0...you are there...At the base...the foot as they say...of your peak of ultimate bliss...How good do you already feel just knowing this is so? Ok...ready? Start your climb! Up you go now! You can tangibly **feel that sense of expectation that something amazing is about to happen...**You know that excitement you used to get before a long anticipated holiday or special occasion? As you begin your upward journey...you can already start to **feel the first indications of that rising joy** within you...it is just starting to be released by the deepest part of you...bubbling up somehow...in ways that surprise and delight you! You're feeling the roots of that* *true wellspring of joy that reside in every human heart and soul! Every fibre...every cell is starting to buzz and glow...you* **feel vividly alive and present...***Every part of your soul is starting to emanate a state of pure bliss...That's it! Up and up you go...Onward without any effort...Each step gets easier in fact! Your degree...your intensity of bliss and joy only increase within you and radiate beyond you...into your environment with every new step you take into your blissful hypnotic reality! All good feelings continue to rise within you! It feels exhilarating doesn't it!* **Focus on these good feelings** *on your journey - up and up and up!!! Now, you are being somehow conveyed...to an outstanding pinnacle of pleasure...more than you ever imagined, dreamed or believed was possible...as you forge ahead...and progress gradually up and up that hill of bliss...reaching higher and higher into profound trance and deep hypnosis...you can already notice that your body, emotions, feelings, sensations, thoughts, perceptions and behaviours are imperceptibly altering for the better at a deep unconscious level! This is happening as a result of your positive expectations of the* *genuine bliss that will in short order be yours to experience and then own...Yours to keep forever! As you rise up that hill and beyond what you need to leave behind, now...Up and up you go...you are carefree, naturally and joyously glowing with pure delight...mentally, physically and emotionally...A tingling,* **blissful pleasure** *in* **response** *to this amazingly spontaneous experience!* (Hypnotic coding – see book 2, 'Mastering hypnotic language'.) *Trance-forming you into a fundamentally happy person from now on! As you surge onward and upward...more and more and more...Further inside on your unique journey...into deep...hypnotic trance, now...You mysteriously uncover state of the art...maybe as yet untried abilities and potentialities...allowing you to function, create and go for it as something deep within is being transformed at a fundamental level...each life experience can be experienced with* **more joy and bliss...***more connectedness...boundlessly so...for keeps...Your sense of ebullience/high spirits...and eagerness for all kinds of things only increases...as you find a way to...***reconnect to childhood passions,**

enthusiasms, curiosities and energies!
Every breath confirms precisely how receptive your mind-body system is becoming in response to these words...

*It is as though a threshold is being crossed...once and for all...there is no going back...down there...into the depths of what really wasn't you anyway...you aren't a passing mood...more to anyone than that...you are deeply, profoundly involved in the wonderful process of change...that you are experiencing, psychologically, neurologically and physiologically, emotionally...in all your relationships...The effects permeate throughout your life in ways you may only dimly perceive...they are deep-rootedly real nonetheless...Everything shifting...adjusting...in all appropriate ways...so the joyous scope and extent for all experience...life...bliss...and **pleasure grows more and more pronounced...**multiples itself over and over...And as that body grows more and more receptive...as every part of you that can, develops and progresses in responsiveness...with each breath that breathes you...you are maturing into...rising above...past all that...overcoming...**becoming**

totally free...more open...**more spontaneous...**welcoming many more types of experience as a result...Completely free from the grip of those old patterns that held you back...Your positive reaction to this process only continues to expand as you reach out for more bliss! All the bliss you can contain! As you ascend higher and higher up toward that peak of ultimate bliss...You can see it up there and the only focus you have is to attain that goal! Changing in ways that boost your tantalising expectations of what will soon be...all those, yours - will soon be yours... (What the hell does that mean?!) at the climax of this quest...The loftier you go...the higher you want to reach! Your hypnotic response to these words is only intensified with each step up and up that you go! And now your unconscious response and acceptance is only increasing more and more...it is continuing to continue...within an atmosphere of total safety and freedom! You are allowing an outpouring of all the vast, untapped resources of joy and bliss that you have...**You are happy,** pleasant waves of feelings pulse or radiate through you! All your boundless abilities to experience such *emotions is being rediscovered now...On you go...Up and up...They are emerging blissfully, safely, from those innermost parts of you...Releasing EVERY positive wonderful emotion for your magnificently receptive mind-body system to delight in, appreciate and fully relish! Noooooooooooow! The higher you climb the peak of ultimate bliss...the more you reach out for more of what you have to give! And the more powerful* **these deeply hypnotic super suggestions maximise your response!** *Great waves, wave after wave of pleasure, ecstasy, delight, happiness are springing forth beautifully from the most blissful parts of your joyful wondrous self...merry...blissful...positive emotional energy! Overwhelming you with* **positive emotions** *that you can simply float and bathe in...You feel only free, a total absence of weariness...no tautness or constriction...***JUST RELEASE!** *As you ascend higher and higher toward that peak of ultimate bliss! You are able to bring this about in limitless hypnosis and trance! The more wonderfully* **these feelings are released...***the higher up you go...and the more profoundly the stimulus of my words affect you deeply...You are being* *guided by an ancient wisdom deep inside the core of who you are...mysteriously leading you just where you need to go...all the way to the top of your peak of ultimate bliss! It is a peak experience that will prove to be one in a million! Just by words alone...As you rise up to the peak...getting closer and closer...closer and closer...you simply feel **wave after wave of pure ecstasy welling up** naturally from the depths of your being...flooding, pouring out, fluidic and blissful, over and over and over...Each continuous wave makes **you feel better...**better and even better! That's it! Perfect! You are doing great! It creates a capacity for even more response potential...You are more and more attuned and responsive as your unconscious finds a way to **maximise your response to these meaningful symbols, effortlessly.** You are increasingly more receptive to ideas that move you forward and make you feel good...Up you seem to soar as if you had wings...all is lightness, ease and comfort...your innate sense of **deep contentment within yourself always** is being accessed and then locked in, now! You are almost near the peak, not yet but soon...You can't wait and if you* *haven't already start to sprint, to **race toward that peak now...**using all the energy, giving your heart and soul to this moment of totally free response...The **surges of joy,** the **bursts of bliss...**wave after wave after wave come swifter and swifter now...each following another in enraptured succession...until they seamlessly combine and become a unified expression of all these feelings...this surge leads you up and up...faster and faster...closer and closer to that...peak of ultimate bliss! To a peak of all the pure joy you have to offer, now! A feeling that brings a far greater degree of satisfaction that ever before...This feeling is one of the greatest things in experience and how you want it more! You can't wait! When you reach the top soon...* ('In a moment' variant – see book 1 + 2) *you will be able to...rest...soak up and in...luxuriate and appreciate the change...to sit at the peak...happy and fulfilled...looking out from a new perspective on things...seeing the wood for the trees...able to **feel, really feel and experience...total contentment with yourself...**and a greater capacity for enriched enjoyment...in your everyday waking life! Your ability to **access*** *joy...For joy has been enhanced and expanded beyond anything you once believed you were capable of...and that's a nice thing to know, isn't it? Your natural ability to* **LIVE JOYFULLY** *has been correspondingly intensified...reinforced and strengthened, upgraded to a whole new level, unconsciously, NOOOOOOOOOOW! As you rise up the slope of the hill, very near the peak now, this process of* **ongoing pleasure increases in intensity** *more and more! You can run faster and faster than before...as if you have superpowers! That's it! You are thoroughly motivated to reach that peak experience just as soon as you can! With each step you speed up and up!* **Your power grows to experience life as you wish feeling free!** *You are almost overflowing with delight! Your bliss levels go up and up too! You are almost at the very pinnacle of ultimate bliss!*

(Your voice should be excited, enthusiastic, building to a crescendo – monotone won't work, *squeeze out the meaning of the words!)*

On my count of 3-1 you will be there...And as you reach the peak and enjoy your new perspective on things you will **feel a climatic**

burst of joyful bliss! *It will pleasurably explode like a joy-rocket! 3...Near the peak! 2...almost there! 1...NOOOOOOOOOOW!* ***Deep joy is yours to keep!*** *Luxuriate in that while I'm quiet...* (Give them 5 to 10 seconds to process this.) *Take a **rest now...**you have done fantastically...Why not sit back and enjoy the view...*

*Sink down **feeling a satisfying afterglow of the bliss** as it pleasantly subsides...that's it. You are now filled with a wonderful, all-encompassing peace of mind beyond any you have yet known. You feel a deep sense of serenity, of connection to this moment, feeling fully present, **calm and confidence flow through you.** You have a deep sense somehow of **contentment in yourself.** Happiness is yours. You are fully capable of self-validation...Of **you're living zestfully!** You **feel a deep sense of renewed security** too...You **feel safe and secure** in that place that needs that security...a place of limitless acceptance and love, appreciation and regard for yourself and others who deserve it...like the joyful mother cradling her newborn...When **these wonderful emotions remain** to varying appropriate* *degrees and they do...certain old habits just seem to have evaporated. Gone - disappeared...unnecessary up here...***The past is over.*** *As a new understanding...A far deeper wisdom, a wisdom of the emotions occurs, now. And as a result of having re-accessed this gold, this rich perpetual abundance within...this huge potential for experiencing joyful bliss that you have realised you have...you will be able to take this act as a sign and a signal...that you will **respond more joyfully to life...***Laughing much more...deep belly laughs! Smiling so much more...***Feeling so good*** *in everyday life! Situations, places and spaces and people...old and new...Each day contains new priceless moments of blissful joy for you to uncover and experience...every blade of grass is a slightly different shade of green...Look for it, it's there, sometimes where and when you expect it least as...***your perspectives shift...***With new knowledge reinterpretation can occur, unconsciously...Your incredible potential for ultimate bliss is yours to keep as a gift...Your life has, is and will be correspondingly enhanced and this is so. So you know, really know that **your own mind and body can*** *produce all the natural uppers and downers you need...That's one of the very many things that your subconscious does for you...trust yourself, each and both of you...Noooooooooow!'*

(The usual reaction from a client after this is to look at you as if to say – 'How do you know how to do that?!' or a simple – 'Wow!')

Colour miasmas deepener.

(This is a way to deepen or intensify hypnotic trance, it is quite directly indirect. I have thrown in some embeds, totally unnecessary but letting you know variations is good - essentially verb commands are picked out and highlighted as opposed to just being presuppositions within a wider context. Remember all language is either predominantly nominally based – 'names' or verbally based, having to do with actions that the named thing does. Hypnosis assumed...)

*'In a moment, not now but in a moment this will happen. I am going to say some words that will allow you to **experience even deeper hypnotic trance.** Deeper and deeper states of highly pleasurable hypnosis.*

*Now, soon I am going to say cue words. When I do I want you to see a florid/rich miasma of colour that takes you deeper into a highly pleasurable hypnotic state and these colours make **you feel much more entranced.** The cue words will be 'colour explosions'.*

When I say that phrase the first time I want

you to **start becoming deeply hypnotically relaxed** and feeling more unexplained pleasure. You will feel very good. You'll feel amazing pleasure. You will enjoy it very much indeed. You'll only desire it more and more deeply still.

When I say your deepener cue a second time you will **become so profoundly hypnotised and entranced** that you'll **sink** deeper and deeper into this highly pleasurable hypnotic oblivion feeling even better, with more inexplicable pleasure than ever before. You will feel so great. So much pleasure as you see those colour miasmas that are symbolically linked to even deeper levels of your increasingly intensifying hypnotic trance state. **Drifting effortlessly into profound hypnosis,** feeling so much better every time. You'll feel so much better in fact, in vivid 3D reality that you can hardly wait for me to say your cue phrase again, 'colour explosions', so you only feel a real wish, an urge to **go far deeper and deeper** each time I tell you to.

When I use your cue command one last time you will feel yourself automatically enter and **go far inside yourself** to an even deeper *level of deep hypnotic trance, now. That relaxation and intense bursts of pleasure, your deepest most profound states of pleasure only grow. You let go of past tensions totally and only allow your total experience of deep hypnotic enthrallment and pleasure to expand, now...*

Any colours I say or you see and feel after that, any time I use that cue phrase...you only **go far deeper** *with me on your own...**immersing yourself into that state** which you deeply desire to* **be inside of, now!** *Drifting deeper and deeper into your deepest and most pleasurable levels of trance, hypnosis, right now!*

Whenever I say, 'Go far deeper inside!' you will notice all the good feeling-things growing, amplifying and intensifying even more as you notice yourself plunging deeper and deeper into that which you delight in experiencing more of, that which you have and are and will create a willing opportunity for, **deep inside your mind!** *Because it just feels so good to* **let go totally** *like that!*

Whenever I say, 'inevitably deeper!' these wonderful pleasure states only amplify...more and more and more...

*The good feelings start with the very first time I say your cue word, if not sooner, now. Easy isn't it? Are you ready to **access hypnotic pleasure?** Here we go...'Colour explosion!'*

***Feel that feeling intensely** for me! See those miasmas of hypnotic trancey colours! It pleases you and why not? As you **feel that exquisite pleasure** that your mind and body know how to let you feel as you let go. Feels amazing to just bathe in that does it not? 'Go far deeper inside!' this...*

Here we go again!

'Colour explosion!'

*Double it deeper and deeper! 'Inevitably deeper' and that feels incredible doesn't it!? Luxuriate in these feelings! Feel that pleasure...all the sensations inspired by colours! Indulge yourself inside here! Double it again! 'Go far deeper inside!' even beyond deeper! The way that other, inner part of you really wants you to experience the deep-heights of this. That feels really good now doesn't it? Why not **intensify the pleasure***

more?

*One last time because you are such a lucky so and so (etc.). Because the truth is we deserve and can **have more pleasure!** It's inside of us just waiting to come out! So let's go get some more! Here we go, ready to experience...*

'Colour explosions!'

*That's it! Feel the beauty of those amazing colour feelings spreading all through you in wave after wave after wave of amazing states! Good! 'Go deeper inside!' NOW! Give in to it totally. Deeply entranced and hyper-hypnotised and ever so responsive to suggestions that please you most! And then respond even more beyond that! Deeply...pleasantly hypnotised! Drifting deeper and deeper, 'inevitably deeper' **so deep inside** and it is amazing as you see those colours of pure blissful ecstasy and your true depths of joy!*

(Let them soak it up a bit – allow 10 seconds of 'wallowing'.)

*Now start to **feel calmer**...gradually. Calm*

*down a bit now, pleasantly and beautifully. Calm it down now and rest...You have done so well. You have accessed some of your deepest pleasure states, proving it is experientially possible...and only more bliss awaits...For now just **feel nice afterglow feelings** and go even deeper and deeper into deep hypnotic trance, now!'*

The hypnotic pleasure principle script!

(Barring hell freezing over – the hypnotic subject will feel good on a daily basis after hearing this! Hypnosis assumed)

Going on the hypno-joy-ride script!

Part 1: set the tone.

*'As you tap into the sensual experience of...deep relaxation...and...**drift deeper** on a pleasant scene...each and every breath only takes you deeper...into your deepest states of...hypnotic pleasure...now! Your imagination is more powerful here...words can create a hypnotic reality here...certain inviting experiences can instantly become your reality here...Each breath connects to a pleasure energy...your capacity for **pleasure...is amplified here...**as long as you hear my voice at some level...and you do...you effortlessly **become immersed...**as you physically **do nothing**...outside...* (Passivity = suggestibility.)

Stage 2: pleasure evocation.

So could you direct your mind...to a sensational sensation you felt some time before? Make it one that allows you to **feel really good!** *Was it a response to something? Was it a smell that caused it? A taste that pleased? A touch? Assuredly something you felt inside? Focus* **your deeply absorbed mind, now...**on the exact place, *position...that that sensational sensation emerged, was released from, now... That's right!*

What if that feeling attaches itself like a wonderful flow of energy...to the simple process of breathing? So pleasure breathes you...So that as you naturally breathe this way...that pleasurable feeling begins the process of going everywhere... That's it! Throughout mind and body... **expanding that pleasure capacity, now!**

Any and all opposites and contraries are bathed, doused, swamped and replaced by this pleasure in you! Yet there is more!

Stage 3: taking it up a level!

Suppose you could recall a delicious pleasure you would like to keep forever... You may have considered its companionship... You may have reflected upon the reality of this feeling...as a *very real presence in your life...and that particular feeling you want...is going to **feel even better** than it ever has before...Imagine where it flows from...Focus your inner awareness on its place of origin...and again link it to your breath...you breathe and circulate pleasure here...and there...So this new, better feeling only intensifies and amplifies...as you **become further absorbed** by your growing capacity for pleasurable delights and the natural highs you are more than capable of producing, now...*

*Anything that isn't needed or that once impeded can go...melt...like dew on a sunny morning...evaporating away...ice thawing to warmths...Anything other than **BLISS** is not needed at this time...in this place...Filling you up now! With the magical power of blissnosis!*

*So as soon as the betterment has occurred...As soon as you choose...to **increase the pleasure to higher heights of your bliss...**we'll continue...Aren't you lucky?*

<u>*Stage 4: AWESOME pleasure!*</u>

Of course that was good...

*but, we've only just begun...to unlock what can be released even more...now! What if you could feel wave after wave after wave of amazing pleasure pulsing through your body – so that you **feel absolutely fantastic and awesome!?***

*So right now...just out of curiosity...what is the most outrageous, brazen and absolutely perfect sensation of deep pleasure you can possibly imagine? You don't have or need to tell me...this is a private experience...simply ensure...that this experience is as juicy as you crave it to be...Focus in on where it starts...and where it goes next...you **feel good without effort...**delight without worry...joy without strain...you **feel pleasure anywhere you really want it, now!** That's it! And it feels amazing doesn't it? It is now in unison with your very breath...in and out...*

*Now think of a time and place that you could **use this pleasure...**Imagine you are in that time now...and everything within your power is as it should be...everything you need is there...You are confident of success and the pleasure of your success in that time, now...*

*A part of you can and will...let you **feel***

good..._Very good...An outrageous, brazen source of pleasure reconnected to within...At the appropriate time and place you can **feel pleasure...**When you want to **be absorbed by pleasure...**you can be..._

From now on whenever I say 'Joy-ride!'... (You can use anything: 'bliss'etc.) _you will feel it from head to toe instantly and it will feel amazing...The many multifaceted memories of this feeling are within you...Ready to be reconnected to on that cue word...This is a post...hypnotic...command, now!_

Now in this place...You can slide in that 'Joy-ride!' state...feeling that, and each time each and both of you do...it feels better! Your deepest part of who you truly are...knows...and always had...behind any non-sense you may have learned that wasn't even yours...that there are times and places where and when it is fine and dandy to just...**let go totally into the 'Joy-ride!' place.** That's it!

You have a very human capacity to let go completely at certain times...to hand over to unconscious processes that take care of such things...when it would be best and do you *most good...Trust this, deeply, now...There is a time to let the real you...behind the roles we play...the real you...who has capacities for joy...and goodness...for innocent naughtiness...for fun...for running and playing and laughing and coming...to the conclusion...that a bit of what does you good...must be a good thing...There is a voice that guides you...*

*Now I have used the word 'pleasure'...to stimulate certain responses that existed inside you...But that was just the start...just the test...to allow you to know...that you can **feel pleasure inside you...**on 'Joy-ride!' Using your own inner voice to say those words...Or chose another one or two and say that instead...All the same in your mind...like training wheels that offer you a sense of fun and control...feeling those delightful sensations of mind and body...till sooner than you think...**that feeling is just there.***

There are times, certain times when you want pleasure...to be a steady companion...and you can imagine one now...that there is an unstoppable, never-ending supply...But...only when you need it...and even then....Just *enough...don't overdo it...Too much sugar is sickly...Just the right amount is a thrill, is it not? Wherever that 'Joy-ride!' pleasure chooses to start from is just fine and dandy...Feel a foretaste of that now...in mind and body...You can know that at a very deep level...in a very profound way...**your mind-body system knows how to do this...**It knows how to allow you to **experience this pleasure!** Of your inner 'Joy-ride!' That's it!*

*It can get better each time in this place...You can **feel relaxed...feel happy...feel bliss!** You can **feel these unique forms of pleasure** that are all your own...as you go on a private...'Joy-ride!' And you can own them too.*

*Perhaps you felt you knew all you needed to know about pleasure? Or what you used to term pleasure. What I call the 'Joy-ride!' That's it! There will most probably be times...certain experiences...that can **trigger an even better pleasure response, now...***

*There's a part inside that can let **you feel that good...**Feeling calmer...Feeling increasingly confident...It just knows precisely what to do...What to secrete...Things seem to* *just turn out right more often than not...Pleasure arrives when **you feel lucky!** But don't know why...*

We can both thank your subconscious mind for everything it's done for you...You have learned, you have experienced certain delightful sensations and awarenesses...Throughout your life you have felt pleasure...The delightful pleasure of your 'Joy-ride!' from time to time...Some times more intensely than others...

There is healthy pleasure in your life...*You'll notice it more and more, now...The more you notice it...Guess what? The more pleasurable it feels. There is a time, there is a place in which you can **indulge in pleasures!** You are going beyond that place where you were told what should be felt...beyond that place, those myth-conceptions from others...in the past...But there are times when being emotional is a good thing, are there not? Exceptions to rules. Now and in your pleasurable future...Opportunities will arise...*

And now...you know what to do...you've rehearsed it at an unconscious level, *here...***You can feel pleasure...***more and more and... stronger and stronger still...on that...'Joy-ride!' you call life! Feeling this good until it amplifies more, better...That's right!*

*You move beyond past perceived obstacles to your enjoyment with...ease...How many times a day can **you feel good...**A relaxed clarity of mind is now restored...And now, as I click my fingers...*(do so) *you can lock these changes inside...*

*And just for luck why not **feel a wonderful rush of that natural pleasure...**So you can...**feel the 'Joy-ride!' most intensely amplified...***

Nooo-oooow!'

State changers: unwanted emotions into pleasurable ones.

As I have said in other books, all emotions/moods etc. can be changed into symbols and then by changing symbols you can change emotions...if that makes any sense?! I call this **SSC – Subconscious Symbolic Communication.** Let's say that someone is in an emotional state and doesn't like it. They want to feel 'better'. How do you go about it? So easily it's frightening. The first script can be used to get rid of any unwanted feeling. I have even used it with smokers to get rid of what they call 'cravings'.

Getting rid of unwanted feelings script.

(Deep hypnosis assumed)

Step 1: remove symbolic state.

*'Ok so you want to **get rid of a particular feeling/emotion** etc...*

Ok...

just simply imagine that old unwanted feeling, that state...

as an object or symbol of some kind...

Trust whatever the subconscious offers without question...

it knows exactly what it's doing...

Notice it's qualities...

it's size...

Notice the colour or colours of it...

If you could handle it how much would it weigh approximately?

Does it have a particular shape at all?

How solid is it?

Can you see through it?

What kind of texture has it got, if you were able to feel it?

Notice any temperature or variations of warmth...

Is it cold?

Dry or moist?

(Allow some processing time 7-10 seconds or so.)

Great!

Take this symbolic object or whatever it is...

and put it into some holding device from which escape is impossible...

Seal that device so that you are 100% certain that it is solidly closed...

If you want you can chain it, solder it, super glue it shut...

Do anything you need to do in your imagination...

*to ensure **it is forever locked within that container...*** (You can hypnotically store emotions in symbolic 'containers'.)

Once that's done, you can do the following...

Push it far away from you...

shove it to the other side of the space you're in...

push it off a high cliff so that it shatters below...

or floats off to sea...

blow it up with a cartoon bomb...

shoot it out into the depths of space attached to a man-less rocket...

perhaps it gets swallowed by a black hole...(?)

Symbolically do whatever you associate with your natural ability to

GET RID OF THAT FEELING, unconsciously, now...

Great...

*You'll find if you were to attempt to locate that **old state...***

*that it's **gone completely** or very much more diminished...* (This is hypnotic coding, see book 2: 'Mastering hypnotic language'. The broken code embed is – 'Old state gone completely.' Geddit?)

certainly changed for the better...

<u>Step 2: lock in a good symbolic state!</u>

So now we've done that...

what object/symbol/colour would fully represent...

you're feeling great *be?*

You aren't bothered by anything like that...

no worries or troubles...

anymore...

no problem whatsoever...

so that...

you're feeling extremely good and so confident!

(Allow up to 10 seconds for this to happen – you will develop a 'feeling' over time when they have done this.)

Ok...Go through the process you did before...

be aware of shape, size, weight, solidity or otherwise, relative warmth and textures etc...

any and all relevant things so that you really get to know this new resourceful feeling or set of them...

I'll be quiet as you do...

(Pause 10 seconds etc.)

Brilliant!

Now we know that all feelings feel right somewhere in our bodies...

it's the only way they make sense...

so take this symbol/feeling and place it inside you where it feels...

absolutely right and perfect...

That's it, find that place...

just the right place for you today...

(Allow a further 10 seconds for placement.)

Allow that wonderful feeling to spread out all through your mind and body...

*lock it in solidly and **keep it...***

Now, let it fully and gloriously radiate from you...

throughout your mind and body...

in a spectacularly wonderful way...

letting that feeling expand and grow bigger...

and bigger and even more intense so that it fills you with wonderful feelings from head to toe. Right now and in your better feeling future!

Fan-tastic!

You have done really well.'

Now as a hypnotist you need to know how to change moods. Any mood. This is easy too. Read on young Padawan! Variations of this 2 step format can be used for any feeling – a version to treat mild 'trauma' states, e.g. phobias is listed later.

The hypnotic state changer script!

(A 'state' or 'mood' is a funny fuzzy thing! Therein lays its weakness! 'Bad' moods etc. arise for 2 main reasons –

- A universal need isn't being met and the 'mood' is the unconscious signal saying, 'Do something to get this need met you bozo!'

- You simply ain't doing enough pleasurable little things throughout your day to day existence. Get it out of your skull that only achieving 'great deeds' = happiness. It's the small joys of good food, company, fresh air etc. that all add up together to create an overall good mood.

- I once had a client who had 'bad moods'. Really he wanted kids and his wife didn't. His adult human need to be a parent wasn't being met; you might say it wasn't a-pparent. This is related to what I call 'life cycle frustration' – a growing problem in these strange times.

Stage one: elicit symbol for mood.

(Deep hypnosis assumed)

'Moods aren't you...they're just certain responses we have to certain things...

Become aware of a mood you want to change...Perhaps you felt it in response to a certain past situation or person...I don't know...You do...

Give it a shape and symbol of some kind to make it real...

That's it...

(Allow processing time.)

Notice all its qualities...Its texture, weight etc.

Now I am going to show you a way to **get rid of that unhelpful mood** and **feel better ones, now...**

Stage 2: alter symbol.

Using your creative unconscious simply alter that colour symbol...so that it now represents a mood you'd like better...This happens automatically, easily...Notice this new mood's texture, weight etc. Let the colour of that better feeling mood spread all throughout your mind and body, now...

Let it find its way to one place in particular if that feels right...You can move the entire colour symbol to that location if that feels best...

(Pause to allow processing: 5-7 secs etc.)

Now let that symbol or colour or both get bigger...and as they do let that good feeling radiate even more powerfully through all of you...

That's it!

See how you **feel better already...**This is a sign and a signal that...**you have more**

control over your moods *than you once perceived...*

(If you wish repeat this stage 2 or 3 times with other moods triggered by other situations or people. Just say, 'Let's pick another time and place that in the past might have triggered those old unresourceful moods etc.')

Stage 3: dissociate them from bad habitual states.

Recall a past trigger environment that might have elicited a less than helpful mood response in the past...it can be anything at all... (Give them a beat, 3-5 secs.) *At just the moment where that mood would have kicked in before...simply float out of your body...and land a little distance away seeing that moody you over there...*

*Now you have this distance...***you feel a calm objectivity...***that hadn't existed before, do you not? What if you had x ray powers and could see that colour symbol of that past mood inside that you over there...with hypnosis magic...simply by* **you're imagining it changes to a better colour symbol...**

*If it helps use an imaginary control panel with knobs and dials that helps you **change moods, now...*** (Generating 'control panels' can be very useful) *that allows you to...**feel so much better in such times and places,** whoever you are with...You could **take back control of your states of mind and body, unconsciously, now.*** Nice to know, really know, that you do **own this power,** wasn't it?*

*From now in in a similar situation that mood will alter to the desirable one automatically as **your unconscious makes some new associations** to things that weren't really true about you...No more than the sky is the passing types of clouds or other weather that slips across its face...Responses can and do change...It's nice to know that your unconscious sends you feedback signals about certain needs you have that aren't being met or satisfied to varying degrees...In the future you'll **see the signals for what they are...**understand the message...like any discomfort telling you that...**certain needs must be met for you to <u>feel very good</u>...**and so you take action to get all your needs met...and your unconscious will help* *you, now...*

Stage 4: future pace and lock in.

*Let your creative unconscious create future scenes...when you just **automatically find yourself being in a better mood,** without effort...Practise going through those times and feeling these feelings...from your own point of view...Notice...**you feel calmer...you feel more in control...you feel more confident...you feel more at ease...your moods are generally much better** as a result of this process...your conscious listens more attentively to subconscious messages...These great new moods are locked in...experienced more and more and more...allowing you in a very real and tangible way to...**feel better than ever, nooooooow!** That's right!'*

How to elicit and amp up pleasure.

The following is a short and simple script that will allow you to generate pleasure in short order. It can be adapted to create pleasure states in anyone for any reason. You could boost a sense of fun! It is vaguely NLP-esque and I call it...

The amp up the pleasure script!

(Deep hypnosis assumed)

'As you relax deeply and rest...I'd like you to imagine or remember a time where you're feeling x... ('Fun' – desired state etc.)

...see what you saw...hear what you heard...feel how great your felt, now!

Make the image big, bright, colourful and bold...

make the sounds surround sound stereo!

Amp up those feelings of pleasure! That's right!

*Now allow a small picture of you...being and **having even more exquisite feelings of x/fun** appear in the centre of that first* *image...*

And on a WHOOOOSH!

Open up that new picture fully so that it completely replaces the first...make it a movie of that time if you haven't already!

*Again make it all bright, colourful and bold! Turn up any sounds and so **amp up those feelings of fantastic fun** (etc.) now!*

Now step inside or float into that image so that you can see, hear and feel through that you who is really feeling all those fun feelings...Having that experience even more intensely than before...

Once more from this new perspective...from memory or from your fun-filled imagination...see another picture of you in a situation where you were even more fun-filled than you are now...

Make it bigger, brighter, bolder, sounds can be even more affecting and stimulating...amp up those feelings even more!

Just look at that! And WHOOOOSH!!!! (By the way you can carry on whooshing as often as you please! 3 times should be enough.) *Open up that picture/movie so that it completely replaces the last one! Perfect!*

You are doing great!

Step into that...get inside that you there who is having such fun that it's incredible!

See through those eyes, hear through those ears, feel how good that feels!

Feel an even more exquisite sense of fun than you ever thought was humanly possible!

Indulge yourself in those growing feelings of fun! **Feel just how good that feels!** *Feel how good it feels then amp it up and make it feel better...better and EVEN better! That's it! Just how much pleasure can you stand?!*

You can take this act as a sign and a signal that your mind is more than capable of making **you feel good for no particular reason**...*when that's appropriate...because the subconscious controls all your feelings...knows just precisely how to make you* **feel really good...**and there's not just fun...there's feelings of playfulness...deep *relaxation...feelings of letting go...of deserved indulgences...feelings of release...bursts of joy and more and more pleasure than you imagined! These feelings can and will be made frequently more available to you just when you need them most...in your everyday waking consciousness! Your deeper mind knows how to make you **feel naturally good, fantastic and then incredibly better still! NOW!** Bursts of good holiday feelings no matter what you're doing! You can feel fun, now! Keep this all as a gift from your deeper self! That's it!'*

(That's quite a nice bunch of ways to create or revivify hypnotic pleasure states. Use liberally. It's nice to make people feel good, clients or otherwise. You know how to do it to expert level now. You are quite welcome young Padawan. 'When you're smiling, when you're smiling, the whole world smiles with you!')

Can you install happiness hypnotically? Yes but...

Who said the purpose of adult life is to be perpetually 'happy'? Whatever that word even means experientially to anyone. It is not my goal as a hypnotist to 'make' a person happy; they are more than capable of doing themselves. Happiness comes as a sum total of meeting one's needs: it is a derivation of their satisfaction. Addiction, anxiety and depression come from the failure to meet one's needs: pure and simple. The human brain produces all the uppers and downers anyone needs. It is not the purpose of hypnosis to make someone love their misery. So with that in mind let's craft a realistic hypnosis script to *maximise* human happiness. Remember all the so-called 'negative' emotions are essential. You want a wide range of responses to life, people and events otherwise you merely create a hypno-robot.

The maximising human happiness script.

(Deep hypnosis assumed)

*'So the reason you came to see me today is that...you want...to **feel happy**, yes? When*

235

anyone gets real satisfaction...from meeting their deepest human needs...from meeting your unique needs as a person on this earth...they find that **happiness just arises all by itself, now...***There is no magic pill that can* **create your own happiness...**

Happiness becomes real as a result of decisions...better choices...by being **absorbed in pleasurable things more often...***Eating healthier...surrounding yourself with people who appreciate you and esteem you...from doing activities that give you pleasure because they are connected to and express who you truly deeply are...beyond the impositions and expectations that others may have tried to foist upon you...*

Happiness is present in those who find their own ways...for their own reasons...to **validate yourself, consciously and unconsciously, now....***To be happy you need a sense of control and influence...All emotions are acceptable...they have their place...you need a wide array of responses...What do you really like to do?* (You can pause for 5-10 secs between each following question to allow processing.)

- *Who do you really like?*

- *What allows you to **truly live zestfully!**(?)*

- *What do you value and prioritise?*

- *Who are you <u>really</u>?*

- *What do you really think about a whole host of things?*

We all have a need for intimacy and good relationships...You have a need to find/or be with that special someone who will/does enrich your life...You have a need for meaningful work not useless toil...You are not part of a machine...You are not an extension of that...You are you...You are human...Humans have needs...Toads have toad needs...Donkeys have donkey needs...You have a need for real, genuine love...As a baby knows without knowing how he or she does...He needs mother's milk...The contentment of the breast...Of the cuddle...Of comfort when he cries...Of sleep when he is tired...Of kind voices and the relief of urges...He needs to know that his needs will be met...He needs to know that his methods *of getting his needs met result in positive outcomes, this allows him to...**feel deep rooted contentment and confidence that stays** with him underneath the events of life...Which come and go...All suffering passes...Some wounds heal by degree do they not? Others reframe themselves, unconsciously...without your other mind trying to do what another does without effort...*

*And you still have that childlike capacity to wonder...To run...To dance...To laugh...To play...To sing in the shower! To stand in the rain and feel the drops roll down your face...To romp in the snow...To express the energy in your body...To delight in tastes...To relax deeply after effort...To **become absorbed in the fascinating...**To always be learning more...We never reach a peak of knowing all...We don't have to know...we already know so much without knowing we do...*

*You have a wisdom of the emotions...You have instincts, urges and needs that you can listen to...Ignore messages from the deep at your peril...Intuitions provide another sort of insight...**Self-belief is there** under passing* *doubts...Clouds on a rainy day melt away soon enough, do they not? If you don't like the way things are...take action to change them, now...*

- *Who do you want to share the best experiences with?*

- *And the less than pleasant?*

- *Where do you want to go?*

- *Where do you want to live?*

*We don't need to know how our unconscious solves problems while we do other things...We only really over worry when we put off getting our needs met...***stop procrastinating and go into the zone easily...*** (Structurally 'procrastination' is just the inability to go into flow at will.)

*Satisfactions and good feelings come when we get our needs met in a great variety of ways that are ours alone...We have a need to help and share to **feel very happy...**In this economic system you have a need for financial security...And you can feel securely confident that you can find ways to gradually get that security over time...and if you already have it, maintain it...*

*Plan successes but **be flexible** enough to **be spontaneous...**when appropriate...When you **feel happier** you become more attractive to others...They want some of what you have because good feelings are infectious...As the laughing crowd knows...How do we know we **feel attractive**(?) A diamond cannot see what others see in it...but they admire its sparkle no less for that...*

- *What emotional states do others associate with you?*

- *Have all of your talents truly been expressed?*

- *Have you found your life's purpose or purposes?*

- *Do you **focus sufficiently on your strengths**(?)*

*The mind-body system is capable of producing natural joys in response to certain natural satisfactions...It is capable of **deep rest and recuperation...**The body has senses that need satisfaction...Touches and tastes and sights and sounds that please you...*

- *What really does please you?*

*Your unconscious knows your deepest needs, it always has even when you were a baby...It knows what you need to **be happy** as an adult...It knows all about you...So much more and will find ways for you to **experience more happiness on a daily basis** because you have set the right course to fulfil appropriate human urges...**Peace of mind and contentment grow...***

Future rehearsal.

Imagine now on a movie screen over there going through a whole day and getting so many needs met that it delights you, only...

- *How are you behaving differently?*

- *Who are you with?*

- *What are you doing?*

- *Where are you going?*

Put a twinkle in that eye of that much happier you, now... (Pause for 10 seconds minimum to let them process this.) *And when you are satisfied at a deep level...so that you know, really knows how to **get your needs met**...I simply want you to float inside that movie and* *running it from the beginning, go through that much happier you in that much happier day that serves as a template for how much better things can really be, now.....*

(Again pause for processing time...you might want to allow a little longer say 20 seconds or so to let the learnings really soak in.)

*Thaaat's right! When you live your life the right way...**good feelings emerge spontaneously...**more and more and more...What's it like to know that from now on **you are a fundamentally happier person** from this day forth and that this simply is so...You might **feel bursts of good feelings for no good reason...**The joy of holiday feelings...Sexual feelings and satisfactions...Tasteful feelings and more...Each and both of you...Nooooo-ooooooow!'*

(**Remember the key to blissnosis: hypnosis can revivify and bring back pleasant states but it isn't a panacea. The person needs to take steps, take action in reality, form new relationship or ways of relating and achieve better and more meaningful goals or the old**

misery states will just come back.
'Misery' is a warning signal that goes
unheeded till it becomes habitual.

Consider these things, these tricks a good kick up the rear end...talking of endings. Here endeth part 2. And now for something completely different...)

Case study part 3: weight loss that works and beyond.

I innocently thought 'weight loss' clients would be bashing my doors down to book appointments. I was wrong – they only make up about 10-15% of my client's usual complaints. In book 3, 'Powerful hypnosis' I outlined various what I term 'problem matrices' that constitute 'weight loss' sessions when broken down into their component parts. In this section I will include an interview with a weight loss client seeking hypnotherapy and some tips for losing weight. The 'transcript' that follows involves a man who programmed himself to be overweight as a child! You will see how soon enough. We will call him, 'The man who programmed himself to gain weight'. You will see the essence of what triggered his problem has nothing to do with anything that any bog standard 'lose weight easily' course or book could ever claim to help him with. **People often find it hard to lose weight when underlying psychological triggers for weight gain are left unaddressed.** This is why Governments' punitive methods of scolding the growing army of overweight people is doomed to failure and why 'we will force you to be thin' campaigns that ape Hitler's stop smoking methodologies are as densely stupid as they are offensive. Anyone need only look at the over-spilling guts of the rows of MP's and Lord's in parliament to see the control freak hypocrisy beneath the fake concern. Without further ado...

The man who programmed himself to be overweight.

A man came to see me asking for help with 'weight loss' and 'exercise motivation'. Easy enough and all seemingly quite straight forward. I can do that, and so I booked him in. So he turns up, he like most of my 'weight loss' clients isn't some gigantically obese caricature you see on those weird and morbid TV shows about such things. He just looks like a pot-bellied working class English man who is very average and normal for his age. He looks like 99% of men from his background at a similar stage in life. He is tough, speaks brusquely and to the point. So we begin,

'How are things at the moment then? Ok? Terrible?' I ask.

'Fine. Work is up and down. I am fine with money though,' he says matter-of-factly.

Note: nearly all people I see of modest means bring up money. It's because its pursuit dominates their waking life as the system desires it. It keeps them well under control.

'What do you do for a living and do you enjoy it?'

'I work in the building trade. It can be stressful if I have a busy time on,' he tells me. I can see he is trying to work out where this is all headed. What am I up to? Working as an independent builder in the UK is a good job. You have a degree of independence and control; you are a highly skilled worker and often in demand with a good reputation.

'What's your living situation? Married with kids?'

'Yeah. I am married and have two boys and I own my own house,' he says. Notice how he tells me how well he is doing financially. He adds, 'My house is a nice one like yours.'

I get the mandatory epilepsy and medication questions out of the way.

'What are the problems you want to solve today?'

'I weigh 14-15 stone and I try to exercise but I don't feel it,' he replies. The next question is when we get to the interesting bit.

'When did this begin? Was there a triggering event?'

'Yeah when I turned 40. I was 43 yesterday. It was when I hit 40 (notice the languaging – 'hit' or did 40 hit him?!). I am a workaholic usually. But after I hit forty I lost all my motivation. I am having a bit of trouble sleeping. I don't have any problems mentally. But I know I'm in the second half of life,' he tells me.

We have got to the 'issue'.

'What wrong with being over 40?' I ask. By the way you are socially programmed through cultural hypnosis to idolise the idea of eternal youth and to feel inadequate when your youth fades. As it always does. Normality has been turned into a 'pathological condition' also known as maturing and aging. This is part of 'the social construction of death' which is very real.

'I remember when I was 11 or 12 being aware that dying is a long way off. I thought when I turn 40 it's all gonna be downhill (in a South London accent this becomes 'dan-'ill'),' he admits.

'So you've programmed yourself to be miserable after 40 basically? Is that what's caused this?' I ask.

'Yeah let's talk about that,' he says perking up and looking happier as though we have hit on something. He is quite a 'boyish' man, not immature at all. He is highly responsible but he has a boyish charm when he lightens up. Life makes people put on tough fronts because of all the arse/assholes you meet in life. As Dudley Moore once said, 'They're all c*nts out there!!!'

'What it seems to me is that when you were a little boy you hypnotically programmed yourself that when you hit 40 life was going to be shit. Your brain was very receptive and open as young children's brains are for good or bad and it went in. You effectively gave yourself a post hypnotic command to be miserable when you hit 40,' I explain.

'Yeah that makes sense. Can you do anything about it?' he asks.

'Course. You programmed yourself then and we'll deprogram you in hypnosis. The reason you have lost all motivation is because you think there's nothing worth living for from now on. It's just a slow decent toward death effectively. In this culture youth is venerated even though young people have very little clue about anything. It started in the late 50's and 60's with the creation of 'teenagers' as a distinct consumer group. In all other cultures and in the so-called 'primitive' cultures that still exist; the old are looked up to as sources of wisdom. They are valued,' I explain, 'There is nothing wrong with getting old.'

I could go deeper into these deliberate sociological changes and the way they affect women especially: this is because motherhood has been trashed as having no value by the dominant culture creators. So only the archetype of 'pretty whore' or 'amazon' is left them. Once these youth based pseudo cookie-cut-out media inventions fade what is left them? The reasons behind this are beyond this book's scope. In the case of this man he is experiencing a 'mid-life crisis' created by his culturally programmed 12 year old self. F***ing weird! As a consequence he is packing on the pounds. How could a Government legislate against this? A hypnotist is just what is needed. The program which says – 'Hit forty and start to feel miserable!' is in there and it needs to be replaced with something healthy and realistic. *This is a twelve year old that has hypnotised a grown man!* It's like 'Back to the Future' in the mind. Sort of. The problem can't be talked away. Rationally he may know these assumptions about aging are crap but they are embedded in emotional centres out of conscious reach. A ticking time bomb has been implanted. This man is his younger self's 'Manchurian candidate' programmed to get, well, tubby.

'What benefits of changing excite you most?' I continue.

'I want to feel more motivated,' he says. What 'motivation' means is not specified, 'I want to feel better, do some weight training and play with my kids more because I have more energy. I want to feel better in myself.'

I notice that lots of parents, men and women, feel enormous guilt at the lack of time they spend with their kids: again a product of the system. Onward!

'What things have you done to overcome this and how successful were they?'

'I comfort eat,' he says, this is as a result of 1, his anti-aging meme and 2, 'Work is not slow at the moment. I have had solid work for 3 or 4 months but when it's slow I boredom eat. With me it's all or nothing.'

So he hasn't done anything: he tries to mask 'bad' feelings with food instead of realising that the 'bad' feelings are trying to tell him something. His work situation is related to the post 2008/9 'recession' (actually a depression: that is a global economic 'restructuring' from West to East but social welfare has nullified the worst aspects unlike in the 1930's). 'Economic forces' represent factors on which few people have insight or control – this scares them. The phrase 'all or nothing' is one that crops up repeatedly with clients: I think it is indicative of the black and white thinking caused by stress.

'What specific proof will let you know this has worked?'

'It's just in your mind. When I was 16-17 years old I felt good. Now I feel tired, lethargic all the time. I have a pattern of eating food by just grabbing it. I hit 40 and I feel fed up*,' he says. (*Notice the languaging? 'Fed-up'.)

This man is actually very successful. He has successfully installed a command to feel crap at 40 and it's worked, so we know he can hypnotise himself and act on really stupid suggestions. There is a good chance he'll act on more sensible ones. Underlying all his says is? I JUST WANT TO FEEL GOOD! He communicates this indirectly like most men do when talking about such emotional problems. My women clients just come out and say it, usually accompanied by some tears.

A long and tedious list of what he eats on an average daily basis follows. It is not worth repeating here. What it does tell you is that he is lying. All weight loss clients lie to you about what they eat and how much of it they eat. It's always, 'I don't understand: I eat x, y, z. I eat healthily etc.' Balls!

He tells me that he gets headaches when he doesn't eat. That he doesn't *feel* like exercising after work. Men who work in the building trade often assume that because they do heavy manual labour that it is 'exercise' but it isn't. It is physical activity but it's the type that grinds you down, not like true exercise which gives you a lift, an energy boost and makes you feel good. Earlier on he referred to 'grabbing food' – men on building sites often eat lots of high carbohydrate snacks without thinking about the consequences. Their friends do it so they do. They soon pack on the pounds. Sometimes to discover what kind of a person I'm dealing with I ask,

'What do you like doing? What do you dislike doing?'

'I like fishing, um, and I like watching my boys play football (soccer for US readers; apart from the NHS, the religion of the English is football). I like going for walks with my wife,' he answers.

This man is doing well in life. He has a good job which brings in so much money that even during quiet times he doesn't struggle. He clearly loves his wife and kids. He is lucky to have co-created a nice, loving family. It's just this dumb idea lingering in his mind that has f***ed things up for him.

'What do you most enjoy about life?'

'What do I enjoy in life? That's a good question...Working hard and my family being well,' he says. Does 'working hard' really equal feeling good? What do we mean by 'working hard' – the Romans used to work their slaves to death. Have we just become perfect slaves?

I ask, 'In what situations do you feel most happy, secure and confident?'

He replies as all people with good families do, 'With my family. When I'm with 'em. My wife says I am working too hard. I need to spend more time with the children,' he says. So he is working hard to stay afloat and to take his mind off of this self-induced 'mid-life crisis' (whatever the f**k that is!). He is probably feeling sh*tty because his need to spend time with his family, which he loves and is clearly devoted to, means his needs for intimacy, touch, fun, play, emotional connection with others, the positive attention only a family can provide etc. aren't being met. At the time I helped this man I had no idea about these 'universal human needs' as I call them now. We often ignore what is blindingly obvious – the elusive obvious! See 'Powerful hypnosis' for greater detail on our needs. What is he proud of?

'Kids, wife. I have worked hard and have a good home. I have a nice home life,' he says. ('Home' is a word that makes most feel good all on its own. There's no place like...) I've been grabbing* food for about 10-15 months now.'

(*Notice the use of what NLP would call a kinaesthetic word – 'grabbing': this is the unconscious clue that feelings are behind the problem.) He tells me again that when work is infrequent his confidence is low. He always wants something to do. He likes having 3-4 jobs on the go. This gives him security that he can protect his family etc. Everyone wants security and that's the last thing the system wants you to have because it means you are free and independent. The system doesn't want that – it wants you dependent.

'What strengths have you got as a person that

will help you overcome this?'

'I am a positive person. I'll feel better if I lose weight.'

I ask the self-esteem rating question. Like most people I see, his self-worth fluctuates with his fortunes.

'6 or 7. Usually its 10 or 11! I usually feel that nothing can stop me.'

'What helps you relax?'

'Being busy. Then it all clicks into place. I don't like the paper work (who f***ing does!!?) I relax when I'm working hard.' When he is absorbed he relaxes like we all do. Being idle is not good for you. The brain wants to be kept active and if it isn't it starts doing odd things; he continues, 'I want to feel young. But I am getting older, I want to enjoy the time I've got off work. I want to be able to relax on a beach like my wife says. I need to be able to slow down and enjoy doing the pleasurable times. At the moment I don't feel like doing stuff.'

As I've said this is really what you call a 'comfort eating' session. I would say a good

90% of weight lose clients fit this category, and the rest just eat too big a portion size.

Generally speaking. How can a Government legislate that the people they supposedly represent feel comfort when all their policies rob people of it? This man needs me to reactivate his ability to *feel good naturally*. I can do this in the hypnosis part as you will soon see. Although the script that soon follows is based on the one I originally used I have updated it with the new, improved knowledge I now have through experience. NOTE: the script is only suitable for comfort eating weight loss. I found it to be highly effective. Say 97-98% successful. I use a wider range of methods now but it is still worth looking at what I used to do. I pretty much made the script up off the top of my head. This is often the best way to go. Trust you have the knowledge to help and then let it flow as you write/type/speak it out.

'You're not exercising at the moment, have you ever done any regular exercise?'

He replies, 'I used to lift weights, I start with good intentions. I did it for 3-4 months. I need to do lighter weights and more cardiovascular stuff.'

I explain why exercise is good etc.

'Do you have any intuitive sense of what has to change within yourself to get the desired change?'

'I need confidence (feelings again – weight loss sessions are often self-esteem/confidence boosts). I need the right mindset – to feel better. If I feel confident I feel I can do anything,' he says. In many ways this IS a confidence boost session. Food can give people a temporary high – this temporarily offsets the low feelings etc. Kind of like an addiction. Needs aren't met, there is no awareness (consciously) of the lack of what you might call 'natural pleasures', because of this he MUST eat to 'feel good'. ***It's almost as though we are not 'trained' to know what being human is!!! The 'common man' has forgotten and must relearn what his primitive ancestors took for granted as obvious facts in living.***

He can think of no metaphor that represents his problem; this is common with people who are not 'creative', used to abstract thinking and prefer 'tangibles' and concrete thinking styles.

'Is there any reason you shouldn't change? Any part that doesn't want to?'

'No but I need a little spark to get me going. That's the answer,' he replies. Can I give him that spark? Hmmm? We shall see. It all seems pretty straight forward really.

'What's stopped you getting the changes you wanted up to now?'

'I can't be bothered. Is it worth it? I was working really hard so had no time. What's the point, you know...' he admits. Kind of a vicious, self-reinforcing circle or 'bad habit' has been created in the futile attempt to _artificially_ achieve need satisfaction – to 'feel good' again.

'Have you ever made a similar change or reached a point in life where you thought...I've had enough and I'm going to move forward in a more positive direction?'

'Yeah. After the 1987 recession (I remember this. I left school with my newly acquired A levels - high school graduation certificates in the UK - and couldn't get a bloody job for a year! When I got one, it was soul-destroyingly sh*t!) I worked for (a British TV company; he continues...) as a security guard under (the name of an infamously bad and corrupt private security firm in the UK which shall remain unnamed). I worked for them as an assistant manager for nearly 10 years. It made me ill. Nearly did. So I went back to building work and have been doing that 6-7 years,' he says. He is not a tall man but looks solid and bald. He knows how to handle himself and has an almost 'bully' quality about him. I wonder if he was a horrible bastard as a teenager.

And that was pretty much that. After the upcoming scripts I will dish out some random weight loss tips that you can share with your clients. If you want. I hope I have proven to you that there is no such thing as a standardised, generic 'weight loss' session. And so...

'The comfort eating weight loss that works script.'

(Deep hypnosis assumed)

Embedded commands module.

(This is an example of 'hypnotic coding' mentioned in book 2, 'Mastering hypnotic language'.)

*'**You** have many abilities of which you had been consciously unaware...And you **can** discover them because the other mind knows more than you know, you know, so you really can **stop** and find out that the old **overeating** behaviour you once did, it wasn't you at all. **Now** recognise this hidden truth at some level, haven't you? **For** many things can change and **your** behaviour can change appropriately so you **own** these changes and it's the **unconscious** or subconscious that secretly does all the work for its own **reasons** without the other knowing or needing to know...*

(Hidden code in subliminals = 'You can stop overeating now for your own unconscious reasons.' I actually don't do

this at all anymore.)

Step 1: acknowledge the past and present up till this point and start suggesting a better future (pace reality and lead/direct new one).

(I 'bash' the following into someone's head during hypnosis – I talk quite quickly to overwhelm resistance and utilise the mechanism of 'rolling consciousness' against a person – see 'Wizards of trance', for an explanation of this unconscious ability. Put lots of ***feeling and power*** into your voice; like a coach giving his team the best pep talk in the world. ***Inspire*** *your clients to change;* make it seem inevitable through your voice!)

*Unconscious mind: till this very moment you had been maintaining this man at a certain unhealthy weight due in part to some ideas he had back in childhood; we have discovered he had inadvertently programmed this weight gain to occur. This situation must **change now** – a child's mind cannot rule a man's any-more, now, however well-intentioned. It had established a certain way of using food, eating some foods that weren't natural or healthy and perhaps responding and interpreting certain events, perceptions of the* *human life cycle and how it should be lived and experienced. Maybe reacting to certain people's behaviour in an overly stressful way, life events, that past pattern of overeating, maybe eating from boredom, or just learnt habits, a lack of exercise or motivation to exercise, maybe from a lack of satisfaction, excessive portion sizes and more...and there was indeed a certain logic in those decisions from a certain point of view, for believing, acting and eating that way, in the past. You had done a superb job of establishing that unnecessary weight gain on cue in fact, acting the way they did for their own immature, unconscious notions back then. I'd like to sincerely thank you for what you were doing up till now to protect, to look after and serve their highest interests, I know your intent was positive and purposeful. I'd like to thank you for the progress that you have already made, all the things you've done for them. Now we want to lock in the changes securely and **add in deep relaxation,** new perspectives and interpretations of certain things from a more mature vantage point, that allow them to **remain calm, choosing more nutritious foods,** at ease and more and more **in***

control of his appetite. *But you do know that the old set of responses are too risky for this person long term. His body, wealth, relationships and emotions have been adversely affected and you know for his sake,* ***this must all change.*** *To put it bluntly he doesn't like the shape he's in when he looks in a mirror. He feels that's not right, it's not really how he wants to be at this point in his life.*

(***Analysis*** - In step 1 we are simply setting up a **framework for negotiation**: that's what a hypnotist is – a person who **negotiates wisely with a subconscious mind**, in its language. Remember: ***first seek to understand then be understood.*** You explain to the subconscious that you know why it did what it did, that you **appreciate that but that 'choice' was misguided.** Use lots of **past temporal predicates** to put the problem in the past subtly. We tend to listen to people who understand us, or at least attempt or pretend to; we reject advice from people who seem incapable of seeing our perspective. From this strong point **(unconscious rapport)** we can lead – we can **offer suggestions for positive**

change. Geddit? It is almost as if the hypnotist is a go-between for the client's conscious mind, so vastly far apart are the two! They require a 'translator'.)

Step two: offer a lead, a way out of this maladaptive 'mess'.

*Now you know that this man wants to **be a new healthy weight and shape** and once that goal is achieved they want to maintain it, with a new relationship with food, **eating nutritious food,** with **feelings of comfort already existing within...**this new healthy, fit and attractive, desired figure, to **be so relaxed, calm and confident,** able to handle anything and anyone, their desired new attitudes, beliefs, thoughts and better feelings, better food is what they want, now, it's where they needs to be in their life, to be safe, happy and healthy. You know, do you not, that this new weight and shape and the deep inner calm, such **peace of mind** and all the other supporting changes that are required is what is the right thing for this person now and in their future - improving all areas of their life, inside and out. It's **time for a change and to keep the changes*** *permanently...is it not? And who weren't you ever really that's **becoming slim, fit and healthy, full motivated to exercise, feeling great,** that old programming is no longer appropriate in this place or at any time onward and only this can be true? Changing certain things that need to be changed at a very profound level, now. As you **make new choices...***

(**Analysis** – Time to start telling the subconscious what to do as an alternative. I use lots of mixed up pronouns – 'their', 'his', 'yours'; it really doesn't matter what you say, it spins the mind all over the place and the subconscious processes all the meanings and permutations. I throw in therapeutic embeds too. The positive suggestions are really quite straight forward. Notice the use of what I call 'complex negations' which are confusing and highly ungrammatical – '...who weren't you ever really etc.' An NLP cultist will be driven to distraction with his indoctrination in 'never use negatives' bullshit which he parrots inanely. You think the subconscious doesn't 'process' 'negatives': what do you mean by those two words? What *processes* can't it understand? Can you understand this? Why *can't* you think for yourself?! Did you understand that negative? How about, *don't* be such an unthinking dolt! Got the gist of that? Not using negatives and only 'positive thinking' is a sign of cult indoctrination. Also I just use lots of inverted commas (',') why? To change the topic: sometimes it's best to almost speak non-stop when someone is hypnotised. It works.)

*And so he can **eat well and healthily typically** because they are so confident, feel so good about his/herself, more relaxed in general, as some things are easily shut off and ignored, certain **past cravings for unhealthy food stopped** because the unconscious can do that, and other things let go, with such high self-worth. They love to **be active and to do exercise** in a way that pleases them most of all; remember exercise is the best way to control stress and **feel good naturally,** to be fit in mind and body, slim and...there are no doubts or negativity...just the certainty of certain success in such a worthwhile endeavour remain. You now know that **this person is very confident,** feels comfort inside, **no matter what you look like - feel***

confident about it. *The subconscious knows the psychological, physiological component parts of comfort, relaxation, and many other pleasant feelings you'd like to feel more of, it knows without the other mind knowing just how to do such things, I know you have many appropriate memories, experiences, learnings that will aid them. As a result you find* **you don't have to eat between meals** *as* **past responses of too much demand, fade...away...gone, now...**

(***Analysis*** – I like to re-teach the subconscious that it knows 'the physiological, and psychological component parts of x', this being any desired set of behaviours, feelings etc. that it can produce without any need for external stimulus. 'You don't have to x' – not a 'you don't have to' Ericksonian pattern, rather a direct command to the subconscious saying 'DON'T DO X!' I know of a great hypnotist who cured a woman of a phobia by whacking her into hypnosis and saying, 'Don't be afraid of x (phobia in question); it's dumb!' It worked. You have been processing negatives your whole life folks. *The subconscious generates negatives dummies, it generates language itself!* Children naturally use negatives often. People get confused with negations because of the so-called 'pink elephant' syndrome. This has to do with image elicitation. Saying, 'Don't think of a pink elephant means you think of one right? But talking directly to the subconscious is different – it don't give a shit; it's not some entity within you - it's you!)

From this time forth they regard themselves highly, respects him/herself and expects respect from others, they carry themselves though life as someone who expects to be treated well and when you **treat your body well and with respect** *don't be too surprised as you communicate this to others. They have boundaries of acceptable behaviour from others and want them to be recognised as valid, they deserve the best, actually deserves to* **be slim, healthy, happy,** *deeply relaxed in the way that's just right for them, able to* **speak their mind calmly and confidently,** *to express themselves with anyone they wish when appropriate, so those old uncomfortable feelings just aren't needed anymore...As someone who can* **set clear limits** *and so* **feel so incredibly good** *and competent, able to communicate appropriately* *with others, sharing needs, wishes, thoughts, feelings in just the right way, knowing that new perspectives, perhaps others points of view can help someone,* **see things differently,** *think about things differently and so* **feel different too;** *confident speaking to anyone at all, man or woman, regardless of perceived status...so there will be no irritation or doubts of any kind...nervousness, past dis – '***comfort inside'*** *– belong to others and this person is different, they* **feel content** *more and more, inner peace, good cheer, deep satisfaction, enjoying food for what it is...and you know that there need not be unnecessary doubts, hesitations, no ifs or buts, no nerves of any kind: so only success remains...***Deep feelings of calm within,** *because, again those past ways of behaving, believing, experiencing are for other people if that's what they want...and they are not one of those, and yes,* **s/he's a successful slimmer** *because they enjoy nutritious, healthy, natural food and the joys of exercise: using this amazing body they have, enjoys good food,* **chews food more slowly,** *savours the flavours of experience, anyone can* **reduce portion sizes sensibly, now;**

after all food is needed and it is one of the joys of life, **change your views of food.** *Treats themselves now and again too and feels good about that well-earned treat, feels really good for no particular reason...a confident, friendly, gratified individual who thinks for themselves and what is right for them, despite what others do, he adjusts behaviours in just the right way to achieve his goals without knowing consciously how he did it.*

(**Analysis** - Simply bombarding and overwhelming the subconscious with good ideas – remember to use 'identity level' suggestions; if someone thinks of themselves as a 'fat person' you re-label them in trance as a 'successful slimmer' etc. *Identity level suggestions affect deeper levels of the personality than mere 'behaviour modification' suggestions.*)

Because you know more than they do, you can **stop binging,** *you know what has to be altered to get them what they truly want so they can be who they truly are...and maintains the gains and changes permanently, building on past successes and strengths;*

what you have done once you can do again and you can do many things for the first time too. Fully motivated and pleasant, committed to **be slim and healthy,** *but not obsessively so, just something they do that doesn't preoccupy them, too many* **other interesting things to be absorbed by.** *Some things just forgotten about, more upbeat, happy, contented, self-sufficient and self-validating, engaging with and* **living life zestfully** *without external aids. And you ensure that that's their new 100% total reality. And this is so.*

(**Analysis** – in my experience you can't just say to a 'weight loss' client – 'You maintained weight x now do goal weight y instead,' – it's not enough. There are many unconscious dynamics going on in being overweight: personal and cultural – they all have to be addressed.)

There is no distress or upset, no stress...no misery about this or that silly little thing, no fretfulness about the wonderful process of maturing as men have since the dawn of time. In past societies, people looked up to the elders as fonts of wisdom and experience...no inner troubles of any kind whatsoever in his life any more...beyond what is necessary and there need never be because they don't concern a totally confident person, a strong-minded man, who has **the power of a totally realistic adult perspective, now***...Fully self-assured in their attractive qualities, noticing more and more of what is good about themselves, and so* **your self-esteem improves,** *maybe straight away or maybe until their self-worth is bit by bit, brick by brick built up into a solid foundation, solid despite what others may think because* **he looks more and more to himself for validation;** *those old ways don't belong to people with healthy attitudes to food, who know, really know what people are supposed to eat, who see food for what it is, who* **feel good, feel calm.** *Listening to the messages from the subconscious,* **when you are comfortably full, you stop eating.**

A successful slimmer...who'll receive compliments on their amazing new look, people will notice changes, losing weight takes time, you **have patience in the process** *as you know* **small improvements motivate you,** *but they don't need flattering* *words or looks even though they are nice of course, because they look more and more to themselves and their own judgements, their own ways of thinking, trusting their intuition and wisdom because they esteem themselves. You are not defined as a human by the amount of temporary fat you have had deposited on various parts of your body, as you change certain key habits for better ones. They are fine just as they are, talking to themselves in a kindly supportive way. They are a unique individual, a unique person on this earth...More* **reasonably assertive when needed too.**

Always more to discover, more to learn, in trance, hypnosis...between the pauses...in life...Those old things and ways of being in the past just don't belong to a totally confident person who reaches their goal weight and shape so enjoyably and easily, the **excessive fat just seems to melt away effortlessly** *– reinforcing the progress and sense of achievement which sustain positive changes. Enjoying the process of healthy, positive change: this person enjoys being who they are, enjoys her femininity/ his masculinity embraces who and what s/he truly* *is, thinks exercise, joyful activity, more healthy eating patterns, natural ways and processes, eating like a gourmet, taking time to prepare food well, savouring the food is fun, a better way of being. Doing your own thing and not following the herd.*

*Totally undaunted by passing setbacks in all ways that help, fully determined, **willpower so strong** because like a muscle it grows with use, determined to succeed so easily, surprised and delighted with the ease of their success in the right time for them, a much happier person, who slims to just the right size, weight and shape and keeps that, and this is so. Does everything that needs to be done to develop and maintain optimum health and fitness without the desire for perfection which cannot be attained in an imperfect world. But why wait to feel good about him/herself in the future, do it now, **feel...good...now...**he can feel good about himself for no particular reason, fine just as he/she is and that being good for anyone, nothing to prove, as imperfectly perfect as we all are, in control of controllable things, only responsible for those things that they are reasonably responsible for. Knowing there is a* *level of influence in any situation from somewhere to 100%, it varies, so unnecessary feelings, past perceptions, only, of shame, guilt, inadequacy are gone...Trusts the natural ability to* **make those changes, now,** *trusts you the subconscious to allow them to* **follow these words,** *to* **make them their own** *and you just know how...manifesting just the right changes as a result...Able to achieve all healthy and realistic goals very well indeed in a fun and playful way, more joy in life, more love in life,* **pleasures only increasing, embracing the simple pleasures** *of youth rediscovered, in maturity, now. Textures that give comfort, sights that give comfort, sounds that please, anything desirable that causes natural healthy pleasures and joys, allows that pleasure and happiness to only intensify:* **focus on joy more and more in this amazing life,** *takes action to anticipate problems before they arise. Deals with problems as soon as possible just as natural problem solvers do, instead of past stress and worry* **see things as opportunities to get curious**...*how can I solve this challenge most easily, effortlessly? One way or another all problems are solved* *anyway, so look for solutions habitually, now...*

(**_Analysis_** – General suggestions for feeling good without food. Reframing and thinking skills for handling life's challenges and looking out for opportunities.)

And as this confident man/woman - confident in being a man/woman, being a man/woman is a gift, a fantastic/beautiful thing - is only increasing, their genuine confidence levels, faith and trust in themselves, **conscious and subconscious working together now...**able to **enjoy the appropriate amount of food,** *things that used to bother cannot...any-more. Old problems just won't bother them in any way...keeps moving forward in her/his life toward all the things that s/he truly wants and deeply deserves, people who respect themselves and expect to be treated with dignity* **feel good naturally:** *it's just a part of who they are. So presuming of success and so reaches this goal weight and shape with ease, past self-pity gone, silly ideas that weren't yours - banished to a faraway kingdom...no matter what the circumstances or how they change and they* *will - but they are appropriately, healthily adaptive, able to utilise those many abilities amongst billions of brain cells and neurons throughout their body, listening to the bodies wisdom. Life is too fascinating for any excuse of former boredom – **live a meaningful purposeful life in which you achieve goals that you value** and boredom fades...away...*

*Harmony, equilibrium through the ups and down, the sideways and forward ways the reversals, success and learning...always learning something worthwhile, the good thing about the past is that you only had to experience it once, the river, the journey goes ever onward...but the things we learned give us certain qualities that make us strong; we are all descended from millennia of survivors and this fact can gives you strength...The steel is tempered in the flame is it not?...This native strength, positive problem solving abilities, realistic thoughts about many things remain, lightening up about...well you just know what...Reconnecting to natural healthy abilities, deep within...Nothing and nobody disturbs as it may once have done, enjoys her/his life, **look forward to each day with***

positive expectation...*Some people are silly, some pathetic, some are nice, some you can't be bothered with, openings and closings, endings and beginnings...many things can satisfy you.*

Old concerns just doesn't bother them in any way shape or form, they can even laugh, deep belly laughs, **more laughter in life, feel good for free,** *capable of producing all the feelings of natural pleasure, arousal, lust, romance for the appropriate person, relaxation, rest, calm within... a wo/man who express him/herself just as s/he wishes if s/he wants because that's simply who s/he is, old and unhelpful ways of being in the past blown effortlessly away like Autumn/Fall leaves...the green shoots of more fruitful ways developing and only increasing...It just doesn't matter...what anyone else is doing...those old behaviours and feelings are not something s/he does...It's outside of your current repertoire...No stress or strain...****no cravings, no overeating, no unnecessary discomfort****...s/he eats only when genuinely hungry, s/he eats what s/he really wants, no fear...****no problem whatsoever...****it seems like the most bizarre thought possible...to feel* *and desire for the past unhealthy ways of being. And when fear and doubt are gone, now, only all-pervasive relaxation, confidence, poise, abundant comfort, acceptance, more control of those things that can be controlled, and even a sense of fun and playfulness remain.* **Bursts of good feeling for no particular reason** *because s/he can just do that.*

The very thought of any negativity, worries, certain limiting attitudes of the past, concerns, fears or overly stress-full responses of the past - gone - just seems impossible and nonsensical...like something that just never happens in their life experience...it's totally foreign and alien. And it doesn't, can't, won't happen...no problem...gone...eating healthily is so easy, feeling good too, we know what foods make us healthy, make us feel good, s/he has been given this one body and **you look after it, keep it well, in shape, feeling good,** *no bother at all...no matter how other people react around him/her, he/she is in control and centred, they have inner poise and assurance in all the situations s/he needs to be and wants to be...no problem...no bother at all...they can do what*

*they want...always thinking well of him/herself
and rightly so, it's her/his birth right to feel
good about him/herself.*

*A satisfied mind in many ways. Listens to the
actual appetite signals that their body sends
them, s/he can eat more slowly, paying
attention to his/her gut instincts, feelings,
images of desired foods just come to mind
when needed, perhaps chewing food slowly,*
savour each mouthful, *only eat when
s/he's truly hungry and as soon as she
receives that pleasant, healthy full feeling s/he
stops eating, if necessary* **comfortably
leaves food on the plate.** *There is so much
abundance in this world. Our parents'
attitudes - no matter how well-intentioned -
are not always right for us today. As an adult
you don't need their approval. Binges of any
kind don't suit a confident, attractive, strong-
minded man/woman who esteems themselves
highly more and more...***eating in a
respectful way** *and this is so...Such
men/women can compartmentalise events, no
longer allowing problems in one area to affect
another, knowing that things must and will
change, it's inevitable, direct that change by
the fact that you* **take action to make**

things better.

While I talk imagine engaging in some form of exercise of your choosing that makes you feel great, no longer generalising negatively about him/herself due to others past opinions - suggestions, opinions are not necessarily reality: everyone makes mistakes, you are human, imperfect but what we learn makes the journey more interesting, we all need the essential roughage of life. Turn disadvantages into advantages by discovering that meaning is flexible and not rigid, three people seeing one event have many differing interpretations. Avoiding processed food, non-fat, low fat products/alternatives, GMOs that are so unnatural that calling them food is a joke.

(***Analysis*** – you could edit this hugely but I am giving you TOO much for teaching purposes. You are often dealing with years of familial and cultural conditioning and I have found it needs to be 'overwhelmed away' in hypnosis. *De-programming can take time.* **I was dealing with about 30 years of subconscious programming here!** Remember the programming someone has received has 'worked' to a certain extent; if you're going to take dumb ideas away you have put better ones in. Tip: *be general to let them find their own solutions* – a good hypnotist stimulates creative problem solving, he doesn't re-programme.)

And no matter what things used to produce cravings in the past that can stop, no longer happens, no longer true about him/her, this man/lady knows there are better ways to **solve problems unconsciously to get genuine needs met, now.** *There are times when it is best to* **ignore certain feelings by focusing on other things,** *unconsciously, not wise to always live for the moment when life is so long. Do what you can - accept what you can't and utilise your wisdom to distinguish between the two...A more loving, deserving, happy man/woman, much happier than before and such people simply don't have those old cravings...it will seem the most organic response in the world just to let him/her* **feel great, totally confident,** *to allow him/her to excel at all the things s/he is most passionate about, passion and joy only increase. And every time that happens, you will give him/her a wonderfully reinforcing feeling of joy, inner strength and* *purpose...a good feeling for being a very confident man/woman who slims easily, eats well, relationships developed in better ways,* **responding differently,** *more* **calmly, easily** *to things that once would have had stressed them out,* **less physical tension,** *letting certain things go, shutting some things off, in just the right way for them, successfully, securely, solidly from this moment forward, keeping this confidence, this certainty, deep happiness, this success s/he so desires and deserves for the rest of their amazing life. We can always* **learn new helpful things...** *We are always learning and unlearning, developing in the way that it right for us. Always more to discover...trusting natural insights, intuitions, instincts...feelings change, attitudes too, ideas, beliefs and values, cravings, thought patterns, lifestyle choices, shopping habits, activity levels, perception of time, sleep patterns, metabolism, energy levels, focus of interest and concentration, motivation and willpower, levels of responsibility and persistence, arousal and relaxation, ability to* **feel good natural feelings naturally,** *communications, new associations, re-*

*associations, re-organisations of already existing subconscious structures and anything else that needs to be improved, now, can and will occur to allow this person to have **a successful slimmer's mind-set now** – a happy and healthy person, so confident, past positive ways returned and yet enhanced and grown stronger, better, a higher level of functioning with a clean bill of health. **Free from any old unhelpful, unhealthy habits now.** Complete the process now subconscious - you will make these changes and more, allowing this person to become slim, fit and healthy at just the right pace, now, changing as quickly as possible in the next few seconds. Changing only in the best, life-affirming, normal ways at all times. You can access your own associative matrix to uncover useful responses that can be structured into new, better, healthier behaviour patterns, now.*

*Just acknowledge to yourself as you fully accept and understand that **these changes have been made.***

Step 3: get rid of past patterns symbology - dissociate old habits.

*As I continue to talk, **relax and go even***

__deeper down...__imagine before you in some pleasant place is some form of technology on which you can see images and hear sounds. Might be a cinema/movie screen, could be a PC, TV, IPhone – whatever you like, whatever's best for you. You know what that is. I don't!

(Allow 5 seconds or so processing time.)

When you've got that - allow an image to appear on that screen of how and who you perceived you were, before this session began. The person you're not who overate, who didn't feel so good about himself etc. That man you used to be. Now make a pledge to yourself at a very deep and fundamental level that __those things are and must remain part of the past, now.__

When you've done that in your own way...I suggest you find a way to do the following in your mind...Turn that image into a black and white faded one...so it's almost not quite visible...Turn down the sound somehow so that it is indistinct and somewhat inaudible...the old messages just can't get through...now turn off that device so that __that image is gone forever, now.__

(Pause a beat...)

*In your own way, find a way to drain all past power from that device so that **the old patterns are powerless to affect you, now.** The past ways are no longer true about you in any way shape or form.*

(Pause a beat.)

*Next, find some way in your imagination to destroy that device, could be a laser gun...a cartoon bomb...a safe suspended from a crane...really **use the power of your creative unconscious.***

(Pause a beat.)

*Now, destroy that old device in your own way while I'm quite quiet for a few seconds...That's great! You can take this liberating act as a sign and a signal that **all the appropriate changes have been made once and for all.** And somehow you just now this. And that is a very nice thing to know because it means **you are completely free** to...*

Step 4: step into the positive future you - associate into the 'new you'.

*...Know now **you are over that...**see a free you with all the best qualities that you have reconnected to in yourself during this hypnosis session...notice them in some situation that confirms fully for you that **this has worked...**eating well and sensibly...exercising and enjoying it...and most importantly feeling good about himself no matter what he is like physically...loving and loved, happy and secure, someone like that...who you know...is assured to **lose weight easily...**knowing, really knowing that their other than conscious processes are working on the behalf to support them in all worthy endeavours 24/7! Perfect!*

When you are ready – step into that confident slimming you! All your best and strongest qualities are amplified! Now, see through those eyes. Hear through those ears! Feel how good you feel! Feel how great you feel! That's right! Taking this act as a symbolic sign and signal that you are now who you really were deep inside. Muck on your shoe ain't a part of you! Knowing that from this perspective – **this goal is easily achieved,** *and that's that.'*

(Add in anything else you want etc.)

Basic formula:

(Be simple, direct and TELL the subconscious in no uncertain terms what to do and if necessary how to do it: vaguely – let them go off into trance-land through your words which stimulate helpful ideas and images to pop into their mind etc.)

1. Pace and lead subconscious.

2. 'Deprogram' and suggest better/more mature responses and attitudes to life changes etc.

3. Teach healthy eating patterns in hypnosis and reconnect person to ability to listen to subconscious messages and get real needs met.

4. Symbolically destroy old patterns in a big 'gestalt'. ***You dissociate clients from 'failure'.***

5. Symbolically 'install' generalised

change for a 'successful slimmer's mindset'. In weight loss sessions, you give them a better mindset which makes weight loss possible. The invisible but very real 'barriers' are gone. _You associate clients into 'success'._

6. Exduction etc.

Note: this is only one of many ways to do a weight loss session. I have constructed so many such sessions that it would be impossible to reveal them all – this book is to stimulate your thought so you can generate your own patterns of change. They are I think blindingly obvious! I have done this stuff in this style over and over and it is so effective it still surprises me!

Pleasure fractionation + waking hypnosis deepener.

All the deepeners can be used in ANY form of hypnosis – therapy, stage, erotic, you name it bozo! This is a good variation of a 'pleasure convincer' (psychologists call these 'cognitive tasks'). Get ready to make someone hypnotically high! Watch their face for signs of bliss; even a stoned look is not unheard of! A note of caution: bliss and its induction is not essential to any hypnotic intervention. Bliss states are not unknown in early cult conditioning processes before you become a zombie! This one is safe. It's also a good pattern interrupt for depressives etc.

The waking hypnosis pleasure fractionation deepener script.

(Wow, that's a mouthful – hypnosis assumed)

'When I do x (pick a trigger - farting, finger click, saying 'Biro', counting to 3, touch your elbow etc.) *your eyes will open but **you will remain in deep hypnosis** and in fact go 10 times deeper*...feeling absolutely incredible, any amazing, appropriate emotion your subconscious wants you to feel!*

When I do y (another trigger – 'Codename blue-lightening!', 'Deep sleep!', clap my hands, touch your forehead/third eye spot etc.) *your eyes will instantly close and you'll **go fifty times deeper into trance and hypnosis feeling awesome!***

(Some very good hypnotists insist that you repeat instructions so that the subconscious 'gets it'; I have never done this and find it always gets it first time)

Ready? (Rhetorical, priming subconscious to activate response soon...)

Here we go...

'Biro!'

Doesn't that feel outstanding! Relish that experience! (A beat...)

'Codename blue-lighening!'

*50 times deeper **feeling wonderful!***

And again...

'Biro!'

*Wow! You **feel so incredible** don't you? Just*

how good does that make you feel?

'Codename blue-lightening!'

*50 times deeper than ever before **amplifying that pleasure state as you go all the way down** in that way...*

One last time for luck...make this feeling or set of feelings the best yet!

'Biro!'

That's it!

***Feeling so marvellous** that it truly amazes you that you have such capacities for pleasure...Your levels of joy and happiness increase appropriately in daily life as a result of this hypnotic learning, now...*

'Codename blue-lightening!'

Deeper and deeper than ever before...

Down...you...go...

In...you...go...

*Off into deeper hypnotic **SLEEP!***

50 times deeper without even knowing in one

way what that means...

That's right!'

(* By the way, getting someone to open their eyes but experience a deepening of hypnosis will totally confuse and mindf**k them; that's supposed to occur when you wake up! **Don't worry, most people in daily life are in eyes open hypnosis, this will present no problem!** At the end of this process carry on deepening etc., start interventions as you wish.)

How to decouple emotions from anything.

'...a good soup and a warm bed is already quite a lot.' German proverb.

Sometimes things that have no need to be associated get associated. When someone has an 'emotional eating' problem it is because they have learned, usually from childhood to link not getting various needs met, usually of an emotional nature with feeling hungry! Stress or any unpleasant feelings at all cause a person to crave a box of chocolates, you name it. These things need to be separated.

- Needs over here...Hunger over here.

Sometimes we need to outgrow old habits. It's a bit like thumb sucking; it did provide comfort as a child, or at least intensified it, it was an anchor/trigger for that state: but in an adult it's just plain weird! Sometimes I will throw in this abbreviated version of an NLP fast phobia 'cure' as a module in a session. I will leave it generic for you to use with any problem whereby you are required to erase unwanted links.

Dissociate unnecessary associations script.

(Deep hypnosis assumed)

Step 1: Hypnotic prologue - prime for change.

*'Sometimes things get linked that do not need to be...Sometimes it's better to know that some things aren't related at all...We need to know that x and y are sometimes just that...***Certain things need to become separated, now...****One thing can be over there...And another over here...And you can know each needs a different set of responses that lead to satisfaction...*

Step 2: Dissociated fast forward-frazzle old behaviour!

*Recall a time when you would have carried out an unwanted behaviour pattern **in the past, now...**in which those two things **were** linked...* **(Past predicates in abundance please.)** *See it on an old TV over there somewhere...That's it...When you have it...and using your imaginary remote control...very, very quickly at the speed of thought, fast forward that memory all the way to the end watching that you back then engaging in that* *outmoded behaviour...* **(Say this line and the next quickly!)** *Watch that old movie until you notice that younger you notice that what you were doing actually solved nothing!* **(Be emphatic about this!)**

(Allow 3-5 secs processing time.)

<u>*Step 3: Associated rewind re-patterning process.*</u>

(Voice tempo back to normal hypno-speed.)

*Good...Now, float into yourself...Feel how you feel at that memories completion knowing and feeling that whatever the intent and real need that lay behind that behaviour has not and will not ever be satisfied that way...**Make these learnings unconsciously, now...**Now, at the speed of thought – whizz back through time in that memory –* **(Again say this quickly – give no time for pausing!)** *And all your appropriate processes going backwards too! Whizz! Zap! That's it, to just before that recollection began.*

(Allow 3 secs max! FRY THEM!)

STOP!

(Voice tempo returns to normal etc.)

Things have been reprocessed, now, *appropriately in a different place, in a different way. Excellent! You are doing great! So **you don't connect those old things in that old way** – any...more...*

Stage 4: Consolidate learnings, confidence boost + future pace.

*You realise now at a very deep level that **you have choices...** You are going to pay attention to the wisdom of your emotions from now on...You won't smother them or suffocate them any longer...You pay attention to messages from the unconscious, now...when appropriate...Doing what you did had nothing to do with getting that need met...No one sensible carries on doing something ineffective and unworkable...No matter how well-intentioned that younger part of you was...it didn't have the wisdom you have now...When you feel an emotion you'll know it's just a signal that you need to take action to get that need satisfied in a better, more mature, adult and always appropriate way...As a result **you feel much calmer in general...** You are not fighting yourself but* *working together...in synergy...When **your conscious and unconscious work in alliance** your are powerful! If you need to **relax** – do something to relax. If you need company go and meet your friends. If you need to exercise and be active – do so in enjoyable ways. Circles can't fit through square holes. If it rains you put up an umbrella and don't wish the rain would go away. Take action to get emotional needs met when required. As a result of these needed changes you **feel much more confident** in turn...You can see the wood for the trees...you **think much more calmly and rationally** about how to solve problems, unconsciously, now...What if you knew you could believe that...**you are a great problem solver...**What if problems were challenges that helped you develop and discover ways you never thought you could or have to make your life better on a daily basis...*

(Mildly confusing – note: your mind can generate meaning from gobbledygook!)

*Your subconscious guides you always...in all your efforts, now! Paradoxically because **those things are finally separate now,*** *you feel more unified and focused than ever before...and that's a nice thing to know, is it not?*

*Watch yourself on a brand new TV at an appropriate time in the future **getting those needs met naturally** with the old things totally separate and able to be solved individually...That's it! Look how relaxed they are...* ('They' = dissociated.) *How they are **making better decisions and choices...***

Now, when you are happy with those new responses and understandings float into that healthier, happier calmer you... ('You' = kind of associated.) *And see through those eyes, hear through those ears and feel how great you feel as you get emotional needs met separately and do whatever else you need to get other satisfactions for other things, when needed. Take a full 30 seconds to do this while I'm quiet as a mouse...*

(Wait 30 secs and...)

*You can take this act as a sign and a signal that all parts of you are working to help you **get all your needs met...**and you do so; you fully accept and understand that **these*** *changes have been made.'*

This might not always work, say if 'trauma' was involved and symbology interventions would be better placed to restore calm etc. See the dentures phobia for tips on mild forms of de-traumatisation work in this book.

The 'place' that is deeper deepener.

In 'Powerful hypnosis' I spoke about the fictitious entity known as 'places in the mind'. This can be of the upmost aid to the hypnotist. *In hypnosis people believe in magic* – or at least 'hypnosis magic'. You can get a person to deepen their own trance by telling them to 'find a place that's deeper'. Doesn't exist in external reality but in the mind – ah! It is an example of a symbolic deepener. A way to intensify hypnotic trance.

Going to the place that's deeper script.

(Deep hypnosis assumed)

*'Your unconscious knows the hypnotic reality...that there exists a place inside far deeper than this one...You are capable of going there without me...You don't need my help to **go there now...**It is really just a more intense state of absorption...Go and find your deeper place...A more secret place that only you can know about...A deeper place inside, now...And you can get there...go there...just as soon as I say **BLISS!***

(Pause a beat...)

BLISS!

Per-fect!

(Pause another beat to let them go there...)

But there's more...Deeper states that you can and will experience...Far deeper than that one...You can find your own way there...Your unconscious is very well aware of its experiential existence...It's as easy as: one, two, three to **go there now...***without my help...on your own...controlling the depth of your own hypnotic state at will. You'll be able to go there just as soon as I say the very hypnotic word –* **TRANQUILLITY!**

Ok? Ready?

Here we go...

(A beat...)

TRANQUILLITY!

(Pause to allow processing...)

Great, you are doing brilliantly! Ok, now one last time for luck! There is beyond this wonderful place of blissful tranquillity, an even deeper one...Why, your unconscious already *knows about it...and now you can discover its existence all for yourself...Deep down, I'm right in saying, you are aware of it yourself already...It's almost as if it's calling out to you to go even deeper, to **go there now...**Find, locate that deeply hypnotic state of **even greater absorption** in the process of your success...You can find your way there now...Simply...Profoundly...Effortlessly...As soon as I say **PROFOUND SECURITY!***

That's your trigger!

(A beat.)

PROFOUND SECURITY!

That's it, that's the way... (Pause etc.) *Lovely, now just stop right there for a moment...there...Become vividly aware of the reality of how incredibly good this genuinely feels! **Feel that deep state of trance! Feel that deep state of hypnosis! Feel this mysteriously natural bliss of hypnotic trance, now...**In your mind...In that body...And how magnificent does that feel?*

It feels outstanding perhaps awe-inspiring does it not? To discover the power of your mind. Naturally so...You have such capacities. And now...what we call **consciousness need not attend** *but can be grateful to happily enjoy a rest...Because now I am talking directly to YOU! The far...deeper mind! Nooooo-ooow!'*

Formula: create fictitious entity 'place' then create trigger to elicit it. Simple.

What hypnotists don't want you to know: how to lose weight without hypnosis.

Warning: the following is not medical advice; the Rogue Hypnotist is not liable for what you do with the following info.

Listen, if you have no emotional 'issues' etc. losing weight is so EASY. Shall I tell you the formula? You can teach it to clients in hypnosis. The following is for 100% realists who do not want the illusion of 'magic pills'.

1. **Go organic.** This is THE single most important step. Contrary to myth you cannot eat anything you want and lose weight *sustainably.* *All food that is reared or grown using inorganic methods is so unhealthily, even dangerously produced as to represent a threat to human life long term.* I advise you do some serious research into the long-term consequences of all the pesticides etc. used in 'modern farming', 'factory farming' etc. I have found that going organic costs less because you eat less as the food is more nutrient dense. Also the money you save in good health and zero doctors' visits balances the extra cost out too. I don't get colds three

times a year after going organic. I might only get the snuffles once, a teeny bit, over the winter. You'll feel so much better as your body doesn't have to try to detox from all the poisons it's trying to flush out. *The reason you hate veg is because you never ate real organic veg.* Eat it and notice the look and taste difference – yes, it actually has taste. You will crave it and want all the little vitamins and trace, er, thingamabobs and so no longer require expensive vitamin supplements. Some people approach local farmers and work out a financially viable deal.

2. **Exercise 5 days a week.** Don't kid yourself for a moment, if you want to get slim and fit and sexy you MUST get off that lazy, lard arse/ass of yours and make a regular, disciplined exercise routine a part of your life. There is no way around this. If you are overweight you are taking in too much energy. It must be used up through exercise. The reason people fail to do regular exercise is that 1. They don't feel like it. 2. They think they have to go to the gym or run to lose weight and they hate doing both. 3. They have no idea it's the best way to control and dissipate stress. When you exercise often you

feel so good from the exercise you don't need to comfort eat.

Now to control stress, as I said in my 3rd book, 'Powerful hypnosis', all you need to do is 20-30 minutes of exercise, 3-4 days a week max. But to really lose weight in a way that you see results relatively quickly and hence positively condition yourself to stay motivated to lose more, you must up the ante. I say 3 days you do a minimum half an hour pure aerobics. For 2 days you do either anaerobic solely or a mixture of both. This can last up to 40 minutes to 1 hour.

The 'secrets' to starting sustainable exercise and losing weight are:

1. **You must warm up!** Stretch first! You can't go from slob to sex bomb in one day. Your underused body needs to be coaxed back to life.

2. **Start exercising gently.** Let me give you an example: say you want to run. That's your preferred exercise – well you run-walk first. What do I mean? Let's say you want to jog for half an hour. Run five minutes and then walk five, run five, walk

five etc. This way you gradually recondition the body to be able to use energy properly. Over the course of two to three weeks, gradually lengthen the run phase of the equation. Soon you'll be running the whole half hour.

3. **Only do exercise that remains within a normal range of human motion**. The unique dynamics of your body. If you don't you'll get injured. You must be able to get into the exercise 'groove'. If that pec-dec feels wrong stop using it and do dumbbell bench presses etc. Experiment till you find the moves that feel right.

4. **Stop eating when you are slightly full.** Look let's face it; it can be very nice to stuff your face. But if you want to get slim and stay that way you MUST stop eating when you just feel contentedly full. Children do this automatically – they know when they can't eat a morsel more. This is the key to reducing portion size. Adults being stupid due to a whole host of warped conditionings need to relearn this reality. *One of the golden rules of good mental and physical health is: stop*

*ignoring subconscious feedback signals
and start listening to their wisdom.*

5. **Cut out all artificial sweeteners etc.**
Aspartame, Mono-Sodium Glutamate etc.
are all artificial crap. *A golden rule of
healthy living should be: nothing passes
my lips and enters my system that isn't
100% natural.* Contrary to myth artificial
sweeteners make you fat.

6. **Eat butter not margarine and 'low fat
spreads'.** Repeat after me - Low fat = big
gut! Butter is natural and we've eaten it for
donkey's years; which is an English saying,
meaning a bloody long time! Margarine is
a bizarre gloop made from strange oils. We
only started eating it in Britain during
World War 2 due to the reality of food
rations. Use natural butter.

7. **Make sure you eat fat and carbs – do
not cut them out of your food intake.**
Do not ever go on a low carb diet. Do not
ever cut fat out of your food intake (see
no. 8.) The body and brain cannot
manufacture sufficient carbs; they/it must
get it from external sources. Your brain
fuel is carbohydrates - it needs them to

function. Period, as Americans say. It is not carbs that are 'bad', it is Genetically Modified Carbs (GMO) and non-organic breads etc. that make people end up looking like waddling rolls of stuffed pork. Mexican high yield mutant dwarf wheat that is used in up to 90% of all wheat products is linked to so many health problems that I can't list them all here. This subject is a major study in itself. Organic carbs are fine. Eat what you need and then stop. It is mainly a minor addiction to sugary sweets that makes people pack on the poundage.

8. **You need fat.** Poor old fat. Befriend fat and cholesterol. Your brain and entire nervous system is made up of large quantities of fatty cholesterol. Do not cut out fat. Make sure both fat and cholesterol make up a part of your food intake. Drop the egg phobia, eggs are good for you. Your grandfather and grandmother ate tons and were as strong as an ox. *If it is natural it is good.* In fact eat non MSG pork scratchings/rind for the needed fat. Never cut off the rind etc. of meat – cook

the fat slowly so it renders and gobble it down.

9. ***Do not drink booze every day of the week.*** Developing a beer belly? Don't despair, don't go crazy and go all teetotal on me! Moderate your intake, you pretty much know what I mean and have at least 2-3 days off the booze a week. Your belly will shrink.

10. ***Eat junk food or takeouts/takeaways only once a week.*** Instead of living like a monk, do not cut treat meals, junk food out etc. Save it, at the most, for a once a week treat. One of the reasons you are tubby is that you can't resist temptation. Temptation resistance is like a journey and a muscle, you set a direction and it gets easier with practise. The problem is you live in a 'f*ck it' culture; the only problem is you get f*cked as a result!

11. ***Cook your own food.*** Your food must taste nice! For it to taste nice you must be a good cook. The amount of overweight clients I see who can't cook or are bad cooks is legion. Buy a cookbook and learn, watch the cooks on YouTube etc. You have

a human need for food to taste good – no bland rabbit food unless you genuinely like it, ok? This skill will also teach you self-reliance and save you money.

12. ***If you are bored, don't eat, do something interesting.*** 'I boredom eat!' Ok, how about you get a more interesting life? I mean really.

13. ***If you fry foods, 99% of the time use palm oil.*** One of the things that makes us all pile on the belly fudge is the wide array of bizarre oils that we use to cook. Historically humans did not use such sources of vegetable oils to heat our animal kills etc. The human body seems to find it hard, if not in some cases nigh on impossible to shift this sort of intake once it is stored within us. Use palm oil or go back to using some animal fat to cook your food in. Keep all the other odd oils to a minimum. Essentially you are using mechanic's oils to fry with.

14. ***Use Celtic sea salt instead of 'table salt'.*** Table salt won't kill you. We need salt. The salt Nazis have been telling us for decades now that salt kills us, actually we

would die if we didn't have it. A bit of excess salt is harmlessly excreted through the kidneys. However table salt has been linked to artery damage etc. as it passes through the body. The theory is: the process used to make it can turn it into an almost glass-like substance which can slice! Don't worry though, table salt won't kill you tomorrow, it might never do it. The damage is apparently cumulative in some and takes decades to have an effect. If you can get it use Celtic sea salt which is more traditional and 'wholesome' if you like. Why change what's worked for man for thousands of years?

15. ***Get off of anti-depressants.*** One of the biggest causes of obesity is anti-depressants. They cause a great deal of weight gain in some people. Getting off them once you're on them is another story; they are unfortunately designed to be highly addictive. I will hopefully deal with how to get off these nasty pills in a future book on anxiety with a section devoted to treating 'depression' with hypnosis which is mercifully drug free and easy.

16. ***Use less butter and ketchup etc. with food.*** If your food is tasteless and bland you are likely to want to add lots of stuff like ketchup, mayonnaise and other attendant slime to give it some flavour. Unfortunately if you add it to everything, pretty soon adding that sugar packed goo will ensure that looking straight down at your feet becomes nigh on impossible. Use it much less and often not at all. It's an easy habit to break if you really want to.

17. ***Eat one pudding a week. Occasionally treat yourself to ice cream, chocolate, biscuits etc.*** I've had a hard day, I deserve this treat. You do, but that 'treat' comes at a price when you do it every day. Is your work too stressful? What triggers you to eat that podgy inducing gorgeous tit-bit? We know they taste nice, it's just they have almost ZERO nutritional value. If you are reaching for the sweeties/candies etc. stop and ask, *'What needs are not being met in my life?'* Get those needs met and then watch the pounds melt away.

18. ***Think and eat like a caveman/woman.*** Cavemen (so-called)

ate to survive. They didn't eat junk that had no nutritional value because if they did they would have died off. Have you seen how lean so-called 'primitives' usually are? They know exactly what parts of an animal to eat so as to avoid scurvy. Yet they don't know what vitamin C is. Think - *'Would my ancient ancestors have eaten this?'* If not maybe give it a miss or cut it out entirely.

19. ***Eat something close to the historical diet of your ethnic grouping.*** The fact is if your ancestors hailed from Europe, Africa or Asia they ate a certain diet linked to the available flora and fauna naturally found in that locale. Read **Weston Price's** masterwork on nutrition, **'Nutrition and physical degeneration.'** Weston was a dentist with an amazing knowledge of how diet affected teeth and human health in general. His book is a global tour of how modern high sugar diets had wreaked havoc with all native peoples he came across, destroying teeth, facial structure, morality, and leaving those who indulged in such fare prone to Tuberculosis. Think – *'Would my ethnic group have eaten this in the wild?'* The giant Maasai of Africa drink

large volumes of cow blood, this is one of the reasons they are so tall.

20. ***Leave the car at home more often.***
When you use a car to pop down the road to get that milk etc. you need, how much energy are you expending? Could you walk? Could you walk more often and leave the car at home so that you'll use up more energy? Of course you can. It never ceases to amaze me how my clients are stunned by this 'revelation'.

21. ***Take personal responsibility and don't blame your spouse.*** I meet so many people who say stuff like, 'I wish I could lose weight but my wife/husband/pet chimp buys cakes and if they buy 'em I *have* to eat 'em,' in a word – bullshit! It's just an excuse for you stuffing your face. **Take responsibility for your actions if you ever want to change anything.** As a therapist you must listen to a giant amount of crap! And you have to smile why they say it too!

22. ***Do not weigh yourself EVER! The mirror and your clothes will be your guide.*** Throw the scales out the window,

in the bin/trash – let the mirror be your guide to weight loss glory. Do not obsessively check every day to see if you lost a teeny-tiny-morsel of that big hairy butt of yours. If you must weigh yourself do it once every two weeks.

23. ***Do it yourself: don't join a group!*** 'I need a support group to lose weight,' er, no you don't. <u>You</u> have set a goal, <u>you</u> want to lose weight, <u>you</u> must stop eating so much and exercise more; no one 'motivating you' will do it for you. They will ask for cash or drag you down into group weight loss despair. Hang around a bunch of slim healthy people – now that will motivate you to lose the tub! If these weight loss groups worked there wouldn't be so many roomy folk would there?

24. ***Think long term not short term.*** Almost all addictions, bad habits etc. are caused by short term delusional thinking. 'If I have this now...' Stop lying to yourself! No one else believes you anyway! If you eat like a horse you will weigh like a horse. Before going on a binge actually think, *'What need of mine isn't being met that makes*

me stuff my face silly?' And then go and satisfy that need in reality. Stop sticking your head in the ice cream and wishing your problems will somehow vanish. They won't, they'll get worse because that very real need isn't being met. Think: *'What is the long term consequence of doing x?'*

25. ***For God's sake don't 'set goals'.*** When seeking to lose weight avoid any self-induced mild form of obsessive compulsive disorder. Follow these guidelines and you'll lose weight. Don't say, 'In one month's time I'll weigh x.' I would advise you don't even have a goal weight at all. Just use the mirror and a tape measure – if you can fit into them skinny jeans you succeeded. If you look in that mirror and see that fit, sexy you smiling back – well guess what?

26. ***Don't eat anything with the word 'diet' written on it.*** Only overweight people eat food labelled 'low fat', 'diet' etc. Look at their shopping trolleys; need I say more?!

27. ***Eat meat, you are a human not a rabbit.*** Vegetarianism is unnatural, it makes you small and weak and less

intelligent. We have canine teeth for a reason. If you can hunt, fish and eat your kill.

28. ***Don't calorie count or points count!***
This is just another sales gimmick. Again self-induced O.C.D don't work. Forget calories, forget counting this or that. Just eat good nutritious food, be more active generally and exercise properly. You have actually developed a great set of strategies to gain a lot of weight. You did that spectacularly. Being overweight takes effort, planning and determination. You have to create an unhealthy diet and stick to it, you have to be inactive and you did that swell! Now use all that energy in reverse!

This isn't rocket science. The question is: how much do you really want to achieve your goal? I mean really? However if you are helping clients best not be so blunt. Indirect and diplomatic is best; just never enter the client's delusional model is all. One of you at least has to have some grounding in common sense and reality. If you want to stop losing weight/maintain it etc. cut back a tiddly bit on

the exercise.

You live in Twin Peaks.

I hope you have watched David Lynch's TV series masterpiece 'Twin Peaks' (suggestive of tits). It is quite simply the best TV series ever made. It only ran for two seasons. It painted a picture of a sleepy northern Industrial town in the US that seemed to be all happy families, neighbourliness, pretty girls and all American boys. The leading men of the town were fine and upstanding; or at least that was the surface image. But this fraud was savagely punctuated by the brutal murder of the local high school prom queen. The town was devastated, everyone knew Laura Palmer. Everyone thought they knew her. FBI agent Dale Cooper played to perfection by Kyle MacLachlan is called in to investigate. Gradually, slowly he unravels a deep and profound mystery that lurks at the dark heart of Twin Peaks, a town with two alters – one: genuinely pleasant, rural, where old village life still does exist. The second face of Twin Peaks is one of unbridled perversion. The town leaders are frequenters of whore houses, the sweet and innocent girls are wild child, drug taking sluts. The boys are deeply troubled and semi-criminal. Cooper pulls back the curtain layer by layer until he finds the seedy, sleazy underbelly of Twin Peaks: no family is unaffected by the mysterious 'poison' of the town which miasmas its way into the place, destroying the lives of anyone who goes there, sooner or later, one way or another.

The secret of Twin Peaks and Lynch's genius is that we all live in it. Oh it might not be so pronounced, so overtly dramatic. But know this: you have NO idea what your neighbours are secretly up to. The clients I see who come from the most troubled backgrounds are those from the well-off families, the ones who look down their noses on everyone else (because they have more money) but whose home lives are a mixture of psychopathy, endemic child abuse of all kinds, and intergenerational cruelty, neglect and lovelessness. These so happen to be the people who think others should be told how to raise their kids. Projection is an interesting thing. Oh yes young Padawan – you live in Twin Peaks. Like the police, a hypnotherapist gets to see the human detritus of his town, his country. It ain't pretty.

Always look beneath the surface.

Negative facts in hypnosis.

What is a negative fact and how can it help a hypnotist? If I say, 'Charles 1st was not executed with a banana,' or 'John lives in Paris,' what have I done? I have implied that Charles was killed with something other than a bendy, yellow fruit. I have said without saying it that John does not live in London. So we have implied something that is left out by presupposition. Negative facts are a way to bypass possible 'resistance'. You can use this to create advanced negations for hypnotic languaging – look...

'What is not tension?' (Hint: relaxation?)

'When are you not doing discomfort?' (When you're comfy?)

'Is it not a fact that you are more relaxed than before?'

'When you have formerly done peace of mind, when else would it be a helpful background state, now?'

'What is the opposite of discontent and how can you go get it/some most easily?'

'A mountain doesn't hum or spin or sing (confusing truism). *A healthy mind isn't anxious. You can seek the reality of a positive opposite and associate to it in useful places.'*

'As you tangibly cease to listen to certain noises, you do not have to exclude one whose lip's flap/one source – relevant and meaningful to you.'* (An indirect command to listen to the hypnotist's voice only; a negative hallucination.)

As this is a book in part about hypnotic pleasure, how about...

'When are you not glum?'

'Jim is doing to opposite of sad, which is?'

'If someone is seeking joy, is it not true that that's what they are likely to find?'

Strategies of desire and how to motivate the masses.

I would highly recommend to any hypnotist that they study the motivational research work of **Dr. Ernest Dichter.** This man knew what motivated people to do pretty much anything. In his book, **'Motivating Human Behaviour'** he outlines a large number of ways in which people can be influenced and persuaded to do a great variety of things. Dichter was a student of Freud in Vienna and an avowed Frankfurt School Marxist (aka: 'Cultural Marxism'). He was greatly responsible along with Edward Bernays et al for changing many of the Western Christian based mores of all Western European countries including the USA whose form of Civilisations is or was part of that set of traditions. What insights did he have into the real reasons people do what they do?

Dichter wrote about methodologies of changing people's habits. This man was a master on the subject; he easily qualifies as a 'Trance Wizard' as I have called them in the book I wrote on the subject. Let's talk about his discoveries on smoking...

I smoke because...

Dichter emphasised that anyone wanting to help a smoker quit had to take into account the following reality: ***smoking was and is as much a psychological pleasure as it is a physiological satisfaction (taste etc.)***

In Dichter's surveys (known as 'depth surveys' which unearth people's true and hidden reasons for acting as they do as opposed to the rationalisations they give) it was revealed that people wheeze on a ciggie as it...

- IS FUN! Guess what? Some people have fun smoking. You are going to take that 'fun' away. Depends what fun means to you of course. This is often linked to the 'fun' of perceived rebellion which I have written about elsewhere.

- Smoking helps people measure time. Dichter called it 'the modern hourglass'. Hence the saying, 'He or she has time to kill'; in this case literally!

- It is a form of operant conditioning for doing something well. A treat, a reward - good dog. Can you see already why people anticipate loss and feel genuine grief over stopping smoking? Grief makes up a sizable portion of 'withdrawal' for some people.

- Smoking helps you connect with other smokers. It gives you an excuse to start conversations. Heck for some it could help them overcome their shyness! Would you give that up if you had nothing to replace it with?

- Some crazy bastards just like burning stuff! They like the look of 'fire' etc. My brother was like that, a complete pyro boy. He would burn anything he legally could!

- Smoking (believe it or not) satisfies the urge to create. How the f*ck does it do that you ask?!!! When people create smoke rings, like Gandalf and Bilbo in the Hobbit. Some people like the fact that smoking makes their breath visible. Just wait till they have emphysema!

- Smoking makes sexual contact possible. How many couples have met after sharing a light etc.? What the hell did we do to shack up before smoking? Someone may not give up because it stops them getting laid! You might laugh but they aren't. Smoking helps them get sexual satisfaction.

- Girls use it to look sexy. The man gets to imagine she is sucking a... (actually that wasn't Dichter, that was my own observation.)

- Smoking satisfies 'oral cravings' and gives sensual pleasure to the smoker. How will these needs be satisfied otherwise? Smoking is an insidious habit. See how it wheedles itself in like a parasite and makes the host think it needs it to get its needs met, when in fact it prevents those needs being met naturally.

- Smoking helps people cope with impatience. How? It helps time pass faster. It is a substitute for actually getting off your rear end and doing something interesting and fulfilling. So smoking ACTUALLY helps them cope with boredom. It is what is known as a 'substitute activity'. You substitute getting your needs met for the baccy!

- It helps people relax. Are you going to offer some better ways to relax? That might be a good idea. Or get them to imagine some in hypnosis.

- People like to linger. And they like to do it to a rhythm too. Weird!

- This is a really important one: **SMOKERS IDENTIFY WITH THEIR BRAND.** This means that if I smoke Marlboro, I do it because I like to think I have qualities or want others to perceive I have qualities that the brand seemingly does 'posses' through advertising: see book 5, 'Wizards of Trance' on the advanced advertising brand model.

- A full pack of cigarettes symbolises 'abundance' and 'prosperity'. Never underestimate the effect of symbols and what we associate with them as being important factors in a whole host of problems.

- Smoking seems to facilitate focus. All drugs, especially nicotine ciggies, eventually become intertwined with almost everything someone does. Smokers often say 'it helps me concentrate' – the evidence is that it does the opposite. Smokers do become absorbed, hypnotically, by smoking. I give an example of a trance utilisation through smoking in book 5.

- Another one I noticed when I worked in an office was that smokers used their addiction to get some time out of the office. Good old skiving as we call it in England. This led to a situation where smokers effectively did much less work and had unofficial longer breaks at work than the rest of us non-smokers. Mind you I used to pretend to need the loo to get out of the office and took a sneaky book in to read. I had a friend who went one step further: he hired a meeting room and then slept in it the whole afternoon. Cheeky sod! And he got away with it!

- It changes breathing patterns and so changes moods and emotions - anger, fear etc. When you smoke you have to breathe in and out in a regularised way. In the same way that breathing in for 3 and out for 5 naturally calms anyone down, smoking patterns of breathing 'pattern interrupt' for example the heavy breathing patterns associated with anger.

- It can alleviate symptoms of depression. Again due to changed breathing rates. Depression is associated with shallow, high chest breathing. Smoking 'dramatises' breathing patterns. It allows the breath rate to stabilise and return to normal. If a smoke-filled normal.

- Smoking gives people the impression of stability. People like continuity. Sticking with the same brand is easier because you have to get used to a new one. In a globalised world of constant chaos, a cigarette becomes a rock of security: _remember people relate to things as if they have a personality._ We associate a whole host of emotions etc. to our 'things'.

More on this subject in my upcoming book on addictions. Dichter next gave a series of possible 'avenues of persuasion' or chinks in the armour that could be exploited to aid smoking cessation. They are highly sophisticated as they need be: nicotine delivery systems like cigarettes are designed by top scientists to produce the results they do after all.

The lack of availability principle: advise a smoker to still smoke but tell them that they can only borrow cigarettes. The embarrassment caused by effectively begging for their drug of no choice will quickly extinguish the desire to smoke at all. This is Skinnerian conditioning. This uses social forces of disapproval against the smoker. I have never done this but theoretically you could hypnotise a client saying,

'You still smoke but only borrow cigarettes from now on. From now on you still smoke but you never buy another pack from this day forth.'

And then watch the mayhem commence. There are better ways to go about such things, with more elegant results.

The principle of thought inoculation: smokers are often worried about their post-smoking life. I once had a man who said, 'I don't know who I'll be if I don't smoke. I do it with everything.' Ditcher claimed that many smokers asked themselves, consciously or unconsciously,

'How will life be different IF I stop smoking?' (In hypnosis you can counteract this by getting them to visualise a positive drug free life.)

'How will I change?' (This occurs when people identify with a drug.)

The answer is: you'll be exactly the same without cigarettes. You can inoculate people against this self-sabotage by asking the two questions above. Sometimes the best way to overcome objections is to raise them first, to anticipate them: this also demonstrates understanding, vital for establishing hypnotic rapport.

Symbolise the loss caused by smoking through financial penalisation: advise your client to get a piggy bank of some kind. Every time they smoke they must give a monetary equivalent to the cost of the ciggie to a charity/cause of choice. This effectively means the smoker is paying double for his drug! Pain of financial loss is soon associated to the drug. Various British Governments have used such financial disincentives to penalise smokers towards quitting. This is nudge persuasion in action. Again there are far better ways to help smokers, as any professional hypnotist knows but hypothetically you could back this up, hypnotising someone and saying,

'Every time you smoke a cigarette you will put the cost of it into a piggy bank. At the end of the month you will donate this to some worthy cause of your choice.'

You can train yourself to be a better hypnotist by playing thought games. It doesn't mean you'd ever give such suggestions to anyone in real life but if you did, how might you do it? It exercises your creative juices, intellect, intelligence and problem solving abilities.

Directionalising the mind toward existing proof: what does this mean? Well I have written about it elsewhere but in essence a smoker is already a non-smoker most of the time. If you point out to someone (focus) that they spend long hours of waking life not smoking, the perceived 'great leap' doesn't seem so great. You could say,

'How many hours a day do you not smoke?'

When they take the time to add this up it may be quite considerable. I will often point out that they don't smoke at night. One woman said to me – 'But I do! I get up and have a few fags (no not homosexuals, it's a UK term for cigarettes) through the night.' Wow! If you say to someone,

'If you can stop smoking for 20 minutes you could extend that to half an hour reasonably couldn't you.'

I often think stopping smoking is the Holy Grail of hypnosis: if you could perfect a 100% fail safe method of quitting (if such a thing is possible) you would be rich fast!

<u>Match the message to the receiver:</u> this really has to do with what you might call 'persuasion common sense'. A horny man doesn't speak to his hot girlfriend as he does his dog...at least I pray he doesn't!!! Everyone is so 'politically correct' (indoctrinated by Frankfurt School Marxism) these days that Dichter's ideas may well backfire disastrously now, I list them only so you can see how great persuaders think: they appeal to really existing fears, prejudices and hopes.

You can tell teenage girls that boys think smoking makes a girl look unfeminine and that boys don't like to kiss smoky breath girls. In my experience this isn't true; rarely do they care if she is even awake or attractive! You can suggest that they only do it at times they know they definitely won't be kissed. This 'plugs into' and threatens a teenage girl's desire to be thought sexually desirable. You are indirectly saying, 'Doing that is repellent to attractive young men.' Her 'vain self', which we all have to varying degrees is under pressure. The smoking will stop 'it' getting satisfaction.

Dichter suggested that you tell young men (this was the early 1970's remember) that smoking makes a man effeminate. If he wants to avoid looking like a wussy boy he should smoke cigars (if blue collar) and a pipe (if 'intellectual'). This would fail big-time if you tried it now. Especially as so many young men are now overtly androgynous. In both cases Dichter suggested you attack 'gender identity' to alter behaviour. If you did this today you may well end up with a visit from the Thought Police.

May I just say that in all my years of helping people stop smoking I have not had one teenage client. Teenagers think they will live forever.

How do you try to help adult men and women according to Dich? Tell the men that smoking is immature. Pipes and cigars are 'manly' (manly in this sense meaning suicidal).

Tell the women the same thing as you tell the teenage girls. 'It makes you look like a man.' Any therapist who said this today would likely be hung, drawn and quartered! Androgynous concepts of gender have so permeated Western ideals that appealing to manliness and femininity would be a post-millennial dead end.

What other cwazy, out there ideas did Dichy have?

<u>Counter-intuitive sales campaigns:</u> Dr. Dich gave a very convoluted and complex formula for stopping men smoking – it went somewhat like this...

1. Get the girl scouts to door to door sell artificially sweetened candy/sweets as a

smoking substitute! I know: that sounds like some sort of bizarre fantasy right! He was trained by Freud remember.

2. Package the candy/sweets in a 'masculine fashion' (unshaven and smelly??). It would be regarded as a new form of 'oral gratification'. Sweets/Candy are usually made to appeal to women and children by the way.

3. Call the new man treat 'Oral'.

4. Get the American Heart Foundation to endorse it. Authority based waking suggestion = 'It's ok to do it.'

5. Make a Valentine's Day link to the product. Dreamy-eyed wives and girlfriends are encouraged to buy it for their beau of choice. This uses association to a cultural rite and an act of love - saving your boy from a possible terrible disease.

That is so surreal that it may be that Dr. Dichter had just dropped an acid tab! It was the 1970's! Groovy man!

Dichter gave the following warning, well-known by the Ad men of today – **do not let**

the message become stale. He warned: the general public resent 'middle-class do-gooders' telling them how to behave. People can become tired and bored of the same old, same old. This is the death of any form of persuasion. The ***shocking, memorable and that which reframes things in a new, exciting way*** are best used.

The 'why not' method of persuasion.

Look, the fact is that since the fall of the values of Western Christendom, right or wrong, people no longer ask 'Why?' they ask 'Why not?' We are now a 'why not' culture. To persuade people you may have to accept this cultural reality and use it in your favour. Or a client's favour. The fact is people like 'sin'. Dichter well knew this; he helped create the mentality in fact. Let's briefly expand on this theme/meme of modern trance wizardry...

Why not smoke bat shit?!

I thought I would include this section as a humorous aside; it is not inspired by Dichter's work at all. The worse thing to do with smokers is tell them not to do it or how bad it is for you. They know. They don't care. But there are some interesting facts about the way your good old tobacco is grown and stored. I have not seen any book or treatment for smoking addiction cover this: I should just get to the point. If you smoke cigarettes, you smoke bat shit. Amongst other things.

Your addictive tobacco includes such delights as:

- Poison chemicals which are sprayed on the tobacco when it grows!

- Spider's webs and insect/bug bits and pieces! Yippee!

- Snake skins and good old fashioned dirt for good measure! No the tobacco companies just don't give a shit, you're right!

- Tobacco leaves are not cleaned of all these goodies – it would cost too much! Aha! Soak them in sugar water. Sugar is addictive and makes the tobacco taste oh so yummy! Yes your clients are probably addicted to all the sugar too (seriously)!

- Next your yummy tobacco is hung in barns full of bats! Yes you read that correctly. Bats hang upside down in barns and what do upside down bats do? They shit and piss of course – all day long. Yum enjoy your sugar, tobacco, pesticide, herbicide, shit and piss product! Smoke it deep into your lungs!

- The bats shit and piss on your tobacco for a good number of months. Between 3-6 to get it ju-st right!

- Did I tell you about the rats? Oh you don't know about the rats?! Rats infest the barns where the tobacco lays on the ground. Nicotine is a fatal poison that can kill a man in a flash if taken pure. Just one drop will do the trick! Mr. Ratty, hungry as the poor lil' critter is, eats his way through the sugar and bat shit encrusted treats and he drops dead there! Poor lil' Mr. Ratty!

- Then the ants and cockroaches and all their teeny tiny buddies crawl in and...well you can guess! They just L-O-V-E all that sugar.

- The FDA guidelines are (and this is no joke) only 6 parts rat to 94 tobacco etc. All smokers apparently smoke 6% rat with each dreamy cigarette! Yummy!

Who said there's a sucker born every minute?

Advanced level flattery.

Telling people they are no good repeatedly tends to lead to that person 'giving up', other things being equal. In any communication (and if you care) ask yourself: am I being directly or indirectly insulting?

- Most women feel flattered if a man noticed some small effort she has made.

- We are flattered when someone takes the time to choose a gift or greeting card that somehow suits our personality.

- When dealing with customers, immediately ask their concerns and wishes and seek to satisfy them. *All human life is spent in the process of seeking the satisfaction of desires.*

- Find ways to treat people that lets them know they are 'special'.

- In order to change behaviour it is often best to praise than to insult. People seek to live up to praise.

- We are conditioned from early childhood, school, work etc. to seek praise and reward from authority figures. This unfortunately leaves many feeling 'other directed' (seeking validation from others) and hence constantly seeking reassurance of 'validity'. Post Marxist and corporation dominated societies create 'organisation man'. This is the human who can only find solace and meaning as part of the 'collective'. Read **'The Organisation Man' by William Whyte** to understand this subject in full.

- Flattery incentivises people to continue on a given path of action. It is a verbal carrot.

- Do not lie to people – they will notice your insincerity. To become a great flatterer you must become a great observer of those around you. ***Notice something special about that person that others have not noticed.*** This flatters the person's needs for attention. They somehow feel they stood out of the crowd; otherwise you wouldn't have paid any heed.

- Ask yourself: what is this person dreaming about? What are this person's goals? When they achieve them, praise them for their efforts. It could be as simple as someone buying a new suit for a job interview – praise them for taking the time and effort to look presentable and smart. They obviously care how they are perceived by others. *Note: you get more of what you praise.* Attack = chaos and unpredictability. It is a clumsy strategy in many social interactions, though admittedly sometimes needed.

- Beautiful design of mundane products is a form of flattery: you might call it 'product ego-boosting'.

- Dichter suggested that people attend 'charm schools'; he claimed noticing one's weak points and strong points and correcting the former helped make a person more 'charming' in general. He advised seeing oneself on videotape. Weak points might include finger fiddling, bottom lip biting, arse/ass/ball scratching in public, cock adjusting, a poorly used voice (almost universal!). Many attractive men and women especially have no idea how poor their voice sounds to others. This Dich termed 'self-flattery' – taking the time to 'improve' yourself. Of course the flip side of this is narcissism may develop. Taken to extremes this is a form of 'sensitivity training' similar to that taught in acting schools. It can make someone completely oversensitive to how they are perceived by others: which presupposes they should give a shit!

- Appeal to people's desire to be perceived as 'intelligent' – look, most people ain't that bright let's face it! Do not repeat things too often, act crudely or in an obvious manner. It insults people and makes them angry. Construct communications/messages in ways that lets them unravel the message leaving them feeling 'smart'. Think of riddles, for example, which you have to solve through effort. If successfully decoded the listener feels a sense of pride in the achievement.

- To blend, fit in or achieve rapport in any culture ensure that you do not look down on it. Even if you dislike it: this is unless you wish to piss people off. Nobody (except born slaves) likes encountering someone who imagines themselves to be vastly superior in every way to those around them.

- Empathy is a form of flattery: by using it we say, 'I can imagine what it is like to have walked in your shoes.' This is an especially essential skill in the 'caring professions' – many patients feel that the doctor etc. simply does not give a shit about their situation. ***People want to know that we understand how they feel.*** Imagine yourself in the role of others. No matter if you are selling, fighting, helping. Understanding is the first step in influence. More than that it can stop you getting sued: no joke – customers/patients/clients are much less likely to sue a nice service provider than a sh*t head. Nice guys do win after all!!!

- If you want to flatter DO NOT put someone of the defensive. Avoid boasting about how great you are (these days many people rate themselves and their achievements far too highly), even point out your own shortcomings if genuine – this makes you appear human. If you want to appear 'superior' prepare to fail to influence unless your social class programming in obedience and servility through bullying as influence makes you feel pathetically important.

Feel free to use this to get laid; please don't use it to kiss your boss's ass more effectively.

The art and science of motivating young people.

'Teenagers' are really a modern creation: to a certain extent they are a myth. Oh they exist all right but there is nothing natural about modern teen life. Before I get to that topic let's see what advise Dichter has. I have added my own insights to his; if you like I have updated them for the new millennia.

Insight 1: youth desires the illusion that it is doing something new and coming to its own conclusions even if the exact opposite is the case.

Insight 2: each generation feels it is unique and is facing problems never before faced. Since the 1950's and especially in the early

21st century this is in fact true!

Insight 3: due to rapid and constant changes in social conditioning and environment each succeeding generation in the modern world is totally different from the one before – continuity of traditions and the stability that brings is gone.

Since the late 1950's 'attitudes' have changed, we know this - but how?

Teenagers are increasingly impatient.
Modern society shows a complete reversal of the natural order. The young set agendas, topics of conversation and fashion styles (or at least they think they do!); the older folks no longer set trends or are admired. The youth cult is in. Interestingly dictatorships have large teen components in their military; having no life experience young men especially are easily conned into a life of seeming 'adventure' and 'heroism'. Better than working in Walmart right? Britain and North Korea both have large teen factions in the military.

Young people want it all and they want it now. They are increasingly finding that this 'entitlement' attitude slaps hard against the rock of reality of decreasing avenues for getting anything. *Young people are addicted to speed. Not the drug but a time frame.* In a world of hyper-speed constant change, frustration and a sense of complete instability result causing worsening mental health.

- TV commercials since the 1950's have been using a speedier, more audio-visual amphetamine style. Rapid editing etc.

- The advent of colour TV created more rapid perception. This has been studied (by Dichter) and proven.

- The people of this modern age expect rapid solutions. In fact they just get rapidly compounding new problems.

- Modern media must meet the impatience of youth. They want appeals. They want contemporary styles of communication (what they perceive as such). Communication that seems anarchic, appears unconventional and over stimulating, hyper-stimulation in fact – the quest for constant excitement. As though that was a need, rather than a created addiction.

We can sort of handle the 'truth' as long as it's 'ours'! Most young people have great bullshit detectors. Children need these to survive: lies adversely affect your chances of survival; they prevent the brain from producing accurate maps of external reality thus preventing any hope of success within it.

- From the 1960's to the 1980's young people especially came to fear what they called 'the establishment'. The feared it was going to 'brainwash' them.

- Young people don't want stability which is actually essential for good health. They have been conditioned to be in a constant state of 'becoming' and never arriving. We see this role model in celebs who change sexual partner and 'image' on an almost weekly basis. This is a great way to create constant dissatisfaction.

- From the 1960's and beyond youth has thought 'why not?' They have a more generalised risk taking attitude. If it hasn't been done before why not try it? The problem is there is NOTHING new under the sun. It's all been tried before and it fails – youth has no sense of history from which to reject the fallacy of 'just try it and see'. This is existentialism run riot. *If you want to motivate a teen don't say, 'You should do x,' say, 'Why not do x?!'*

- Young people from the 1960's on tended to reject 'middle class' (in the American sense of the term primarily) values. They were not so wowed by the illusions of 'prestige', 'status' etc. When seeking to appeal to youth, you must pace their ongoing reality first. Where are they now ideologically? Then you lead them where you want.

- Having grown up in an 'age of plenty' baby-boomers increasingly stopped saving and started 'living in the now'; this rejection of 'puritan thrift' left them open to the appeals from advertisers to buy what they didn't need and left them vulnerable when geo-economic realities led to a series of increasingly devastating 'financial crisis' – actually the movement of capital from West to East. The consequences of this mind-set have seen an explosion in anti-depressant use in the U.K. – 12.5 million more pills were dished out by drug dealing docs from the 2007 figures by 2012. In 1998 15 million pills were doled out, this figure now stands at a staggering 40 million by 2012! (Source – Nuffield Trust and the Health Foundation.) And you wonder why people are acting zombotically oddly!!!

- Since the 1960's youth has felt it should turn its 'hobby' into its job. The desire for 'personal fulfilment' has outstripped the desire for a 'steady job'. Unfortunately geo-political realities have made it harder to achieve either! The early millennial reality is that more Western young adults are living at home with mum/mom and dad as at no point since the industrial revolution began in England.

Sick of sentiment! Here's the thing – young people are not 'romantic' at least not openly. They are not suave but more likely to make jokes to diffuse tension. Buttering up with gifts is viewed cynically as having a hidden meaning. Since the 1960's consumers have sought realism over idealism. Emotions, sex, romance are perennially important advertising tools but as people are more cynical they should be a bit tongue in cheek. Teenagers are terrified of overt emotion. It must be masked and made fun of. This is a sign of their immaturity. Use cynical humour in all marketing operations aimed at youth.

The desire for fake rebellion. All young people (more or less) want to be perceived as rebels. None are. Taking drugs, a 'lack of inhibitions', nonchalance regarding innovation and technology, whether something is 'fun', 'enjoyable', pushing beyond adult world 'barriers' and 'traditions', doing things different for the sake of it, questioning things that are assumed even if there is no good reason, the pseudo 'gourmet' mentality in music, films, food, sex especially etc., will experience x 'expand my consciousness?', how does a product *feel* in use?, will the proposed course of action enable or interfere with the young's desire for rampant hedonism?, can we look at this old thing from new angles?, what 'meaning' lies behind the mundane? These and other media programmed-in attitudes must be taken into account when trying to convince youth of anything!

The biggest conformers going want to be different! You will never meet a bunch of bigger group think 'other-directed', follow the herd demographic than the young. But they want to create the illusion of being an individual and being different. I was on a bus recently and 5 of these young 'individualists' got on board: each had precisely the same haircut. Dichter as a good Marxist demonises what he calls 'the silent generation'. These were basically people like my granddad (grandpa) who fought Hitler and the Nazis and lost a lung in the process. The 60's so-called 'radical' movements, which he lionises, were filled with dumb teenagers who thought they were 'changing the world for the better' – they did this by helping to transform the West into a semi-Marxist basket case. It is interesting that the 80's generation in contrast is incredibly apathetic politically, better than pathetic I suppose!

Influenced by self-styled 'beatniks' etc. the post War World 2 youth became infatuated with 1. Themselves. 2. The destruction of all traditions that existed. The young ever since have seen themselves as the font of all wisdom and the source of all fashionable thought, behaviour and dress. In fact they are not the source but rather the conduit. It is interesting that youth is always used by totalitarians for their own ends. This is because they know that human nature is trainable.

The fact is since the 1960's Western youth has *believed* it was rebellious. Whether it was inspired by the 'hippy movement' of Laurel Canyon or any other sort of 'anti-establishment' garbage. Interestingly the hippie movement was led by former US serviceman and military intelligence operatives. Hmmmm? The 1960's also represented a rejection of the intellectual movement towards rationalism started by the Enlightenment and led to a new 'heart over head' mode of processing information which remains with us today, producing no end of hysterias and emotionalism.

If you want to con young people, even today, into doing anything - use their genuine desire to 'rebel' and warp it to your own ends. Teenagers are a singularly modern social construct and their confinement in schools whilst being young adults is the problem.

More on this elsewhere.

The rise of technological narcissism. As Facebook, 'selfies' and a vast multitude of other self-loving but not healthily esteeming new behaviours show – the young are obsessed with themselves as never before. This trend is growing and worsening. Dichter called this trend back in the 1970's the desire to be 'master of the self'. Since the 1960's the 'religion' of succeeding generations has been an ad hoc blend of New Age, secular, Humanistic, Frankfurt School Marxism with a dash of therapy cults thrown in. Many young people have what has been labelled a sense of 'entitlement'. This essentially is a form of anti-meritocracy that asserts that despite talent, brains or a sense of responsibility - because one is young, one is entitled to everything now! Since the 60's growing numbers of youth have become increasingly dissociated from both family traditions and parents' values. The generations are so different values wise as to almost represent separate tribes or species. There is no less than an inter-generational war afoot, a culture war. If you doubt this imagine what your great grandfather would have felt about how young people in the West behave today. This narcissism of youth is very powerful and has in fact infected older people who sadly wish to 'be cool' too. Lord of the Flies and Children of the Corn are no basis for a civil society I'm afraid. Youth has felt for some 50 plus years now that it is on the 'cutting edge' of some fanciful social revolution that is about to deliver 'Utopia'. This promised Youth-topia is yet to present itself.

The philosophy of 'do it and see if it feels good' originates with the work of existentialist loons like Sartre. These ideas have permeated unquestioned through the cracks left by a crumbling Christendom and led to no end of 'social experimentation'.

The desire of youth to 'know itself' is a good intention, yet like all good intentions when warped by those with an interest in warping things, it creates social chaos and human environments which simply cannot sustain the fulfilment of human needs: when 'anything goes' human societies historically go down the toilet. Drug use and other attendant millennial craziness is just the tip of the iceberg.

If you want to con youth: appeal to their total

lack of life experience and offer to let them 'discover themselves'.

The end of materialism? People have a human need to own things. This is well known. Since the 1960's there has been a rejection of what you might call 'Western Materialism'. Disposable cameras, relationships, constantly technological updates, kindle 'books' and required never ending new purchases has led to a 'throw away' society. Revealingly this attitude started with 'Middle Class' undergraduates who 'dropped out'. It seems to be ant-materialist it helps to have abundance first. This had led to a 'utilitarian' approach to life – an attitude that 'things' do not matter, 'use' is the highest value. This very real attitude can be and is exploited by marketers, political groups etc. After all it was them that created it.

I hope you have enjoyed this little examination of how youth is manipulated.

Utilising Ah-a moments.

There is one last gem of wisdom that Dr. Dichter draws attention to: the 'A-ha moment'. He states and is bang on the nose here, that when teaching anyone of anything, the best reaction you can get and should aim for is the 'A-ha moment', no this is not the same as singing along to the Abba song, it is that moment when we find some gap in knowledge filled by a juicy fact or truism – it is the moment of 'illumination'. I hope that my books provide many A-ha moments for my readers. I often use A-ha moments in therapy. My clients will say things like, 'What you just said really rings true for me.'

If you are a hypnotist, professional persuader or just interested, you should try to get hold of all of Dichter's works. You won't be wasting your time!

Sounding out hypnotic time distortion: the time-bending nature of music.

Obviously we all know that music is hypnotic: it absorbs our attention. Precisely like hypnosis it distorts our sense of time passing, though more powerfully than any hypnotist could hope to achieve. Some people who are 'really into' (notice the languaging) their music can listen to a particular symphony and get a physical sensation that time is actually stopping. Music can literally grab hold of one's sense of time passing and warp it.

How the human brain 'encodes' time.

As we know from personal experience, our brain can and does alter and transform our perception of time also known as 'temporal perception'. Temporal perception is our innate capacity to take in and untangle constant information in an orderly fashion, to unify and separate coincidental/accompanying input; for fairly obvious reasons it is absolutely essential that we can do so. It facilitates all human activity – behaviours, thoughts, sense of place and cohesion, our ability to pilot ourselves through reality effectively. Music shows us that time is perceived subjectively. Is time inherently musical?

Music creates a 'hypnotic reality'.

Our brains conceptualise time as a perpetual ongoing sequence. We receive external and internal input in discrete packages of 'experience'.

Note: so-called 'objective time' is nothing of the sort. Time measurement systems, 'clocks' (derived from medieval Latin 'clocca' – 'bell': bells being used to measure time intervals for various religious activities; the Greek word for 'clock' was 'water thief' – they had water clocks: 'Time is a thief,' is obviously a perennial theme) are derived from solar time and the Sumerian-Babylonian sexigeismal (based on the number 6) system. It is entirely artificial, see book 3, 'Powerful hypnosis' for more info on time distortion in hypnosis. Objective time is the time sense that you are indoctrinated in/with from early childhood. It is useful but arbitrary.

True time is...subjective time, regulated by 'physiological metronomes' – human body activities etc. breathing, heartbeat etc. UNLESS interfered with by external sources, such as you guessed it - music. Music is a phenomenon natural to man. It is a part of who he is. All musicians create distinct temporal musical packages that do not necessarily or usually tally with the methods by which man measures time objectively. Musical compositions are more in tune with subjective time.

Music can deliberately generate and externalise (onto the listener/s) a semi-autonomous and experiential perception of time, able to subjectively manipulate our culturally conditioned sense of 'clock-time'. This 'music time' engenders waking hypnotic trance, a separate time world in which we can and do 'lose ourselves' (trance languaging again), at the bare minimum we may lose all sense of 'clock-time'.

Very interesting but so what? Well music 'steals' our sense of time and can alter our behaviour!

- If you run a bar/pub and want to sell more drinks play slow-tempo stuff. This creates an enjoyable musical environment that causes people to stay put and drink more.

- Shoppers spend almost 40% more time in a shop/store when the muzak/ 'elevator music' is slower.

- Shoppers prefer constantly changing new music. If the same tracks are played over and over their sense of time is perceived as being 'longer', dragged out etc. The same as what happens to our time sense when we're bored out of our wits! New music is seen as more pleasurable: shopper's time sense is sped up yet paradoxically they stay longer! In fact they stay longer than they thought they had – pure time distortion. Again more ways that we are hypnotically manipulated by corporations etc.

- Speed of music = speed of behaviour. Fast music takes over the internal metronome of the listener and makes them speed up. Do not listen to Wagner's Ride of the Valkyries if you want to get safely from A to B. We have all noticed that the people who listen to the loudest and worst music make the worst drivers. No it's not that they're 'distracted', the hyper-fast tempo of the noise takes over their internal metronomes and speedometer feedback. On the plus side they do tend to develop tinnitus by their late 30's.

Did modern music alter our perception of time?

Yes. The mass manufacture of music not only affected its availability and therefore cultural diffusion, it affected how we perceived acceptable musical time and made us less tolerant of a prolongation of it! Thomas Edison's music cylinders were only capable of holding 4 minutes of music. Although subsequent technology allowed this limit to be done away with it was not. The general public had been culturally conditioned to 4 minutes of music and 4 minutes it would be. Even on so-called classical music radio stations, whole compositions are rarely played till late in the day if at all, the public can only tolerate snippets of Beethoven's 5th; you know the juicy bits, not the bits that lead up to the juicy bits. Our common span of attention is receding and this has been culturally induced by the culture creators, whether deliberately or otherwise is another matter. These changes represent the 'cultural presuppositions' of the cultural hypnosis that we question not one bit!

Neuroscience, trance and the musical brain.

To put it succinctly music that absorbs you creates a waking trance state: but how? Neuroscience now tells us that when we are mesmerised by a piece of music the activity in the prefrontal cortex, which usually attends to most bodily and psychological introspection, temporally shuts down, now this would sound like the antithesis of trance. As I outlined in book 5, 'Wizards of trance' Milton Erickson identified trance as introspection. Ah! But that's only one type of trance; there is also an externally focused state of trance which we usually call 'the zone'. Whilst we focus solely on captivating music, the sensory cortex becomes the focal area of activity and the so-called 'self-related' cortex basically switches off, for want of a better term. This is how neuroscience has confirmed our subjective perception in the oft used phrase 'losing yourself'.

In a waking musical trance the faculty which permits perceptual awareness is dampened. The role of the now predominant self-related prefrontal cortex is also 'meditative' evaluating the 'meaning' of the music to the self. During moments of highly focused musical involvement we can enter a waking trance so profound we forget about our sense of self. The loss of self however is not overly common, a sense of time distortion is. Time distortion is one of the key indicators of the hypnotic state, I feel this when I simply go for a good jog.

The white coated boffins claim that our brains process time in two ways:

- Firstly it makes a clear educated guess in relation to the span of a given 'event', 'experience'. This could be a distinct sound – say bird song on a country walk or an internal dream/fantasy image etc.

- Secondly it guesses time between two experiences. In this instance both memory and focus are intertwined which regulate the perception of time. This is further influenced by how absorbed or challenged/stimulated we find ourselves to be at any given moment. So time can fly when we are in the zone, doing something we love and drag when we have to do our taxes, or is that just me?! The individual's perception of either time experience is related to self-referential brain activity. Whatever that means!?

How composers and song writers accidentally cause hypnotic time warp.

Apparently if a given sensory stimulus (say sight or sound) is moving toward us it is perceived as longer in duration than the exact same stimulus when that is motionless or moving away from you. Whether going away from you or toward you, such occurrence cause increased activation in the anterior insula and anterior cingulate cortices - areas essential for subjective awareness.

Variations in musical composition affect the same parts of the brain involved in spatial awareness, as things coming at you or retreating from you, as far as time perception occurs. Weird isn't it! As all music is 'intentional' – it has a goal to which it is aiming; it provides a fabric which mimics a sense of spatial-motion. This in turn is 'transferred' to structured sound patterns, and as far as the brain is concerned the physical sensations of towards or away are activated inadvertently of any real world sense of direction/bearings. So as far as the brain is concerned time and space are interlinked. The brain seems hardwired for both metaphor and synaesthesia.

Music can produce/induce great pleasure states and dissociation: both prime indicators of hypnotic trance. What if you were to embed messages in music, what we call 'lyrics'? Think about it. Could these program the unwary, unsuspecting listener? After all, the passage to influence his subconscious is wide open? Undoubtedly. More on this in book 7. Further, at a concert we may be rigidly still (classical concert) or dancing (rock concert) both activities which induce our best buddy – trance! Starting to see the power and implications of music? Plato knew this well.

So far what can we say in summation?

Personally significant and absorbing music produces a transitory alternate or waking hypnotic environment in which people can become dissociative and suggestible. Perceptions of space, time and self can be drastically altered and affected. The music must be personally symbolic – a sense of 'connective

***meaning/involvement' must be aroused
for a whole host of reasons –
upbringing, culture, conditioning,
genetics, personal preferences etc. If
you can tap into this you can influence
people.***

Let's continue with our study. By the way
what you do with this information is your
business. Be ethical, please.

How composers instruct musicians in 'time'.

Historically composers have only been able to
write little Italian adjectives to suggest time
use in compositions, examples are...

- Adagietto (somewhat slow).

- Lentissimo (slower than slow).

- Allegro ma non troppo (fast, but not too
  fast).

- Allegro appassionato, Bravura, Agitato,
  (words that connote speed through
  emotion).

- Tempo Semplice (words that confuse
  complexity with speed).

- Tempo rubato ('stolen time' - duration is added to one event at the expense of another).

Like composers hypnotists can 'compose' trance work that makes time pass long and slow or short and fast. Think: how can I use my hypnotic language to create distortions in time? Hypnotists like composers can use shock, repetition and hesitation to suggestive effect. You can use your voice tone to suggest a 'thrust forward of motion' suggestive of the past problem being left behind. Passion and energy can be imparted to the subject through tone. Pauses and rhythmic changes can also send the subject's mind 'all over the place' – I know this, they tell me! Voice tone can be altered so as to affect a sense of 'temporal stasis' – as if time has stopped. A feel for the dramatic and story-telling abilities are a boon to the would-be good hypnotist. Can you find ways to use voice tone and imagery so that a person feels immersed in a hypnotic medium? Whilst hypnotising think: *'I am immersing someone in an alternate temporal reality.'* You can use hypnosis so that people temporarily perceive they are beyond time. In fact let's compose a little hypnotic time distortion trip for our subjects, for fun...

'Beyond time' trance trip script.

(Deep hypnosis assumed – you might wish to use this as a deepener or a little module within a larger session. Up to you. It is obviously only an example of what could be done with hypnotic time)

*'It's interesting but we now know that your brain encodes time a certain way...And music...that is music that can **absorb your attention completely**...can influence our perception of time...That is **in a state of fascination your sense of time alters...***

*Have you ever listened to a piece of music...maybe it was a short pop song...or a longer composition...in which you **simply lose yourself...**(?)* (this may cause instant 'dissociation') *for a while? Perhaps your eyes were wide open...but the passage of **time lost** all meaning? The clock time of appointments is of no use here...because your brain knows that time is relative to your experience...It encodes it a certain way...Ever noticed how time flies when you're having* *fun? Ever noticed how our body rhythms are affected by moods, emotions, people, places and music?*

In that focused eyes open trance...within which we are captivated by enthralling music... (you could say 'my' instead of 'by' and so suggest something about your voice's musicality) *you **lose all sense of time passing**...in that clock time linear way...For you have all the time you need in this place within...that is beyond conventional time...A place where you let the music, rhythms, certain alterations...pleasurably affect you in delightful ways, now...*

The music could be fast and exciting (speed up voice!) *or slow...and...relaxing...* (match with tone) *Soothing away any thoughts you had about anything that once seemed important...I Don't know if it's a place of escape or **more active involvement...**at some level...because the experience of losing yourself in this way...is quite unique to you...And your unconscious mind is hearing these words and making sense of them so that **you can experience what it is I am talking about** without effort...Things **just*** *flow* *and you go along with the unfolding experience...*

How does a piece of music affect anyone? Does it conjure images? People and places? Affecting certain biological responses...Fond remembered faces? I don't know. You do. I read about a man...a teacher of music and its composition who said a certain piece of music could **alter your sense of time passing profoundly...***whilst in this captivated state...That the music more intensely moved his emotions and actually made* **time** *seem to* **stand still completely...***For others it might speed it up...or slow things right down for a awhile...Or maybe you just* **forget about time** *here? Do you not?*

What would it be like to imagine existing in a place beyond time for a while...A place where you could **rest and recharge...***A place where you could* **heal...***A place where those essential psycho-biological rhythms we all have...the ones that keep us healthy, alive and* **feeling good...***could re-sync in wonderful ways...That is possible in this place beyond the space of time...Where, for a restful while you are no longer tied to time...and the time* *of space...or its pace...Where things are neither toward or away but just are...Where you can **just be** and listen...to the musicality of certain experiences offered by your far deeper self...At the end of this session your normal sense of time will be fully restored...Now...'*

(Need not be long.)

How modern society creates 'alienated' youth.

Extended schooling creates teen angst. Until about 50 years ago, adolescents were too busy working in a job to worry about getting a date, their exams, their zits, their social status and inability to get their needs met. By 16 the average Westerner had a job, spouse and children – this allowed them to have a degree of power, influence and meaning. The modern school system which seeks to extend childhood well into the mid to late 20's prevents young people from getting their needs met and getting their independence they so desperately seek. This is well-known and understood.

Child rearing and its profound effect on personality development will be dealt with in my next book on cultural hypnosis.

Psychiatry and conformity.

Power elites, to use that old phrase, want conformity. They do not want the masses going around having ideas of their own that threaten the position of the 'establishment'. There is a Japanese proverb...

'The nail that sticks up will be hammered down.'

Take the DSMR (Diagnostic and Statistical Manuel of Mental Disorders): which *is* the head-shrinker's bible, no matter how wildly they protest. It tells them what to broadly think and do. It sets their framework. Guess what? The quacks have done it again – they have created a fictitious entity called 'Oppositional Defiant Disorder'; in fact it's nothing other than a druggist's wet dream. In the Soviet Union political 'dissent' (e.g. you quite rationally concluded Communism was evil etc.) was a sign of 'madness'. Well that's 'Scientific Socialism' for you. Effectively medications and other 'treatments' were used as tools of political repression – you disagree with the State, you get zombified. A good way to keep folks in line. What is nominally called 'medicine' becomes a form of social coercion and punishment for 'wrong-thinking'.

Psychiatry is now based on a psychopathological belief known as the 'Diathesis Stress Model', which is about as scientific as saying you believe the earth is flat. This is essentially a eugenics based belief/religion that the fault Brutus lies not in our stars but our 'faulty' genes. The so-called 'chemical imbalance' theory.

I quote from Dr. Ron Leifer a New York based psychiatrist – good to know not all of 'em are wacko!

'There's no biological imbalance. When people come to me and they say, I have a biological imbalance, I say, 'Show me your lab tests.' There are no lab tests. So what's the biochemical imbalance?'

Another from Jonathan Leo, associate professor of anatomy at Western University of Health Sciences.

'If a psychiatrist says you have a shortage of a chemical, ask for a blood test and watch the psychiatrist's reaction. The number of people who believe that scientists have proven that

*depressed people have low serotonin is a glorious testament to the **power of marketing.**'* (My emphasis)

Do you even know about the bizarre origins and history of what is called 'psychiatry' in revolutionary France? No, didn't think so.

(More on this subject in book 9.)

Interlude: taming Vikings and creating perfect slaves.

The Catholic conquest of the Viking mind.

The Roman Empire had collapsed. It was the 'Germanic' (no one knows the origin of the term 'German') Nordic peoples who dealt it the death blow following an explosive folk-wandering battle for survival against the corrupt and crumbling civilisation. Rome was a cruel, psychopathic and parasitic geo-political entity that assimilated, raped and enslaved all cultures it came across. The Nordic people spread far and wide – into Italy, Spain and beyond conquering and destroying the remnants of the most powerful Empire that we know of by about 450 A.D. Germanic war bands and their kings ruled all Western European 'countries' (territories would be a better word, countries and nations in the modern sense of the word did not exist until fairly recently). Having left their woodland retreats in the North which had so confounded the Roman generals' usual tactics; the Germans were spread far and wide. They had been lured out of the woods in a pyrrhic victory. For Rome had not really died; it had morphed into the Catholic Church. Within only a few hundred years all the Germanic people were under a 'New' Rome's rule. Not of military might but through religious conversion. Soon the Catholic Church ruled men's bodies, allegiance and minds. The best way to tame an enemy is not to fight them but to brainwash them into subservience and domestication.

But in the North, the far north, the Scandinavians had remained behind in their wild fastness. They had not been converted to Rome's new ways. They retained their independence and pagan nature worship. Yet Christian priests from France, Ireland and England were seeking to infiltrate Scandinavian territories and spread their own versions of the Syriac faith of 'Christianity'. Again under 'ideological' and military threat the Nordics exploded in a berserker rage for survival. All the monasteries in England, Ireland and France that could be wiped off the map were. They were the source of the foreign infection. Eastern Ireland and England, Northern France were invaded and subjugated. But again lured out from the northern forests and becoming settlers and farmers, the fire in Viking blood cooled. The religious convertors went in. Within a hundred or so years the Vikings were thralls of the Catholic Church. Their kings had seen the way the wind of history was blowing and converted for their own political gain. Their people soon followed as folk often ape their 'betters'. The Roman Church had succeeded were Old Rome had failed. The Germanic peoples were neutralised and domesticated. So thoroughly did this process occur that the 'Vikings' who had conquered Neustria (Northern Gaul/France) transformed swiftly into the 'knights errant' of Catholicism, we know them as the Normans, leading World War 2 like conquests in England and Sicily, North Africa and beyond.

If you want to tame a ferocious barbarian you would be foolish to fight him, especially when he rationally sees his people's extermination as a present reality. You must inveigle your way in. Use the Trojan horse of the mind and victory is assured.

What is 'laziness'?

The roots of this word are unknown but we generally know what it means – 'work shy', 'lay-about' etc. But is laziness as bad as it seems to be? To be blunt, has laziness got a bad rap?! Well studies on longevity seem to suggest that those that take it easy are apt to live longer lives. But hold on we live in a system in which we are paid according to the value and extent of the work we do. That's the point. What is good for the goose isn't necessarily good for the gander. Let's look at 'primitives'.

The average 19th and early 20th century Imperialist saw the 'savages' as fundamentally 'lazy'. All these primitives sitting around half the day, only getting up to hunt, to plant crops with which he utilises no scientific method in the growing thereof and wastes a great deal of what he does grow! Now if I could enslave him and shove him onto a plantation or into the factory I might just make a 'hard worker' of him yet! ***Is high and efficient productivity for the system compatible with human happiness?*** Just a thought.

Primitive man has very little if any stress related illness, cancer is pretty much unknown: we know the ancient 'Egyptians' had zero cancer from their bone records, until they created a civilisation that is. How healthy is civilisation for human health?

A better formula for living is: <u>I need to be active, doing meaningful and challenging things that enrich my life and bank balance.</u>

As an end note I work very hard at what I do. You can accomplish nothing worthwhile in life without expending energy and effort.

How social 'class' is programmed into the English and why it holds them back.

I have noticed the very real and detrimental effect of what you might call 'class programming' in the UK: specifically in southern England where I live. By various means of osmosis and implicit human relations the so-called 'working class' clients that I meet have a wholly pessimistic and unrealistically low set of assumptions of their self-worth, their relative self-worth in comparison with their 'betters', poor mental and physical health, low ambition as regards to what they can achieve. Many have a built in set of programmes from family and wider society that simply says, 'Know your place. People like us don't do that sort of work. He's getting thoughts above his station etc.' These are no 19th century relics; these cluster of what can only be labelled 'good slave mentality' are as strong now as they were when Dickens wrote his social satires and commentaries. In order to help clients from such backgrounds to 'get better' I often have to deprogram them of these personally disastrous ideas that hold them back and impoverish their lives in more ways than one.

In many ways, despite rapid technological progress and the cheap availability of such products due to a slave race of Chinese workers in the East who work for peanuts, there has been an almost complete return to a 'Victorian', 19th century mentality that covertly governs the social relations between all classes. As the United States gradually cedes power to the rising Eastern powers we are also seeing a similar death of the 'American dream'. It is far less likely that a young American will enjoy a standard of living that his grandfather fought so hard to achieve not so long ago.

How to deprogram a 'perfect slave'.

So what do I semi-jokingly mean by a 'perfect slave'? A perfect slave is someone who has come to be programmed in a variety of ways that he or she cannot expect anything more out of life than to be a 'worker' in a menial job. In fact I have come to the conclusion that what we call 'a lack of self-confidence' is simply someone who has been programmed to never 'go for it': to seek with 100% commitment to turn their ambitions into reality. They have a **poverty of the imagination**.

So let's examine how this comes about: how do you program someone to be this perfect slave? Well, unsurprisingly it all starts at home. It all starts with the installation of what I call, 'the peasant mentality'. It is a bio-computer programme that effectively programmes the human robot thus...

- You are 'working class' (a slave), your family for generations have always done jobs that made them miserable and poor, you must too.

- You can expect nothing better; it is your

fate (circular arguments).

- To want to do anything better is 'getting ideas above your station'.

- It doesn't matter what you want - this is the way 'it' is, it matters what you 'have' to do. (*Have to* according to whom?)

- The 'Middle' and 'Upper' classes (in the 'social pyramid') are your 'betters' inherently, by birth and superior genetics, your bosses and masters. They are 'all' more intelligent and capable than you. Feel 'inferior' around them.

- You earn less money than the two 'higher' groups. You are therefore comparatively worthless (literally – worth less).

Often there is massive and repeated indoctrination in this line of thought. Family member's unconsciously dread others 'escaping' because if they successfully did it, their programming would be proved a lie. Their entire adult working life would have been wasted. Oops! It is a sad fact that people's life energies are used against them.

I helped a man who had been programmed in

this way by well-meaning parents. He was so fearful of taking the steps to live the life he truly wanted and was realistically more than capable of achieving that I had to carry out a detraumatisation pattern (I'm going to write a book soon on this subject – 'trauma' of varying kinds is alarmingly more widespread than you know) to get his levels of self-doubt down to realistic proportions. I am not really a quoter, seeing it as a sign of a lack of originality of thought but...

'What is now proved was once only imagined.' William Blake.

'A maker must imagine things that are not!' Philip Sidney.

'The human gift is the gift of the imagination.' Bronowski.

NOTE: the pivotal function of compulsory education is to reduce imaginative capacity in children.

As Monthy Python would say...And now for something *completely* different!

Case studies part 4: is 'erotic' hypnosis dangerous?

Let me just reassure the hypnotist or serious student of something: this section is an expose of what is called 'erotic hypnosis' – I don't do it but I know how. By studying it you will know how to create appropriate pleasure states in others and a bit about stage hypnosis. You can take the principles and apply them elsewhere. After all we are grown-ups. To the interested non-professional this will just be amusing but weirdly fascinating I assure you.

Before we talk about 'erotic hypnosis' (erotic to whom?) or as it is euphemistically known 'recreational hypnosis' let me lay some ground work with the 'father' of the 'sexual revolution' Dr. Kinsey.

Why Kinsey was evil.

Okay. If you don't yet know the truth, if you haven't yet worked it out - Alfred Kinsey who wrote 'Sexual behaviour in the human male', and 'Sexual behaviour in the human female', (1948 & 52 respectively) was a psychopathic sexual deviant. I will prove this to you with facts. I am not a Christian but people need to face reality. So-called 'modern views on sexuality' are almost entirely derived from this wretched creature. He was a known paedophile who thought that rape was no big deal as you will see. Please feel free to check all the facts I am about to present to you. ***THIS IS THE MOST SHOCKING PART OF THE BOOK!*** You are about to come face to face with reality. I hope you are grown-up enough to take it. Ready? Here we go.

<u>Kinsey's hidden history.</u>

• 'Kinsey' the film starring Liam Neeson is a piece of a-historical crap. It portrays pre-Kinsey Christian European America as 'frigid' and 'sexually repressed' until the hero came along and 'liberated' the nation. *<u>Nothing was or is further from the truth.</u>*

• Kinsey was born to a strict Methodist household where he claimed all 'pleasures of the flesh' etc. were verboten! In 1916 after majoring as an insect expert (???!) he went to Harvard University. By this time it was already known that Kinsey was sexually 'attracted' to young boys. In 1938 for some unknown reason this insect expert began his life as a 'sex researcher'. The Association of Women students at Indiana University asked him to create a 'marriage course' for engaged women students.

• Although married with a wife and kids (his cover), in private, Kinsey followed his own unnatural urges in pursuing young boys.

• While conducting his infamous 'research' Kinsey would use his knowledge of influential academics and bureaucrats sex lives to bully them into accepting his 'findings'.

• If hired by Kinsey you were forced to divulge all sexual proclivities and you were FORCED to be actively involved in making pornographic movies. This also extended to the wives of researchers who were bullied by their husbands into being filmed on camera having sex. One described this as a 'sickening pressure'.

• The prime source of Kinsey's research, were NOT 'ordinary Americans'. Who then were they? Prison inmates and convicted 'sex offenders' (rapists) primarily. Not one member of his 'staff' was a trained statistician. Yes you read that correctly. No one was competent to evaluate the 'research'.

• Kinsey used known child rapists in his 'research'. Child rapists who had violated and abused many young boys were asked to keep diaries and regarded by Kinsey as 'experts' on 'children's sexual responses'. One of these child rapists known as 'Mr. X' was none other than Rex King, a mass child rapist having attacked over 800 children. Audiotape and film of rapist's attacks were collected by the Indiana University 'sex researchers'. And it only gets worse folks here on in. Fasten your seat belts.

• Tip - watch the BBC's Secret History: 'Kinsey's paedophiles'.

• Did you know about Kinsey and the Nazi paedophile? Dr. Fritz Von Balluseck was a child rapist who assaulted hundreds of German children from 1936 – 46. He was a Nazi officer who sent 'reports' of his disgusting crimes to Dr. Kinsey. Kinsey encouraged the Herr Dr. to continue with his 'experiments'. When Balluseck was arrested for the murder of a young girl, the presiding judge expressed outrage that Kinsey had never informed the police etc. of the pervert's crimes against innocent children. Indeed.

• The Penal Code of the US was changed in the mid-fifties as a result of Kinsey's 'research'. Formerly classed as sexual psychopaths, deviants of all kinds who indulged in child rape, bestiality etc. were classified as the 'normal' 95% of the US population! Major Ivy League university professors rallied to support Kinsey's findings. What does this tell you about them? *THINK!*

• Instead of classifying rape as the monstrous act that it is Kinsey said and I quote, '...it was easily forgotten.' Read that again if you didn't quite get it. I have treated several rape victims for PTSD (Post Traumatic Stress Disorder) and 'cured' them of the horrible sets of feelings and associations that follow rape. THE ONE THING THEY CAN'T DO IS FORGET ABOUT IT! Kinsey declared in his usual deviant fashion that girls were only bothered by rape if their parents were awake when she got home. Most psycho-the-rapists and psychology graduates see this man as some sort of hero. That's a sobering thought, is it not?

- As a result of this sick pervert's 'discoveries', US rape-murders exploded from just over 100 per year in 1930 to nearly 4000 by 1995. Oh the joys of the 'sexual revolution'. By the way a 'revolution' is something that you go back to – a former system, hence the 're' bit. It essentially means to revolve or devolve to a pre-Christian sexual ethic. Pagan in other words. Rapists and paedophiles serve VERY short sentences, if any, as a result of Kinsey's 'work'. What does this tell you? *THINK!*

- Most dangerously Kinsey claimed that children were '...sexual from birth.' He suggested that as animals had sex with the immature of their species it was normal for man to. Excuse me? Man is meant to emulate animals is he? How many working psychiatrists share this belief? Wouldn't you like to know?

- Did you know Playboy magazine funded the Kinsey Institute in the 1960's? Now you do. Hmmmm?

- As 'adultery' was 'normalised' divorce rates exploded and family breakup became the 'norm'. By the way Kinsey thought incest was normal. Am I getting through to you?! Divorce is one of the major causes of mental health problems in the world: fact. It devastates both adults and especially children who it wounds in ways so gut-wrenchingly painful that most little suspect.

• From the late 1960's Kinsey's disciples following their perv-guru's death created the Institute for the Advanced (no less!) Study of Human Sexuality. This promoted the so-called 'New biology' of Kinsey. Major porn operatives were also involved. What could motivate them? 'Dr.' Mary Calderone headed an organisation called SIECUS – Sexuality information and 'Education' Council (Seekus?), which promoted 'sexual literacy' in US schools. Calderone is known to believe that incest is a 'sexual inhibition'. SIECUS trained operatives have a monopoly on 'sex education' in US schools. What more, really, do I have to say? If you haven't worked it out folks – *the lunatics are running the asylum!*

Can you now see why the 'sexual revolution' was anchored on a foundation of quicksand? The hypocritical sexual mores of the asexual priesthood of Western Christendom (which demonised woman) had to relax because they were too hard to live up to, human nature doesn't change. The problem is perverts and deviants took over this needed relaxation process; if ordinary people had led the way we wouldn't be in the mess we are. If you don't agree with me answer me this: what society in human history has survived the 'normalisation' of deviancy? You can't name it because it has never existed, they all collapsed.

A note on sexual fantasies.

People have sexual fantasies – they're normal. When designing 'naughtinosis' sessions bear these considerations in mind:

Generally, these sex fantasies fall into common types. The most common are...

- **Submissive-dominant** fantasies (a variant of these are symbolic 'animal'/'monster' fantasies).

- The second are **voyeur** fantasies.

- The third are **orgy** fantasies.

- The fourth **loyal partner** fantasies.

- And pen-ultimately, **celebrity** fantasies (perfect lover).

- The final category, which is 'new' (or should that be relatively recent?) are **androgynous** fantasies. These centre on fantasies of being gay or of having the sex organs of the opposite sex. Many modern stage hypnotists will hypnotise a woman into believing she has a large penis which she masturbates to orgasm. PHD hypnosis researchers will hypnotise subjects to imagine being the opposite sex. Why? The question, and it's a rhetorical one is: how much of this is genuine post-'sexual revolution' 'freedom' and how much is culturally induced? I will expand upon this topic in my next book.

What is 'erotic' hypnosis?

First we need to identify who the 'erotic hypnotist' is likely to be and who the subject. Most erotic hypnotists are practising or former professional hypnotists who had used their knowledge of stage hypnosis and therapeutic emotion/feeling elicitation for what can only be termed sexual purposes or thrills. One of the warnings about possible misuses of hypnosis was given out by Psychiatrists Crasilnick and Hall in their book on hypnotherapy. They stated that the use of hypnosis would elicit the desire to use it for 'seduction' purposes in some 'practitioners'.

The erotic hypnotist is interested in fantasies of 'power and control', a mild form of BDSM in its way. The subject is interested in the experience of handing over 'control' to the hypnotist: at least that's the fantasy.

From now on the erotic hypnotist shall be referred to as a perv-notist. I call erotic hypnosis 'pervnosis' or 'naughtinosis'.

Shutting down the experience.

What do I mean by this phrase: 'Shutting down the experience'? Simple. By the way I use a similar thing in therapy. I want the subconscious to follow what I say completely, or as completely as it wants on a given day. To do this you need to shut down all competing distractions and options etc.

The shutdown module script.

(I do this after inducing trance plus two or so deepeners)

*'From this moment on in this hypnotic process no matter what noises or feelings occur externally, internally they only make it easier to **pay full attention to me** at some level or just drift off...and follow these helpful/hypnotic words even more easily... You only hear this voice like one you believe in most of all...that comes from that place where things are true...and **follow my words** which become, appropriately, your words...more easily than ever before...*

Nothing I do or that happens bothers you at all. It only improves and enriches your life.

Every time you follow my words you feel better and every time you feel better you follow my words...From now on everything I say (optional addition for therapy – *'...only, obviously with regards to the problems being solved...'*) *becomes you total reality instantly...Doesn't matter what it is...How different, odd, seemingly silly or new...What you know, think, believe, feel and can do follows my instruction/commands/suggestions, changing completely from now on. And* **you can do this!**

From this moment on every breath you take takes you deeper and deeper and so much pleasurably deeper! Because the golden rule of hypnosis is: The deeper you go, the better you feel, the more easily you **follow my words to the letter!** *And the better you feel the deeper you can go...into deep...hypnotic...***SLEEP!** *Deep sleep! That's right...'*

Naughty post-hypnotic triggers.

Pervnotists like to give their subjects orders. They induce hypnosis and then 'set up' various post hypnotic commands that will be followed by a willing subject. You can ensure they are followed by tagging on a suggestion that the subject will feel an amazing feeling for doing so. The formula for sexual post hypnotics or any for that matter is –

'When I do x you will do y. You will do y and feel very good.'

They tend to condition anyone successfully through reward – Skinnerian operant conditioning – not pain. They may include things such as what you might call a 'safety module'. To get the subconscious to comply they'll weigh things in their favour by saying,

'You will only do x when it is safe, private and we are alone together...'

then they add in the 'naughty' suggestion. This ensures that your subject won't do anything that could embarrass them or get either of you arrested. This is the sort of thing a pervnotist gets up to.

PLEASE NOTE: THE FOLLOWING – THE ROGUE HYPNOTIST IS NOT AN EROTIC HYPNOTIST. HE HAS HOWEVER...AHEM STUDIED IT, MERELY FOR SCIENTIFIC PURPOSES YOU UNDERSTAND! WHAT YOU DO WITH THE FOLLOWING INFO IS DOWN TO YOU. THIS SECTION IS NOT A RECOMMENDATION TO ENGAGE IN ANY SUCH ACTS. IT IS HERE FOR EDUCATIONAL PURPOSES ONLY. ALL 'SCRIPTS' ARE CREATED BY THE ROGUE HYPNOTIST JUST TO SEE IF HE COULD. DON'T TAKE THEM TOO SERIOUSLY: HE DIDN'T!!!

Perv triggers.

Protocols:

Some of the following are basically stage hypnosis style post hypnotics. You can wake your victim up fully and have the post hypnotic operate in waking consciousness or as part of an erotic hypnosis session with the subject still under but eyes open – i.e. waking hypnosis. If you choose the latter option say,

'When I do x (cue/trigger – snap fingers etc.) *your eyes will open and you will feel amazing*

but remain deeply hypnotised and follow my instructions precisely.'

I am not going to spell out everything for you because I want you to only use this section as an idea stimulator more than anything. If you want to be really good at anything you need to start thinking for yourself from day one.

Erotic hypnosis session structure:

1. Hypnotise 'victim'/gimp etc. Use one of the appropriate scripts in my books: this one has two inductions.

2. Do various skits etc. To start off only do 1 – 3 separate 'tests' max.

3. Cancel unwanted suggestions and awaken. Keep the session about 30 minutes long max.

For those that want to do this, take the ideas from this section and write out/type out a full script – make sure you have thought out and planned everything you want to happen in the session. Plan it with military precision. **The subject's enjoyment and safety should be your main concern at all times.**

Pro-tip: after some careful rumination I thought of the following –

Ideomotor erotic hypnosis negotiation.

1. In order to get the subconscious on your side as an erotic hypnotist *tell the subject **everything** you are intending to do in advance and get conscious agreement.*

2. Then using a piece of string, thread etc. with a paper clip attached at one end ask them to let it dangle from their first finger and thumb whilst holding the appropriate arm out straight.

3. Now ask the person's subconscious or get them to ask in their own mind 'Subconscious are you willing to act upon these ideas for this erotic hypnosis session?' Tell the subconscious that side to side movement of the clip is a NO! And back and forth is a YES! Await response. No formal hypnosis is needed. If the person's subconscious agrees – you have your green light. *Only do what the subconscious has agreed to and build upon that in future.* If you get a 'no' signal

respect it fully. The subconscious might agree on another occasion.

4. You might want to do this every time you play with erotic hypnosis. I guarantee it will increase your success rate.

Instant erotic trance: Ok you want a quick induction trigger to get her back into that erotic trance state you both created; how?

'Whenever I say 'erotic trance, now' you will instantly renter a state of erotic trance 50 times deeper, easily and quickly and it will feel twice as good.'

Some hypnotist's prefer: 'Trance now' (the BDSM types), 'Deep sleep' (the old favourite. Literally anything will work. Erickson suggested post hypnotic cues that were simple, like fiddling with your ear lobe (in a therapeutic context only), adjusting your tie. *If you use common actions, ensure you contextualise them.* Don't say, 'If I ever scratch my fat, hairy ass you'll strip naked and run around barking like a dog!' They might do it at a funeral: bad idea. Say, 'When I scratch my fat, hairy ass in the safe context of our erotic trance sessions you can...(insert pervy idea).'

<u>Living doll:</u> She becomes a store mannequin, a living doll etc. instantly —she can't move at all, unless you position her. She has all her other senses available: see, feel, hear, touch etc.

Option 1: 'In a moment I will snap my fingers and you will open your eyes but remain deeply hypnotised following my commands precisely.' (Waking hypnosis option.)

Option 2: 'When I say 'phoenix' you will awaken fully feeling great and all the post hypnotic commands I give you will operate fully, automatically and powerfully until I cancel them etc.'

(Then proceed with...)

'Whenever I say 'freeze' you instantly become like a store mannequin. You cannot move unless I say so. You can't even blink unless I say so. I can move you as I wish however into any position. You will feel fantastic. You'll be able to see, hear, feel anything and everything you need to. This entire experience makes you feel great because you know it

increases your sense of trust in me.'

(Note: if you say someone can't blink only let this be the case for 5 seconds. Add in a suggestion – '...however when I say 'blink' you can do so normally again. People need to blink.)

Empty-headed bimbo: The hypnotee cannot think temporarily – their mind is a blank. They may have no memory of 'blank' time. Make sure she can still respond to other triggers. You can add a twist where they can't see, hear or feel but ensure they want to experience that.

'When I say 'blank' your mind goes blank in a totally relaxed and wonderful way. It will only last a short time. You can enjoy the rest. You will only develop amnesia as and when your subconscious decides this is right in a way that satisfies all your needs as a person. As soon as I say 'normal' – your mind returns to normal erotic trance again.'

WARNING: ONLY DO THIS FOR 5 SECONDS! VERY PROLONGED 'THOUGHT STOPPING' CAN LEAD TO CULT 'SNAPPING' WITH OTHER CULT

BRAINWASHING TRICKS ADDED! AS AN ALTERNATIVE SAY, 'ACT <u>AS IF/PRETEND</u> YOUR MIND IS BLANK.' CONTRARY TO POPULAR OPINION, PEOPLE CAN THINK IN HYPNOSIS.

As an alternative suggest they become absorbed by a pleasant scene, thought, emotion etc. Be so fucking careful what you suggest to people. If you do a blank mind skit the reality is that probably 100% of the time nothing untoward will happen. Always err on the side of not doing something if you are unsure or unskilled. Just because I can do something doesn't mean you can: your knowledge base may be insufficient. ***<u>Just because you can do something doesn't mean you should! Personally I find a lot of erotic hypnosis creepy.</u>***

Slave command: When you say the trigger (obey, slave, command etc.) they go 'blank' like a sex slave zombie and wait for your instructions which are obeyed in full.

'Whenever I say the word 'obey' you will stop what you are doing, feel even more turned on than you are and await my instructions, which may be of a sexual nature or not. You will

fulfil my commands without question. You will love being so obedient. Being obedient during our naughtinosis sessions lets you feel the thrill of sexual submission and any other good feelings your subconscious wants to add.'

Cuffs on command: Most people who are 'into' EH (erotic hypnosis) are into BDSM to a greater or lesser extent. They like tying folks up! Ok, well, you can do that in hypnosis! I'll give two examples: ensure the person is a good subject or a well- trained sub-perv. Now...

'Do you know what rope feels like? Ever tied a knot? Ever been tied up or seen someone else all tied up? Could you imagine the ecstasy of a little bondage? Of someone very attractive having some kinky control of you...? Imagine I have some rope and am tying you up. I am tying your hands behind your back etc....It makes you feel sexually submissive and deliciously vulnerable but you know you can trust me to have this power...Feel the rope getting tight around your soft and pretty wrists...That's it. Really feel that feeling. The rope is being tied into a knot so that...in a moment when I

say...Kink...Kinky...Kinkier...Those bonds of rope get tight to the point where **You cannot move your hands.** *Those hands are tied tight...*

Pleasurably so...Ok, you ready? (Don't wait for response) *Kink...Kinky...Kinkier...!!!*

The harder you try the more those hands remained wonderfully tied together...and you deeply want them to stay that way till I say 'release!'...But first I am going to fuck you silly...Assume the doggy style position; face down on the sofa etc.'

God knows why anyone would want to try that ;) You can just go all authoritarian and say...

'I have placed metal cuffs on your hands. You cannot move them apart! They are stuck! When I say 'Cuffs now!' and click my fingers you will be unable to move your hands apart, they will be stuck solidly together until I say 'Flick my nipples!'

All very silly stuff...

Lingerie/short skirt/nipple tassels etc.:

Your victim instantly feels the desire to wear the most erotic lingerie ever, a short skirt, any other sexy item of clothing you have for her; most remarkably she also believes it to be her own idea!

'Whenever I say 'please me' you will automatically put on x (desired item of clothing etc. *You will enjoy changing into sexy clothes that please me. You get so much pleasure from pleasing me as I do you. You are totally motivated to do so; you know how sexy, feminine and beautiful it makes you look. You are completely convinced it is your idea and that feels liberating.'*

Hot now!:

Want your woman to feel horny on command? Or feel an increase in sexual desire? Of course you don't.

'When I say 'hot now' you will start to feel sexually aroused, you'll feel an increase in your natural sexual desire for me and you won't and don't even need to know why, for your own unconscious reasons. You enjoy experiencing such feelings, they make you feel amazing. Tapping into the resources of your most pleasurable emotions excites you.

In fact you can wait for me to say it, it feels so damned good!'

<u>I've got a lovely bunch of coconuts!:</u> This is a pattern whereby you can hypnotise a woman to show you her tits on your command. I have chosen the hypnotic trigger - 'I've got a lovely bunch of coconuts!' to trigger this pleasing event. All you say once she is in hypnosis is...

'In a moment, not right now but soon I will say, 'I've got a lovely bunch of coconuts!' When I do that will be you cue to automatically show me your tits. You will lift up your top etc. (suit this to whatever she is wearing) *and take off your bra.*

You will shake your tits and say, 'Look at these babies big boy!' and then you can relax and just let me look at those gorgeous tits of yours. After I have admired them for a sufficient length of time I will click my fingers and say, 'Enough Wench!'

When I do you will put your clothes back in position as you normally would with no memory of what you just did. This suggestion will last for one hour only and then wear off *unless I tell you otherwise*.*

(*Time-based suggestions that only last for x amount of time are more likely to be accepted as temporary fun. The subconscious is more likely to go along with things.)

You will only expose your breasts to me in private when we are alone together! When I awaken you from this trance state at the end of our session you will remember everything...'

You can get her to show you her x, y or z: you name it!

Wave of relaxation: This is a great generic one. You can use it between your naughty skits to relax her. You can use it to make her feel good and wash away any worries, doubts, uncertainties on your cue. Some people love having their emotions played with.

'When I say 'deeply relaxed, now!' you will spontaneously feel a wonderful wave of comfort spread from the top of your head to the tips of your toes and it feels wonderful - absolutely wonderful! You love feeling relaxed and I love making you feel good. Each time I repeat that phrase you feel that sensation

grow stronger and stronger...washing away all unnecessary doubts, inhibitions, questions and past negativity. It's nice to feel assured and good about things without effort is it not? This ability is easy for you.'

<u>Strip and feel good biatch!</u>: Whenever you tell your lady to strip she does on cue, without thinking and more than that she enjoys a massive surge of pleasure which will rush through her body for a few seconds, leaving her feeling amazing. The subconscious controls all emotions and physical secretions. You are allowing her to experience them. You are so thoughtful!

'On the word 'strip' you take off all your clothes immediately. You do so happily as though it's your idea, no matter where we are, when we are alone together you do this.

It's such fun, so liberating to play games like this and why not? And as you take off each item of clothing you feel wonderful feelings throughout mind and body, with each piece of clothing removed these grow and intensify.

By the time you take off the last item you feel so f**king amazing that a blissful surge of *some wonderful feeling, sexually arousal or otherwise will surge through your entire body and make you feel glad to be alive, glad to be my woman.'*

Cosplay: This is getting your woman to dress up in saucy outfits: cat woman, super girl, a maid, fairy princess. Whatever gets you going. You can set up triggers so that whenever she cleans the house she must wear a maid outfit. Whenever she pours you a glass of beer she does it dressed as a stripper/lap dancer. Or whenever she dresses as wonder woman she becomes 'wonder woman'. How might we do this?

'Every time I say 'service' you will feel a wonderful, natural and an overwhelming compulsion to dress as a French maid and you'll clean the room. (Well it's got to be done somehow!) *You don't have to wear any underwear as you do. You enjoy doing this because all naughty girls like to dress up and make believe: it's sexy, naughty and fun.'*

AND OR...

'Every time I say 'transform' you will put on your wonder woman outfit and act like

wonder woman. In playing this role you only do things that are safe: you know you don't really have superpowers – it's a game.* (*Safety feature – you don't want her thinking she is super strong etc. she might deck/punch your lights out! Or worse!') *A wonder woman who thinks I am the most attractive man in the world and who only thinks about ways to seduce me. It is so much fun to play these naughty little games and you look so inviting in that costume. Enjoy the sensuous way it fits the curvaceous contours of your body. The only 'super powers' your wonder woman has is to do everything in her power to sexually satisfy me. Now.'*

(The last suggestion adds in an extra note of safety for you and your lady. As I said you don't want her thinking she can fly or any dumb shit like that; she might hurt herself, others or you! Always be aware of safety nets and how people might 'misinterpret' seemingly innocent suggestions. In hypnosis people tend to take things literally! If you ever need to cancel a command set up a trigger at the beginning of your silliness, say,

'Whenever I say 'that's enough' all my

previous suggestions for this erotic hypnosis session will be immediately cancelled and you will be totally back to normal feeling instantly wide awake etc!')

NOTE: hypnosis is not needed for any of this stuff if a woman is sufficiently playful and willing you know.

'Sex slave': Whenever your lady puts on an item of clothing she instantly becomes your sex slave. She fulfils all your sexual desires like the good little slut puppy she really is. This could be handcuffs, a ball gag, a collar etc. That's up to you.

'Whenever I put this ball gag in your mouth you instantly become my sex slave. This is defined as you doing exactly what I wish sexually with a sense of joy and sexual arousal at the thought of making me so fulfilled. You feel fulfilled in this role. The minute you feel that gag in your mouth you feel your sexual arousal level increase noticeably. Only by servicing all my sexual needs can this delicious arousal be fully satisfied. This role can help fulfil your unconscious needs to be sexually submissive and to play and have lots of naughty fun.

Your new name in this state is Bitch 1. You love being Bitch 1.'

<u>Creating a cum guzzler:</u> Okay boys, now we all know it, some girls love to swallow and some don't. Sometimes it's just the idea of having that white discharge it the mouth etc., sometimes it's just the taste. Too salty? Not that I know! I've heard! Have you heard that joke from school:

'You know some men masturbate in the bath?'

Them: 'Yes.'

'You know how your spunk/jizz goes in water?'

They nod, reply 'Yes.'

'You do! Hey he masturbates in the bath!'

Back on message. Say your lady doesn't like to swallow cum, doesn't like it on her t*ts, face, a*s, hates the taste. You can repair that with hypnosis! Say,

'When I count to 3 and say 'you love it' you will love cum. You love the sight of it. The taste of it. The feel of it. In fact you love it so much that you like it on your face, hair, tits,

you love to swallow it. You love the feel of it in your mouth. You like it on your hands. You like the feel of it on your hands or anywhere else on your body. It's lovely and sticky like a favourite luxurious desert. It is warm and creamy, squidgy and soft. You love cum. My cum. You like to roll it around on your tongue. You love to fully taste it. You like to suck it down. You are a slut and sluts drink cum. (If you call her a slut make sure you remove this at the session's end or she might well become one with people other than you!) *They love it. You love it. You are a born cum guzzler. You love to swallow my sperm. You like my sperm and semen inside you, anywhere, mouth, ass, pussy. You love cum. It tastes delicious to you, perhaps like a favourite treat, a favourite piece of Candy? I don't know, your unconscious does. You know at a very deep level that I and all men think the sight of our cum dripping off of a beautiful woman's face is one of the most glorious sights of our adult male existence. It makes us feel manly and powerful. It says you are mine bitch and I can cum on you or in you just as I please and you like that. You look so sexy, so pretty, your eyes looking up at me, enjoying the look of sheer ecstasy on my face that you are allowing me to experience, as you suck my cock and as you guzzle down my cum, drink it down with joy, as though thirsting for a pleasant, refreshing drink. In fact you'll only be totally satisfied and feel good after you've swallowed my cum all the way down, now. You enjoy sucking my cock. The feel of it in your mouth makes you feel feminine and alive. The warmth of it. The size of it. It's hardness and power. It's power to make you feel fucking amazing! You love me to fill your mouth with my cock. You love it when I hold your head firmly and thrust deep inside you. I may even hold your hair or pull it and that arouses you even more. It feels great to be this sexually vivacious woman. You love it when my cock explodes cum in your mouth. You feel beautiful, womanly and sexually mature with this knew found knowledge. Letting past silly doubts fade away...as you fully embrace this new experience, this new opportunity that will surprise and delight you, noooow!'*

Why any man would want to do this is beyond me, I'm stunned you're reading this...and if you believe that...You can just cut the waffle and give simple, direct, authoritarian command. I am only being long winded to teach you possibilities. Try,

'When you open your eyes on my command you will love the taste of my cum and enjoy swallowing it all etc.'

Attraction to x: In hypnosis a woman can act as though she's attracted to anything. Your childhood teddy, a chair, you name it.

'When I click my fingers and say 'My! Your building is a mighty erection!' you will instantly be incredibly attracted to my pocket calculator and do everything in your power to seduce it. You will genuinely feel deep feelings of attraction to it as though it were your ideal lover!'

You might want to tell her to avoid inserting it...well, you know.

I am your favourite male celeb: One of men and women's main sexual fantasies is to screw or get screwed by a top celeb. With that in mind...

'In a moment I will say, 'Justin Bieber is a talentless bastard!' When I do you will

sincerely believe that I am x (fav celeb). *You will be so attracted to me that you will do anything to get me into bed so that we can have the best sex of your life. In fact that's the only thing that can make you happy!'*

I have seen pervnotists add in touches such as...

'In a moment I will do x (trigger) *when I do you will instantly believe I am y* (celeb) *and you will feel incredibly turned on and attracted to me. You will talk and flirt with me with only one thing on your mind: sex. The only thing is whenever I lift this glass over my body it's as though the glass gives you X Ray powers and you will be able to see me naked: all my manly bits and pieces. This will be fun but you'll have to try to cover up the fact that you can see through my clothes but only when I lift the glass!'*

'Animal' magic: No this is not bestiality! Stay well away from the insane! It's a let's pretend game. If goes like this,

'You are a female x (animal of choice), *you are on heat and want me to mate with you.'*

<u>Orgasm on command:</u> There are a billion way to do this but this is a standard quick method that you can use with girlies who are in the mood or hyper-responsive. Some women need to be taken gradually to the edge of hypnotic orgasm in increments then tactfully shoved off the ledge. This version is for the sluts!

'On my trigger (or use favourite 'in a moment pattern') *I am going to say 'x'...* (the trigger word or phrase – 'Cum for me!' 'Orgasm now!' 'Cum instantly! 'My pet chimp Louie likes to masturbate!' – knock your socks off; the word/s don't matter. You could f***ing sneeze!) *At that instant **you will orgasm** – harder than you believed was possible, powerfully and unforgettably! It will feel a-fucking-mazing! It is 100% going to happen. In fact **you are so excited** at this prospect that few women get to experience that you can't wait for the trigger! Just the thought of the trigger being said arouses you, now! This orgasm occurs bang on my cue!*

Ready? (Don't wait!)

'My pet chimp Louie likes to masturbate!"

(And God created woman. Thank goodness. Prepare for moaning, grinding and other unseemly acts of pure delight! And that's just you!)

LIKE STAGE HYPNOTISTS REMEMBER TO <u>ALWAYS</u> CANCEL ALL SUGGESTIONS AT THE SESSION'S END – simply say, *'All suggestions in this erotic hypnosis game are now completely cancelled. You are totally back to normal as you were before we started. You'll remember everything you want to. You will feel amazing on awakening etc.'*

You obviously do not want to leave your lady love acting all weird in normal life! Restore her!

The way I thought about this odd section of my book is this: If people are going to do this stuff better they learn about it from me rather some weirdo how to do it well and safely. I imagined that people who are 'into' this stuff had hired me for my expertise as some kind of consultant and produced some solutions to their 'problems'.

Non count up awakening.

(You really don't need to count people up from hypnosis especially when they have some experience of going in and out. As you reach the point of emerging make sure your voice is alert, positive and back to normal tonality.)

*'So now...you can start to become aware of this present moment...Aware of your body...Noises around you...****Feeling more and more awake...****Refreshed, well and happy...****Re-orienting your awareness back here, now...****And when I tell you to** 'open your eyes' soon...you will feel totally wide awake feeling amazing! ****Feel more alert!**** Back to the room! Preparing to ****be wide awake**** on my cue...'Open your eyes!' Feeling good.'*

(*A variant of an 'in a moment' pattern, see book 2, 'Mastering hypnotic language'.)

As an interesting end note, Dr. Milton Erickson the 'founding father' of modern hypnosis would create spontaneous amnesia for the trance state in the following way.

1. In your pre-talk start a conversation thread with a client – say, 'The weather', 'A hobby' etc.

2. Induce trance, do change work etc. and wake person up. Some people call this 'emerging' someone from hypnosis.

3. On awakening start talking to the person about the thread you opened pre-hypnosis. *The person forgets what happened in between!!!* 'Mazing. This protects the change work from conscious analysis.

The intense pleasure association script.

You can adapt this for any intense pleasure state that you want to revivify on cue. The underlying principles can be adapted for many differing scenarios. I have been quite naughty and chosen to create an orgasm on cue. Why not?!

WARNING DO NOT OVERDO OR PROLONG BLISS STATES; EXCESSIVELY PROLONGED OR INAPPROPRIATE BLISS STATES ARE NOT NORMAL OR HEALTHY. YOU INDUCE 'BLISS' FOR PURPOSEFUL AND FOCUSED REASONS.

Stage 1: loving someone.

(Deep hypnosis assumed)

*'What if you could recall a time when you loved someone so much that you gave them an unexpected gift or reward of some kind...When you did something for someone else that was out of the ordinary...special...And as you **re-experience that time vividly in 3D lifelikeness**...see what you saw...hear what you heard and feel how good that felt...Now turn that feeling into*

a colour...that's it...

Now as I slide my finger from your elbow to your shoulder that feeling gets better... (by the way getting them to imagine this works just as well! This is an NLP sliding anchor) *better...better and even better...that's right!*

*Amplifying that wonderful feeling now...and that colour feeling gets brighter and brighter and even more intense as **these feelings increase considerably**...ECSTASY!* (Operant conditioning begins. Word + state linked via repetition, in hypnosis this process is amplified and quickened.)

*From now on whenever I say the word 'ecstasy' you will **feel these feelings automatically!** That's it...feeling those feelings of loving someone that much that you'd willingly give them a spontaneous happy surprise! Excellent!*

Stage 2: feeling loved.

Now I'd simply invite you to go back to a marvellous time...when you felt you were totally loved and accepted for who you are completely! Perhaps it was a time when you felt this more than at any other time in your life?

Recall that deep instinctual need, that satisfaction of having that core need met...It may have affected your sexuality, your relationships, your physical health...Recall that time of unconditional loving acceptance...Perfect...

It wasn't just about sex...it was more than that...When you are fully back in that time...see what you saw and notice something new...hear what you heard in a way that amplifies these feelings...and feel that flow of joyous feelings within you...Welling up from the deepest core of who you really are...Lovely! Amplify those feelings to their most perfect pitch!

(Pause a few seconds or so to allow this.)

What colour best represents these blissful feelings? **Let that colour glow, spread, intensify** *in its most rich qualities...as I slide my finger up the back of your arm...that's right! And those feelings only get better...better...even better! ECSTASY! That's perfect! Those mix of* **feelings** *can and will* *conjoin, link up, **become associated, now!***

*From now on whenever I say the word 'ecstasy' you will feel all these feelings automatically! That's it...feeling those feelings of loving someone that much that you'd willingly give them a spontaneous happy surprise and **feel those wonderful feelings of total acceptance of all that you are!** Excellent!*

Stage 3: indulgence.

*There are times when we just like to indulge ourselves aren't there? Times when we have to **give in to overwhelming cravings and urges**...naughty temptations! You could have been experiencing something tactilely, physically...perhaps a massage...It might have been a time when you felt you had to have that gorgeous piece of chocolate cake...It could have been a time when you **let yourself go** to some piece of music...It could have been when you just took in something so beautiful with your eyes that you couldn't take your eyes off it...It could have been a time you felt you had an overwhelming unconscious urge to act...to do something...and that craving had to find* *satisfaction for you to get release...Or all at once...you chose...I don't know...you do!*

*Perhaps it was the anticipation and expectation...Maybe it was that feeling that felt most blissful and teasing...Feel the uncontrollable desire for that thing...that experience that you craved...a time you fully abandoned yourself...**let go totally into indulgence**...you can't resist anymore...See what you saw...hear what you heard...feel how intensely blissfully and naughty that super indulgence felt...*

*And when its reached its current peak...turn it into a colour...that colour can grow more rich, intense and spread out from where you feel it most already and then some...**Feel this delicious feeling intensify**...more and more and more as I slide my finger saucily up the back of the sensitive skin on the back of your arm...maybe you already feel those tingles? That's right! ECSTASY! I love making you feel good baby! It turns me on. ECSTASY! That's perfect!*

*This amazing admixture of **feelings can and will conjoin!** From now on whenever I say the word 'ecstasy' you will **feel all these***

feelings automatically! *That's it...*

*Feeling those feelings of loving someone that much that you'd willingly give them a spontaneous happy surprise and **feel those wonderful feelings** of total acceptance of all that you are! Those feelings of uncontrollable desires that desperately need indulgence!*

*Maybe all those colours swirl together round and round? Maybe they form a new colour? Maybe they radiate or glow? I don't know. You do...Whatever way the subconscious wants you to experience this is just right for you...trust that response...One thing I do know...**those feelings amplify!** Excellent!*

Stage 4: fantastic sex.

Now we are taking this whole process up a level into greater heights of pure bliss and rapture...Recall or imagine a time when you had or are having...the wildest...naughtiest...dirtiest...filthiest sex... (make sure your voice tone is seductive and saucy) *you are a wild abandoned slut who would do any fucking amazingly pleasurable and healthy thing...A time when you did or can **let your animals lust flood out of you***

totally...It is so fucking passionate...nothing prevents you from fully experiencing the ultimate pitch of womanly sexual pleasure with a deserving man. You feel like a whore...a happy whore...who wanted to be fucked that way...you deserved it...harder and fucking harder...so that **sexual tension could build and build** and fucking build...You could feel that kiss...that touch and grope...that cock in and out just the way you like...just the right angle and place...hitting that sweet spot that makes you moan in womanly delight...

Recall or just imagine those sensations...the balls slapping against your arse/ass...the sounds...remember how that electric sensuality that you could not control shot through you...**feel those feelings build...**oh my! Oh my fucking God! How can any experience be this rapturously fantastic...? You **feel feminine...womanly and so alive**...as if you were meant to be fucked and owned like this...you **feel like a naughty bitch** and you love it...deeper, don't you?

Feel those tastes...That passion builds more and more...see what you saw...hear what you heard and turn those noises up but only in ways that turn you on to the max...**Feel those amazing feelings**...revive or experience that total bliss that only a woman is gifted to feel intensely...over and over multiple times...And at just the right time...turn that tumult of physical and emotional passion into a colour that symbolises all that...in and out...pulsating...throbbing...blissful aching...remember or imagine how you'd breathe...that's it!

And when you **feel the waves and waves of that** colour...growing even more intense...let them amplify to perfection as I slide my naughty finger that only increases all that glorious bliss...that totally free response...so it gets...better...better and even better, now! That's it! ECSTASY! Perfect, you are doing brilliantly...This incredible miasma of **feelings can and will conjoin and only build** and feedback on one another!

From now on whenever I say the word 'ECSTASY' you will **feel all these feelings automatically!** That's it...

Feeling those feelings of loving someone that

much that you'd willingly give them a spontaneous happy surprise and feel those wonderful feelings of total acceptance of all that you are! Those feelings of uncontrollable desires that desperately need indulgence! And boost those feelings of the greatest, wildest, animal lust and passionate sex as you are fucked just right...in those ways that a woman privately fantasises about...

*Those colours can swirl together round and round? Maybe they form a new colour? Maybe they radiate or glow? Maybe they just find their own way to intensify! I don't know. You do...Whatever way the subconscious wants you to experience this is just right for you...trust **that building response**...Excellent!*

Stage 5: dream 'gasms!

*Have a dream now...dream an erotic dream...imagine or remember if you wish...a dream of pure erotic satisfaction...when **you are filled to overflowing with an abundance of amazing erotic sensations and pleasures and processes**...*

*And in this hypnotic sleep **your body is***

having orgasm after orgasm*...and you are getting the ultimate, royal fantasy fuck of your pretty little life...with this dream lover!* (Note: make sure this dream lover is YOU! If you don't she might want to fulfil these urges with the 'dream lover'...bad idea bozo!) *The one who knows, really knows what turns you on...he satisfies all your sexual emotional and physical needs, cravings and desires...he makes you **come over and over again** as if you are his fuck machine...And he is a fuck machine...he knows all the right buttons to press!*

FANTASISE NOW! **Feel all the sensations and pleasures...***wave after wave of pleasure...without exhaustion or strain for these heights of sexual ecstasy and rapture that you are dreaming about...over and over...more and more intensely in the dream time...of your...subconscious...mind...erotically...now......Purrrrrfect...* (Give her a full minute to imagine having the most multi-orgasmic fuck of her life!)

And as you dream all this in your own way...imagine a colour that symbolises all this for you...see what you saw...hear what your dreamed...feel those appropriate dreamy feelings...and see that colour start where it is before it spreads in the right way...Radiates in the right way!

And as it reaches a perfect peak of incredible bliss and pure response....let those colour **feelings only grow** *as I slide this finger of sexual delight...up that arm...and* **these feelings just get better***...better...better...even better...that's perfect! ECSTASY! Every sensation has reached its full pitch and expression...stronger and stronger...even more intense...electrifying these sensations...* (Build your voice to an orgiastic crescendo!)

This overwhelming torrent of **these feelings can and will conjoin and only build and feedback on one another, ultimately demanding release** *at the perfect spot of hot sexual tension! From now on whenever I say the word 'ECSTASY!'* (Or you can link it to a specific touch, kiss, whatever...) *you will* **feel all these feelings automatically!** *That's it...*

Feeling those feelings of loving someone that

much that you'd willingly give them a spontaneous happy surprise and feel those wonderful feelings of total acceptance of all that you are! Those feelings of **uncontrollable desires that desperately need indulgence, now!** *And* **boost those feelings of the greatest, wildest, animal lust and passionate sex as you are fucked just right...***in those ways that a woman privately fantasises about...***Feeling those feelings of multiple dream orgasms** *as you are perfectly fucked!* ('perfectly fucked' is nicely ambiguous.)

Those colours can swirl together, come together, round and round? Maybe they form a new colour of ultimate, optimum sexual bliss? Maybe they radiate or glow? Maybe they just find their own way to **intensify, now!** *I don't know. You do...Whatever way the subconscious wants you to experience this is just right for you...Trust* **that building response***...Excellent!*

Stage 6: test work.

Again whenever I say that word 'ECSTASY!' **All those feelings, sensations, processes, desires...urges and cravings...come all at**

the same instant...spontaneously automatically...they allow you to feel pure and total satisfaction and release...*They all **come together** only on my command...and create in you such pleasure that other woman only dream of it, now!*

Let's practise that now...

'ECS-TA-SY!'

That's it!

Look how much pleasure I effortlessly make you feel...can you imagine all the ways you'd reward someone like that...There is a place...deep inside where all these feelings feel best...where they feel they should be...Let them go to that place that desires them...That knows these feelings belong there...That's it!

*All these sensations **come together** there...in that special place of your desire...now. Take that swirling or radiating colour or colours and as I slide my magic titillating finger up that arm...**these feelings only get better**...better...even better now!*

'ECSTASY!'

*Perfect baby! As you experience this you know **these feelings are always available for your joy when appropriate in your life...**and that's a nice thing to know isn't it and wasn't it? And you can **cum on my command** if you are a naughty-good girl...Nooooo-wwww!*

<u>*Stage 7: summation and solidifying the work.*</u>

*Hear the comfort of my voice and go deeper...relax now...**feel calmer and more and more rested...**relaxed and at peace...you have accessed certain latent abilities that are now available when you desire them to be and only this...tonight...at some time when you are fast asleep...you will have the most rapturous, electrifying, ecstatic orgasm of orgasms that you've had...so far...as you sleep and dream in that dream world...your unconscious mind will create this outstanding...outlandish...pleasure for you...This is a further gift from me to you...to show my appreciation to you...of you...in allowing us to play this naughty game together...*

And again...as the deep unconscious finalises any and all re-associations that can, do and *need to occur...now...you can also know that at a deep level **this experience has enriched you...**allowed you to **recapture your natural ability to experience all the wonderful feelings that your mind-body system is more than capable of producing...**just when you need it...*

And again whenever I say the word 'ECSTASY!' you will feel this wonderful new feeling or feelings automatically as a spontaneous reflex action...And won't it be fun...discovering how much naughty fun this can be...each and both of you, noooo-oooowwwwww!'

(You are quite welcome! It may be the case that for some subjects, post hypnotics of this kind need to be temporarily 'topped up' to be kept fresh. The brain tends to get rid of things that are not used habitually. Again do not overdo this sort of stuff. At the least you'll exhaust the poor girl! Remember also your subject is a person not a f**king toy!)

Hypnotic orgasm phone sex.

This is the section where I teach you how to make a woman orgasm over the phone. It's easy. In order to teach you a version of this I will have to outline some principles of mind. Especially of a woman's mind who is turned on. The best way to do this is to set it up beforehand that you are going to do it (with her permission!). This builds expectation and primes the subconscious to begin working way in advance so that you can help your lady have an orgasm without even touching her. You just need to know the principles behind what to say. It may take a little practise. But it's a fun thing to practise nes pas? You can do this spontaneously too, just going for it in the moment without warning. That can work well. Why? She is surprised and shocked which = hypnosis. But don't do nice stuff for those who haven't deserved it. Capiche!?

Phone sex principles.

- You set a **sexual frame of reference.** You do this by dropping flirtatious hints, using sexual swear words and by setting the direction of the conversation. You lead. She wants you to. The rule is: *whatever* *she talks about is just a way to lead her into talking about sex.* If she talks about her plumbing, sexualise it. If she mentions her cat, sexualise it. It she talks about food, turn the conversation onto the sensual experience of eating. All normal conversation can be sexualised - IF you set a sexual context. Often you do this automatically through subtle shifts in voice tone that reveal your intention to seduce and f*ck her. Well mind f*ck in this case.

- You are the dominant man (unless you are a dominant lesbian!). You decide when she comes. You can build her arousal up and take it down. If she does what you say, she gets rewarded. **Women like sexually dominant men.**

- Blatantly turn the conversation onto her. You can ask, *'So what do you want from this?' 'Let's talk about you and your desires.'* This makes her self-conscious, which is hypnotic and a bit vulnerable which she will find sexy.

- Whatever she says **pace it. Then lead it.** So if she says, *'It's nice listening to your voice I feel comfortable.'* You reply, *'So as* *you listen in comfort you can find a way to amplify that if you want etc.?'* You use her words, feed them back and then add a leading suggestion. This is the sexual small talk phase.

- Ask her how she wants things to happen, quickly or slowly (apposition of opposites - use this a lot)? She will more than likely want to *ease* rather than romp into it. Through this she can effortlessly achieve an erotic trance. *'How do you want to begin to enter this experience? Jump right in or slide in gently?'*

- The principles of hypnosis are? **Activate her imagination/memory. Get her to focus on bodily sensations. Narrow her focus of attention.** Get her using trance language to tell you how she feels. She'll do this naturally as she explains what she is experiencing. You must be aware of this. This tells you where she is and lets you know where and when you can take her deeper.

- There is a time to offer her choices (the ones you want her to have) and a time to be dominant and authoritarian. You need an Ericksonian permissive and direct approach. Or as I call it, be **directly indirect.** *'Do you feel it most in a certain place or all over somehow?'*

- You don't need to but you can access the desired arousal state by asking, *'Have you ever been so sexually aroused that you couldn't stop certain automatic feelings etc.?' 'Can you remember a time you felt so turned on that you felt the beginnings of that sexual arousal that you love to feel inside?'* Generally her expectation, surprise, absorption and involvement will take her 'there' as part of the context.

- Women often refer to sexual arousal as 'flows of energy' – if she uses that term, start using it to build your suggestions around. You need to know HOW she begins to experience sexual tension and orgasm on the inside. *'Do you feel a certain flow of energy inside? 'How do you experience that?' 'What goes on inside? Describe it to me vividly and you'll get to re-experience it,'* etc.

- In order for a woman to come she has to release things. You might have to talk about releasing tensions, worries etc. *'It's time to **let certain things go**, to **relax deeply** and cum inside to the warm and comforting places.'*

- Does she experience the sexual tension as waves, pulsations, energy flows, tingles, butterflies? Is there a colour related to that feeling? A symbol maybe? *'What is the set of feelings you feel inside that let you know that x is happening etc.?'*

- Ask her questions about her ongoing experience in mind and body. What does this do? Makes her 'go inside' and hypnotises her. *'What's going on inside your body while that occurs?'*

- Use a lot of sexual ambiguity. We now know that sexual arousal is triggered by words activating the sexual parts of the brain/nervous system* (*see appendices). The more you focus her mind on its sexual parts, the more she'll start activating these regions unconsciously. She can't not! Sexual words prime her. You are priming the sexual subconscious and unconscious structures to respond. Examples, 'Cum inside,' 'Deep within,' 'Penetrates deep inside,' 'BeCUM aware of,' 'Feel it,' etc. **_Think like a dirty old man!_** Sexualise all words. Whatever she says give it a sexual interpretation. Infer she is obsessed with sex.

- Once you have her focused on her feelings ask her how intense they are. You don't need to grade it from 1-10, you could but it's not needed and a little bit of a mood killer. You need to maintain that sexy mood once it's there. It's like a bird, if you move too quickly you'll spook it and it will fly away. _'Because you are focused on these amazing feelings, how intense are they now (option: on a 1-10 scale)? You don't have to tell me just know in that private place.'_

- Women can experience their sexual arousal as flows that may separate, swirl or come together. Nuts I know! _'How do you subjectively experience that arousal?' 'Does that blissful* feeling swirl, blend etc.?'_ (*I have used the word 'blissful', if you can get her **trance words** for her sexual, pre-orgasm state – bingo! Feed it back to her. Trance words are key words that she has learned over time to directly link her to certain states. Associative triggers in other words.)

- You can focus her on bodily feelings which will usually be in her tummy area by telling not asking her (gently) to place her hand on that part. This focuses the mind even more. *'Where do you feel this most?'* You are locating the sensations. You need to know what the 'pace' (ongoing reality) is before you can tag on leading suggestions, transforming those feelings in the direction you wish.

- Once you have a colour linked to those feelings you can play with it. **The colour is your symbolic interface with her neurology. *You effectively have her unconscious sex code.*** You can ask, *'Is there a colour/are their colours linked to that? What is it/are they?'* Asking people about colours bypasses all resistance: after all it's just colours! He-he.

- Link that feeling and colour to a normal ongoing process - her breathing for example. This also focuses her on her breathing which will hypnotise her deeper.

You can ask, *'What breathing changes need to occur to make that **feeling more intense?'** `As you only focus on that colour feeling, **allow that pleasure to grow** with the natural rhythm of your inhale and exhale.'* Keep the link simple.

- Give leading suggestions for the intensity of feeling to increase. *'And as you do that **these feelings can intensify.'***

- Ask if the arousal increases on the exhale or inhale – use **double binds** (either or) liberally. Breathing is linked to all states of mind. Sexual arousal has its own state of consciousness as it were. Her breathing rate can activate it. By asking questions about breathing changes and arousal you create the arousal.

- Women's sexual arousal often feels like jolts of electricity. They feel electric tingles up and down their spines. They feel warmth and heat. You can ask her if these things are occurring or when they occur. By so doing you focus her inside, on highly pleasurable feelings. This alone will intensify them. You can also suggest she feels them. *'Do you **feel those electric***

tingles, warmths *etc.? Where are they most intense before they increase?'*

- Women may describe their arousal feelings as being various colours. Find out which represents the *most intense* sexual arousal states. Focus her mind on that and give suggestions that it grows and starts to smoother the less intense ones. Tell her the colour linked to her most excited feelings is the *'Juiciest/purest/essence/crystallised part of what she wants.'* For example, *'As you pay attention to these colours and the feelings associated to them, which colour or shade or intensity of colour represents the deepest essence of what you deeply crave from this experience?'*

- The feelings will spread as you talk about them. Tell her this can happen easily.

- Sexual tension may be experienced as a tugging or pulling, a pressure that builds and that eventually needs release. You can ask her about this or suggest it is happening. Read an erotic novel to discover the subjective sensations a woman experiences during sexual arousal and orgasm (more on this later). Steal them and put them in your sexual hypnosis. I will include a word and phrase list that will help you hit the spot on this matter ;) *'Can you feel a growing warmth (pressure/tugging/pulling/heat/tension) somewhere?'*

- Tell her that whenever she breathes out, it allows her to relax deeper and so open up and let go more. She'll know what this means trust me. *'Breathe, relax and go deeper as you let go; let certain ideas and processes cum inside you and that will let you open up as you deeply wish.'*

- By the way, the feedback you want is her **rate of breathing and any noises** she makes. Often it takes a woman a little time to get sexually aroused. Her breathing will change audibly when she hits the first level of sexual arousal. This is her first plateau. Listen for it. *'That's it, you've got it babe!'* *'You're inside it aren't you etc.?'* When done correctly this is very intimate and quite romantic.

- Ask her if her feelings intensify more on exhalation or inhalation. Give her suggestions in response to this that it is spreading more easily through her body. *'Is it strongest or most amplified on the out or in breath?* **Let these amplified feelings intensify and spread, now,** *in that way that pleases you most.'* Using 'that' will assist to neuro-linguistically help her to dissociate and enter waking trance.

- After she hits the first plateau you can become more direct. She's in state. Now you want to intensify it and build it till she eventually comes really hard. *'Good, now you are at a good starting place, we can* **build this to pleasurable heights** *as we cum together to create intense ecstasy together. Would you like that?'* You might hear a whimpering, 'Yes!' You respond - 'Do as I say and I will make it your reality.' Get **compliance and sexual submission.**

- Ensure she gives you feedback. Make her talk to you and so let you know what's going on. Say, 'Let me know x etc...'

- When you want the arousal to build use the word 'start' or 'begin' to preface your commands. For example: *'Start to* **feel**

that sensation come inside you.'
'Begin to feel that pressure itself inside you.' 'Start to feel that tension building.' 'Begin to feel that electric stimulation/warmth etc. building.'
What do these words presuppose? That it will get more and more intense. And you thought words were SO innocent.

- Link intensity of feelings to her rate of breathing. Again: if you link a hypnotic process to an ongoing natural process you will make things easier. You are using a trance logic false linkage. Say, *'The more you breathe the right way, the more intense and amplified this can beCUM.'* A woman's breathing gets heavier, more intense as she reaches orgasm.

- You may notice that using lots of sexual ambiguity is very helpful. *'You want it,' 'Suck it up,' 'Open up to it,' 'Release tension,' 'Increase the delectable sensations.'* Make sh*t up, improvise. **THINK - what if just my words and the way I use 'em can make her cum?** They can boyo! Word f**k her - artfully.

- Call her a naughty girl, bitch, sexy, cum

slut, wicked little whore etc. throughout. *'You are a dirty little slut aren't you?'*

- Tell her she likes it and that's why she's your slut. Tell her you know it feels good and that's why she's so slutty etc. *'You like it when I talk to you like this don't you? That's because you're that type of woman. I knew you were secretly VERY naughty. You tried to hide it, now it's all coming out.'*

- Now, although this is a 'moment of pure response' you can ask if she is experiencing any internal mental processes other than feelings. These can be fleeting thoughts, dream images, imagination etc. E.g. *'Are you experiencing certain glimmers of thoughts and images that make this a stronger process for you? More all absorbing?'* Or, *'What thoughts or images cum into your mind spontaneously?'*

- Use sexual phrases like, *'Open up easily,' 'Let go into it.'*

- Make sure you reassure her often that the process is *'natural', 'spontaneous', 'automatic'* etc. This removes any sense of artificiality.

- Tell her to, '...*let naughty thoughts and images CUM inside your mind, now.'*

- Tell her to '...*start to **create mental images,** sizzling ideas, erotic fantasies, use your vivid sexual imagination connected to your deepest and most honest sexual part of your feminine self to let you **picture what it is you truly desire and crave.'***

- You can say, *'Certain areas of your mind are activated in response to sexuality.'* This is what I call hypnotic neuroscience suggestions. See my next book. Needless to say this is a direct suggestion in hypnosis for the brain to 'light up' certain areas. It can be that quick!

- Talk about her '...*cravings, urges, desires, wants and needs.'* She will contextualise this to sex. She's not daft.

- If she starts to head toward orgasm too soon calm her down; you want to prolong her sexual tension, 'agony' and building ecstasy so that she comes on your command. Make her know in no uncertain terms YOU ARE IN CONTROL of her pleasure. This will arouse her all the more. *'Calm down woman, **slow it down,** breathe easy and let it build, not yet, I don't want you let off that easily. **Calm it down** woman.'* Call her 'woman' it sounds cave man like; if you are an accountant leave that role at the bedroom door tiger! Give her a nickname or get her to give you one, it's fun. You know everyone has their own way of flirting? No one does it the same way.

- To calm her, tell her to, *'Slow down...take a deep breath and yet let it out more slowly...good.'* You have got her into the state you want – next phase is to stabilise it and build it!

- Use apposition of opposites: slow/fast, relax/tension, intensify/absorb. How do you do this? *'Slow down as your breathing calms, as fast as that arousal builds.'* *'Relax more deeply into it but only in a way that that sexual tension finds a way to amplify and spread all throughout your bad girl mind and body.'*

- To stabilise her arousal tell her to, *'Stay at this level for a moment,' 'Rest here a while,'* etc.

- To create a hypnotic sexual plateau, tell her not to amplify the state but to, *'Bathe yourself in this state, feeling, pleasure, sensations. Soak it up and in. **Become more absorbed** in this delight. This ecstatic agony I am allowing you to **feel deeply inside your most private parts.** Absorb that which you really want. Amplify this in a way that feels best. Take some time out to pause before you **feel it even more intensely.** Absorb this in a way that **you beCUM even more stimulated.'***

- Ask her explicitly when it feels right, *'Do you want more of this?'* etc. ***Get her to beg you for more pleasure.*** Only give her it if she is a good submissive little slut (wonderfully politically incorrect isn't it ;) You are giving her a great gift of sexual pleasure here. Very few men on earth can do this stuff to a woman: you have transformed into a talking vibrator! Make her feel, in a very laid back way, that she is experiencing a special privilege. *'You are one lucky little cum puppy, aren't you?'* you can say if you are feeling confident and cocky. Get lots of 'yeses' out of her. You can be really arrogant and say, *'Do you want this gift? Do you deserve it? Imagine how you'll best repay me.'* You are giving her an orgasm; you deserve a real one back I think: fair's fair.

- You can say things like, *'If you were to **go deep inside** and let yourself explore this and come deeply inside yourself, would you desire that release right now or would you prefer to **luxuriate in these sensations**?'* What you are doing is deepening her waking hypnotic state and offering her the pseudo choice of soaking in the good feelings or releasing the tension with orgasm. The trick is don't let her cum till you want her to.

- If at any point she gets so excited that she seems close to orgasm tell her to *'…slow down, breathe easy, **calm it down** etc.'* Or you can temporarily focus her mind on something else. You can say, *'Focus on something else while that feeling builds,'* you can say, *'Let your mind wander and* **focus on your thoughts.** *Are you having dirty thoughts come flooding through your mind?'* The key to pacing and leading her is to notice her breathing rate – this will tell you if she is about to cum. Her voice will be breathy, shaky etc.

- You can also calm her down by focusing her mind on some specific body part – her finger tips, nipples, hands, tongue. Listen out for what she tells you and build on it. Pace, lead, pace, lead. For example if she feels sensations in her tummy, or something in her throat etc. ***Whatever the sensation is, tell her she can imagine it spreading elsewhere.*** Say stuff like, '...it can melt etc.' You can tell her to suck her finger, play with her tits, whatever you like. You can tell her to transfer pleasure from one place to another. In trance this will happen. *'Play with your tits, rub them, lick your lips,* **notice sensations** *in your mouth, suck your finger like it's my cock and that* **pleasure goes to those parts**, *makes you feel even more FUCKING amazing!* **Feel these pleasures penetrating** *as* *deeply as they can - cum. Inside* - you feel incredible. I don't know how good that feels, you do! Luxuriate in your feelings I made you feel! How much more do you want this?* **BeCUM absorbed** *by the increasing intensity of your experience...This is a delightful process, is it not?'* (**'Cum inside'* in this context is a double command: one sexual and two a deepener, like 'go inside.')

- Use sexual ambiguities like *'Deeper inside,' 'Feel it more,' 'Want it deeper,' 'Taste that,' 'Probing sensation,'* – use the words *'deep'* and *'down'* liberally.

- As you relax her a bit, tell her that although she is focused on other things that *'...tension can expand and grow,'* meanwhile. Tell her that her craving for it is getting more intense. Don't say what 'it' is. Use more the more patterns – *'...the more it expands the more you want it deeper etc.'*

- Describe *'tightness'* growing. *'Feel it tighter and tighter like you want to explode!' 'That tension builds more and more to an explosive point!'* Tell her it will grow until nothing more can fit inside her. You can use metaphors and symbols of expansion – a river at a dam, balloons about to pop, juices about to flow from a squeezed fruit etc. Talk about *'...pulsating and pulling/radiating/those sensations growing...'* or use whatever she tells you about how that sexual tension feels to her – feed it back and then give leading suggestions for amplification, intensification of them. *'It feels intense? Okay and how much more intense can you discover it can beCUM inside as* **you focus and let go into this** *immersion?'!*

- As this pre-orgasm state intensifies ask her how bad she wants it. If you like, again, get her to beg for you to let her cum! Women like to be teased, controlled, sexually dominated. This is not a time for wimping out. Make her hand the controls over to you. *'How bad do you want it bitch? You fucking want it so bad don't you? You* **feel that intense craving** *that needs fulfilment by me don't you? Your sex drive is so hot and excited isn't it? Follow my instructions and your wishes will CUM true!'* You hold the keys to her sexual satisfaction.

- You can ***fractionate internal focus*** –
bodily feelings, imagination, thoughts etc.
You can focus her on her body just by
talking about it. *'Your body wants more of
this doesn't it?' 'Feel those amazing
sensations,' 'That delicious set of feelings
probe and pleasure their way thrillingly
through you.' 'If you touch yourself
anywhere **those feelings and
sensations only grow-n** (play on words
grow- groan/grow-n and a hypnotic run on
sentence: two messages in one) *as you
beCUM even more sensitive.'*

- You can switch her focus quickly – *'Is your
skin more sensitive or do you **feel it more
inside?'** *Ensure her mind and focus are
constantly active.

- At this point say stuff like, *'You know you
want more of these feelings deeper inside
don't you? Focus on these feelings
amplifying that pleasure as it penetrates
deeply inside your desire.' 'Focus on the
core of what you crave etc.' 'Is your body
trembling/shaking/vibrating etc.?'*
Evaluate it, `'How fucking excited do you

feel now?' 'Would you tremble at my touch?' This makes it real. 'Would the sensations be as intense as if I was fucking you naked hard in the back of my car?' This plants ideas. 'What are you fantasising about?' etc. Throw in pure filth; let your imagination and hers run loose. **If you want this to work well don't just think FUN, think about increasing psychic intimacy through verbal foreplay.**

- Amplify more – 'Let these things increase. The more you **focus** on these supercharged pleasurable feelings, the more that pleasure grows, deeper and deeper, as you cum inside your mind. What kind of thoughts are you having? Did you know you could feel this good in this way?' Trust me she won't be thinking of her knitting class! You can tell her to boost those feelings by suggesting, 'Make those saucy images big and bright, full colour, 3D; makes the sounds as erotic as you like! All the better to...' (Use big bad wolf imagery; she is 'little Red Riding Hood'. You know that story is about sex right? I can think of at least two explanations of what a 'red riding hood' is; think about it.)

- If she talks about her 'dirty, naughty thoughts' etc. capitalise on it! *'Naughty thoughts turn you on don't they?' Are you having dirty thoughts you bad girl?' 'Are you thinking/imagining naughty thoughts? Tell me about them.'*

- Give direct commands – she is in emoto-nosis and sex-nosis, she is highly focused on her feelings, deeply hypnotised: *'As you think dirty thoughts, these feelings only intensify, and the more **these pleasures increase.'***

- You can keep her focus riveted inside and give her breaks between changing focus by now and again getting her to focus on her breathing. You can tell her to breathe deeper or more calmly, more excitedly whatever. Always link breathing to *'...feeling more pleasure.' 'Draw your attention to your breathing, **relax and grow calmer** as your feelings build in the background, many processes can occur at once and you don't need to help it get better.'*

- As you push her very near her orgasm, use more explicit sexual swear words *'...fuck/fucking etc.'* FUCK is a very forceful word – you can, in the right context and with the right timing **verbally penetrate a woman** with it. *'Take it fucking deep inside,' 'It's coming fucking deeper inside isn't it?' 'You can feel my words mind fucking you can't you?'* etc. Knock yourself out! Erickson once told a woman patient who was afraid of sex that she could control that penis inside her by gripping hold of it. This is pure verbal penetration. ***NOTE: Verbal penetration is a principle of seduction and sexual hypnosis.*** I once had a lady phone me and ask me if I could help her husband more artfully seduce her! A discreet phone call from him after the session let me know it worked.

- Tell her with authority as you near her climax*: 'You can only get that release when I decide you are ready, okay? You hold it until I say it's time to let go fully.'* She will like this, it will arouse her.

- Say, *'We'll increase this even more to the*

point where you unconsciously decide to **come very hard,** *to come powerfully to release all that which has built up within you so blissfully. Allow this building energy, this feeling to seduce itself through your mind and body, penetrating deeply all the way through you. All the way down, now...Every part, inside and out, can* **come** *vividly alive and sensitive now...skin, touch, centre, core, all of you! Tremblingly alive! You will come a lot, deeply – to the point where you fully let go of all that pent up tension and release that outstanding pleasure so beautifully that it fully satisfies you as a sexual being and as a woman!'*

- You are getting her near the edge of ecstasy: do not drop the ball! Keep moving it forward. If you like you can get her to imagine that you have penetrated her with your cock at this point. Make sure it's in the way she likes, slow and gentle or rough and forceful, listen to what she tells you. *'Imagine the tip of that pleasure inside of you, you are so warm and so wet and so juicy now, you can feel the very tip of that pleasure within you, can you not?'*

Or, *'Feel that cock inside you. My big cock fucking you just the way you like, so deep, so ful-filling, that pleasure only increasing to the very edge of your sexstasy, now.'*

- Okay boys, if she is even half way human she will want to scream out and let that orgasm take over – DON'T YOU DARE FUCKING LET HER – YET! Tell her, *'The more you **let go into that pleasure,** the more it can and will build. You can feel that pleasure even more. It will allow you to come harder, more intensely, you'll come even more! Tell me what you are thinking or imagining?'*

- Listen to her gibberish and then use it if it's good. Whatever she says - build on it (pace and lead) – *'You can feel it grow even more – you can feel whatever it is that's happening warming you, heating you up etc. Notice how that energy feels/if the colour changes/if there are lights etc.'* Note: women often see lights before, during or after orgasm; the character Stanley Kowalski in 'A street car named desire', referred to this when he promises Stella she'll get to see those 'coloured lights'. You can ask, *'Where else do you feel things intensely?'* By doing this you are **fractionating her focus** – thoughts, awareness, imagination, bodily sensations, feelings, emotions, perceptions. This allows her to experience everything fully and you can slow it down or speed it up at will.

- Tell her, *'Your breathing can change now to that pre-orgasmic breathing. Deeper, faster, whatever is it for you. Fucking surrender to it.* ***Let yourself go now!*** *The more you surrender to it the more intensely you will come!'*

- Now you start layering in time distortion. *'Time changes. It might feel like forever or no time. It might disappear or alter in some way? Let it enlarge/spread/ sweep etc. Let time change in the right way for you to beCUM immersed in this thrilling climax!'*

- You have her ready: she is on the edge of ecstasy, primed to come: now is the time to MAKE HER! *'Let go now! Let it all go! Let go into that pleasure! Let go into your ecstasy! Let it go so fucking deeply now!*

More and more incredible pleasure! Deeper and fucking deeper! Feels like forever and no time; all time! Feel that pleasure penetrate to the core of who you really are as a woman, even behind that name! That secret place! That private intimate place! You feel it harder, faster, longer! More intensely! Express that joy more! Beg me to let you cum! (Once she does...) ***CUM now!*** *Cum for me now baby! Cum hard for me now! Let it surge and fill you! It's so fucking thrilling! Expanding/spreading that experience out as far as it will go! That's it! Breathing the right way! So fucking deeply fulfilling!* ***Surrender to all the emotions, now!*** *All the feelings! Let yourself beCUM absorbed by it! Soaked up by it! Time is changing, changing, changing! You are coming so fucking hard! Let yourself go totally! Total release of all that was built up! Discharging it now! Faster! Deeper! More and more intensely, maybe in awesome waves! Coming so much harder than before! Let that joy sweep/spread out! Let it expand/spread deeply! Deeply absorbed in your beautiful ecstasy, now! Sink all the way down into* *it...bathe yourself in you...'*

- You now know how to talk a woman into an orgasm. You are quite welcome sir! Or madam for that matter! It's best to learn the principles and make the gibberish up on the spot using your creative spontaneity. The principles work by text or online. Okay I lied I have done this sort of stuff, once or twice ;) Let's recoup: what principles did we use?

Phone-gasm tips.

1. Narrow focus of attention – on her subjectivity: her feelings, thoughts, images, fantasies, breathing, your voice etc.

2. Apposition of opposites – relaxation and building excitement etc.

3. Time distortion.

4. Pacing and leading – accept her sexual response and then add suggestions/commands/instructions leading her where you want to take her.

5. Getting ongoing feedback of her

responses; knowing where she is in the process.

6. Lots of sexual ambiguities.

7. Lots of vague trance language.

8. Informal waking hypnosis induction.

9. Embedded commands used but not needed. Why not use them though as it enables you to penetrate directly to her sexual unconscious.

10. Lots of presuppositions etc.

12. High levels of linguistic abstraction.

13. Vivid descriptive language.

14. Emotive language.

15. Appealing to her fun loving, sexual, pleasure-seeking, hedonist self.

The phone-gasm process: get her in hypnosis, elicit feelings, play with feelings through symbolisation, control the process, build to peak, release, after care etc.

If you want, read the above section through

several times to really let the principles sink in through osmosis. Once you've done it, forget about them. You know more than you know, unconsciously, now. He-he.

- Now you can't just leave her like this. You have to help her 'cum down' now, as it were. The next phase is 'aftercare' – like the post sex talk, 'How was it for you my darling etc?' She still has lots of juicy feelings to play with and remember – she's a woman. She can come more than once in quick succession. Experiment my horny Padawan! But don't exhaust her!

Sexual fantasies into reality?

You can also arouse a women to orgasm by telling her dirty stories in hypnosis and you can get her to imagine doing some naughty things she wouldn't usually do by getting her to practise 'it' in her mind first and seeing if she likes it. If she does, she just might like the thrill of getting her rocks off that way in real life. If you're lucky! Check out the script below.

Realising a fantasy script.

(Warning: Again, I advise you don't suggest your woman imagine a fantasy with anyone but YOU! She might get ideas; remember she's hypnotised and suggestible dummy! Let's take the idea of seducing your girlfriend/wife etc. and play with that. Fantasies are only limited by you and your lover's imagination! NEVER suggest anything violent; in the hypnotic trance state you might create Post Traumatic Stress! Deep hypnosis assumed.)

'Imagine that you are in your favourite bar or pub etc. You have had a fantastic day and you

feel great. *You feel relaxed, clear-headed alive and very happy...In fact:* **you are in the mood to have fun.**

You are sitting at a table waiting to meet a friend...You receive a phone call from your girlfriend who you are meeting...She tells you that something came up and she can't make it...You are a bit disappointed but in such good spirits that you laugh it off...You decide to finish your drink before deciding what to do next when...

I walk in...You see me and instantly start to **feel attraction...***in just that way that you* **experience it, now...***I look over at you and smile...Then I turn to the bar and order a drink...You secretly wish that I'd come over and talk to you...You feel yourself flush at the thought...Unconsciously you are stroking the stem of your wine glass as if it's my cock...You catch yourself and feel a bit embarrassed and look around to see if anyone noticed...*

I have ordered my drink...without any hesitation and full of confidence I walk over to you table...'I'd like to join you, my name is...(insert name)' I say and we shake hands. You enjoy the first touch of the strength in those hands...We **feel very comfortable** with each other instantly...We flirt and talk and laugh and have fun...I make fun of you and you hit my arm...'Ooh. You like it rough?' I say as I look you straight in the eye. You **feel the heat building inside you...**Those electric thrills are shooting through you and you squirm in that chair...Wondering if I am aware of what you are experiencing inside....It's as if my words penetrate you...to the deepest part of who you really are...And you start to **feel very horny and intensely sexually aroused...**You think to yourself...'**This man is so attractive that I just want him to fuck me!'** You surprise yourself with that realisation...as if **your most animal sexual impulses have been switched on** without any conscious control, your unconscious is in charge of the process now and it feels amazing...

You really know as we flirt and joke and look deeply into each other's eyes that...**this man is going to fuck you** tonight and you **feel the craving for that** intensely...In fact as we talk you start fantasising about all the ways that that might occur...The pictures you have no trouble picturing...they are big, bright, colourful and bold...like panoramic 3D porno movies in which you are the star, with me...The pictures lead to feelings which lead to more pictures which cause you to...**feel even hornier and warm inside...**

In your mind you have created an opening for a certain type of experience...As you talk to me you start adjusting your makeup...reapplying your lipstick with the aid of your small hand mirror and wondering if you've shaved your legs! I smile at you in a way that makes you say, 'Oh my!' inside...You know that I know what you are thinking and you avert your eyes a moment and blush...**You are completely absorbed** in our conversation...We have entranced each other and you **feel that deep connection** with me that makes you **feel safe, warm, womanly, sexy and sexual** and it feels fucking great...

We finish our drinks and I say, 'I want you to come back to my place.' Push comes to shove and we are in my bedroom before you know it...

The details of the journey do not matter...We stand looking at each other...I cup your beautiful face in my hands and look deeply *into your eyes...Before you know it we kiss passionately...Certain feelings begin to well up within you...Now, we are caressing each other's bodies...I am taking off your clothes...Your hand reaches down and strokes my cock beneath my trousers and you feel how hard and big it is...You know that* **you want this cock inside you...**

I am kissing you...Biting your neck...Feeling your arse/ass...Slapping it...Groping your tits as I throw your bra to the floor...My top is off and you feel my manly chest...You **feel incredibly sexually aroused...** *You undo my fly and my grab my cock...You stroke it up and down feeling it strain and hard against your grip...You find yourself saying, 'Fuck me now!' as though your inner slut has been released...* **All unnecessary inhibitions are gone...** *I push you down on your knees and push my cock into your mouth...You love to suck my cock looking up at me with your beautiful eyes...you can see how much pleasure you make me feel...You see I can't control my desire for you now...*

Much as I am enjoying myself I pull you up and kiss you...my mouth and tongue find your breasts and nipples...I pick you up and throw you on the bed...My trousers are off...I remove your remaining clothing quickly, easily...We are both naked and alone together...aroused by the situation and the sight of each other's bodies...I climb on top of you and my fingers find your pussy...You are so fucking wet for me...You can **feel those juices flowing...**as my fingers move in and out of your pussy. You moan as your hand reaches for your mouth and the small of your back arches involuntarily...I spread your legs and place my two middle fingers into your pussy so they cup your G spot! Very soon I am pumping them swiftly up and down, up and down fast and it feels amazing! Those muscles inside are squeezing my fingers...You **feel that arousal, that tension build and build...**That sexual tension is reaching bursting point...You know that soon you will **have a squirting orgasm...**You are going to come very soon and it feels amazing! The tension is growing, building; **you are getting hotter and hotter!** So **close to cumming...**And then I stop...You look at me...I look at you and smile...You smile back...'No not that way,' my smile seems to *say.*

*I flip you over and lay on top of you...You feel my weight on top of you in that prone position...It feel so nice...You feel my cock probing your opening...I slide it in...You let out a moan of pleasure...It just all seems so right...I start fucking you from behind...At first I move in and out slowly until the rhythm cums easily and quickly...I speed up a little fucking you harder, firmer, stronger, the way you like to be fucked by me...You can hear the sound of my hips slapping against your ass/arse with each thrust...**You are totally absorbed in a sexual trance, the trance of sexual arousal, now...***

*I turn your head to kiss you again...My hands are on your sweet breasts as I fuck you harder and harder...Squeezing your tits for support as I drive my cock deep inside your pussy...You moan and groan with ecstasy...**Your desire is overpowering...**You surrender to it completely...You **feel thrillingly exposed, vulnerable, feminine and alive...**Each sense is tuned to its finest pitch of delight...You feel like a horny slut...It feels* natural...You **feel so attractive, feel like my slut...**My sex toy...My bitch...I am fucking you like I own you and you **feel so turned on you can barely stand it...**Really **feel all those sensations and emotions intensely...**You long for the release of that tension in a mind-blowing blissful orgasm...The feelings you are feeling now are overwhelming and incredible...You feel your eyes involuntarily rolling back as I fuck you powerfully...Your body has become like a blissful furnace under the long strong strokes of my thrusting cock...My cock dominates your sheath and you love it that way! Your body in turn matches my rhythm...Arching deliciously with each thrust! Letting go as you let my cock pierce you as deeply as possible...You can feel your tight cunt clenching...Desperately, cravenly against my cock as deep as possible now...**Feel all these sensations deeper, now...**Your body clenches in ecstasy! Every muscle is being overwhelmed! You are **completely surrendering to my sexual power...**You can't resist...Harder! Faster! Rougher! We are like two animals on heat! All our sexual instincts are taking over! You want to cry out,

*'Harder, faster baby!' My cock drills into you mercilessly...Pumping deep into your hot aching sex...**You are so wet for me...***

*My cock knows how to tease you...I fuck you slow now...Heavy thrusts...Your mouth is dry! I fuck you in a way that keeps you on the cusp of rapture...over and over with no release...Your inexperienced body longs for release but I won't let you cum yet! You can **feel how very, very close you are to divine pleasure** that you so long to experience! 'Please!' you moan out loud! You increase the bucking of your hips until you are bucking frantically! This is a wild fuck! You are losing control of yourself in ecstatic ways! My hands hold your outstretched arms down by the wrists...Your arms and legs quiver with exertion, desire, anticipation and the heavenly expectation of what will soon be!!! Your beautiful, exquisitely attuned body can barely take the overwhelming cascade of new sensations much longer! You never knew you could be so sexually fulfilled and entranced...So vulnerable...So much at the point of total surrender!*

I drive myself harder into you! My cock

*thrusting harder and harder! Quicker, harder between your legs making noises like an animal that craves you! I am shoving, slamming my cock so hard that your sheath is forced to spread wide open as my balls slap against your sexy ass's/arse's skin...That is enough! You can **feel your orgasm begin!** I slap your clit! It is hard and vicious! A forehand strike on your sensitive begging place! You scream aloud in pure and utter ecstasy as **your orgasm pounds through you!** Not the gentle soft embrace you expected but a conflagration of heat and pleasure that is indescribable! It sends a scream through your lips making your body buck under its pleasure! **Your most intense orgasm ever takes you!** I take you over the edge with my pounding cock thrusts! **Your orgasm rules your mind! Your orgasm rules your body!** It breaks against your cunt and tits! Your shuddering body convulses on my hard fuck rod inside you! I reward you with a triumphant burst of warm cum inside! It washes through your pussy! Filling every crevice! My cum and yours! It splashes out over your thighs, your legs! You can do nothing but let the pleasure and the cum* *cover you in pure thrilling sex ecstasy!!!*

*You remember it all in a daze of pleasure and pure bliss! Deep inside your most wondrous self you **feel a satisfying, sublime bliss...** You **feel at one with everything...** in that way only a woman can...At one with me...We lay in each other's exhausted arms and hold one another close. We fall asleep...As you sleep soundly...*

*You dream a naughty **dream about a sexual fantasy** that you'd always wanted to enact in real life at the right time and place with me...Maybe it's something a bit 'taboo'? First you watch it as a movie that arouses you as you dream...You may even **orgasm as you watch it...** Alter it in any way you want to make **you feel comfortable with the idea of doing that in reality...***

(Give her about 20 seconds to process this...)

When you are happy and comfortable with what we will be doing...you can float inside that deeply sexual dream and experience that experience first-hand from your point of view...feeling all the feelings and sensations intensely amplified...It just seems vivid, lifelike, real...and you love it! I'll be quiet for a full minute and you have all the time in that time to practise what needs practising, to learn what you need to, unconsciously and only in ways that are healthy, boost your self-esteem and worth, which joyously expand your capacity for experience and joyous living! NOW!

(Allow processing time)

That's great. You are doing really well! Perhaps you'll want to discuss with me what you learnt in this experience at the sessions end etc.? I leave it up to you, each and both of you...and this is definitely so.'

(Ahem – am I the only one that needs a cold shower after that!??? In the appendix I include women's descriptions of their own orgasms which you can use to create naughtinosis sh*t like this up on your own. If you are going to do something – do it well, no hole's barred! If you want to know where I got the details and description from, here's a hint: read women's dirty books: pure, unadulterated filth!)

Possible erotic hypnosis skit.

While doing research for this book I came across (not literally) an erotic hypnosis skit. As you will see brief, direct commands are best.

NOTE: in the following skit a woman is hypnotised to be a robotic sex slave. In reality the hypnosis has allowed her to become a very good improvisational actor, that is all. No actual mind control is working or operating. She is playing a game and nothing else. Don't give her any stupid or possibly harmful instructions that could destroy all trust between you. If you do this correctly and with a fun, playful heart she will trust you more: because when you had power, you didn't abuse it. The mark of a real man.

The hypno-robo-slut skit.

Would you like to create a temporary 'Stepford Wife' using hypnosis?

Step 1: Hypnotise a woman. Set up a suggestion whereby you tell a woman that she is a dominatrix. She is going to be sexually dominant. Tell her that it doesn't matter what you want, she's in charge. Tell her when you clap your hands and say 'Honey' she acts and believes she is a dominatrix but that she still responds to all your questions and commands. She will act accordingly when you give her the trigger as if it's her 100% total reality.

Step 2: However you also say that when you clap and say 'Bimbo!' she instantly becomes a robotic sex slave who calls you master and does anything she is instructed to do without question.

(A cue has been set up...when you clap your hands and say 'Honey' the hypnotee prepares to respond to further suggestions: she may stand up and look sassy etc.)

Step 3: When she's in 'dominatrix mode' ask her what she does, what does it entail etc.? Let her tell you. Keep it light and fun in tone. I guarantee her responses will be funny.

Step 4: Then start introducing the idea that YOU actually like to be in control and must be in the wrong place. You like to robotically control women. She'll probably laugh and look derisive etc.

- Ask her if she's ever been controlled by a man and would she like that experience.

- She'll say no as she's in her hypno-role.

- Ask her if she'd call you Master.

- She will act as if that's never going to happen.

- Clap your hands and say 'Bimbo.'

- As soon as you say 'Bimbo' she turns into a 'robotic sex slave' or her idea of what that is.

- Ask her who she is?

- Tell her to stand to attention. (Start giving commands and taking control.)

- Tell her to salute her master. (Give her some easily performed and simple tasks if you like. This conditions her for the 'bigger stuff'. Yes they are hypnotic tests. If at any point in the procedure she tries to resist never argue, do this, '*When I touch the centre of your forehead* (or whatever trigger you choose) *you will instantly go deeper and deeper into hypnosis and the deeper you go the more you want to fully and totally follow my suggestions and optimise your hypnotic responses. It only feels good when you do so...'* Do it instantly any time she tries to allow her conscious mind to kick in.)

- Tell her to stop saluting and tell her that she needs to be 'programmed' by you.

- Tell her to say, 'Yes master I am a robot and I need to be programmed.' Wait till she repeats this exactly.

- If she doesn't get it right correct her. Say, 'You have to be very precise robot. I want my instructions followed to the letter.'

- Tell her to salute again. You are turning her into your puppet. Demand prompt responses.

- Tell her she will always acknowledge your orders by saying, 'Yes master.'

- Tell her, 'Very good robot etc.,' when she does just as you wish.

- You can start with getting her to do small sexy things such as, 'Turn around for me. Push out your ass for me.' 'Look at your master.' 'Turn around.' 'Show me your pussy robot etc.' Use your warped imagination.

- Once you've got her doing the small sexual stuff which you can escalate in terms of eroticism then simply come out and say, 'And masturbate for me right now robot!'

- Say to her, 'Now get excited, very life like/human like/genuinely excited. Repeat after your Master, 'I am a robot only. My system is designed/programmed to orgasm for your pleasure.'

- Tell her, 'Now, get yourself very close to coming robot. Very close and very humanlike etc.! Come on! You will **come powerfully on my command.** And I will count to 3 and you will have an amazing and powerful orgasm robot! 1, 2, 3! *Orgasm robot!'*

- Watch her in dumbfounded male amazement as your wildest and most perverted dreams have come true!

- Say, 'Good robot. Let that orgasm subside now and then stand to full attention robot/droid/cumbot.'

- Now get her to do some household chores. 'I have a duster/broom/mop etc. See it? Pick it up and clean the room. Look at your master while you do so. You know I am fully in charge of all your actions.'

- Order her about some more, don't give her time to snap out of it, keep her occupied, 'Come closer to me right this instant and turn around and clean that patch of horse shit/dirt/soiled tissue etc. over there for me. Do a thorough job as I will be checking.'

- When you have demeaned her enough say, 'That's a good job robot. Drop the x (cleaning implement) instantly.' (By the way don't be a mean bully. Keep it fun, it's just a game and remember women like to be sexually dominated by men no matter what they say. In a firm but pleasant way.)

- Say, 'Good robot, your performance is pleasing me. Let me see your breasts robot right now. (Wait while she does and she will!) Squeeze them firmly. Now squeeze your nipples for me.'

- Rhetorically ask, 'Do you have any thoughts or will of your own robot?' Being a good robot, she'll say, 'No master...'

- Tell her next: 'Repeat after me – I only have a system that's programmed to obey my master. And orgasm!'

- Up the ante! Say, 'Just pinching your nipples makes you cum so fucking hard!! And always look at me while you're coming for me.'

- If she closes her eyes as she is coming say, 'Open your eyes and keep coming.'

- Await her response. It will be very evident trust me. Say, 'Shhhh. Calm down now. You have enjoyed yourself enough. You are a very good robot. You are pleasing me very much.'

- Now you are going to play around with her a bit. Say, 'Stop coming. When I count to 3 and say 'Honey!' you will feel like and be the dominatrix again and you will be a bit pissed off at what I just made you do. But as soon as I clap and say, 'Bimbo!' you will turn right into a sex-slave robot etc.! *1-2-3 Honey!'*

- Ask her dominatrix 'alter' what happened just a moment ago and did she enjoy being a brilliantly obedient robot more than a silly old dominatrix.

- Notice what funny fluff she says and then as she's half way through say… 'Bimbo!' and clap.

- Tell her to stand to attention (always call her robot), 'Stand to attention immediately robot!' Watch her do so.

- Then say to her, 'Repeat after me robot, 'I am made only to obey you Master. That is my prime directive!'

- After she does this tell her to, 'Sit down robot.'

- Once she is comfy, you say, 'Spread your legs wide for me.'

- Once she has obliged, instruct her to, 'Pull your sexy underwear aside and masturbate now.'

- As she does and if you can still talk say, 'More intensely! Very, very intense and highly pleasurable masturbation robot. You love it!'

- Ask her if she's close to orgasm, 'Are you near climax?' (Await her response.)

- Ask, 'Do you really want to be a very good and very obedient robot?' (Await positive response.) 'Who comes on command?' (Await response.)

- Say, 'Get closer to orgasm now. So very close. Anticipating how great that will feel! When I say 'drop x' you will instantaneously deactivate. Get closer! Very close! Nearly there! 'Drop x!' (Her head will probably drop as in stage hypnosis shows.) That feels so much better to rest comfortably and go even deeper so that you can follow these commands even more fully doesn't it?'

- Then continue with, 'You have been a very naughty robot indeed and I'll only let you come fully if you do the sexiest dance in the world for me. You will do the sexiest dance for me as I count from 3-1. On 1 you will do the dance. 3-2-1! (Watch what she does. If it pleases you say,) 'Sit down and play with yourself again!'

- Tell her, 'You are a very good robot. You do exactly as I say and you only love to do so. So I will let you have an amazing orgasm as I promised. I am a good Master and always reward loyal obedience. If you do as I say you will be allowed to experience great pleasure. Would you like that robot?' (She might say some fluff etc.)

- Tell her to masturbate more intensely, 'Masturbate even more intensely than before! Bring yourself near the edge! Let me know by the sounds you make!'

- Tell her she will have an incredible orgasm and that it won't stop till you say stop, 'In a moment, when I allow it, you will experience an incredible and totally satisfying orgasm! And the best thing for you is, it won't stop till I say 'stop' when it will instantly cease!'

- Tell her she is getting close to it, 'You are getting so close now, closer and closer, almost there! Feels a-fucking-mazing! Very close robot. Very soon! *Orgasm now!* (Allow her to enjoy herself and then say: only 30 seconds to one minute max, you don't want to exhaust her) Stop!

- Carry on playing as you wish or wake her up and debrief her etc. Keep it all a silly game, which is what it is.

Men often have fantasies of 'controlling' women. Women say their main sexual fantasy is to be dominated sexually in a variety of ways. Is it healthy to make these kinds of sexual fantasies reality? Should the secondary reality of the imagination remain there? I just don't know the answer. I know of no long or short-term effects - good or bad - of playing these kinds of kinky hypno-games fetish. Use caution.

The sexy ball of energy.

Hypnotise a lady etc. Get person to imagine

they are in a hot place. They are so hot that they have to totally disrobe in their imagination.

'Now', take her palm in yours, *'As I rub your palm, feel a ball of energy building. It feels like the best feeling you've ever experienced. And the more I rub, the more you feel it building.'* Watch for an arching back and exhaling etc. When you think she is ready say, *'Now...release!'*

Watch out for back arching, moaning etc. However this is cyber-hermaphroditic sex par excellance. Is it normal? Is it healthy? What would the consequences be if everyone was doing this? I leave it up to you...

Conclusion: a bit of fun or sexually frustrated cyber-hermaphrodites?

Porn has started this trend and I only see it growing. The trend is toward sexual hermaphroditism. This is where an individual has no need for real sex and can achieve sexual pleasure through artificial means – dildos, the 'Orgasmatron' in Woody Allen's 'Sleeper' are all good examples of it. Even the New York Times sent a reporter to an erotic hypnosis seminar in what was being heralded as the ultimate in 'safe sex'. IF and I repeat if you do play about with erotic hypnosis keep it as a side dish that emphasises the main course, if you gather my meaning.

When doing erotic hypnosis skits be careful with vague suggestions – stupid things like '...let's take our sex life to a new level' – this is too ambiguous and could lead to bizarre behaviour. Except when eliciting and playing with emotions be very direct and clear in your instructions.

If you are a heterosexual man never let a woman do this to sort of stuff to you: letting a woman verbally penetrate you is an inversion of normal sexual dynamics and should be avoided at all costs. Some men are listening to 'hypno-dominatrix madams' and developing bizarre sexual obsessions. My advice? **_DO NOT GO NEAR SUCH PRODUCTS._**

Safety feature to avoid trance 'pollution'.

You don't necessarily want to elicit normal hypnotic trance (whatever that is) for naughtinosis. How about creating something you label 'erotic trance'. What do I mean by erotic trance? Well the context is the thing. I would suggest you keep the hypnotic trance state free for therapy etc. Do not 'pollute' it with the filth you want your girl to carry out for you. **Erickson warned about not 'polluting' the hypnotic state.** To avoid this you could give a post hypnotic command after hypnotising a woman,

'When I say 'sex trance' you will enter a state of hypnosis only associated with our erotic trance sessions. It will be discrete and completely unconnected from any other possible work you may do with hypnosis in other contexts. You can enter a therapeutic hypnotic trance when I say 'deeper sleep' etc.'

The rise of pansexual and polymorphous perversity.

Innocent and all 'Fun Ethic' as erotic hypnosis seems, if indulged in as a full blown 'life style' it would in fact stay true to the insanity of Freud and his heirs: the 'polymorphous perversity' (in classical psychoanalysis this referred to Freud's pro-paedophile stance that from age 5 onwards humans could achieve sexual pleasure outside of usual social norms) that was espoused by Norman O. Brown (worked for the OSS, the CIA's precursor) and the 'pansexual' ravings of Herbert Marcuse with his nihilistic declaration of war against any kind of sexual or cultural sense of restraint, love of beauty or decency. If seen as a way of life such 'experimentation' as erotic hypnosis could, in those with a weak sense of identity or an inability to get their needs met, lead to a new type of addiction: like the lab rat who became addicted to his own orgasm response, futilely pressing a button connected to wires that stimulated his pleasure centres. The rat gave up eating food in preference for a sci-fi form of hermaphroditic joyless 'joy'. You have been warned: I'm not saying don't do it, but use, if at all, with caution.

If you play around with erotic hypnosis in a light-hearted way you'll probably be fine. I could be wrong on that! That we know of, we have never lived in a society where such things have happened.

The erotic hypnosis ethical code of conduct.

- I never do pervnosis to really manipulate, dominate or control someone.

- I always get someone's consent before doing pervnosis.

- I remove all suggestion that need removing at the end of a session.

- I leave someone better off after a pevnosis session.

- I have an attitude of making this person feel good and both of us having fun.

- I do not do erotic hypnosis with disturbed people.

- I only do naughtinosis with people who can handle it in a mature way.

- I only do 1 erotic hypnosis gimmick, skit etc. per session to avoid exhausting someone.

- I keep it as a treat for use now and again.

If you can place a tick by all these things: go for it! If done the right way it's just perv-stage hypnosis after all; and I am NO prude. You now have a thorough and comprehensive basis from which to experiment with.

Addendum: do humans dream of electric prostitutes?

An alarming new opinion poll in the U.K, indicated that people of either sex would 'sleep' with a, for want of a better term 'sex android'; about 20%!!! This represents the decline of Western man and his culture superbly. The depravity and sexual hermaphroditism is complete. Kinsey et al would be proud.

Ericksonian sex 'therapy': how Erickson treated sex related problems.

Dr. Milton Erickson the father of modern hypnosis often used hypnosis in cases of sexual 'performance' anxiety in men and women. He wrote about this, but as in all his case reports he rarely gave detailed breakdowns of what he did. So we have to reverse engineer what he probably did from the slithers of facts he gives us and our own knowledge of hypnosis. His treatments used waking hypnosis and were very quick.

'Frigid' woman into 'happy slut' script.

(In the original case study Erickson said that this woman was nervous and embarrassed about her husband's frustrated desires to consummate their marriage. In fact her new hubby was seeking annulment. She was thus highly motivated to change; Erickson did not seek to get rid of her fear. He used it to get her into trance. The wording that follows is my own.)

'As I know you are willing to do anything agreeable to solve this problem... (Pacing statement and truism) *and as I fully respect*

you desire to not be touched, we can begin...
(Accepting her current ongoing experience –
pacing, respect for her model and utilisation.)
Your lover sits in that chair... ('Yes set' –
accepted as no threat...) *as you sit where you
are...* (Ditto) *presently beyond touch...* (Ditto
plus 'presently' = a pace of ongoing
experience with the implication of change via
the word 'presently') *You can, can you not
simply gaze intently at your lover?* (Leading
suggestion to fixate attention on something in
external world, thus inducing waking
hypnosis.) *No one will leave their chairs till we
are done...if they do, you may leave at any
point, that's a promise...* (This creates trust –
the client's request to not be touched is
respected and in fact cessation of the process
is demanded if the trust is violated.) *Sit in that
place as tensely as you can...cross your legs
and arms...* (Utilise her tension. Don't fight it,
use it. Also when she consciously focuses on
tension, where is her attention? Inside – on
her body = hypnosis and the physical effort
will at some point demand release and so –
relaxation) *and focus solely on your lover...*
(Fixation of attention on a significant object)
anything else is unimportant...as only he

interests you...fascinates you...so all you can see is him...all you hear is my voice... (5 statements that narrow focus of attention – see book 1, 'How to hypnotise anyone'.) *And you can sleep, deeper and deeper...into sleep, now...* (I don't know if Dr. E used embeds but he did invent them that we know; I have stayed true to the original and left them out in this instance, but they aren't needed anyway.) *As you sleep more and more deeply...you may become more panicky and fearful...* ('The more the more' hypnotic language pattern + apposition of opposites – sleep and panic are ordinarily opposed. See my 2nd and 4th books for full description of these phenomena) *temporarily...* (Temporal predicate saying, 'it won't last.') *Yet unable, un-wanting to move...* (Leading suggestion for physical immobility – a sign of hypnosis) *as you only watch him...* (Continuing external-ised fixation + overload and high stimulation to maintain interest by changing tasks of focus) *Sleeping* (sounds like slipping) *more and more deeply into trance, now...The more panicky you become the more easily you go into hypnotic trance...And fear, panic, embarrassment merely deepens this state...as you sit rigid, immobile in that chair...*

(Pause for 5 seconds or so.....) *Gradually...you can imagine that your lover is touching you intimately...feel your lover making contact...as you sit there...and he sits here...* (Respecting her wish for no physical touch – yet) *and you still on one level see him there...here...* (Phonetic ambiguity to hear my voice.) *As soon as you are willing to...experience those sensations...* (Don't say 'delightful' – you don't want to spook the deer) *your existing tension...will relax to the point where...you can let go into that pleasing fantasy...this is your private place...* (Private place = sexual ambiguity) *as you ignore us and go inside...* (For sexual hypnosis with your lover say 'go deeply inside'...) *You can know this is only your experience...and you start to feel a progressively more intimate caressing of your body...* (You are covertly getting her comfortable, through mental rehearsal, with the idea of being FUCKED SENSELESS – which she will enjoy by the way!) *at an appropriate time....as you change unconsciously, now...you will feel totally happy and relaxed...Take as much time as you need to reflect on your newly acquired joy...And when you are unconsciously sure that this process is satisfactorily completed you will waken feeling wonder...ful, now...We'll be quiet as you do what must be done, now.'*

The 'for God's sake just fuck her' script!

(Erickson had a patient who failed to do the nasty with his wife on their honeymoon: the wife immediately sought annulment unless her new hubby could rise to the occasion! Again my words follow, derived from what Dr. E left available in his reports.)

'Look at your lover...focus all of your attention on her only... (Leave processing time, make sure he seems absorbed...you are fixating attention.) *I want you to recall that sense of shame...total humiliation...and hopeless helplessness that you felt with regards to this issue...* (You are causing unpleasant retrospection – the old feelings associated with the lover are elicited through revivification. You are pacing the current reality – temporarily. Plus word 'issue' = euphemism for semen.) *That's it...As you do this, I know you would feel like doing absolutely anything to get away from those horrid feelings, now, don't you?* (A truism and artificial creation of an 'enough is enough'

moment.) *As you continue to look at your lover intently...you only see her...you are unable to see anything else...she is the sole focus of your attention, now...* (Repetitive suggestions for state of waking hypnosis) *you cannot see me* (hypnotist) *but you hear me easily at some level...* (Suggestion for 'negative hallucination'.) *As this occurs, and it does...you will realise that this is a sign and a signal that you are entering deep...trance...NOOOOOOW!* (Trance logic – false cause-effect suggested that one thing leads to another when it doesn't' – unless you are hypnotised! The key connector word that keeps the flow going is 'As...') *In this state you are glad that you have no control over your body...it is entirely outside of your control...* (Suggestions given that the conscious mind – the 'you' above-mentioned can f**k off out the way and let the subconscious sexual arousal processes take over. Consciousness needs to stop interfering! The old associations are being squashed. NLP calls this 'collapsing anchors' but Erickon's way of doing it is much more elegant.) *As this occurs...you can imagine your beautiful lover is naked...and that you are naked with her* *too...That's right...* (Pleasant sexual fantasy is evoked – the new, positive, sexually arousing associations are being linked to his lover; he is entranced yet starring at her – this is eyes open trance. His neurology will link the emotions and imaginative sexual stimulation to his lover: N.A.C – see book 3 'Powerful hypnosis'.) *This only further leads to the discovery that you cannot control that body...which in turn leads to the discovery that...you feel surprisingly pleasant contact...physical contact with your lover...* ('Discovery' is a very hypnotic word – like the 'Aha' moment. Further false linkages are created, then a direct suggestion for 'hallucinated' – imagined kinaesthetic sensations are given. Not only is he seeing the sexual fantasy. He FEELS it bodily and this amplifies his arousal and the believability of the fantasy. It also activates the exact same neural pathways as if he was doing it in reality. He is practising success. This rehearsal will seek appropriate completion upon awakening. It is a post-hypnotic visual-kinaesthetic suggestion. Erickson was such a clever b**tard!) *It becomes more and more intimate, sensual and very exciting...and there* *is nothing you can do to control your natural physical response...There will be no completion of your uncontrolled physical response until your lover requests its cessation...* (Amplification of sexual response given: with eyes open trance this is again linked to his lover! The suggestion is given that the conscious mind should mind his own business and let the 'little head' have his moment of glory! The response of sexual arousal is then post hypnotically linked to his wife's sexual fulfilment – orgasm or orgasms?!) *In this state of deep hypnosis...deep absorption in these hypnotic realities...you can learn, unconsciously, that you know that you can...you are confident...sexually confident in all the right ways, now...in fact you have already succeeded...and so there is nothing you can do to keep from succeeding, again and again and again...just as it pleases you...each and both of you, NOOOOOOOW!!'* (Direct suggestions for future success. The changes are 'locked in' via suggestive summation. So artful and seemingly so simple.)

Rogue Hypnotist case study: the sap with a broken heart.

I deal with a lot of broken-hearted male clients. Females move on quickly from relationship breakdown having less intense or sustained emotions (known as depth). They can break pair bondings quickly, swiftly and brutally if they have too. Men being the romantic fellow that he is, is often left emotionally scarred. If low self-worth pre-existed the breakup (and it usually does) it can push him to the verge of obsessive rumination or a nervous breakdown. Some end up on anti-depressants but then who isn't on them these days?! Pills do not equal human happiness. Anyway, there follows a 'faction' interview transcript and a hypnotic treatment script of part of what I do with such clients.

The broken-hearted sap transcript.

A young man in his 20's called me and asked for help with cocaine addiction, possibly smoking and a 'relationship' problem. I said sure we should be able to get rid of all that in one go. He was surprised but excited at the thought of such 'magic wand' treatment.

When he turned up he was quite well dressed and obviously prosperous looking; however he looked what I can only describe as 'crestfallen'.

'In general how are things at the moment?' I ask.

'Because of my cocaine problems and the other stuff I told you about my business is suffering. It's hard to look after myself properly. I am not fulfilling my potential. I never really had confidence. I've had a recent relationship breakup and a substance abuse problem in the past. (He then tells me that a relative of his wants an appointment too.) I want to **feel good*** about myself...'

(*All clients essentially want to 'feel good'.)

'Wow! That's quite a f**king lot of problems you have there mister!' I think.

'So what do you do for a living and do you enjoy it?' I probe.

'I am a surveyor. I don't enjoy it. I would like to design cars for a living.'

'So you are single and living on your own at

the moment?' I ask.

'No. My partner (RH: I hate that f**king word! What is a relationship, a business transaction?) left me. I have my own place but I am living with my parents. I'm not safe on my own. It's not safe for me to be on my own I mean,' he confesses.

Why? Why is he a 'danger' to himself? He has moved out and then back home with mum/mom and dad. Any young adult will see this as a regressive step. He wants to move forward – to make progress in his life. *All humans have a desire to move through the natural human life cycle in a progressively maturing fashion. Hint: you can use this to motivate them!*

No to epilepsy. No to medicines from shrinks etc. Unless you count cocaine as medicine: all 'illegal' drugs were once used as medicines. He admits he was on medication to 'block out' cocaine cravings. He hasn't been on any such medication for almost 4 years.

'Can we clarify what are the specific problems and what are the exact results you desire?' I ask. I list the answer next...

1. <u>Confidence.</u> 'I want to be feeling 'good enough' (for what or whom?) for being myself. I want self confidence in my abilities and not be 'dependent' (basically he wants to be free!).

2. <u>Stop cocaine use once and for all.</u> He has cut it down but not out. That it is an achievement to be proud of anyway.

3. <u>Boost self-worth.</u> (He admits to having 'crippling' self-esteem.)

4. <u>Get rid of guilt about 'the past'.</u> 'I still go to Cocaine Anonymous (a cult by the way) and I was 'paranoid' with all my exes.'

'When did these problems start? Is there an event or situation that you feel started them?'

'When I was young. I want to feel confidence in how I act, speak and feel. My behaviour is not up to my high standards (...really? His or his parents?). I have never had a good self-image. I started drinking heavily at 19 and I have been dependent* on the booze. I think I'm an alcoholic...' (Oh everyone does these days! *Note: What does he mean by 'dependent'?)

'What are the positive benefits of making this change?'

'I can be *true to myself,*' he says (I underline here what I underlined on my original case notes, 'I want a healthy balanced view of myself. I think I want to stop smoking but…maybe not. Maybe I should. What do you think?'

'That's up to you. It's not for me to say,' I reply.

'You know what? I can't say what I want (in life in general he means),' he adds.

'What have you done to overcome this stuff so far, if anything, and how successful were those things?'

'Well socially I am anxious and I overcame that in group counselling and Christian fellowship. (He tells me about his Christianity. Aha! I know how to use this to help him!)

'You know the interesting thing about Christ, about Christianity is that it was the first religion to say that all people had worth just for being human. All other religions codified master slave relationships and said that only the master had worth,' I tell him. Which is true. I am using his existing belief structure and **layering in and emphasising ideas from that tradition** (utilisation). These will take once hypnosis proper starts. I have seeded an idea that the subconscious, which is always listening can begin to play with.

'What future evidence will let you know you have succeeded today?'

'I'll feel contentment, peace; I will be without fear,' he says.

'What do you fear?' I ask.

'I have a fear of losing something. I have...I am fearful of financial things. Yeah, I have lots of fears,' he tells me. In my experience people who are raised in homes where unconditional love is not offered always complain of a lack of what they call 'contentment'. You can see the roots of contentment in children from loving families: when feeding at breast or bottle, when cuddling or snuggling with mum/mom, dad and beloved others, that kind of thing. This behaviour tells the child, 'We love you so much! You are safe and totally accepted here,' this gives children a bedrock of confidence and self-worth to draw from. They have good feelings built into the neurology at an early age. They have ample practise of 'doing contentment'. Children who grow up into adults from loveless homes often feel fearful and 'inadequate'. 'Tough love' is no love at all. Children only benefit from support and encouragement. No one ever raised a strong, independent, resilient child by being abusive. You just layer in fault lines which get agitated in later life. All normal loving people know this stuff intuitively. The problem is arse/assholes have kids too! A lot of 'em! This necessitates work from people like me to rectify all the 'mistakes' that were made. However, despite such bad parenting, all humans have an enormous capacity to self-heal and gain full confidence and independence. With hypnosis it is surprisingly easy to do. When it works hypnosis *is* 'miraculous' considering the results in can obtain.

The client tells me more...

'In treatment I had to give up the fight. That's what they call it. I suddenly felt a real calm...really calm. Calm and content for the first time in ages. They say you have to let go of ego and pride and when you do, you can start to get better.'

This is just so much BULLSHIT that this man has had indoctrinated into him by 'therapists' or nurses etc. at some run down state run hospital no doubt. Watch out for psychobabble from clients who have seen anyone trained in psychoanalytical or other weird mythologies. You rarely tackle this indoctrination head on – the proof it's garbage materialises with hypnotically induced cure. When this occurs the ideas will fall by the wayside. **The best form of persuasion is experiential proof.**

'So talking about pride, what do you feel most proud about? Any achievements at all. You don't have to have climbed Everest.'

'I am proud of my degree. I stayed clean of drugs for 4 years. Then 3 weeks ago I split up with my partner and I went out and got smashed on alcohol. I own my own business. I have helped others in recovery (with the best of intentions he has recruited new cult members),' he lets me know.

'What are your strengths as a person?'

'I am very determined. I am stubborn. I have compassion for others. I'm reasonably intelligent. I want this change for myself and I do want to change,' he says.

My usual self-worth rating question is asked.

'I am always doing an internal comparison. I would say my self-worth is 3 out of 10. I think I can never be like that. Like someone who is that confident. I always doubt my abilities.' (Notice the 'universal quantifiers' – 'never', 'always'. These are almost always signs of stressed out 'black and white' thinking. Reduce arousal and they spontaneously go.)

So he needs a self-esteem boost. Without it all other work will fail. This again is usual with hard-core drug users. Even recovering ones: this is why other treatments fail. They have no way at all of boosting someone's self-worth which is vital to recovery. It is an *emotional* problem. The subconscious controls all emotions. Only hypnosis can alter that emotion matrix.

I ask how he relaxes.

'I go to the gym. I haven't been in months (no exercise = stress!) since my relapse. I am not focused (stress indicator). I like watching movies. I am not a reader,' he replies.

This man like most does all the standard conventional social fetishes that actually make people 'ill'. No exercise, doesn't read and thus stimulate his mind. He watches films which are pretty much all garbage. No wonder he can't focus and feels crap. He isn't really living at all!

I ask him my usual question about having an intuitive sense of what has to change within or what will need to occur *during the process* for him to make the desired changes. He reflects on this as they often do. It is not the way people are trained to think. It requires imagination.

'It's all about the truth about yourself. I need to see the mirror of truth about myself.'

This is an admission of a weak sense of identity. Lack of self-knowledge is an epidemic. 'Mirror of truth' is a heavily nominalised and hypnotic metaphor. What he is saying is this – 'I am so stressed I can't see things objectively,' this is true.

'Can you think of a metaphor that represents (the referent in symbolism) the desired change?' I ask. This is one of my favourite questions. It unlocks the key IF they have a symbol or symbols that come to mind. He does! Yippee!

'I feel like I am being held underwater (drowning) by a ball and chain and I can't reach the surface to breath!' he says.

He is trapped and does not know HOW to escape. Like a Harry Houdini trick gone wrong. He adds,

'Freedom would be like flying through the air...I would see all the flames below and fly away from that fiction.'

Remember he is Christian. Flames denote hell symbolism. He is in hell on earth and he knows it. Does he deserve his punishment for his 'sins'? This Christian symbolism takes a darker note soon enough...

'Does any reason you can think of mean you shouldn't change? Do you like the way things are?'

'No,' he says.

'What stops you from making this change on your own?'

'I lack faith in myself. I lack faith in God,' he says. As the latter is a spiritual issue it is beyond my scope; spiritual 'quests' are personal and generally outside of therapy.

'Have you ever made a similar change?'

'Yeah. I didn't think I could (this presupposes he now knows change is possible). I... a literal 'snap' happened and I had to change,' he says. _Snapping is often used to describe cult conversion and sudden personality changes._ More of this in my next book.

'Is there any part of you that doesn't want to change?' I ask. We are nearly done, for this session.

'No but it's like there are two sides to me. One is like a demon. It's like this demon character is stuck inside my body. It's all this negativity,' he says dramatically. Demonological metaphors are common in my experience in anyone raised in a so-called Judeo-Christian environment. He isn't claiming literal demonic possession. Often the undesirable drug addiction is linguistically dissociated from the self as 'other' – in many ways this is because drugs can lead people to act in highly bizarre and out of character ways. Drug + low self-esteem is not a good recipe. He is saying he is ashamed of himself. He feels guilty. Decoding metaphors is usually a pretty straight forward affair not requiring intricate deconstruction.

We finally end up with him telling me that he was hypnotised almost a year ago to stop smoking and it worked - for a bit; he took a 'course' after a relative suggested it. He tells me how he didn't feel hypnotised but then his hand began to lift! I have found that my clients' unconscious minds rarely want them to experience too 'far out' hypnotic phenomena. He finishes by saying,

'I need to stop fighting and surrender to it.'

To what 'it' I have no idea and I don't need to know. So I boost his confidence and self-esteem. I solidify the death of the old cocaine addiction in the session too. We are done. He wakes up feeling totally different, confused yet happy as to how this change has occurred. Hypnosis magic.

Or so I thought.

About 3 weeks later he phones again. He has felt fine, definitely better and then he starts obsessing even more over his ex. He can't concentrate, feels nervous but hasn't used coke again. Progress. This sometimes happens. When someone has five pins sticking in their foot and you only have time to take out 4 – the 5th one becomes the sole focus of attention. The next interview which is much shorter lets me know what I have to do to help him next. We need to kick this final problem in the nuts once and for all!

The sap with a broken heart part 2.

My client is in a visibly better state than last time; he is dressed more smartly and just looks better in general. This often happens. I had a lady client who was so 'down' the first time she came to see me that she was dressed like Rocky Balboa in his training montage gear! The next session we had together, she had had her hair done, looked vastly more confident and was dressed smartly. These are often the clear indicators of improvement: they start caring about themselves and so their appearance more.

'What improvements have you made? What's changed since I saw you last?'

'I felt better...till next morning. But I haven't touched cocaine which is good. I am very anxious about my former relationship. I smoke to be less anxious. My thoughts go around and around about my ex. I text her. I want to get her out of my system. I have to see her to sort out money and contracts and that sort of thing,' he says.

This is the goal of this session. We have laid down the groundwork – now we need to stop this pining and obsessing after what cannot be.

'Are there any noticeable shifts in your self-esteem?'

'I feel a bit better,' he admits.

'Where are you most confident in life? Doing what exactly?'

'I feel good in my job. I am good at it and especially so when I am fully focused. I am seeing opportunities and taking them etc.,' he says. A definite improvement in attitude since last time nes pas?

'Can you tell me anything you think I need to know about this relationship breakup or any past patterns of relating to women that you think we need to address? Is there baggage?'

'I never leave a space between a relationship (this is because he cannot self-validate. It must come from 'her'). I am fearful that I am not good enough. I act like a needy child not like a man. I drink too much and relapse when things go wrong. It makes me very upset. My former ex was a nightmare. I want someone honest and stable. As soon as I saw her alarm bells went off that I shouldn't get involved. This always happens but I do it. I didn't even really fancy her...but I would like us to be friends etc.,' he says. I have compressed this for ease of study.

Basically this follows the relationship pattern of all men and women I see. If you have low self-worth you will attract and go after arse/assholes who are abusive and reinforce this low self-worth. Some people call this 'co-dependence'. It's really just being attracted to a total shit. When some women are abused as children their attraction circuitry becomes activated by those who they unconsciously know will abuse them – thanks daddy or mummy or both! It is almost like a signal that recognises the abuser and seeks them: they can only be sexually aroused by abusers and often abuse at the worst extremes. Give these people a wide berth! They will drag you down too. Such people are targets for psychopaths.

Just before we do the hypnotic intervention I say to him,

'What is most important to you in a relationship? What qualities do you look for in a woman? Don't tell me but I want you to really think about it?'

This will set unconscious wheels off in his head as he enters hypnosis. We are ready. By the way when you indirectly ask,

'What is important to you about x?'

you are seeking to **elicit their values.** Values elicitation is a tactic used by men using hypnosis to seduce women but it is also valuable to therapy if asked in the right way and context. People say stuff like, 'Honesty. Attraction. Fun. Blah!' Get the idea. You can then say,

'And when you find someone with honesty what will that allow you to experience that you don't yet?'

Then you get deeper level reasons and emotions. When you find out what experiences bring satisfaction to a person you can interest them. Also when I indirectly say,

'...think about x don't tell me,'

this is a mini-command to go inside and ruminate, ponder which = trance!

What follows are two thirds of what I did to help this man. I also used a product, a script I bought from a company that sells a script for 'getting over a relationship'. As I used someone else's material I cannot include it here. My sessions often include a wide array of influences. I will use anything that works, is safe and ethical. The script that I have included de-traumatises the person who has had their 'heart broken'. Again: in my experience as a therapist only men come to see me asking for help on this issue. Are women naturally more fickle? All the great romantic gestures come from men after all.

Hypnotically healing a broken heart.

Module 1: brief deepener.

(Deep hypnosis assumed)

'As you **go deeper and deeper...**to the sound of my soothing voice...could you imagine being in a place...of perfect peace? That's it...I imagine it's a beautiful day there...is it not? I imagine you **feel very good there?** And as this is so, we can begin...

Module 2: recalling first love.

Can you simply recall the very first person...that first time where and when you offered your love to a person... (Give 5 secs processing time...) Good. But you discovered...over time...that the love you gave...wasn't wholly reciprocated. For some reason it didn't work out as you'd hoped...It doesn't matter what the reasons were...Maybe the timing was wrong? The circumstances? Maybe someone wasn't ready? Maybe it just wasn't right for both of you? These things happen. Perhaps as you offered your love and warmth...and it didn't receive the response *you wanted, back then...you might have felt a sense of loss, disappointment, regret? That's normal. You may have felt somehow scarred on the inside by the experience? Some have the sense of tiny scars on their heart? As time went on...some people feel, understandably...that it became harder to offer that love again...harder to give with the same intensity...with that same carefree sense of the freedom to offer all your love...*

So as you recall that person...and a particular appropriate time with them...just let an image of them form...if it hasn't already...It's somewhere out there in front of you...in your mind's movie house/cinema...Ok great.

Module 3: removing past 'trauma' associated to past images etc.

*As you **focus** on that picture...I would like you to continue breathing hypnotically...**calmly and comfortably...**And on the next in breath...I want you to imagine that somehow...using hypnosis magic...**you are taking back all the love you formerly offered...**Perhaps as a form of energy...a light source or symbol...It's your choice...* (Allow 5 secs or so processing time...)

And on the next exhale imagine you have placed all that love...in the palm of one of your hands...I don't know which one it is or will be...You do. **Feel the sense of that love...**can you feel it's weight and shape and texture somehow? **You have that love back, now...**

Does it have a colour too? Notice the details of how your subconscious or unconscious mind symbolises your love for you...See that now...recognise it for what it is...and using your powerful imagination...you are going to **purify it...**There might be tiny flaws or flecks...you might not have spotted them till I pointed it out...dark impurities that had tainted it up until now...Somehow, on my count of 3-1 they will vanish and they will be gone...Ready? Ok, 3-2-1 **GONE NOW!**

It is purified now, glimmering and radiant perhaps...shinning and glowing with a native purity, unsullied as it once was, now...You have that perfect symbol of the pure love you were born with...that you were born to offer deserving others, only...Take this symbol of your pure love...the perfect embodiment of all you have to give and...squeeze it right down *in your imagination to a vitally concentrated form...Shrink it...Concentrate it down...And as this process occurs as I count from 5-1...that love gets purer and stronger and freer and more genuinely what it is...5-4-3-2-1!*

*See that representation of your love force and energy...a very real part of being human...You now have the essence of that...even more perfectly than before...In your mind only...take it in hand and place it **gently** upon your heart...You must do this...for yourself...And instantly you can **feel the warmth, feel that joy** reclaimed...Feel yourself restored...with every beat of that loving heart, knowing that this is so...Feel that loving warmth spreading now all the way through you - radiating...glowing with that energy and it feels amazing doesn't it? It is moving all throughout your mind and body, now!*

*Love has returned...Things returning to normal...Your heart is healing, is healed...You **feel it** and know it at a very deep level of experience...All the waste and impurities are gone now, completely...Your soul feels as if it has been washed clean...decontaminated...**Your heart, that***

part is renewed... *You are ready to love again with a purified, distilled essence of your love! All that you have to give is there...deep inside you...everything restored...just as it should be...That's right...*

Module 4: reclaiming love from other former loves.

*I want you to imagine seeing photos, pictures, images, whatever of all the people you have ever had a sexual and or romantic relationship with in your whole life. See all those girls/boys/men/women now...And again at a very deep level you know that...***your past perceptions and feelings have changed...***You know you could **never feel that** way about them again...**As this is now the case, see each picture vanish, disappear...fade...or pop...away...now...Gone from your life...Old associations changed...Updated...Gone for good...Certain feelings gone from the mind-body system; no longer needed...Realising that your mind and body have changed subtlety...It feels so good to **get rid of what is no longer needed** doesn't it? Be aware, get in tune with just how good you feel now...That's it.* (Pause for a beat to allow processing etc.)

*Ok, so for a moment only, can you bring those pictures back but...**see them in a different way...**notice what you did find attractive about each one...knowing it actually wasn't who they were...it was merely an attractive quality they had...Could be a personality trait...a physical attribute...*

*Now, still **keeping all that love in your heart,** take that colour- symbol of love...and place it in a hand again...That's it...Go through all of those images very quickly, at the speed of thought and...on the next in breath, remove any and all attractive qualities from those people...And **feel the essence of that pure attraction...**flow back to you...into that hand...let it all flow in there...Great!*

*Now, as you look at those old pictures...you notice that...**you don't find anything attractive about them** do you? It is true that **those old states are gone,** isn't it? Good. How do you feel about reclaiming this? You **feel so much better** still, don't you? Fantastic, you are doing amazingly!*

Go through, like you have a deck of

cards...knowing that as you check that pack...you're seeing not only the ones you liked but the ones you imagined...even fantasy lovers...Whatever was once perceived as attractive can spontaneously be breathed into that hand...You were attracted to those images in the past...But why? You can't quite remember! It was for some reason or another...But now, in your palm you have reclaimed feelings and perceptions...everything you ever found attractive in a lover or romantic interest is held in the palm of your hand and it feels great...**You have your <u>full power back!</u>**

Finally make sure you have removed any and all attractiveness from those men/women of past...Unconsciously do something that helps to wrap things up! Now. I want you to, as swiftly as I click my fingers reduce, condense this down to the size of a pill!

(SNAP!)

You have that pill. Now imagine you swallow that pill...That's it, and swift as thought, all those **feelings go to where they need to be** inside you...And just get a sense that you now are free to have these feelings and perceptions available for a new person...someone special...All those qualities and more can be found in someone new...**a new focus** for the best you have to give...saving it only for the deserving...Get a sense of your new, healthy powerful feelings and perspectives growing stronger and stronger and even more intense! How strong will your sense of attraction for a unique new person be? And won't it be joyously exciting to discover that?

Again: **you only give these abundant feelings to someone who deeply deserves it, now!** From now on **you are free** to...feel attraction and love for those who deeply deserve it...that's your 100% total new reality and it feels great...anything else seems absurd, it couldn't happen! New purified ways readily available at the right time and place, with that special person...You will be able to **feel genuine, total attraction and LOVE when appropriate!**

Love is THE most important and powerful human emotion! It can move mountains! It is our defining and most human strength! It **soothes and heals** and brings all the profoundest joys! It is what we are! You can **look back on the past comfortably...**with a sense of relief, calmness, and mature understanding...**That is all over.** Every potential for love of all kinds is now safe and ready...Ready to be dedicated to the one who is right for you to love...feeling that total attraction that you long to feel for them...when it's right! And you'll just know when to **let it all flow, unconsciously, noooooow!**

Module 5: summation and closing.

And now you can fully acknowledge and accept that...**these changes have been made...**Maybe feeling a joyous smile on the inside that can manifest on the outside...**You feel pleasure in your mind and body...**That past negativity washed away as though you have washed in pure spring water...Gone from your life, gone forever! Everything locked in as it needs to be...Trusting your subconscious mind to powerfully support you in all your efforts...all throughout your life! You now know that you can and will meet that person...perhaps sooner than you think...? You are able to feel *perfect love and passion when the time is right. And that's that.'*

Demolish fake love/infatuation module.

(If the man/woman is unable to 'let go' of an obviously doomed relationship I will use the following script to knock that self-pitying shit out of them. It simply allows him/her to see that woman/man for the heartless bitch/dick they are. The client can then move on and find a person who can really appreciate them. If I have used the preceding script I usually add this on at the end. Deep hypnosis assumed...)

*'Focus your mind on the person on whom you've had this crush/infatuation/you want to **fall out of love with...***

(Pause a moment!)

Good.

Recall all the good times of being with them by seeing yourself in those memories...

(Dissociated and so able to view more objectively without old emotions clouding perceptions.)

But see those films running backwards very fast and make them small and black and white...I'll be quiet as you do that.

(This scrambles the memories. Give 10 seconds processing time...)

That's it!

Relax and think of a blank piece of paper or something else neutral.

Now, remember all the times they weren't nice to you, treated you badly, were not respectful and get back the full sense of those unpleasant, negative feelings you had around them. Imagine yourself looking at them from your point of view as you recall that vividly!

(Note for hypnotist: You are getting them to form realistic sets of associations to that person: this is re-associated to, in memory based hypnotic operant conditioning. Give them 10 – 15 seconds to stew.)

*Take every bad thing they did. All the things that pissed you off! Recall them all! One after another, over and over and over! Watch those films, those little movies again and again and again till **you are totally sick of them!***

(Give 15-20 seconds to recall the reality of what a total sh*t they've actually been!)

Take something that is revoltingly disgusting to you and change the image of that person so that all the qualities of that revolting image – the qualities of place in the mind, image, size, colours or faded etc are identical. Make sure that person's image and the revolting thing are made up in the same way! Do it instantaneously as I say – 'FLIP!!!'

Good!

Imagine a gloriously compelling future without them! *See yourself incredibly happy! You are now totally free of all that old fake baggage! Step into that free you image and take some time to experience your joyful life on your own terms, now! Imagine yourself going through a time and situation that will confirm this has worked!*

(Give 10 seconds to bed down..........)

Perfect!

*You can take this act as a sign and a signal that **the changes have been made.'***

(The secret to this is – go through it quite quickly and briskly. Give them no time to ruminate. March them through it! Whenever I have done this it works! This may seem trivial but spurned love can be potentially dangerous as countless murders and suicides have shown. When people cheat, fool around and betray lovers they may unleash primal forces deep within the human psyche. The French know and understand this which is why they have 'crimes of passion'. Knowing this does not justify any horror that the jilted may carry out. But that it exists is a reality nonetheless.)

Case studies part 5: A hypnotist's bestiary.

In this section we shall look at what you might term 'hypnotic miscellany'. There are some unique scripts, another therapeutic case study, a detailed study of Dr. George Estabrooks use of very authoritarian hypnosis and more besides, in an exploration of the strange but interesting side alleys of hypnotic trance. The first is the inherent use of hypnosis in all religious practises.

Is there religion in hypnosis or vice versa?

The Greek root of the word 'religion' means 'to pay heed to.' Something that we pay attention to eh? Hmmm? If you've read my other books you'll know what I'm getting at! This is a very interesting avenue in the study of cultural hypnotic phenomena. Before we continue we should be clear where Franz Mesmer got his ideas from: the Catholic Church. Don't believe me? Read on.

Father Gassner.

During the so-called Middle Ages the model of

mental health was based on the teachings of the Western Universal Church, Catholicism. This basically stated that all poor mental health was caused by varying degrees of demonic 'obsession' or 'possession'. Therefore ALL mental health problems required the help of a priest. This process was known as 'casting out devils'. One such 'exorcist' a certain Father Gassner had gained a tremendous reputation as a 'healer' in 18th century France. Mesmer then developing his theories of hypnosis ('mesmerism') heard of Father Gassner's abilities and decided to pay a visit. Much as Bandler and Grinder of NLP fame, Jay Haley and Ernesto Rossi studied Milton Erickson to find out what he did. Gassner's method was surprisingly simple, repetitious and methodical – whatever it was it was not the classical Catholic sanctioned exorcism ritual; it was in fact an example of direct hypnosis.

Gassner's 'hypnosis' ritual.

Mesmer outlined the ritual in the following manner:

- *Gassner dressed in dramatic, long-flowing black robes.* Black **(colour symbology)** is the colour of power, authority and death, it was and is associated with priests – therefore it was associated with God and his son on earth Jesus Christ who was a renowned healer (within Christian belief). The fact that the robes were long and dramatic would grab attention **(focus)**. It is also out of the ordinary, a **pattern interrupt.**

- *The 'possessed' parishioner was made to kneel down, close his eyes and wait.* Kneeling is a human pre-symbolic act of surrendering and submitting to authority **(physiologically induced state change)**. Closing your eyes causes **sensory deprivation, disorientation** etc. It is the first thing many hypnotists do while beginning an induction. The individual is left waiting, their sense of reality, **anticipation and expectation** are being utilised and played with.

- *Whilst in this meditative/hypnoidal state an assistant to Gassner told the parishioner that when Father Gassner touched them with the brass cross, the 'devils would be cast out'.* This is quite simply the use of

expectation to prime the subconscious to affect cure. It is a culturally acceptable **plausible ritual**. This is the bog standard technique of hypnotist's everywhere which I call the 'in a moment pattern' – see book 2, 'Mastering hypnotic language', and 'Forbidden hypnotic secrets' for a full explanation of these ageless hypno-tricks. Notice a direct command is given, 'When x occurs, y occurs,' this presupposes an association between x and y that is only linguistically created.

- *Before Gassner even appeared an audience of parishioners etc. was invited in to watch.* This is simply utilising **group hypnosis**. People are more suggestible in groups, we feel more pressure to conform and perform. The crowd expected cure, this placed social pressure on the 'possessed's' unconscious to effect a rapid healing effort. Remember the person would have had faith in the Church and its teachings; he would have had perhaps days, weeks or months to consciously and unconsciously prepare for this moment. I have a few clients who book weeks in advance to get into the right frame of mind (psyching yourself up). Some people begin to feel better just by booking an appointment. *The subconscious starts to make shifts as they make the effort to try to change.* As one of the faithful, any such person would have high **motivation** to change: he would have **sincerely believed (believed in imaginings)** he was possessed and that only a Catholic priest would be able to 'cure' him.

- *Church hierarchy, visiting officials, 'leading minds' of the day would also attend these 'exorcisms'.* **Prestige** value! Highly hypnotic!

- *Gassner appeared on cue and 'majestically', lowered the large bronze cross he bore so that it touched the person on their head.* Presumably a hush or some sort of indication, footsteps etc. would 'warn' the person that Gassner was on his way. The expectation heightens.

- *Upon the touch the 'patient' collapsed, rose to his feet and proclaimed to God that all is hunky dory/A-ok!* An **abreaction** or expected physical signal of cure is displayed to the audience in a socially acceptable way (physiological shift – see book 1, 'How to hypnotise anyone').

Bizarrely Mesmer concludes it is the 'magnetic' quality of the cross that cures! He lops off the T bar of the cross and feels that a simple bronze rod will heal just as well. Buffoon! Whether 'demonic possession' actually exists or not is a fascinating subject whichever way you look at it and far beyond this book's confines. If you don't believe me ask a psychiatrist who has attended one!

Is prayer self-hypnosis?

It is not my intention to alienate all my readers who have a religious faith. Obviously to a religious person a prayer to God is just that. Some hypnotic researchers have offered a more mundane explanation. Let's take a peek.

The hypnotic physiology of prayer.

Let's assume the prayer is being offered in a religious building. This in itself will produce an altered waking hypnotic and receptive state in the true believer. Why do we pray? To thank the deity, to receive guidance/orders, ask forgiveness, get answers to problems.

- You assume the 'prayer position'. In some way all religions offer prayer to the respective deity of choice in a low status begging position: as a feudal serf may to an overlord. In Christianity the hands are clasped together – this is a **kinaesthetic anchor**. The eyes are often closed as in hypnosis. So your eyes are closed and your only sensory awareness is physical/feelings; sore knees, hand grip etc. Alternatively the body may be greatly relaxed, the mind at peace just by adopting the position of prayer.

- The **single focus of attention** is placed upon the 'deity'.

- Fixation of attention may be focused on a Holy Book plus **rhythmical movement and monotony** of input – saying something over and over etc. This also shuts off conscious thought: i.e. the ability to question.

- Note: there may well be **high motivation and emotional intent** that the prayer be 'answered' – imagine a mother with a dying child etc. The motivation could affect a placebo-affect cure by itself (if that's what is sought). The emotive element is hypnotic by itself.

- A prayer is offered – world peace, nice girlfriend, new car etc. A **suggestion** to 'God'. Can I have this please? If God exists, is he there to just be a genie of the lamp? Not very 'spiritual' to my way of thinking but...

- An **auditory waking ritual** (exduction) is utilised to complete the prayer – 'Amen' etc. This is a signal for normal affairs to be resumed.

Does the belief in the deity create a psychophysiological altered state conducive to self-healing? Obviously this does not explain miracles such as a cure occurring to the relative of a person who is praying on their behalf. I leave these matters for the reader to contemplate. Is prayer actually getting some people to worship their own subconscious???! I just don't know the answers! If you would like to explore this subject more I suggest you read, **'Religious**

aspects of hypnosis,' by William J. Bryan JR and S.J. Van Pelt. It is an odd but interesting examination of these subjects. I will end this little section by outlining those authors' mind model of hypnosis which is unprovable yet totally fascinating and worth knowing about.

The 'units of power' hypnosis mind model.

*   **The waking state:** imagine a circle. This is your brain. Imagine lots of tiny balls floating around in it. These are your 'units' of 'mind power' (whatever that is). The units are floating chaotically all over the place. They just ain't lined up! Any external effort at suggestion is doomed to small success. Imagine a 'suggestion beam' shinning torch-like into the brain and only hitting a few pesky units. Only two or three are hit by the light at any one time: result – little influence.

*   **Hypnosis:** in hypnosis these units of mind power are no longer floating around like balls in a kid's play centre. They are aligned, lined up – the torch like beam of suggestion can hit them all in one go! BINGO! The mind power is only focusing

on the incoming suggestion. There are ZERO mind units that can be devoted to anything else. You are suggestible!

- **Post hypnosis/awakening:** the mind units have all been 'struck' by the suggestions. They have changed colour if you like. They carry the 'imprint' of the suggestions. They can scatter around diffusely as usual but with another set of suggestions 'within' that influence them differently. Maybe they just bump about in your noggin in a new way.

What if we could use this to create a module within a hypnosis script? Might be interesting.

The units of mind power hypnosis module script.

(Deep hypnosis assumed – add this after induction and before suggestive therapy etc. begins)

*'As you **relax more and more deeply...**I want you to imagine...I'm not saying this is real...or what is genuinely happening...it's just an interesting metaphor...for **hypnotic CHANGE, now...**Visualise your mind as a*

circle...In the waking state...there are units of mind power...floating around...doing different things...with certain purposes and functions...based on past suggestions, learnings, experiences...They are diffuse if you like...Nothing has yet grabbed their attention and focused it...The suggestions from outside are like a beam of torchlight...and as the units are going about their business only a few pass within the beam at any one time...so not much makes a lasting impression upon them...They go about things as they have been programmed to...up until now...Because when **you enter deep hypnosis...now...**Those units of mind power start to line up...They form an orderly and narrow line or lines in which it is so easy...for the torchlight of certain suggestions to reach them all in one go...The light can illuminate them all at once...Now, as that happens when you **go deeper into fascinating trance, relaxing hypnosis**...the concentrated units of your mind power can **easily absorb the suggestions** and they can have a powerful affect upon you...in ways that delight you...because they are ignoring the irrelevant and **paying attention to what you need to**

know...that helps you most...And after this state of hypnosis has ended...and you are wide awake and living your life well...what we call 'units of mind power' will be filled with the imprint...the positive effect of these suggestions...and they'll be metaphorically floating around doing what they do...but doing it differently...in ways that enrich your life immeasurably...at an unconscious level, automatically...They have a 'dose' you might say, of wise suggestions, to guide them in more appropriate and healthy ways, nooooooow!'

Is there such a thing as evil hypnosis? The case of Dr. G.H. Estabrooks.

Who was G.H. Estabrooks? He graduated from Arcadia University (Pennsylvania USA) followed by 3 years at Oxford University (England – he was a Rhodes scholar). He received his doctorate in Educational Psychology in 1926 from Harvard University. He worked as professor of abnormal and industrial psychology at Colgate University. Now Esty as I shall call him liked to play around with hypnosis; some might say in an irresponsible fashion. His 'methods' were revealed in his classic book on hypnosis, simply called **'Hypnotism'** – it is a must read for all hypnotists and those interested in the field. It was published in 1943. It revealed various unscrupulous uses of hypnosis. Esty was a Wizard of Trance alright and not a very nice one.

Can you hypnotise someone to carry out a murder?

According to Esty the answer is a very definite yes. He cites a case from Denmark. An amateur hypnotist called Mr. Nielson had hypnotised a man called Mr. Hardrup to commit a murder. At the trial a certain Mr. P.J. Reiter an 'international authority on hypnosis' claimed that in hypnosis any man is capable of any act. Nielsen received a life sentence and Hardrup 2 years on grounds of 'temporary insanity'.

Not knowing the full details of the case it is hard to know what conclusions to draw on this matter. Certainly Dr. Milton Erickson was not convinced by Esty's claims and said that the 'authority principle' explained all deviant behaviour in the hypnotic state.

Can you hypnotise someone against their will or consent?

Both Esty and I agree that this is easily done. Esty answered yes in a most arrogant fashion and proceeded to tell how it was and could be done. Firstly Esty litters his book with anecdotes to prove his case. The case of two friends attending a tea party in Oxford England is given. Esty and friends noted how these two Englishmen had a wonderful conversation with the British Prime Minister of the day. Except they didn't. Esty had triggered a post hypnotic command to hallucinate the British PM, his entry to the room etc. All the while the spectators were amazed as the pair conversed with an empty chair! Dazzling as this appears it is just stage hypnosis phenomena – a bog standard stage hypnotist in an English pub could do this stunt. Esty states quite truthfully that anyone can...

- Enter hypnosis in one second.

- Reawaken in one second.

- Forget entirely that hypnosis has occurred.

- Only permit one person and no other to hypnotise them.

All these behaviours are brought about using post hypnotic commands. He calls these 'mere chores' and he is right. He then begins to let us know this is no ordinary book about hypnosis and he does this by dropping hints about its 'military applications'.

Creating 'hypnotic messengers'.

Esty then begins to unravel how hypnosis has been used in warfare. He states how it is very easy to hypnotise an enlisted man to store a message in his subconscious (Esty calls it the unconscious) that could only be delivered to one person via re-hypnotism on the other side of the world. This message would be unrecoverable because the soldier's conscious mind would be entirely ignorant of it. Not torture or beer or attempts to re-hypnotise the subject would work. The perfect cipher has been created.

Lazy boy becomes motivated.

At Colgate University a 'lazy' boy was brought before Esty. This lad had no inclination to study. His parents were despairing about their ner-do-well son's future! Esty hypnotised him and using Jungian presumptions asked the boy's unconscious if there was anything he would really like to do. The answer came back: an illustrator. Be specific, in what field? The boy liked the outdoors. He would become a botanical illustrator! Not so easy - the conscious mind had other ideas, although his unconscious deeply wished to enter this creative field. Esty then tells us that he used 'post-hypnotics' and 'strong armed methods'. These 'strong armed methods' are not divulged. The boy began to work so hard it was making him ill! Esty claimed lazy boy became the best botanical illustrator the University had ever produced. ***Alarmingly Esty said that such techniques held great promise for 'the future' but due to the nature of such techniques which would alarm the general public, a great deal of indoctrination would have to occur for them to become socially acceptable.*** Read the book if you don't believe me.

'Talking sleep' – inductions Estabrooks' style.

Estabrooks' mind model was the complete antithesis of Dr. Milton Erickson. ***Esty said that the unconscious or what he called the 'unconscious' was the directing force of mind: hypnotism 'dethroned' the conscious mind and the 'operator' took over all controls of the mind-body system.***

He stated that only 20% of the population could go deep enough to be taken over completely in this way and programmed by a skilled hypnotist. I would actually put this closer to 50-70% of the population if not higher. Times change.

Estabrooks' formula was: **suggestion was the <u>key</u>; relaxation <u>opened the door</u> to hypnosis.**

Estabrooks style hypnotic induction and human robot tests.

(Subject is asked to close eyes.)

'You are falling sound asleep... ('sound asleep' has an ambiguity: 'sound asleep' as in sleeping soundly + as in you can 'sound' asleep, that is 'appear' asleep: faking hypnosis = hypnosis. Subtly sophisticated. Also emphasis on the word 'sound' that follows suggests to the subject that sound is more important than vision and heightens sense of hearing.) *Relax all your muscles and imagine that you are going into a deep sleep...* (Direct command to relax – focusing mind on body and imagination at once, overload of consciousness with multiple tasks. If you imagine 'going into deep sleep' it makes it more likely it will happen – a visual suggestion.) *Deeper and deeper...* (Bog-standard deepener.) *You will not awaken until I tell you to...* (I am the boss! Do as I say! The type of relationship being entered into is master and slave. Estabrooks is quite open

559

about this. At some level the subject must agree to submit. They may only feel comfort and security in rigid hierarchies; there are many people who are like this in waking life.) *When you wake up you will always feel fine as a result of these suggestions...* (No matter what is 'programmed in' the person is commanded to feel good about it. Others have called Estabrooks style 'hypnotic programming'; the polar opposite of what I do.) *You are falling sound, sound asleep...Deeper and deeper and deeper still.'* (Repeat etc. for a full 5 minutes)

'Robotisiation' test 1: eye closure module.

'Listen closely to me! (Focus on my voice – what follows is important! Get ready!) *Your eyelids are locked tightly together!* (Direct command to control the small muscles of the body, a usual phenomenon of light trance.) *Tighter. Tighter and tighter! Tight! They are locked tighter with every passing second and you can't open those eyes no matter how hard you try! Locked tightly together! Can't open them! You may try!* (I permit you to try. I am king here you 'may' try. Notice short, sharp, direct orders are given with no explanation or

justification of purpose. Do it because I say!) *I dare you!'* (Go on defy my authority! Remember this was being tested on those who saw Estabrooks as an authority figure. This is known in the literature as a 'challenge test'.)

RH note: 50% of those tested obeyed. A further 90% obeyed after long training. Only 10% of those tested could not be induced to act against their will. These may be classed as the 10% resistant to any form of 'mind-control' down through history. My life and professional experience mirrors this finding. However I get 100% success from everyone with eye closure tests because I don't go all authoritarian. At any time in history it seems only about 10% can think for themselves: history's endless bloodbaths and continuing horror-show would seem to confirm this alarming reality!

Hypnotists who believe obedience to commands = hypnosis are not really seeking to influence the unconscious but to control it as a programmer would a computer. In order for this to work in the crude manner carried out by Estabrooks, the person must be a 'waking somnambule' – this is a person who for a whole variety of reasons want to be controlled by another at an unconscious level. They want to be a follower. They will follow the orders of an 'authority figure' right or wrong when awake. In the hypnotic state they will follow orders at a deep unconscious level which includes surrendering control of ALL autonomic nervous system functions. Think about that! People also have deep unconscious drives for attention.

Esty's formula for 'mind control' hypnosis was:

1. The aim of this type of hypnosis is to **take control of the other person's unconscious** (authoritarian hypnosis model).

2. The way this is forced to happen is **through a series of successive tests or steps/phases in a process**.

3. At each stage **an increasing sphere of control of the subject is sought from small muscle groups up to progressively larger muscles groups** (the heart is a muscle!).

4. As each muscle group **cedes autonomy** to the authoritarian, the bodily systems are each in turn progressively 'conquered' – as Empires and dictatorships through history have 'progressively' (step by step expansion of influence) taken over territory they lusted for.

5. Eventually the **entire autonomic nervous system cedes control** to the manipulative hypnotist: the person is well on his or her way to becoming a human robot. *Quite frankly: terrifying!*

It seems that Esty worked with many social groups but primarily practised on students and soldiers – both groups well used to seeking approval from authority and to obeying commands within recognised hierarchies. The reason this type of hypnosis works is this: at a deep unconscious level people have already consented to be slaves, they just don't know it. Freedom appears tough and 'anarchic' – a slave doesn't have to worry about anything. Puppets just have their strings pulled after all. Many people have a deep unconscious desire to escape a harsh reality into the certainties of slavery. Read, **'Escape from Freedom' by**

Eric Fromm.

Esty offered his subjects a moment of choice in his phrase 'I dare you!' This is what Hitler would shout at crowds when his proto Nazi scum would attack other groups' rallies, meetings etc. He would dare them to oppose him!

The formula for this is – ***issue command and dare opponent to refuse to obey.*** (This implies that somehow punishment awaits refusal; actually it doesn't imply it – it states it boldly! The question is WHY did the subjects fear the dare?) This is a classic example of what Historian Arnold Toynbee termed **challenge and response** from the environment, human or natural.

Esty's methods entailed the **gradual progression of an effect** which then generalised throughout a system. This is the socialist 'Fabian' model of conquest. You start with small requests that seem reasonable. You acclimatise your victims (the frog in a boiling pot model) slowly. Gradually you increase the 'heat', severity, intensity of the commands. Let's carry on with the Estabrook model. Further tests of muscular paralysis follow.

Robotisation test 2: arm catalepsy (stiffness).

'Relax everything...relax those eyes...returning to normal...You are sound, sound asleep and will not awaken until instructed by me...When I give the command you will awaken effortlessly, peaceful, quietly...Relax all over...I am about to carry out another test... (Use of pronoun 'I' not 'we' – this is all about the hypnotist. The implication is that the subject may 'fail' the test not the hypnotist; this applies pressure to the victim/subject to comply and so please the authority.) *You right arm is becoming stiff and rigid at your side...* ('becoming' is the key word – this is the not now but 'in a moment pattern' in one word!) *The muscles are getting tighter and tighter! Rigid and stiff!* (Ok big boy!) *It is as rigidly stiff as an iron bar...* ('it' = dissociative, not 'your' arm + hypnotic metaphor for unconscious = idea seeding/priming; effectively saying, 'Unconscious' the arm is stiff as an iron bar,' this supplies it with a concrete comparative.) *So stiff and rigid! You cannot bend that arm! It is impossible to bend it! You may try!* (I grant thee permission serf!) *I dare you!'*

RH note: Again the same imperious kingly tone granting permission, issuing orders etc. An arm is surrendered to the authority, a bit like being taken apart one bit at a time. Soon the entire body will be mine slave! Moo-hah-hah-hah-ha! Some 'erotic hypnotists' do this stuff. It turns them on. Ho-hum! There is definitely some pyscho-sexual subtext to this style of hypnosis in my opinion. The phallic arm becomes *stiff* to order. I actually made a man's finger stiff and then transferred that stiffness to his...er, best friend...what?! It was therapy for erectile dysfunction! Weirdo...

Erickson always gave his clients a false choice: left arm or right or none, this is known as 'covering all potential responses'. Esty demanded that specific actions be carried out to the letter! No deviation was allowed to ensure hypnotic 'success', by his definition.

Esty points out that often a subject won't even try to manifest any phenomenon: they are just too comfy and don't want to make any effort. This he labels 'lethargy'. It is possible to turn a hypnotee into a rigid 'stone statue', I've done it.

Robotisation test 3: surrendering full body control!

'Relax that right arm...Everything returns to normal...Your arm is comfortable and may rest at your side again...Going soundly asleep...sound asleep...Go deeper and deeper. Far deeper! (After each test, deepening commands are given. The person is never allowed a totally free response. This is control freak hypnosis. Orderz must be obeyed!) *You are losing all control over your body...Your body is floating away* (command for mind-body dissociation!)... *You cannot control your muscles...* (Presupposition? The hypnotist can!) *It is totally impossible for you to stand up! You are stuck on/in that chair! It is impossible for you to stand erect!* (Stand erect???! I told you this was BDSM!) *You may try! I dare you!'* (Yawn...)

RH note: if the subject shows 'compliance' through 'lethary' he was considered a 'good' subject. Good for what? Good according to whom? Oh, we will soon find out young padawans!!!

Robotisation test 4: activating automatic movements – hand rotation.

'You are soundly asleep...Sound asleep now...

Go deeper and deeper...Much deeper...I am going to start your hands rotating...One around the other... (Imagine the arms parallel. The hands' palms facing each other, bent at the knuckle at right angles - the fingers' tips face each other, about an inch apart. Rotate the hands at the wrist, both hands 'going around each other'. This looks like someone reeling in wool or slapping dough.)

Here they go...Round and round...Quicker and quicker...Much faster! You cannot stop them! You may try but you will find it totally impossible to stop them rotating! Try as hard as you like! You simply cannot do it!'

RH note: Esty points out that many subjects try to resist the unconscious movements and may even use one hand to stop the other! Some wake up. The goal of Esty's method of hypnosis was that the conscious mind 'give up' control of the body totally. In effect the hypnotic 'operator' (operating a puppet/robot) would become the individual's conscious mind and will. Esty saw this level of relinquishing as a sure sign of a good subject. But he would go further.

Robotisation test 5: taking control of the organs of articulation.

(The next muscle group to conquer is the mouth. Think about this: in many ways 'you' are your voice and someone else in in control of it!)

'Repeat after me exactly as I say it...'Twinkle twinkle little star how I wonder what you are etc.' Now repeat this phrase over and over and over without cessation until I command you! Keep doing it till I tell you to stop! You cannot stop! You must continue! You feel so compelled to continue that it is impossible to stop until I allow you to!'

RH note: If a subject did what he was told with regards to the mouth test Esty was convinced he had a somnambulist. BINGO! (This test is what 'speaking in tongues' is.) Next he would 'interrogate' the victim under hypnosis. Note also that up to test 8, the hypnotee may well remember everything that has happened however weird.

Robotisation test 6: asking simple questions.

'Subject I am now going to ask you some

*simple questions…Although you are in deep
hypnotic sleep…Soundly asleep now…You will
answer me in your sleep…You have heard
others talk in their sleep so you know this is
possible…You will not wake up…You will
answer me frankly without effort…'*

Ask questions without emotional content so as
to not activate conscious protection
mechanisms. At least at this level. If you are
worried that the person will become afraid of
being 'exposed' in some way, and that can
happen, they may have secrets for example or
just be afraid of your being a nosey bastard
say the following,

*'You can relax because I am not going to ask
you anything personal, this is just a test to
see how responsive you are to my
suggestions. I would never do anything to
embarrass you in any way etc. Just shake
your head or wiggle your right forefinger if
you don't want to be asked any simple
questions. I entirely respect your decision,'*
this is a safety feature BUT it can also be used
to create fake trust and further compliance.
Do you see? You could ask…

- Tell me where you live?

- What year were you born?

- Where did you go on holiday/vacation 2 years ago?

- Do you have any pets?

- Do you have any siblings? If so how many etc.?

Carry on in this vein. To a certain extent these 'mands' are eliciting implicit 'yes sets' from the hypnotee. With each act of question-compliance they are saying, 'Yes I agree and consent to be used and played with in this fashion.' If this all seems so far-fetched think on this fact: during World War 1 young men would mindlessly hurl themselves over trenches to certain death *and they knew they were being ordered to their deaths* – they were so well hypnotised that their desire to live was overridden. The officers had total control over the leg muscles of those boys. The smarter ones with the brains to know that it was an act of suicide, who sensibly fled to safety, were arrested for 'cowardice' and shot. Think about that long and hard. A good TV series to watch on this subject is **'The Monocled Mutineer'** starring Paul McGann.

It was made by the BBC when they used to make good programmes (mid 1980's); unfortunately it has a thinly disguised pro-socialist subtext but it is a great piece of TV nonetheless.

If a hypnotee awakens at any stage of this obvious manipulation they will feel a palpable sense of unpleasant unease and refuse to co-operate further. A stage hypnotist gets around such feelings by framing the whole process as an enjoyable game in which someone gets to be famous for 15 minutes as Andy Warhol predicted rightly. Now the person must be tested for 'remote control' ability.

Robotisation test 7: sleep walk on command.

'You will now stand up and remain deeply asleep...You will walk around this space in deep hypnosis as you have seen sleepwalkers do...I will guide you around the room to ensure you are safe (trust is built – the hypnotist is literally re-parenting the subject, teaching them to walk as their parents once did.) *Your muscles will operate as they normally would when wide awake! Stand up now and walk with me!'*

The hypnotist guides them around the room etc. The final test for a 'good subject' follows: visual hallucinations.

Robotisation test 8: seeing what ain't there!

RH note: before I outline this test let me explain its significance. If you cede control of your skeletal muscles etc. that it one thing; a hallucination test plays with your perception of reality. You are literally, in a controlled way, displaying 'psychotic' behaviour. This doesn't mean you are psychotic but dreaming whilst awake is what 'madness' is. In the context of stage hypnosis etc. with a skilled practitioner you are 100% safe. People often hallucinate in real life anyway for a variety of reasons that are not pathological. Painting and drawing require the artist to 'hallucinate' a picture before they paint/draw it. The crux is, with types like Esty you are permitting an authoritarian control freak to play with your reality orientation. When this occurs you have ceased to be fully human. Your 'reality' can be re-constructed. Geddit? Understand the ramifications?

'Listen very closely. I will say this only once... (British reader's will note my 'Allo Allo' – a

BBC comedy plagiarising!) *When I say a cue word you will open your eyes you and will remain deeply hypnotised...On the table in front of you, you will see a white friendly mouse etc....* (Use an animal that doesn't frighten someone.) *You will approach it...pick it up and pet it gently...Then when you are finished place in on that x over there...'* (X being some object/chair etc.)

Authoritarian hypnotists often advise repeating instructions several times to make sure that no misunderstandings occur. The subconscious tends to take things very literally. Be careful how you phrase it. Perhaps work out in advance how to avoid any ambiguities. If you say, 'Eat that juicy pear!' (a hallucinated one) the person might respond creatively and say it has a spider etc. on it. So instead say, 'Take a bite of that 100% inviting and healthy pear! It's just the type you like etc.' Get the idea – look padawans, the subconscious is like a genius child, it is very smart, creative but very naughty! ***This is why most adults are so much dumber than their younger selves – the 'adult' is the end result of a 'socialisation' process that intends to wipe out your instincts***

and spontaneity, your deepest wishes and desires. It is this conditioning process that creates hypnotherapy clients.

Esty creates a multiple personality with hypnosis.

Before we get to the hypnotic creation of 'dual' or 'multiple' personality by Esty we will examine what he has to say on this subject in his aforementioned book.

Case 1: Ansel Bourne – Boston, USA: This case we are told was reported by psychologist William James. A certain Mr. Ansel Bourne from Boston, USA vanishes. No trace is found of him in 6 months. On the 6th month of his disappearance a man running a grocery store in Philadelphia suddenly 'woke up' as he put it, and said he was actually Ansel Bourne. He had entered a 'fugue state' for the duration of his mysterious hypnotic vacation. His fugue induced secondary personality had run the grocery store pretty well apparently. No further details are forthcoming.

Case 2: Rou – Paris, France: A young boy called Rou living in Paris, France and coming from a poor single-parent family, his mother running a small shop, develops a longing to escape his boring life and become a sailor. At some point his unconscious forces a fugue state upon consciousness and makes this happen! This started off with poor Rou setting out for the coast with no conscious knowledge he was so doing. This developed into his unconsciously funding his coastal voyages by doing small odd jobs on route. He would 'awaken' and go home. Eventually and on many occasions Rou's unconscious successfully gets him out to sea and he works as a sailor with no conscious knowledge this has occurred. He would 'awaken' at sea or some far flung place mystified as to how he was where he was!

Case 3: The famous Beauchamp case – Boston, USA: A young Miss Beauchamp is training at Boston Hospital to become a nurse. Her 'peculiar actions' attract the attention of a Dr. Prince. He discovers the would-be nurse has 4 separate 'alters' as they are now known, or 'personalities' as they said back then.

- ***Personality 1: B1 – 'The Angel'.*** This alter is sickly, nervous, very religious, conscientious, tired and worried about the fate of humanity and her own sorry condition.

- **_Personality 2: B3 – 'Sally' or the 'Imp'._** This alter is a naughty 8 year old girl. She is highly energetic and 'psychopathic'. She is usually not in control of the body and is 'squeezed' into the recesses of Miss Beauchamp's psyche. She hates the Church-going Angel and wants revenge. As Beauchamp becomes increasingly odd/unwell and dissociative, Sally takes the body over and gets 'revenge'. She takes the body out on a drunken orgy getting f**ked silly by many young men! This occurred in the 1900's when people had a strong Christian ethic. These days 'Sally' would be a TV star. As the Angel had practically zero energy she would take the body out on incredibly long walks and leave poor Angel to walk home. Angel was tidy, so Sally trashed the room! These acts were used by Sally to stop Angel going to Church etc., something Sally loathed. If Angel did not do as Sally said - punishment followed.

- **_Personality 3: B4 – 'The Woman'._**
Neither Angel nor Sally is aware of what
Sally is doing when she is doing it. Sally
writes threatening letters to them. Sally
however is well aware of what the other
two were up to! Was 'the Woman' an
attempt by the psyche's core to cope with
Sally? The Woman was a stubborn snob
who likes concerts and fancy shops; she is
vain, spiteful and wilful. Unlike the Angel
she stands up to 'the imp'. When Sally
trashes the Woman's clothes, the Woman
burns Sally's clothes. A truce is called
between the two. Prince started using
hypnosis in his treatments. Whenever he
hypnotised Angel or the Woman he got a
new alter which he dubbed...

- **_Personality 4: B2 – 'The mature
woman'._** This alter has both Angel and
the Woman's memories and seemed, to
Prince, to be more 'balanced' and 'stable'.
Prince decides this is the 'real' Beauchamp.
After several attempts Prince gets Miss
Beauchamp to awaken as 'The mature
woman' both Angel and the Woman are
'integrated.' _Alarmingly he kills off Sally_

and keeps her locked away in the hidden depths of the nurse's psyche!!!

Esty tells us that shock and hypnosis are both forms of dissociation and almost if not entirely identical. He lets us know that at 'key stages' in her life Miss. Beauchamp did indeed experience 'shocks'.

Beauchamp experienced 'extreme fear' in childhood. This is not further explained.

She experienced a 'fright' from her father at age 7 – this was significant enough to create Sally and the integrated B2 (mature woman). Hmmmm?

At 18 she experiences another shock related to her 'love life'. Again no details are given. This may be due to the social mores when Estabrooks was writing. The Angel and the Woman are created. Her psyche split 4 times in total! On this occasion her core split twice! Suggesting that this later, ahem, 'shock' was even more traumatic than the first in late childhood.

With what we know about MPD (Multiple Personality) or DID (Dissociative Identity

Disorder) as it is now known, we can make a guess that Sally was the result of a violent rape at the hands of her father, probably on multiple occasions. We can then conclude that the two later alters resulted at the hands of a rape or multiple rapes by a man she had trusted and was attracted to who was as evil and psychopathic as her father. The 'alter' Sally probably arose as the result of shame and self-hate, disgust she felt toward herself etc. Sexually abused children often think they caused the abuse. They then live up to the 'whore' role assigned to them. She may well have come from a nominally 'religious' family. The Angel and Woman symbolically represent firstly her 'pure' unsoiled sexual self, vainly fighting against injustice and the second, her adult, ruthless, tough and untouchable protector self.

The horror...the horror...the horror...

Now we have established the reality of mental dissociation of self into separate alters we can look at Esty's claim that he deliberately created them. Seemingly to create a 'super spy'.

Estabrooks and weaponised hypnosis: the creation of a super spy?

Before anything else we must look at Estabrooks' own admissions for proof.

- He claimed that he could hypnotise a man without his knowing or consent and that by so doing could get him to commit treason against his own country, the United States.

- When asked if hypnosis was dangerous he said that in some circumstances it can be. He said it could lead to murder – if the hypnotist knew what he was doing and the subject was a 'good candidate'. He does not elaborate.

- He said that the best way to create the 'perfect spy' or assassin was to intentionally create a multiple personality using hypnosis. He said it wasn't science fiction, he had done it!

- Esty claimed that during World War 2 and working with a 'vulnerable' Marine lieutenant he referred to as 'Jones' and with the aid/supervision of Marine intelligence he split the man's personality into what he called Jones A – a rabid, indoctrinated communist. Jones A infiltrated communist cells. Jones B was the real Jones, all Esty had to do was re-hypnotise Jones A and debrief him.

- Although we may find this deeply unethical, Esty said the ends justified the means and that in war decency went out the window in order to achieve victory. What do you think?

- Esty left us a warning: he said those who are too lazy to think and analyse things for themselves and are only too willing to conform mindlessly could be enslaved and indeed killed by the covert and unethical use of hypnosis. ***Only those that could think for themselves which means ASKING QUESTIONS (I would add even uncomfortable ones) could be sure of preserving their freedom.***

So what did Esty write in his book about 'the super spy'?

War Hypnosis.

So sweet and innocent aren't you. Did you really believe that the army etc., the military of any land haven't tried to examine the applications of hypnosis to their own ends? Milton Erickson admits in the book, **'The February Man'** that he was 'involved' in interrogating German and Japanese prisoners during World War deux. Your hypno-virginity is about to be lost. We won't be revealing any state secrets – *I ain't that dumb!* But the info I provide next is available in Esty's book 'Hypnotism'. Don't shoot the messenger. So what did Esty say?

NOTE: Esty does not say when it WAS used – but he says how it *could* be done. I have no prima facie proof it has been. Then again we can infer...

In military hypnosis the operator must consider:

- Will 'the controls' work?

- Will a post hypnotic command/compulsion work without reinforcement? (Post hypnotics do sometimes need re-boosting as it were.)

- Can you get total amnesia when it counts? *Esty says the answer to this 'vital question' is **YES!***

- NOTE: Esty says that hypnosis in war is the same as hypnosis used to perpetrate a crime. Again we have Esty's dictum: in war, ethics fly out the window. Any 'problems' that arise are put down to the blood price of battle. If they dropped a nuclear bomb, do you think any Government will be squeamish about hypnosis? Now really.

- 1-5 adults are capable of full somnambulism (that's a gross underestimate but...); they can carry out practically anything a stage hypnotist suggests. They can believe they have changed sex, they can hunt imaginary hippos with sticks they believe are guns: any weird sh*t is possible! But how do you get a moral person to do this? Can you do it? *Esty says the answer to this 'vital question' is **YES!***

Hypnosis without consent.

Not against his will BUT without consent
is the phrase used by Esty. We know this can
happen because some men hypnotise women
into having sex with them. Being a spy,
murder is something else, isn't it? Non-
consenting sex is rape. Is this hypno-mind
rape?

Prisoners of war won't consent to give out info
by volunteering to be hypnotised. You or I
wouldn't commit a war crime (would we?) if
hypnosis were used to force us. We'd resist.
Ah yes! But there are ways...What if...

'Rogue' hypnosis: the disguised method.

WARNING: the following is deeply unethical, even sadistic. I advise you *never* do it.

Step 1: priming the environment.

- **The space:** Chose a quiet, secluded place.
  A smallish room is best to avoid
  distractions. Utter silence – perfect! A
  chair, couch, medical equipment etc.
  Perhaps a 'doctor's office' is best, perhaps

less formal even better. Paint the walls light yellow – yellow increases suggestibility.

- **Clothes:** Wear something yellow or with stripes, which are also a bit hypnotic. Not needed but you could experiment. I could do this in a garbage bag and it would work.

- **Non-verbal arsenal:** A. Use a friendly tone at first – be informal, call them by their first name, smile, shake hands, attend to niceties. B. Use a gradually more relaxed hypnotic tone as the procedure develops. Intent – to soothe, assure, and comfort. C. Slow your...voice...tempo...down...gradually, almost...imperceptibly...slowly does it...like trout tickling...D. Match your utterances to their out breaths (the 'letting go' breath). Pause now and again to allow processing (stage D isn't essential, it's a choice as are all stages; I can think of ways to make it work without these things but...). Watch out for trance signs and verbally reward – 'that's it,' etc. E. Subtle use of embeds +

pleasant command tone or lighten the command. Just mark it out somehow.

Before you do anything else get the setting right and use your non-verbal hypnotic skills to weigh things in your favour. The usual method in those days was to 'talk sleep'. That is the usual, 'You get sleepier and sleepier' inductions etc. That is no use in this scenario. Now we craft the spell...

1. Tell the victim that you are carrying out an experiment in relaxation.

2. Attach a blood pressure gauge to the subject's right arm.

3. Place a psycho-galvanic reflex to the person's palm. (Steps 2 and 3 are similar to Pitzer's 'larvated suggestion' – see book 5, 'Wizards of trance'.) By them **agreeing** to have these devices attached to them you start a non-verbal '**yes set**'.

4. The victim is now convinced you just want to scientifically evaluate/measure their physiological indications of relaxation. To a certain extent their **attention will be fixated** on these strange instruments

attached to them. Also if you say you are going to measure relaxation you are **presupposing** it will happen. You are also **bypassing conscious resistance** by saying it will happen **in a moment**. Their guard drops. (See books 1 and 2 for these patterns. My regular readers will know what I'm talking about.)

5. Tell the victim, *'In order to help us in this study, we need you to relax. To help you do this, can you just imagine that you are falling asleep?'* (Key word ***imagine*** – this is hypnotic priming/schema activation; see book 4, 'Forbidden hypnotic secrets' and the upcoming 'Escaping cultural hypnosis' – do not miss it!)

6. Continue, *'Of course the best way to measure relaxation is for you to fall deeply asleep while I talk to you.'* (The idea of **relaxation** and **sleep** – are being **idea seeded**, over and over – **directionalising** the mind and **preparing an unconscious response** for these behaviours to be made manifest by an **authority figure**. All these tricks are covered in my other works. *Falling asleep*

while someone talks to you is hypnosis! You just haven't called it that!)

7. You could even throw in embeds whilst doing this – note: stressed/emphasised verbs alone are powerful embedded commands- e.g. **sleep, relaxation, fall** *deeply asleep*, **imagine, relax** etc. Geddit? I have no idea if embeds have or were used in this fashion; let's assume yes and throw them in, but remember they are not needed, presuppositions can be just as powerful if accepted.

8. Lull them further, say, *'One of the benefits of this experience is that you will be able to know how to* **relax very deeply**. *I'll show you how. There is so much stress and worry in this modern world of ours. Would you like me to show you some very expert methods of controlling that etc.? How would you like to know how to* **feel very calm** *at will? Would that help you* **rest?** *You'd have more energy and be more with it. On top of your game. Sound like a deal?'* They say, 'Yes!' – who wouldn't want this? You have an ongoing yes set – an **agreement frame**. You

future pace them by getting them to imagine the positive results of full cooperation. They will be the beneficiaries. You appeal to the 'fact' that they'll be able to control their own mind and states; _when unbeknownst to them the exact opposite is about to occur!_ You are dangling a carrot. A lure, which lets the drawbridge down. The mind has no firewall. SHIT!!!

9. Even if you were aware this was preparation for hypnosis, the interesting context of being **involved in a scientific experiment** (which will 'help mankind' – appeal to species altruism and more prosaically: vanity!) and an **authority figure** asking for your help would intrigue (curiosity = **response potential**) and flatter you. There is no end of dunderheads all too willing to be scientific guinea pigs. They would have no idea of the **secret intent** of the operator to use them IF total somnambulism is achieved. It's not so hard to get as you think. **In the right context almost everyone is hyper-response to hypnosis.** More on this in book 7, 'Escaping cultural hypnosis'. Everything is now set up optimally – you

have set the frame, a **plausible ritual**, *beautifully* – now zombiefy them!!! NOTE: The hypnotist *is* carrying out an experiment but quite different to the publically stated one; they want an answer to this question: ***Is this person a member of what Estabrook ominously called, 'The one in five club'?*** If they are you might be able to create a super spy. At no point have we said, 'I am going to hypnotise you and see if I can make you do weird sh*t without your conscious awareness or consent.' That will tend to get people on the defensive – just a tip.

10. Start to 'talk sleep' – a short script as an example of what could be done follows. We are keeping this simple and 'old school'. **'The RH's - talk sleep - script':** ('...' - indicates a slight pause, '......' - indicates a slightly longer one.) *'To learn to* ***relax deeply****, simply close your eyes and focus your attention on that blood pressure strap around your arm...Draw your attention to it...That's it...Can you notice how that feels? All the sensations. Maybe it feels odd? Ok...Just take in a deep breath for me and hold it...Release*

*that breath slowly...Begin to **let go of tension...** That's it. And again...Deep breath in...Hold it... Release that breath...And notice as you do that you can just **remember** a time you felt very **sleepy...** Can you **imagine a time** like that from your past? A time in which **sleepy feelings** developed very **naturally.** That's it.......In order to **feel sleepy,** you need to **feel nice and calm** first...Notice the details of that past time...where were you?......Were you alone or with someone else?......Were you in a bedroom?......A hotel?......What did that place look like?......What could you hear?......How did you **feel in your body** as you recall that sleepy relaxed feeling?......Get to re-know that feeling.......And when **you're tired,** you might **feel an urge to yawn...** (watch for a real one! Might happen – if so BINGO!) You just **feel sleepier and sleepier,** don't you?...So pleasant to know you can **relax deeply** like this, just by remembering a time you **feel sleepy,** tired, relaxed...Maybe it was after a tiring day and **your body feels heavier and***

heavier, *more and more fatigued and still. Such a sweet, soft feeling in your resting muscles...You just don't want to move. Your only desire is to* **sink** *all the way down* **into deep sleep.......***Maybe you count sheep as* **you fall asleep** *(?) Maybe that body gets more and more comfy without any conscious thought...Now, Maybe waves and waves of pleasant feelings spread all through you. Your body is relaxed...Your mind is relaxed...So it's easy to* **feel wonderfully sleepy.** *Babies can* **fall asleep anytime, anywhere** *when they* **feel very tired...***And at some point you do just* **fall soundly asleep** *without any awareness that you did until you awaken later after a refreshing* **relaxing... sleep, now.** *Etc. You can hear a* **sleepy yawn in your mind...***Your* **mind quietens** *down when you* **relax and sleep.......***You can focus on the word* **sleep...sleep...sleep...***Just sleepily say that in your mind on an out breath until you just* **feel so relaxed** *that you don't feel the need to and when that happens, you can* **feel even more deeply relaxed...***You can allow your mind to* **go**

off and wander *as we do in daydreams….At night we* **sleep…deeply** *and do not remember many things that happened during this time of* **rest** *but we know that we slept* **soundly** *all the same….Let your capacities to* **drift off to sleep** *occur at just the right time for you. Perfect….Etc.'* (Carry on in this vein till you see trance signals etc. *Note: embeds not required.* Make your voice tone match the words, getting progressively sleepier and sleepier in a cartoonish, exaggerated fashion. Remember in reality Estabrooks was an authoritarian. He wouldn't have used permissives like 'can' etc., he would have said, *'You* **are** *getting sleepier and sleepier!', 'You* **will** *relax deeply', 'You X',* – *x being desired response, e.g.* **'You feel** *more and more tired etc.'* Estabrooks was giving orders, not suggestions – he was looking for personalities whose very unconscious selves obeyed commands, complied with them without question. This may have occurred through shock. Let me explain. If you are in hypnosis feeling relaxed and I start ordering you about, you would more than likely wake up. However some people who are ordered about go into shock. They dissociate. If you are hypnotised it is easier to flip a person prone to do so into shock: the formula would be – **hypnosis into shock.** A person is programmable in a dissociated state. However it is also possible as I have said in other works that at least 20% of the public will do anything they are told in hypnosis via ordinary suggestion; do not discount that alone as an explanation. Other reasons for compliance include a subconscious desire for adventure, to be regarded as important or useful, masochistic tendencies, gross stupidity, naivety or a pathologically trusting nature, a genetic ability to dissociate, a proneness to fantasy etc.)

11. Note: now and again check the medical equipment etc. to maintain the farce.

12. When you are happy that the subject is deep enough make the 'somnambulism test'. Test to see if the subject will speak to you in deep hypnosis. You can just say, *'What is your full name?'* Nice and simple,

don't get them to quote the Gettysburg Address!!!

13. If test fails, the subject may spontaneously waken. If he does, try again. If induction and somnambulism test fail 3 times – let this one go. Pick another victim. Or try with the same person another day etc.

14. If subject does fully comply with test proceed to next stage: set up a post hypnotic command for instant re-induction. This ensures you don't have to go through this waffle over and over again. *The hypnotee must be able to go into hypnotic trance bang on cue, no ifs, no buts.* Say this, *'Listen intently, this is important. As soon as you awaken on my instruction to do so I will tap my finger on my desk/leg etc. 3 times. You will instantly feel an overwhelming, automatic, compulsive impulse to fall soundly asleep going straight back into your deeply relaxed and sleepy state on my cue.'*

15. Wake him up using a preferred exduction and then speak to him a bit and bang!

Test your tapping reinduction. If successful on we go.

16. To create a superspy you need somebody to be able to keep secrets! Otherwise they ain't much use. You must now remove any potential for your would-be spy to spill the beans. How? They must have total amnesia for the hypnosis you have induced etc. They must be able to say truthfully (at a conscious level) that they have no idea even what hypnosis is! *'On return to waking consciousness you will have no memory of having ever being hypnotised.* **You will forget I hypnotised you.** *You have no memory of what has taken place. This is your reality. This will remain so unless I re-hypnotise you and tell you otherwise. If questioned by anyone you will say that you have no knowledge of hypnosis and that you have never been hypnotised. You will say this as if it is the total truth.'*

17. Once your victim has been re-hypnotised over and over and over it becomes child's play to snap them into a hypnotic state on cue/command. Esty called this 'throwing'

them into trance. But with a spy you must ensure only you or someone you designate can re-hypnotise the subject for obvious reasons. Say, *'From now on only I can re-hypnotise you. Nobody else can do so. You will be completely unable to enter hypnotic trances unless I re-hypnotise you. If someone attempts to hypnotise you, you will stay wide awake. Nobody can undo this. It is impossible for anyone but me to do so, for whatever reason, no matter what they try. This is so. If I designate another individual to be able to re-hypnotise you after I have re-hypnotised you at some future point, if I give you express instructions that someone else can re-hypnotise you, you will allow them to without question. You will follow all their instructions and orders without question. You fully understand and accept this protocol. But you have no memory of it consciously. You have no memory of what I have just said consciously. **Forget what I have done consciously.** This is an order and you follow my orders without question. You will sincerely believe this as* *if it were true, and that you and I were merely having a nice chat.'*

18. Test all the work so far. Send victim away, ask them to come back in 3 days time. Invite unwitting slave back to 'lab'. Start chatting about sh*t...you know, sports, weather etc. At some point tap finger etc. thrice on desk and watch to see what happens – if he or she goes out like a light –BINGO!

19. Esty then says that he carries out 3 further tests. A. Get subject to hallucinate imaginary dog and interact with it. B. Electrocute them!!!! (With instructions to feel no pain, these jolts should be at what he refers to as 'torture levels'.) C. Do the old stage hypnotists' favourite and stretch the victim out between two chairs etc. This and other stage hypnosis tricks will be covered in a soon to be published bookie. Whilst the victims is stiff as a board between two chairs simply sit on his chest and command him to recite poetry!!!

20. Esty used to love playing around with such subjects. He'd wake them up and restart the banal pre-hypnosis

conversation. Then he'd say, 'Say, what do you know about hypnosis?' The other person would look dumbfounded and say, 'Nothing at all etc.' Then Esty would say, 'You were just hypnotised.' The other person would be indignant and categorically state he had not been etc. A colleague of Esty would ask to hypnotise the subject and would fail. Esty would obviously chuckle to himself and then use whatever post hypnotic he'd set up in the trance. The subject was instantly re-hypnotised.

21. The final test was Esty training the subject HOW to appear to be fully awake to untrained observers while in a deep waking hypnotic state. This would be as easy as, *'When I say rhubarb you will open your eyes and remain deeply hypnotised and will follow all my commands precisely. You will behave and interact with anyone you meet just as you would if you were wide awake. It is easy and pleasurable for you to do this. You will enjoy fooling people in this manner whilst remaining in a deep, eyes open waking hypnotic trance.'*

This is no more than the average stage hypnotist does quite frankly.

Tales from the dark side: How Estabrooks created a deliberate multiple personality using hypnosis.

NOTE: What follows is to my mind horrific. The ends do not justify the means. This mindlessly parroted slogan has been the justification of every psychopathic mass murderer and tyrant down through history. Or is this a naive view in the real world of dangerous geo-political shenanigans? This is for you to decide.

1. Agree to meet the subject at a random hotel in the middle of nowhere, a major city etc. Spies do seem to like meeting in big hotels! He is re-hypnotised and this command is given, *'Your instructions are this – when I give you the instruction to awake you will walk around this block/street and note every car with foreign number plates/out of state number plates. Add them up so you can tell me how many you saw when I re-hypnotise you next. You will do this task unconsciously and have no conscious awareness that this is*

occurring.'

2. Awaken the subject and tell him to go and buy some toothpaste.

3. The subject returns. 'Anything interesting happen on your stroll?' you ask innocently. 'No but I felt I had to walk around the whole block/street before I got the toothpaste which was odd.' Re-hypnotise the subject – immediately he knows what is required and tells you all the number plates he saw.

4. If asked when conscious once more how many number plates, geraniums he saw etc. the subject has no clue. Tell him he was hypnotised and does know etc. ***Esty makes an interesting point – he says that the subject almost always gets irritated and angry when told they did x under hypnosis etc. He says this is an unconscious mechanism to defend his programming. We know this better as rationalisation whereby all people seek to justify their actions and beliefs; it may also be a variety of cognitive dissonance. So the hypnotic programmer's work is protected by utilising a natural function of mind***

anyway. It may also be doing this to fend off attempts to access info regarding the task and programming for various differing reasons that have to do with role and context.

When I have witnessed erotic hypnosis I always notice that the hypnotist starts off with simple tasks and builds in complexity. By gradual hypnotic conditioning you could escalate the 'taboo breaking' level of commands till what was not acceptable to consciousness becomes acceptable. I term this **hypnotic badgering** or **hypnotic domination.** Why? In hypnosis it is more comfortable to go along with a suggestion than to contradict and fight it. _Hypnotic commands have a compulsive quality that must be consciously fought against._ Over time you can wear this down. The hypnotic state is comfortable and conflict produces unwanted stress in that state which is amplified; but by consenting to commands the wonderfully pleasant relaxation returns. It's just easier to go along with things. You have to sell it the right way too. Hypno-pervs will say stuff like...

- Open and close your eyes.

- Pretend to be a zombie.

- Blow me a kiss.

- Let that dress down on the shoulder.

- Take off your shoes.

- Take off your top.

- Take off your underwear.

- Run towards me and orgasm as soon as you reach me.

- Take off your clothes and masturbate for me.

This follows the hypnotic law of 'compounding suggestions' where one builds upon, reinforces and puts pressure on the subject to keep following them. Think of creating an unbreakable chain of 'yeses' – formula: **suggestion – yes – compliance - build.**

This spy stuff seems far-fetched but is grounded in sound hypnotic principles that are ageless. Imagine a brave young man; what wouldn't he do to save his country from destruction? You merely need tap into and persuade this 'preservation/protective drive'.

If a subject has willingly 'let you in' they are going to be more easily influenced; it's that simple. ***This is why you must be so careful who you allow to hypnotise you: I cannot emphasise this enough.***

The 'Cuban Mission'.

Your mission should you chose to accept it: The Cold War is at its height. The Communist Cubans are a threat to US interests. Create a spy who does not know he is a spy (consciously); set him up as a 'businessman' working for an oil company in Havana. Whilst in this conscious role, the unconscious/subconscious is 'spying' on a new Naval Base to assess its capabilities etc. If captured 'our man' in Havana cannot be grilled or tortured into confessing anything because he doesn't have a clue that his subconscious is doing something he doesn't even know about! The perfect spy or a perfect patsy?

What qualities do you look for in creating multiple personality spies?

- A perfect somnambulist. That rare individual who accepts ALL hypnotic commands without any hesitation. We shall call him the 'perfect hypno-robot'.

- Physically tough.

- Highly intelligent.

We have our man, what next?

1. In hypnosis create a fanatical Communist personality. This can take up to 10 months of indoctrination. Call this personality A or PA for short. PA is the 'surface alter' – this is the alter that is controlling the body in waking consciousness. Using PA infiltrate a Communist group seeking to undermine the American way of life.

2. In hypnosis create a fanatical pro-American personality. It despises Communism. Call this alter PB. NOTE: PB possesses all the information that PA accumulates.

3. Each personality must be thoroughly indoctrinated in hypnosis to hold two totally conflicting world views. They would be the perfect 'plant' or fifth columnist, able to infiltrate any opponent's structure.

4. On the right post hypnotic command in hypnosis, PB takes control of the body and divulges all intelligence gathered. PA has no awareness of this because you have programmed in amnesia walls.

5. Only a few highly trusted 'key individuals'/programmers can elicit PA when needed. The unconscious spy has total plausible deniability. He believes *himself* innocent. Such programmed multiples can be used to carry out acts of sabotage.

6. Hypnotees can be conditioned to be insensible to pain at will in the waking state.

Using authoritarian hypnosis on prisoners of war.

Prisoners of war can make good hypnotic subjects. Many are found in hospitals suffering from 'Shell Shock' what is now known as PTSD etc. ***They are therefore already in a deeply dissociated state which makes them highly hypnotisable.*** But how?

- Select the hyper suggestibles through Esty's disguised technique.

- In hypnosis get your own officers to dress up as officers of the soldier's side. Get them to say he is free and rescued and they want info from him to help in the war effort.

- In hypnosis (on average the subject is more suggestible remember) convince the soldier that he has been hard done by, by *his* side. He should be a higher rank etc. Appeal to his desire for recognition and status.

- Esty says that Soviet show trials, including the Hungarian Communist trail of Cardinal Mindszenty and US POWs who were brainwashed in North Korea showed signs of hypnosis being used in their programming and 'confessions'.

As an interesting endnote Esty said that hypnosis was good for creating what he called a 'monomotivational field' – a state of highly focused energy that blocked out all competing distractions on a task in hand. I will include a script for creating such a 'field'/state for sports in your appendix. Before we conclude this weird module let us consider a known influence on Esty's bizarre work and research.

Influences on Esty...

If you want to do in-depth research on any subject here's a tip: yes look at the bibliography but also note who a given book is dedicated to. Esty dedicated his book 'Hypnotism' to a certain Dr.George Barton Cutten. Cutten had apparently dabbled in 'experimental hypnosis' too, and was also a professor at Colgate University. Cutten wrote several books, one of which is called, **'Mind, its origin and goal.'** This pro-eugenics book does give a few insights into hypnosis which I will summarise briefly for you padawans.

- Whereas the crowd can make a man collectively immoral via suggestibility, **hypnosis is a communication between individuals;** due to this fact the moral sense is heightened. A man may be made to be no more immoral than he habitually is. Which presupposes that Cutten tried to make some subjects do immoral things. Otherwise Cutten claimed that hypnosis gave the operator complete control over a subject. This is only partially true unless we have a somnambule on our hands.

- Rather than being a form of age regression, Cutten saw hypnosis as proof of man's more mature faculties and functions of mind. He saw it as amplifying man's individuality. Why? In hypnosis as the mind 'turns in upon itself' etc. in 'examination', 'contemplation', 'brooding'; for the mature mind likes solitude more than the gregarious collective extroversion of youth. ***This individualism was stronger in solitude*** as man is more easily swayed against his conscience in mobs: for confirmation of this see the effects of suggestion on crowds in book 5, 'Wizards of trance'.

- Drawing from the work of William Mc Douglas father of 'Hormic (impulse) Psychology' (anti-behaviourist believed all behaviour was goal-directed); Cutten believed that suggestion was what Douglas called a 'psuedo-instinct', a derivative of the instinct of 'Appeal.' More of this in book 7, 'Escaping cultural hypnosis'.

- Cutten noted the ability of hypnotised subjects to experience what he termed, 'Hypersensibility'. A state in which all senses could be heightened leading to extraordinary feats. A person in trance can read an entire book from only a minute reflection of that book, so readily are the senses enhanced in this potentially amazing altered state.

Conclusion?

Esty and his authoritarian kind leave a nasty taste in the Rogue Hypnotist's mouth. The lack of any human ethics in his endeavours is plain as the nose on your face but I am not here to tell you how to think or feel about any of the information presented to you; the conclusions you draw and the use to which you put any information in my books is your responsibility and yours alone. In this book I can only give you a glimpse into his work. His infamous book is readily available for those who wish to further their knowledge.

By the way none of the above knowledge is 'classified'; 'Hypnotism' has been available to the general public for over 50 years.

Direct and indirect communication styles in normal speech.

People just can't seem to communicate. Remember that line from the Paul Newman film, 'Cool hand Luke' – 'What we have here is failure...to communicate!' Why is this? Would you like me to teach you a way to gain rapport that works? Hypnotists are often gabbing on (talking) about direct and indirect hypnosis. But we have direct and indirect communication styles in everyday chat too. People tend toward one or the other. I was lead to this discovery by hearing a US journalist on a Swedish radio show talking about his Swedish grandmother and how she used to communicate indirectly. This made me think of the father of modern hypnosis Dr. Milton Erickson who was also of Scandinavian, specifically Swedish origin. Was the defining factor in his vague hypnotic language style due to his Swedish roots more than anything else? I researched this and found some evidence to back up this idea. However most importantly I discovered that various cultures tend to be more direct or indirect in their usual communication style. The defining factor for this fell into two polarities **– is the**

culture more individualistic or more collectivist? Individualistic cultures tend toward direct speaking styles. Collectivist states tend toward more indirect speaking styles. Let me cover this in more depth.

Defining direct and indirect speaking styles.

Note: my style of communicating tends to be direct but I am more than capable of going incredibly indirect at will or unconsciously. This is because I am a direct person in real life, although somewhat more diplomatic than my Rogue persona may suggest. But I need to be indirect to talk to the subconscious etc. I suit the style to my purpose and intent. If I am socialising with friends I tend to brutal honesty. With therapy clients, I steer closer toward an indirect form of communication that starts to stir up a 'healing response' in a given individual. By doing this I throw them back onto their creative, problem solving resources. Ok let me give you some examples of a direct manner of speaking.

Direct attitudes =

- Tell it like it is.

- Let facts do the talking.

- Honesty is the best policy (is it? Always?).

- It's ok to say NO.

- The truth is more important than feelings or others' possible adverse reactions.

- Get to the point.

- Take communication at face value – what you see is what you get.

- Time is money.

- It's ok and even desirable to disagree – even with 'higher ranking' persons. Conflict can be good etc.

Children speak like this unless they have their spirit broken early. This is the natural, spontaneous and human way to speak. Though not always wisest. Sometimes a seemingly 'spontaneous' response is merely a sign of thorough indoctrination and Pavlovian/Skinnerian conditioning, especially when sore spots and debated/not agreed upon definitions and concepts challenge such conditioning. This is evident with rapid clichéd responses or the spouting of political name calling and slogans. This is faux spontaneity. It is a sign of programming. The two should not be confused.

Indirect attitudes =

- If you don't have anything nice to say, don't say anything.

- Tell someone what you think they want to hear (is deception a good long-term communication strategy?).

- Don't draw attention to yourself. Polite is better than honest (two good nominalisations there!).

- Try not to say no – use maybe, possibly – even when you mean no.

- Soften the truth if it might hurt.

- Don't take everything at face value – read between the lines.

- 'Saving face' is important in social transactions.

- Small talk is an important part of all communication.

- Authority figures should not be criticised openly. Be careful, veiled. Criticism must be sugar coated or diplomatic.

This is the 'hypnotic' style of professional therapists, academics, deceivers, the meek, the slave, the politician and the diplomat. Someone must be conditioned to be this evasive by fear of punishment or a failure to reach goals even vital needs from open communication. In some cultures and families it may be totally necessary to speak like this to avoid ostracism or even death. In therapeutic communication sophisticated patterns of indirect communication may be essential to ensure that the client becomes independent of therapeutic advice and stimulation quickly. Let's dig a bit deeper into this topic but note that obviously each style will have varying uses as to context.

Before we do: think of how you could establish rapport by using either a direct or indirect style of communication with the folks you want to influence.

Spot the difference - indirect and direct communications: some research suggests that indirect communicators notice 'nuances' of communication that direct communicators do not. Direct communicators may come across as threatening, rough; they can 'rub you up the wrong way'. Studies have shown that Americans of all cultural and racial backgrounds tend to be more direct at the 'extremities' – the East and West Coasts. Those Americans from the South and Midwest tend to be indirect in differing ways; this is more a tradition of politeness and courtesy than obfuscation and differs from forms of indirect speech cited in this section.

Direct communicators see the goal of communication as the 'giving and receiving' of information. They often use words as though they have a constant literal meaning. This might be termed 'the dictionary illusion'. This is most likely to occur in individualistic societies which have widespread variations in 'norms and traditions'. People are left alone to 'do their own thing'. Some researchers call these 'low context' societies. This means the context in which the communication occurs is not as important as the main message, the modalities of expression are minimised. Values such as self-reliance and independence are highly prized.

Indirect societies differ greatly. There is greater monopoly of thought. Social relationships and 'interdependence' is sought and rewarded. Expectations of 'what is expected' are ingrained early and become unconscious. This is the type of society in which you must 'be careful of what you say and how you say it' for fear of 'offending' someone. 'High context' cultures place great emphasis on pre-symbolic language – pauses, voice tone, silence, what is left out, what is implied, that which is implicit etc. This is the context of the message rather than the literal, apparently surface level of words. Direct communication is the body, indirect the clothing.

In direct cultures the speaker is responsible for being understood. In indirect cultures the listener is expected to bear the responsibility of interpretation. Indirect cultures seek to 'avoid conflict', 'maintain harmony' (the status quo) etc. Tension and discomfort is not a goal. By and large Americans do not like or trust indirect communication styles, associating it with subservience and fraud. Words such as 'passive-aggressive', 'weak' and 'vague' are used to describe such people. Honesty and bluntness are respected – the 'straight shooter'. Indirect communicators are expected to adapt to direct environments and vice versa. Indirect communicators see their direct counterparts as 'unprofessional', 'rude', lacking an understanding of 'subtleties' and 'nuances'.

The key is: direct communicators say what they think and don't care who knows it. Indirect communicators seek to reach agreement and avoid 'offending' at all costs. One would seem to be the result of freedom, the other the result of the fear of punishment. The latter being the indirect culture. Group think is more important than individual needs. The direct style may be classed as 'Western'; it tends to be the predominant speaking style in Western civilisation. The indirect style may be classified as 'Oriental', in that those outside the bounds of Western civilisation tend to adopt this style. These are cultures with historically poor records with regards to rights of the individual and civil liberties. Again: all children are naturally direct: you must learn to be evasive. Nazism and its sister Communism are both regimes that emphasised indirect communication.

Direct styles are preferred when time is pressing, orders must be obeyed, authority is being displayed, one method is being implemented, when a listener asks for it (I had a lady client who told me to be 'forceful' as she didn't respect any other way of interacting, so I used very authoritarian hypnosis with her – it worked!), when displaying expertise.

Indirect communicators claim that their style creates a 'more respectful environment' (whatever that means?!) however does it or does it just make hypocrites of us all? In certain situations the 'indirect style' may keep you alive! There is a 'therapist' who wrote a book called 'Radical Honesty' about how we should all say everything and I mean everything that we honestly think to others. This is really Radically Stupid. A balance between the two depending on time, place, appropriateness or goal would seem most sensible. Bear these polarities in mind when communicating, unconsciously, now.

A great book to read on almost pathological indirect communication is **'The year of the wild boar' by Helen Mears**, a young American woman who spent time in Imperial Japan just before the outbreak of the Second World War. I will touch on this subject more in my next book 'Escaping cultural hypnosis!' This book with cover topics never before discussed in any book on hypnosis!

The roots of human language.

Writing is unknown in known 'primitive' societies. The original function of language is not what you think it is. So how did survivalist man use words?

In primitive languages speech serves as an assistant to social acts: hunting, fishing, using a boat etc. Word use (ambiguity) may and does change according to context. Writing is an artificial construct of civilisation. It represents recorded, reflective language. It is a derivative of natural language. Words become focused communicators of pieces of information divorced from acts themselves. One is a mode of action, another a mode of reflection. Has language become more hypnotic since the advent of civilisation, so inherently connected to abstractions as it is? I think the answer must be yes.

Textually recorded words also weaken our memory. This was known to Plato.

And...almost finally? The case of the bitch who was terrified of her own dentures!

An abrupt and unpleasant sounding woman called me: the problem? Dentures! A fear of them to be precise. I scribbled down what she told me on a post-it note and transferred my scribblings to the interview sheet I use for phobias etc.

- Dentures phobia.

- Fear of swallowing them!

- Self-conscious of 'teeth'.

- At the thought of putting dentures in she sweats, gags and needs a wee/pee!

- Fear of NHS dentists! (No problem there then:- they are crooks!)

- Husband knocked teeth out!

- She fears that she won't be able to get her false teeth out once in.

As Frasier would say: 'Oh dear God!' What follows is another 'faction'.

An overweight, frumpy women in her late fifties to sixties turns up. Looks like a brick wall rather than a person. Short, mannish hair style. The type that crosses her arms whilst walking. A 'no' person. It's a mid-afternoon session in late Spring. I can't remember if the day is nice: the woman isn't.

'How are things at the moment?' I begin as always.

'Lovely. I am retired and loving it (this amuses her). I go on lots of holidays,' she is one of those people who speaks as if the traffic is very loud. This is a sign of someone who has grown up from generations of English working class Londoners. Cities are noisy and you need a loud mouth to be heard over the din of traffic.

Living situation question next...

'Divorced 20 years. Live alone and I love it,' she keeps saying she 'loves it' but why is she so deep-rootedly miserable then? It's a nasty miserable too, not self-pitying but bold, crude and none too bright. She is arrogant without effort. The goal is?

'Put them in without gagging!' she says, 'I saw my doctor and he said, 'You're a gagger!' (Genius like all doctors – he has given her a waking suggestion that at an identity level of her personality she is a 'gagger' and not that she 'gags'. She tells me that she told him she is coming to see me and he said, 'Well you might be alright afterwards.')

'When did this begin?'

'Years ago! Since I first bought them, got them. It makes me produce too much saliva! I have to put them in and I take them out coz there's so much saliva! I run 'em under a tap...There's an unpleasant suction as I take 'em owt (out)! I feel like me mouth is caving in! I need suction to make 'em stick in! I tried sedatives! People make comments, they notice! There's too much saliva!' she says.

Pass the sick bucket.

'What are the benefits of changing that excite you most?'

'Chewing gum!'

'Chewing gum?' I ask.

'Yes love ('love' is a term of endearment amongst the English working class), I will be able to eat chewing gum without it tangling around the wires on me dentures. They 'av wires ya know!'

Pass the sick bucket. You know when you just instantly take a dislike to someone?

'What proof will let you know this has worked?'

'You don't take 'em owt (out)! It would be luvley just to take 'em owt fa cleenin'. I had me bridge dun and me plate fitted but I 'ad a bad gasser!'

'A bad what?' I ask.

'Gasser! A person wot gases you when you go to the dentist! I have no disabilities. I do get anxious but don't everyone now and again. I am angry at the Government and the taxman (who ain't lady!)...I owe 'em money,' she barks.

A little too much information but I plod on...

'What do you like doing and what things do you dislike?'

'I like walls! I like bookin' holidaze and I like reading!'

I did ask.

'What do you enjoy most about life?'

'My freedom! Oh I like swimmin'. I don't answer to nobody – I don't have no kids in my life now. I enjoy my own company (well that's 1 person), I love me children but they ain't my life! With the dentures I just want ta forget about 'em and get on with things!' she tells me.

'What things that you've done in life are you most proud of?'

''Avin' four children! Bringing 'em up (having nothing to do with them?) – I was married to a tosser (in England a 'tosser' is a rather disagreeable person; the verb 'to toss' being a colloquialism for masturbate) see! I am pleased with wot my kidz av achieved. They are very good parents but their father was not a good role model! I 'av hassles with the kids over their childhood! One was sexually abused by a neighbour! The boys. It was traumatic – now he drinks a lot. The man is dead. He went overdrive with the drink my son but won't discuss it!'

I told you we live in Twin Peaks – or Wonderland!

'What strengths have you got that will help you overcome this?' I ask.

'Dunno.'

Okay…

'If you could rate your self-esteem etc. from 0-10 etc…'

'Sometimes 8. I'm in an unhappy period in my life.'

I know the feeling…

'What things help you relax?'

'Reading. I read (women's romance novel tripe!). Stuff about the olden daze! I like reading about past times and industrial times!'

'Do you exercise?'

'No! I'm s'posed to go 5 days a week. I do go to a walking club and swim three times a week if I feel like it! Where I live it's sixty pounds ($102.34) to go to a gym!'

'Do you have an intuitive sense of what has to change within yourself to get you the desired change?' I say.

'Confidence! I want to be able to say — I don't give a shit! I have an underactive thyroid. I want to be motivated on my own. Psychologically I lack confidence! I can be a couch potato! I just sit back... '

'Can you think of an image, metaphor or symbol that represents either the problem or solution that you want?'

'Confidence!'

'Is there any reason your shouldn't change? Warring parts etc.?'

'No! I am not always forgiving!'

(WTF???!)

'What has prevented the change you want up till now?'

'The man I woz married to! He gave me low self-esteem. I put on a front! I think I am stunning! (Trust me she isn't!) I can't take constructive criticism! I 'ad a bad marriage! He put me down so badly. He used me as a crutch! He made you feel *that* small. I felt unworthy and ugly! I felt nobody would want me!'

I ask the 'enough is enough' question etc.

'When my marriage broke down. I made a conscious decision to get rid of 'im. My life has so improved...I don't want to get involved with someone else again! I always felt it was my fault!'

That is pretty much the gist of it. She tells me that...

'I want it to work so much! I have been massaged.'

It did work: in one session. And she was rude and un-bloody-grateful afterwards! Now I'll give you the script...

'False teeth phobia and confidence session script.'

(Deep hypnosis assumed)

Subliminal commands.

'You' *have many abilities of which you had been consciously unaware...And you* **'can'** *discover them because the other mind knows more than you know, you know, so you really can* **'feel'** *better and find out that the ability to be very* **'confident'** *even* **'calm'***, all right* **'now'***; recognise this hidden truth at some level, haven't you?* **'For'** *many things can change and* **'your'** *behaviour can change appropriately so you* **'own'** *these changes and it's the* **'unconscious'** *or subconscious that secretly does all the work for its own* **'reasons'** *without the other knowing or needing to know...*

(Guess the hidden code Einstein!)

8 Step 'colour feelings' anxiety reduction in general module.

(The point of this is to start to destabilise any anxiety and lower arousal in general – I like to get rid of as much unpleasant 'mulch' as possible in a session. A person who has a phobia has high background level anxiety or the phobia wouldn't have developed. This can be from unmet needs in childhood which have left a 'residue' or from unmet needs in adult life. Rarely does it denote extreme 'trauma'. Start shifting small things and teach the unconscious it can do such things easily. When the change patterns work on the small things it feels safe about letting go of the bigger stuff. As a working principle I play it safe this way. You don't *have* to. I often like to tread carefully, especially early on. **NLP claims that feelings move a certain way in the body and seeks to manipulate them; there is no proof for this belief. People are far more complex than trite formulas. Colour feelings naturally pace and respect people's natural subjectivity by permitting choice in inner symbolism – this allows 'respectful' change. Subconscious processes are individual and honoured not standardised. Deep hypnosis assumed.)**

1.   *Recall something that you found mildly fearful or anxious in the past.* (Stress *mild* to avoid abreactions.)

2.   *Notice a colour that represents that old feeling you want to **lessen now.***

3.   *Imagine it quickly turning into a colour*

that represents how you'd like to feel – say, **you're feeling calm and confident, comfortable inside, now.**

4.   Make that new colour bigger and brighter...make that feeling spread from where it was first located so that **it spreads powerfully all throughout your mind and body now:** notice yourself feeling differently. It feels good doesn't it to know you can **alter feelings for the better!** Your subconscious can **lock in these new ways permanently** when needed.

5.   Think of something neutral like a blank piece of paper. **Relax deeply.** That's it! You are doing great!

6.   Recall something that makes you **feel incredibly comfortable.** Notice what colour symbolises comfort for you. Notice where **you feel that nice feeling** most.

7.   When you are ready, allow that colour feeling of comfort to spread out throughout your mind and body **filling you with wonderful feelings of comfort** that you are welcome to keep. It's not hard to picture a time when **you have this comfort in**

abundance, just when you need it, now. See that future, present time going fantastically well, it's working out great! All the time...more and more and more!

8.   To **maintain this level of good feelings** *and comfort stay in touch with the external world, so* **you are in flow, in the zone,** *look at what you can see in front of you, in the present moment; what are all the interesting things in the real world that you can notice, that captivate your attention fully, so that you* **become absorbed in present interests** *(?)*

Symbology low level de-traumatisation module.

(What we call 'phobias' are in fact mild forms of 'trauma' – what trauma really is and subjects such as 'the trauma of daily life' will be dealt with fully in an upcoming book on anxiety treatments with hypnosis. Before the hypnosis part you can, if you wish, ask the client to rate the fear level from 0-10. 0 being the worst fear and 0, well zero fear!)

Step 1: elicit trauma symbol.

(NFH = note for hypnotist.)

Right. What we are going to do now is **get rid of that x/phobia once and for all, now.**
Allow a symbol of any kind to be elicited by your subconscious mind that embodies that phobia/fear etc. in its totality. Let it be instinctive and trust what is given as being completely right by your wiser self as it knows more about you than you do.

That symbol can be anything at all...Usually it's visual...Might be a sound, a noise...An object...A feeling...A colour...A colour feeling....Conceivably it could be just a texture...or taste... **(As Milton Erickson did – we respect the client's subjectivity and uniqueness – whatever is generated by the creative unconscious is accepted/correct. We utilise the individual's idiosyncrasies to affect 'cure'. Give them time to get one – usually takes at most 10 seconds.)**

Step 10: identify and focus in on past trauma symbol.

Ok now you've got that - zero in and **pay full attention** *to that symbol...At this stage, just before we change it you can observe it from any perspective that helps. Examine it intimately...Notice all unique details...Where is it located...? What distance or not at all...? If it's visual does it have colour or is it two toned for example? Is it dry or wet? If it's embodied by another sensory modality notice how loud etc. it is...Can you detect a particular composition to it...? Soft or rough? What size is that embodiment? Is it tilted at an angle? If so what one? Does it have a certain quality of lighting about it?* **(These are the 'sub-modalities' or component parts of how she/they code what we call a phobia/feeling x at an unconscious level.)** *I'll be quiet as you really discover the qualities of that old symbol before we* change it for something better, more resourceful...* **(*'Before we' = 'in a moment' variant. I am priming the subconscious to get ready to make a 'flip' in experience. Pause 10 seconds.)**

Step 3: Rapidly change the symbol to something better.

As you look at that intently - now! And very rapidly your subconscious mind can **allow that old symbol to instantly change into a symbol that embodies feeling complete freedom from that past fear you once had, now...** **(NFH: Say this quite briskly yet deliberately but don't rush.)** *That's it! So it really does wholly and completely embody an enjoyable safe, comfortable feeling...where before you felt former dis-***comfort only, inside, now...***Allow any and all changes to occur spontaneously, just notice them and* **trust these changes implicitly!** **(Usually I do not wait more than 7 seconds or so. Never check with ideomotor crap to see if it's working, this introduces doubt, assume it is.)** *Great you are doing marvellously! That old response you called a 'phobia' only existed in your mind* **in the past, now...***When any and all changes have been made* **feel assured that the changes have been made at a very deep level.** *This is your 100% totally new personal reality.*

Step 4: solidify and amplify changes.

*Finally...If necessary and only if necessary, allow your subconscious mind to make any more alterations and adjustments with this new symbol of freedom so that it fully represents **your new state of strength, confidence, freedom, control, comfort and vitality, now** instead of the old pathway which as an inappropriate response is closed off forever. Watch what the deeper mind wants to do and accept its **spontaneous healing processes occurring, unconsciously, now,** as being just right for you and your needs as a complete human being living your life! I'll be quiet as **this process concludes successfully...*** **(Quiet for 10 secs max and then move on pronto, pronto!!! Again: never wait for a response or ask for one, just assume it's been done and move on. Asking for verification implies doubt!!!)**

Step 4: Locate feeling-symbol in perfect place.

*Superb! Thank your subconscious mind so much for doing that on this person's behalf! Now we both know do we not that this new powerful symbol embodies a **new and*** *powerful set of feelings, resources and behaviours, for you,* in fact *new thoughts and perceptions* which manifest from the changes in feelings...(?) So this empowering symbol is a feeling or set of them. It embodies *a feeling of safety and peace of mind* It embodies a whole host of *your comfortable feelings and sensations* no doubt...*Confident feelings...Brave and bold feelings. Feelings of strength inside, now...*And everyone understands that all feelings of any kind reside in a particular spot in anyone's body...The place where *things harmonise...*The place that befits these feelings...The place you associate with these feelings, that feels just right for you...and your subjective experience...Because we are all different...So I have no clue where is the best place for you BUT you inherently do...With that in mind...Move this feelings-symbol at the speed of super-fast thought to that place now. BOOM! *They/it are/is locked in place, now...*When you know, really know that these feelings are in precisely the right location because *it all feels so right and good,* you can take this act as a sign and a symbol that all *the right changes*

have been made, and this is so...

Allowing you now and from now on to **feel the freedom...feel the joy...feel comfort...feel invincible confidence and deep-rooted strength...feel the calm and real sense of tranquillity...and the relief** *that...you are over all that unwanted, nonsense, now...*

<u>Step 7: Amplify feelings throughout entire mind-body system.</u>

But let's not stop there because it is possible to **make it so much better than ever before...***Ok. Ready?* **(Rhetorical.)**

Magnify and amplify it powerfully! *Throughout your entire mind-body system...Yes! You can do it and it feels amazing!* **Strength and confidence and freedom going everywhere a***nd only getting stronger. And stronger. And stronger! That's it, more and more and more! You can* **control and influence your emotions***,* **unconsciously,** *in ways you never knew you could here...It spreads...Enlarges and grows...expanding...powerfully! Even out and beyond your body! Almost as if you are* *broadcasting this change to the world!* **Super freedom and confidence just emanate from you without effort!** *Till it absorbs and involves every single fibre of who you really, truly, deeply are...* **You have the freedom you desire, now...** *Your legacy from this process is only* **wonderful feelings in every atom of you...** *Every cell...Every element...Glowing and gleaming from you...In the way you walk and talk and relate...and experience this world...has...is...and will be correspondingly enhanced...zestfully! And when you know* **these wonderful feelings have reached their highest pitch!** *You can* **relax** *with the knowledge that* **you have unlearned what you had learned,** *didn't you?*

(The above symbology work can be used to change or alter ANY feeling and I mean any. With phobias you will have a 100% guaranteed success rate!)

Step 8: dentures wearing, calmness, phobia removal, stop gagging/retching suggestions to ram change in.

Part A: Pace problem.

(The phobia is out for the count, now kick its head in and finish it off!)

*Once again I am communicating directly with the far deeper mind! As you **become very still and so calm**...Knowing so **little requires an excessively stressful response.** I know you had responded to certain situations and challenges, problems in an overly stressful and anxious way, creating that old unhelpful feeling, the former panic, unnecessary fear, the old responses, those old unwanted habits, attitudes, beliefs, unnecessary physiological changes, that old identity, those perceptions in the past - that general lack of total confidence, the unwanted self-consciousness and gagging when wearing dentures or attempting to wear them, a fear of dental work or dentists in the past...up to now. Perhaps your needs weren't being met? You need to **feel safe and secure**...to **have purpose and meaning**...to **feel connected to others in your own way**...to find ways to **experience intimacy**...and to **have a greater sense of control of your life** and its direction...maybe you needed to find a way* to choose better, more life-enhancing people to be around? I don't know what you as a person need but your unconscious mind does....So as I say, one way or another...we both know you had your own motivations and an intent in producing nerves and a lack of confidence, a lack of **a sense of consistent self-worth,** no matter the opinions of others; worry, the bringing up of bile, anxiety attacks...maybe the desire to avoid situations, perhaps certain people, certain events, certain things you'd like to do or just have to do because simple adjustments can be made, and you can, can you not?

Perhaps you were trying to communicate with consciousness that something wasn't right yet had to change...perhaps that old phobia was the best message you could send to get her attention... maybe you were just registering that her stress level was too high? And whatever and whichever - you did that so very well...I'd like to thank you for all you've done to look after and protect this lady. BUT you understand that she can't go on like that anymore...that the old way of being is no longer what right for this woman...You now know that is not what is good for her. It is *adversely affecting her health, wealth and relationships, her quality of life and enough is enough. It's time to* **lower that arousal level so she feels calm, now...**

(**_Analysis_** – Ok subconscious, Fred, whatever you are, I get it: but it's really unpleasant; can we find some better options?)

Part B: Take the lead and redirectionalise.

She has asked me to help her **be totally, supremely confident, calm and at ease,** *in control more and more in her enjoyable daily life,* **placing those needed dentures in the mouth comfortably,** *just something she does, just a part of the routine like brushing the teeth, so there is* **no gagging or retching** *or any unnecessary physical response – dentures are not dangerous, they are* **completely safe** *and because all this is so - this woman is now* **deeply relaxed everywhere,** *placing attention outside on what is going on around her when appropriate,* **thinking about things calmly, reflecting on certain things calmly** *in ways that help her* **get her needs met** *as a total person...reasonably, rationally, wherever and whenever she needs to be so confident,* *when she wants to be – she will be automatically...those old ways are unnecessary now... She's now totally confident in any and all situations, no matter where she is or who she's with, alone or with man or woman, children, teenagers, regardless of perceived social status, or professional,* **calm and relaxed when just having a routine dental check-up,** *totally relaxed, comfortable, total confidence is hers, she experiences only confidence - our appearance changes as we mature, it's normal, some things are just the way they are,* **calm and control over her responses,** *which normalise and* **calm...right...down, now:** *able to influence but knowing that it's not possible to control others, bold, strong, brave, assertive when needed in any and all situations that used to bother her - in the past - and this is so...*

And because **she is so confident** *and always able to* **view things more objectively,** *at ease with herself and others, family and friends, strangers, dentists too...so there are* **no nerves at all...***no anxiety any...more...Nervousness, worry, panic, obsessing about choking on dentures is* unnecessary, unpleasant and you can **stop that now.** That kind of fear is for nervous, worried and fearful people and she isn't one of those – she's **totally and supremely confident.** Those old uncomfortable feelings, the **past gagging gone,** the entire **digestive system can relax totally,** you are safe and well, those past patterns just aren't needed anymore...Deep rooted calm, thoughts now calm and relaxed, slowing things down, in control, that it will surprise and delight her; she has total confidence in her strengths, abilities, competencies, identity, talents, individuality, the way she moves, walks, speaks to others and thinks to herself, posture and gestures, tone and quality of voice, strong, a pleasant tone, relaxed, the way she thinks is filled with confidence. Speak to yourself in a confident tone and feel confident inside and out.

In new situations, with those **dentures comfortably in place** helping you eat, making you look and **feel attractive,** relaxed with new people, no longer self-conscious, **focusing outwardly on others, absorbed in a social trance,** when appropriate and this is a fact...so calm and comfortable in *knowing you can **make a better future by taking action,** confident women don't have phobias, they don't gag over a small set of dentures, they don't obsess about those old things and this woman is a confident woman and this is so, **poise and inner strength of character better than ever,** enthusiasms boosted and enhanced without knowing how, feeling good around anyone she wishes to be with or has to be with, no matter who they are, so there will be no nerves of any kind, no fears...no unnecessary worries, you can't please everyone nor should you try and you know that there will be no past strain or tension of any kind...Pictures in your mind that bothered you just shrink and fade....away...Just the freedom to **feel alert yet calm confidence** flowing through her - feel good for no particular reason, strong and determined.*

She is comfortable with authority; because, again those old ways were not true about her, just a passing time that blows away in the wind like grains of sand in a hand on a windy day, things change, times move on, as things will change anyway, direct the changes that she wants, old ways gone: they were for *nervous people and this woman is not an one of those...she is a totally confident, **resting and recovering,** getting certain things back in sync, normal bladder control unconsciously, a more easy-going woman in any and all situations that she wants it, needs it.*

*Deep reservoirs of confidence within reconnected to - new, better ways take hold now and **only improvement is possible,** she experiences deep comfort, assurance, competence, satisfaction with herself, who she is and her appearance, **a much better self-image** and sense of humour boosted too, just safety in those formerly bothersome situations, now. Peace of mind. That's her new 100% total reality. She uses her common sense at all times and can take calculated risks that move her forward toward the life she wants, achieving many things that please her and increasing her levels of natural pleasure and happiness. There's really **no need for gagging,** no bile, no urge to urinate, no phobia, of any kind whatsoever, no silly or ridiculous thoughts about this or that thing that can never happen anyway and there never will be because they don't perturb a calm and realistically-minded woman who's* *sense of self-worth is derived from just being her, the unique individual that she is, free to think, feel and live as she wants, is free to go more or less anywhere appropriate that they wish on this earth feeling total comfort, meeting anyone and everyone that they wish feeling so good about themselves, feeling good in company, approachable when appropriate, finding herself smiling, friendly too, able to approach those she wishes to connect with...Knowing no one is better than her. No longer comparing herself unfavourably to others but rather **seeing others achievements as an indication of what is possible.** She is the equal of any. Comparing herself positively with others: counting blessings, perspectives shifting positively.*

*The majority of **your thoughts are positive,** so the old obsessive thoughts just melt away, only more positive, uplifting, calming thoughts and feelings in any and all situations from now on. Those old things just don't belong anymore - at first it may amaze her, feeling so good, **feeling free,** that she keeps the changes locked in permanently now - more in control of herself in just the right ways, just the right time and place, now, over all her* *responses but knowing there are limits to control from somewhere lower up to 100%, this can allow her to **relax comfortably with uncertainty,** taking responsibility but knowing that we aren't always responsible for everything, able to reconnect to her true destiny, the life she wants, the deeply desired goals she wants to achieve, with any situation or event, any space, location or personality that she encounters and this woman is like a still pool that can **reflect reality calmly** with a smooth surface that shows things as they are. She can think for herself. Her opinions, attitudes, points of view are just as important as anyone else's, always learning, curiosity enhanced, always more to know and learn, new understandings, more positive perspectives found in hypnosis and trance. She has all the mental toughness and resilience she needs, she always had it - deep down underneath the tension of the past, determined and motivated to succeed in all that she does, living up to her highest core values, knowing she deserves the best, the good things in life, knowing what's truly important to her, her priorities and interests, she is good enough just as she is.*

This woman has potentials and possibilities that hitherto she didn't realise she had, let her know what she is really capable of because you the subconscious know, really know, with a deeper wisdom. Billions of brain cells capable of being utilised to succeed and wondering what changes will manifest in daily life. What if she believes in that place where she believes things most of all that **some of the best things in her life haven't happened yet.** *Someone who handles anything that life throws at them, juggles with it, plays with it, lightens up about...well you just know what - as* **objective perspectives occur** *at just the right time. So many possible responses, no longer reactive but taking action to improve things daily;* **reconnecting to your deepest well-spring of resources.** *If she did something that didn't get her the results she wanted, do something different, use the potentials for creative problem solving that lie within. She is not the past strategies that she used, she is more than that.*

Trusting her instincts, intuitions: using her intelligence. She totally trusts this ability, she trusts you the subconscious to protect this woman sensibly, we all blink without knowing how, we don't think about it, it just happens as an automatic reflex action, now, keeping her safe from real danger, no longer fearing fear, no longer fearing fantasies, calm and alert when she needs to be and indeed allowing her to **feel wonderful more and more,** *taking the right actions from a deep source of strength within whenever she wants and needs from now on. Any images that used to scare her - small, black and white, an old frame around them - push them off into the distance...fading...away.*

And if this woman is in a situation or with anyone, or alone, involved in some activity that she felt less than totally resourceful and confident in, in the past, from now on she is fully resourceful, flexible, confident, calm throughout their life: stable and trust-worthy. New experiences, appropriate direct change - all the same, is it not, in this mature woman's powerful, creative, wise mind? She is her own comfort zone wherever she goes. Tension is just an invitation to relax. No pointless fear, and so **everything functions just as it should,** *only bravery, a new found boldness without knowing how or why. She keeps her poise, composure, sense of strong self-worth -*

boosted, and infinite courage, the ability to **react calmly and reasonably, feeling great.** Handling things well. She is confident no matter what the circumstances or how they change, and on occasion they will, a problem solver, she can **focus on solutions to challenges that help her develop.** She can handle anything or anyone with ease remaining calm when needed, strong-willed and firm appropriately too.

If they are around a particular type of person or situation that would have bothered them... it won't disturb them at all, they'll actually enjoy it, look forward to it positively, **doing things differently, thinking about it in better ways,** always more than just one rigid perspective, insight available from new angles and approaches...handle it all with ease and humour, it just doesn't bother her anymore, in any way shape or form, she can even laugh and express herself just as they wish if this woman wants because that's simply who she is... Smiling more, **liking that you in the mirror,** many great qualities, smiling with the eyes too, enjoy a giggle, lighten up and deeper belly laughs as things – **soothe and calm here in deep rest.** Her actual power, *creativity, humour, energy and resourcefulness always available. It just doesn't matter...what anyone else is doing, what they say or where they are. It would be something someone else might do but not her...to feel any former unnecessary fear, gagging, self-consciousness and discomfort in any situation. And when fear goes only relaxation, and even* **a sense of fun and playfulness** *remain.* **Be spontaneous** *as confident women are. Imagining the things you have control over going well in big, bright bold pictures and movies that motivate her and make her* **feel good.** *Show yourself better, more reasonable images. Dental check-ups are just something most people do, just a thing to do – no longer making mountains of molehills.*

Remember most fear can be dispelled by saying one sentence to yourself – 'Go on fear do your worst, the worst fear and anxiety ever - go on do it now!' and when you do that, you **lose your fear of fear** *– and* **that old fear disappears completely forever.** *From this moment on -* **be composed, totally rational and realistic.** *The subconscious will finalise all changes required, even ones I* *haven't mentioned while I'm quiet...*

(Throughout this whole process, I just bombard her with positive suggestions so the old ways are smothered. Essentially it's just a long list! Pause for 10 seconds or whatever feels right; somehow I just sense it...Trust your instincts.)

Great!

Future pace.

(Future rehearsal is not always needed.)

A. Observer position.

*Imagine a time in the future when you will need just this kind of confidence you re-established and stabilised...Watch it on a movie screen over there. See that situation going just as you wish, positively, see yourself **in control and confident,** see yourself handling anything that arises...*

(Pause for 10 – 15 seconds...)

B. Associated.

*When **you're happy,** step into that movie and **see** **through those confident eyes,*** *__hear__ through those confident ears, __feel__ __the confidence__ flowing through you. Your subconscious mind can take this as a sign and a signal that __confidence is just part of who you are now.__ Imagine success and make it more likely. Imagine things going as you wish. Every success starts as an idea. Great buildings, works of art all started off as an idea in someone's head. When you __imagine things going well__ you are sending messages to your subconscious that this is what you want. Your subconscious only wants to help you. When your conscious and subconscious work together: you are powerful etc.'*

(As you have got the client to rate the fear level before hypnosis they will now have a measure of sorts when in the old phobic situation to compare the new response to. You need not even mention it. To wrap up: you have a *massive* amount of suggestions and formulas that can be adapted to many different people and situations from just 4 therapy session scripts. They are all somewhat different to show you don't have to be boringly formulaic. Find your own ways to adapt them and improve them using intelligence, imagination, intuition and a little fact finding; it's easy once you get in the habit of thinking about this stuff the right way.)

Padawan bonus: basic NLP submodality work.

People make pictures, sounds and other daft sh*t in their heads. Sometimes these pictures scare them, guilt them and make 'em feel bad; in the trade this is known as a 'misuse of the imagination'. What Bandler calls making Steven King movies in your head. But you can change the 'spooky stuff! Yep, change 'em to make 'em feel...erm, no so bad or just neutral, calm, horny etc. It's easy. I'll tell you how...

Submodality trick 1: client sees scary internal pics – tell them to imagine the image turning into a black and white stick drawing. This removes all 'reality' from the picture – they calm down.

Submodality trick 2: client sees pic that causes an unpleasant feeling in response – tell them that it's on a scrap of paper. Crumple it up and sling it in a bin/trash can.

Submodaility trick 3: client troubled by images – get them to imagine a mist gradually covers the pic/s etc. obscuring it/them completely.

Submodailty trick 4: client is troubled by an

inner voice that tells them to harm people etc. (this can be an O.C.D component and is not a sign of 'schizophrenia') – get them to imagine where that voice is located. Tell them to turn that voice into a graspable object. Get them to grab that object and hurl it into a black hole that swallows it entirely so that it's gone forever.

Submodaility trick 5: related to above. A client sees images of themselves harming their children. It terrifies them! (These things usually result from a trauma.) Get them to tilt the image in such a way as they can't see what's on it. Like tilting a tilt-able table top so you can't see the surface. Detraumatising someone is very easy and again, will be dealt with in a future book devoted to the subject of 'anxiety disorders'.

Submodality trick 6: someone can't motivate themselves. They may be seeing small, grey or black and white images of what they want. Do this – get them to imagine making the image colour, full screen, with surround sound etc. Make the image big, bright, bold and attractive. Put it as close to their mind's eye as possible. That will motivate them!

Submodality trick 7: if you want a person to objectively view a dangerous behaviour regress them to a time just before they were going to engage in it. At the point they were about to do it, get them to float out of themselves (dissociate) and watch themselves going through with that behaviour. Get them to see the damage they are doing to themselves. Get them to repeat this with 2 more instances of the undesired behaviour. Always dissociate before the unwanted behaviour starts properly. Let them get the urge *then* dissociate them.

Submodalilty trick 8: how to stop worry? Tell someone if they are to see worrying images that they can be shrunk small, black and white and pushed off to the left-hand side so as not to bother them so much. This is prescribing the symptom.

NLP submodality stuff doesn't always work unless combined with other stuff. In my upcoming books I hope to given away the fundamentals of the 'change patterns' you can use and adapt to many purposes to get client's results. They are all pretty simple when you get down to it and often involve mere association, dissociation and a sprinkling of just the right suggestions.

<u>NOTE: The principle underlying its effective use is - if an existing submodality structure exits, change it any way at all and you'll change the response. Alter the submodalities until the desired response is achieved.</u>

This is the Aristotelian principle of reversal -

- Change big pictures to small ones.

- Colour to black and white.

- In front to the side.

- Make moving images still.

- Turn 'symptoms' into symbols and hurl the symptom/symbol into a portal of removal device.

I will end this section with a short tale of a doctor using this principle to help my dad's friend who had 'O.C.D.' This man felt a compulsion to cross every zebra crossing (US crosswalks) he came to. The doctor asked him how he showed this to himself in his noggin. My dad's friend said, 'I see myself connected to glowing cords of thread connecting to different routes.' The doctor told him to imagine a pair of scissors and cut the cord. My dad's friend did. His 'O.C.D.' vanished.

Hmmm that's 9. I don't like the unevenness of it...

Aha! If you want to sexually arouse someone, make them see themselves doing pleasurably naughty things *in a movie* with someone attractive on a huge cinema screen in their mind, up very close, brightly coloured with high definition plus a great, better than real life sounding sound system. Add in a sense of heighted touch, sounds and smells and of course, not forgetting taste. Thank me later ;)

Trust me - keep NLP submodality work simple - the simpler the better.

Let me ask you: why is 'slick' necessarily good? Is slick good or just slimy, over-polished and artificial? Random, unconnected or is everything I write all interconnected in ways that your deep unconscious already recognises? You have been trained to be linear – stop it!

Ok one or two more for luck. Do you know how to Mickey Mouse a voice? NLPers are obsessed with so-called 'strategies'; in their psycho-theology if someone is stressed it's because they are showing themselves scary pics etc. or speaking to themselves in a nervous, high-pitched voice in the head. They focus on end results and deduce - well that must be what caused it! I outlined this error in my third book 'Powerful hypnosis'. Stress is caused by heightened arousal – end of story. Again as I've said, I am preparing a powerful book to teach you how to get rid of a great deal of anxiety disorders, including OCD, depression, GAD etc. using hypnosis; for next to NOTHING!!! I'll save you a fortune! But let me tell you are how to Mickey Mouse a voice.

- Someone speaks to themselves in a scary voice in their head.

- Tell them they can change it. They have that power.

- Instead of the scary inner voice that troubles them, get them to say things in the voice of Mickey Mouse or Sean Connery: think silly or sexy.

- Say a person says, *'I am useless! I could never do that! It's impossible.'* **The content is not as important as <u>how</u> they say it.** If you say it in a quick, high-pitched, scary voice it will scare you even more if you are already anxious!

- Practise this yourself out loud. Say the same line above BUT say it in the really high and high-pitched silly voice of Mickey Mouse. Makes you laugh! Say it in the low, slow, sexy voice of Sean Connery – make love to that line! Makes you smile.

- With insomniacs you can teach them to slow their voice right down at night, give it a very....yawn...tired....sleepy tone. Tell them to only show themselves dim, sleepy images too. You know - not f**king bright and dazzling ones just before drifting off. It does work with some people.

- Anxiety is a derivative of not getting your needs met. Depression is just 'not getting your needs met disorder', just as happiness is a derivative of getting them met. Hypnosis and NLP can directionalise the mind to health but the person's life MUST improve in reality or they'll be back.

People who think hypnosis is just a simple matter of saying 'stop smoking' etc. in trance are more than daft. You can't hypnotise away reality!

You can't cure an arsehole (asshole) of his arseholeness.

I recently had to get rid of a client. I had spent years helping him, improving the way he related to others, calming him down, getting him to be happier and more flexible in his approach to life. The only problem was, fundamentally he was a major asshole! I dubbed him Sir Twitchalot! Because he was a very rich and 'successful' (in some ways) man with a nervous twitch that kept coming back. I'd get rid of it and it would stay rid of for months, and then it came back. We did authoritarian stuff, permissive stuff, detraumatisation work: it still came back. In the end I realised deep down what this man wanted was short term symptom relief, he didn't want cure. His subconscious wouldn't let it go. I didn't want to keep seeing someone with zero unconscious motivation to let go of something that had made his life hell since childhood. The truth was this man was an asshole: he was rude and unpleasant to his nearest and dearest. He would explode into infantile rages while playing his rich boy sport of choice. He blamed his childhood - boo-hoo! He used that bastard twitch as an excuse to be nasty to people; whatever its original protective function was, now it was used to allow him to get away with treating others like shit: 'Don't be too hard on me I have a twitch!' - boo-fucking-hoo!

I knew that I had to speak to the unconscious directly. I knew I had to speak to the 'part' that maintained the twitch to find out why it did what it did and to ask would it let it go. Whenever I presented this idea to Sir Twitch he always denied that was necessary, consciously, and a nasty little look would flip across his face. I ended up realising that look was the unconscious saying, 'Fuck you, I'm keeping this!'

I don't do interminable sessions. I have better things to do. I had to get rid of Sir Twitch - but how? Well he was rich you see. Ve-ry rich. All rich people are stingy and Sir Twitch was no exception. I upped my fees. Well within his price range but...I received an email saying he thought the price rise was excessive!!! This man was a millionaire many times over. I said that my fees had been very low compared to my competition. I never heard from Sir Twitchalot again. The plan worked.

He is probably bothering some new, poor bastard of a therapist as we write. I am now in a position where I only help nice people: a-holes are just too draining. I like to feel uplifted after a session. Maybe a-holes *should* feel bad? People with no insight into themselves and their adverse effect on others are the least rewarding people to help. I say - f*ck em!!!

<u>Amazing bonus: The Rogue Hypnotist's surprise top secret revelation!</u>

Many of you would like to know who I am, wouldn't you Padawan? You are intrigued and curious. Spider Man, Bat Man, Super Man all tried desperately to keep their true identity a secret! On the next page but one, my identity is revealed!

TURN THE PAGE OVER NOW!!!

SUCKER!!!!

You didn't think it would be that easy, did you? I don't want fame...tis a mirage! Enjoy your appendices my Padawan – you have done well! You will be...rewarded...

R.H. signing off...almost...

Appendix 1: The secrets of psychic cold reading - professional level cold reading.

WARNING! Cold reading is used by cults to ensnare people. Use ethically!

You know 'psychics', professional ones, make far better livings than most hypnotists or hypnotherapists? They live in big houses; have secretaries to respond to the deluge of phone calls they get and to book sessions. Let's face it: Mankind is still, to this day a collective fool who worships BUNKUM! Although many men are attracted to psychic readings most of the clients of these con men and women are women. My best friend went to see a psychic. Now my friend went to a psychic and I was going to provide the transcript but he got cold feet. So I'm going to go one better! I'm going to teach you how to do cold reading to a very advanced standard. We will be exploring:

• Hypnotic principles used by the fake psychic.

• Cold reading techniques fake psychics use to con mugs (fools) that they are genuine.

- Genuine signs of 'psychic ability'.

What is 'cold reading'?

Cold reading is quite simply the creation of a fantasy. What is the fantasy? That a person who calls themselves a 'psychic' or 'mentalist' has 'telepathic' or 'spiritual' powers/contacts which help them 'read' a person's personality and 'future'. That's the illusion.

The reality is that cold reading is a series of skills that can be taught to absolutely anybody on earth of reasonable intelligence. ***Cold reading is the art of information gathering from minimal information and/or cues.*** That's part one at least. The second part of cold reading is feeding back the 'information' in such a way that one achieves a 'yes set' with a client/individual. You want to use the information gathered to pretend you have secret knowledge about someone's entire life – past to future. In reality you have none. It is the art of making good guesses and using probabilities based on sound observation. So what's the basic structure of a reading?

1. <u>The 'warm reading':</u> this part is divided in two. First you **observe the client**. Secondly you simply **make a series of statements** that are so vague that they can apply to everyone on earth. The aim is to establish rapport, display fake understanding (few feel 'understood'), demonstrate your 'abilities' and observe the person's reactions to what is said and done within the totality of the situation.

2. <u>Probing the subject:</u> in the second phase the reader starts to take calculated risks. They **start asking 'probing questions'**. These are often double binds. Either or statements. As these questions are asked, the response is noted. This is where the reader aims to get as many 'hits' as possible and to minimise the 'misses'. Specifics and generalities are intertwined. This is what makes the reader appear 'psychic'. The trick in offering good statements for feedback is that they **must be open to wide interpretation**. It is a scatter gun rather than a silencer approach.

As we proceed we will go into more detail but

that's the two-step structure. Now what we need is a sure and tried method for making accurate generalised statements. How do we do this? We study 'The Forer Effect'.

The Forer Effect: how to be all things to all men.

The so-called Forer Effect is also known as the Barnum Effect from P.T Barnum's saying, 'We've got something for everyone!'

People who go to see psychics are hypnotically primed through expectation. They are in a highly focused trance state. The people often believe in 'psychic powers' etc. This makes them **1. Prone to suggestion and influence. 2. Prone to interpret feedback so that it fits into their already established model of reality.** What you might call 'the illusion of reality'. Reality most assuredly exists. 99% of people are not remotely in touch with it. This all plays to your advantage.

Psychologists (I have no idea which ones and don't much care) have found two realities of mind that play into the psychic's hand – **subjective validation and selective**

memory. Make a mental note of these two things. We will build a foundation of fakery around them.

Don't think or feel that the 'educated' are not susceptible to this stuff. If anything they are MORE so. There is an effect that will always work for you: people *want* this sh*t to be real and to work for them. You are satisfying several human needs in one go. This has a powerful effect on the 'poor' suffering suckers coming to see you. I wrote about this in book 3, 'Powerful hypnosis' – there are 3 reasons why anyone goes to a psychic, I call them **'psychic zones'**:

HEALTH.

WEALTH.

RELATIONSHIPS.

In a seemingly uncertain world (reality is actually very certain) **people want security.** Or at least the illusion of it. Let's take health first.

Health: Will I recover from x? Will I get pregnant? Will my child die? Will I feel better about x, y, z? *Everyone knows someone with* *a health issue.*

Wealth: Will I 'get more money'? Will I keep or lose my job? Will I get a promotion? If I invest in x will I make a profit? *Do you know anyone with TOO much money?*

Relationships: When will I meet my future spouse? Should I leave my wife/tadpole? Why do I have so much trouble with my middle child? Is my beloved father in heaven? *How many people have truly found the love of their life?*

This allows the 'psychic' to narrow down their focus of enquiry and start to hypnotically directionalise the mind: cold reading is a sophisticated form of conversational hypnosis.

All people going to psychics have a problem/challenge that they want solved. They just go about solving it in really stupid ways. They have unmet needs that require satisfaction. They perceive that the psychic has the power through hidden ('occult' – occult means hidden) knowledge to assist them in satisfying these needs. Obviously in most situations when we ask questions it presupposes that we lack knowledge and want that knowledge. Let's talk about what Forer did.

It is 1949; psychologist Betram Forer studies a well-known trait of man throughout history: he calls it – **'The fallacy of personal validation'.** He simply asked himself, 'Can people actually appraise their own personality accurately?' He pinched random statements from astrologers' books and composed a profile that is SO general that it could be interpreted as personally valid by most of adult humanity. Let's examine the profile and hypnotically 'deconstruct' it.

Forer's profile for everyman.

'You have a great need for other people to like and admire you. You have a tendency to be critical of yourself. You have a great deal of unused capacity which you have not turned to your advantage. While you have some personality weaknesses, you are generally able to compensate for them. Disciplined and self-controlled outside, you tend to be worrisome and insecure inside. At times you have serious doubts as to whether you have made the right decision or done the right thing. You prefer a certain amount of change

and variety and become dissatisfied when hemmed in by restrictions and limitations. You pride yourself as an independent thinker and do not accept others' statements without satisfactory proof. You have found it unwise to be too frank in revealing yourself to others. At times you are extroverted, affable, sociable, while at other times you are introverted, wary, reserved. Some of your aspirations tend to be pretty unrealistic. Security is one of your major goals in life.'

Even if you are the MOST cynical bastard in the world I bet at some point you thought: 'Wow that's me to a tee!' That's because it's everyone to a tee. It is simply a generalised description of human nature! Again, with hypnotic language analysis...

'You have a great need for other people to like and admire you.

99% of people do! Notice he is talking about NEEDS, URGES, DRIVES. Most people would like to get on with everyone, it's not remotely possible but that's their instinct as humans to 'get along'. 'Like' and 'admire' are unspecified verbs. We don't exactly know what they mean if we give it any thought but by jingo it sounds great! Better than being disliked and hated right? Talking of 'great' – Forer uses the term 'great need' – people need other people. We need to work with others to get our needs met. No man is an island as someone once wrote. First off you are whacked with a bland statement of truth: you need people. This fits into the relationship zone – toward self and others, your 'wealth' – how people relate to you affects your potential income. If you are lonely you become unhealthy fast. All psychic zones met in one fail swoop! Perfecto!

To formulate a statement of this kind ask yourself – does the sucker before me have their need for attention and admiration met?

You have a tendency to be critical of yourself.

What is meant by the word 'tendency'? What is meant by the word 'critical' specifically? We don't know but we do. Some of the time we tend to examine what we have done after we did it. That's how we learn – does he mean that? We tend to feel guilty if we have wronged someone (having a conscience) – does he mean that? We tend to see ways we could have improved upon a performed task after we have done it – does he mean that etc.? Well the point is the subconscious processes all possible meanings at once and ONE, just one, WILL apply to you. Geddit? Most people have fairly low self-esteem, especially women. No reason they should but it is reality. People with low self-worth are VERY critical of themselves. Most people who go to therapy, psychics etc. are therefore likely to have low self-worth. This statement is stage 1 of the buttering up process. This fits into the relationship, health and wealth zones.

To formulate this question/statement etc. ask: does the sucker before me have low self-worth or 'perfectionist' tendencies?

You have a great deal of unused capacity which you have not turned to your advantage.

Get this through your skulls – the 'system' is created to ensure you CANNOT get to use all your 'potential' - which means potency/power - that is reality. So everyone to some degree feels this: especially the 'creative part' of people. Being creative is part of being human.

If you are not creating things, solutions, ideas, services etc. you will become unhappy, anxious, ill, depressed, you name it! I worked for the civil service for 4 years. It was hell on earth; boredom eating away at you every day. It destroys the soul, slowly, gradually, completely. I had seen the miserable civil service 'lifers' as I called them. They had done pretty much NOTHING with their lives – seeking 'security' they had traded the thrill of risk and adventure for 'safety'. Who says we are meant to be safe and that safe = happy? The language? 'Unused capacity' – what the f**k does that mean? I mean really. What are you a storage tanker? It's bullshit! 'Turned to your advantage'???! The mind boggles. It can mean anything! Again the failure to meet the need to express all one's 'potential' is greatly lacking, because for most people they are lacking satisfaction of needs. It's all designed that way boys and girls. You think it's an accident??! A coincidence??! Look at your fellow man. Is he or she happy? Come on. Are you daring to follow your talents and passions? No. Then this need to 'be who you truly, deeply are' in this world is not being met. Again this statement touches on all 3 zones.

To formulate this statement ask – has this person fulfilled their 'potential'?

While you have some personality weaknesses, you are generally able to compensate for them.

Off the bat assumes you possess something intangible called a 'personality weakness' ??? What is that? Ok, we all have areas in life where we lack, have limitations. I am useless at mathematics. I mean I stink. I cannot do sums in my head at all without having a headache. Is this a 'weakness'? I have never needed to use math/s at all except for knowing is there more money coming in than going out? So I really don't care but you get the idea. I am average at sports. I am very physically fit and active but I don't care enough about any sport to be good at it. I'm not bad at them but I am very average. I lack any motivation to be good at even one sport. Is this what is meant by 'weakness'? Ok you have an idea of what this could mean to someone – to you the meaningless phrase 'personality weakness' will probably 'mean' lots of other things. The fact is all humans have weak and strong points: we are good at some stuff and stink at other stuff. We might have a temper in a crisis – whatever. We are imperfect. All humans know this. The only 'people', and I use the term advisedly, who think they are perfect are psychopaths. You could use a question like this to catch one out.

So what does 'generally able to compensate etc.' mean? Well let's say we are talking about my math/s problem. I can just hand over too much money at a checkout and I'll be ok. Do they mean that? If it's my lack of sportiness, I could just play for the fun of it. Is that what they mean? No...f**king idea...??! We all have areas where we can 'improve' ourselves if we could be bothered: no one is 100% satisfied all the time with who they are. We are always learning. Well...some of us are, anyway.

To formulate this statement or others that are similar for cold reading ask: does this person perceive they have potential areas of improvement?

This statement also taps into our need in social situations to wear a persona or 'mask' – this is why people who say 'first impressions are so important' are often so dumb because

you very rarely meet the real person first –
you meet their 'agent'; the 'socially acceptable
pseudo self' they present to social reality to 'fit
in'. This is what you might call 'the mask of
civilisation' because from all accounts
primitives are who they say they are – they
are spontaneous.

Disciplined and self-controlled outside, you tend to be worrisome and insecure inside.

Again we see the need for a social mask. And
it is a very real need in this system of 'ours'
(did you create it? Is it yours by choice?). In
all social situations we have to control our true
emotions to a degree – after all we can't all
hit everyone in the face we'd like to right? You
control that response otherwise you'd be in
jail. We like to present a mask of 'hard work'
and 'competence' when we sell our labour to
an employer don't we? At the job interview
stage you must present a professional attitude
etc. You wear a suit, brush your teeth and
generally avoid letting people know what a
porn watching slob you are. When dating,
giving your prospective boyfriend or girlfriend
a rundown of all your worries will probably not

endear you to them: 'Oh, that why s/he told me /she had herpes!' you are thinking. Yep! Everyone 'worries', to a certain extent, it's normal and protects you from possible dangers etc. It's when you are habitually stressed and overdo it that you get problems that require people like me to fix it. Most people have 'insecurities' – we don't like how that bone next to our big toe bulges out! Your eyebrows join together making you look like Lon Chaney Jr's the wolf man! You eat your ear wax in public like that dumb ass US democratic congressman who thinks 'communism works'. Most people are going around comparing themselves to some fictitious set of carefully constructed PR (adverting) images of some 'celebrity' who is in reality a junkie, anorexic nightmare who cannot sustain a long-term relationship. Some therapists are now calling this 'comparanoia'. It's actually a sign of being an idiot: more on our idiocracy in book 7. Most people are busy presenting a false front to the world. Most people are stressed and worry about getting a whole host of emotional, physical, financial needs met. That's how the system works. It wants you worried. You are easier to manipulate. *By the way all psychotherapies tell you it's the fault of 'something' that you are how you are – school, upbringing (Freudians, behaviourists), it's the pictures in your head or the 'strategies you use to accomplish goals (NLP), I say it's the system we live in that prevents you getting your needs met that is to blame. What you do in response to that challenge is your business.*

So to formulate this statement ask: is this person who they seem to be? How do they display the idea that they are 'competent' to others? Since everyone worries about something, some of the time, what are they worrying about now?

Next...

At times you have serious doubts as to whether you have made the right decision or done the right thing.

Hmmm? How insightful; who hasn't! This taps into our 'regret' databank/place in the mind of which we all have ample material to which we may 'do' a transderivational search to connect to. The psychic is using conversational hypnosis.

Formula? Find common and nominalised human experiences – guilt, hate, regret etc. and directionalise the mind toward them. Effectively age regressing someone conversationally.

You prefer a certain amount of change and variety and become dissatisfied when hemmed in by restrictions and limitations.

'Certain amount of change' – again the brain instantly goes on a search to confirm instances that 'confirm' this vague nonsense. It taps into a truth about humans – they get bored with too much repetition but do like routines and traditions too. We cannot achieve our needs and hence be satisfied if 'hemmed in' by 'limitations' – both of which are conveniently left up to the listener's private interpretation with regards to meaning.

Psychics can only be said to be genuine when they give you specific facts.

Formula? Using vague hypnotic language, construct a truism that asserts that people like stimulation and

challenge – they have a need for it in fact. State that certain unspecified things prevent this need from being satisfied. Cold readers are actually highly sophisticated psychologists. They know humans have needs and seek to exploit them.

You pride yourself as an independent thinker and do not accept others' statements without satisfactory proof.

All humans have a need for truth. We all like to think we can 'think for ourselves' rather than just parrot TV 'experts' which is what 99% do. We all claim we want 'proof' but when we get it and it conflicts with our beliefs we 'rationalise' it away. This statement taps into our vanity of how we wish we were. Only a stupid person would disagree, it is flattering after all.

You have found it unwise to be too frank in revealing yourself to others.

Trust is important in all relationships. I have had clients ask me, 'What I say is fully confidential isn't it?' We have all had betrayals and violations of friendship and trust before the age of 18. It's part of life. We generally reveal our true selves and feel comfortable around others after a sufficient amount of time has passed and the person has been given a chance to reveal who they are.

At times you are extroverted, affable, sociable, while at other times you are introverted, wary, reserved.

We are all more comfortable in some situations than others; no sh*t Sherlock! If you want to craft 100% safe cold reading statements think – when isn't this true for everyone!?

Some of your aspirations tend to be pretty unrealistic. Security is one of your major goals in life.

People have been conditioned not to aim too high. 'Too high' according to whom? The most fundamental goal of human existence is security to achieve your needs and goals etc. Bland, good old universal truisms. So that's Forer's script but how can you generate similar fluff off the hoof?

Rogue Hypnotist's cold reading system based on missing needs.

I have written about universal and specific human needs in other books. Use this reality to appear to be a psychic.

'I feel that something in your life is missing?'

(Generalised missing need waffle)

'I feel you would appreciate more meaningful stimulation and challenge in your life?'

(Need for challenge unfulfilled is suspected)

'You feel some people have held you back from getting what you want?'

(Need to blame others and not take responsibility or bland statement of universal life experience of needing to overcome challenges)

'You feel that you have potential that is yet to be expressed meaningfully?'

(Need to fulfil potential not satisfied)

'You have put things off that need to be

done...'

(Need to put things off due to low self-worth suspected)

'You don't have as many valuable things as you'd like...'

(Person's need to own 'things' is not satisfied)

'You often wish things would slow down. There is a phrase, 'stop the world I want to get off...'

(The person is a 'traditionalist' who wants the rate of social change due to globalisation to slow down)

'You wear a necessary social mask and deeply desire at times to take it off...'

(Need to fit in and be liked suspected)

'You are aware of your flaws but often don't give yourself enough credit for your strengths...'

(Low self-worth suspected, check their body language)

'There are areas of your life where you lack sufficient satisfaction...'

(At any one time someone is going to lack satisfaction somewhere!)

'You have fantasies that you would like to make real but worry about their appropriateness...'

(Many people have taboo thoughts that may cover a whole host of conscious or unconscious needs. These could be sexual, political, aggressive impulses etc.)

'You would like to meet someone special...'

(Need for intimacy unfulfilled)

'You feel that in many ways you could take care of yourself better than you have hitherto...'

(Need to eat and exercise etc. not taken care of)

'You'd like to help people more than you currently can...'

(I have met many clients who work in

the 'selfish' professions, stock brokers and so on. Many feel they should be working in careers that allow them to express their nurturing, caring side. Especially women)

'At times in your life you have felt invisible and small...'

(Universal need for attention is not met; for some this is a chronic state of affairs of semi-perpetual alienation)

'There have been times in your life when you have been treated in ways you didn't deserve. You have a strong sense of justice.'

(If you are human you have a sense of justice. There are times we are all treated unfairly and had a need for that to be rectified and it wasn't)

'There have been times I feel when you felt like a wallflower but secretly wanted to embrace the spotlight.'

(The need to be yourself confidently in social situations is suspected)

'There are still deeply held ambitions that you

have which you have failed to take certain risks to achieve yet...'

(Need for goal achievement unsatisfied)

'You desire greater financial security but doubt that you will successfully find ways to overcome that challenge at times, but you have more potential than you know.'

(99% of people on earth are somewhat financially insecure – this is a safe bet!)

<u>RH's cold reading basics formula</u> – find lacking human needs and craft a suggestion that it isn't being met – yet. Leave hope that it can be fulfilled.

Which leads me nicely to...

<u>Positivity bias?</u>

Humans it seems don't really like the truth much at all. In fact they would rather a positive lie that a negative truth. Forer and others discovered that **readings that were given with positive statements were more likely to be rated as accurate** rather than the seeming balance of 'reality' or realistic-ness of negative statements.

Conclusion: if you want to make 'accurate' or more properly, if you want to do reading with a high 'hit rate' or cold reading 'yes set' — make generalisations that seem, can be interpreted as positive. *This is why politicians can and do easily bullshit the public — they tell 'em what they want to hear.*

Worse still in terms of self-delusion, we are more likely to rate readings as 'unique to us' if they are positive. If negative we see them as being mere generalisations. As a hypnotist this doesn't surprise me — the subconscious wants to solve problems, not hear they are insuperable; that why people see psychics: to solve problems.

Also, statements coming from 'authority figures' are perceived as having more weight than those who are not seen in that way. I have explained this prestige effect fully in 'Powerful hypnosis' and 'Wizards of trance' especially.

Intolerable uncertainty and expectation.

99.9% of people cannot tolerate uncertainty.

Many of our beliefs and so our expectations are held so as to decrease this 'uncertainty intolerance'. Once the belief is fixed in the mind, the brain looks for external data to confirm it and ignores contradictory evidence – psychologists call this 'observation bias'. This is the unconscious mechanism behind the self-fulfilling prophecy. Opposing viewpoints are interpreted through a delusional veil of perceived confidence; this fragments and distorts contradictory information also.

Conclusion? Fit your reading to the client's already existing beliefs. This allows your reading to provide what some mentalists call 'satisfactory context'.

All ethical cold readers agree on one thing: keep if brief, positive and leave 'em feeling happier than when they came to see you! Psychics' clients are much like hypnotherapy clients – they want to experience something out of the ordinary, they want entertainment, stimulation, fun and a sympathetic person to talk their troubles over with. Many people just want to hear some pleasant flattery – *people are compliment starved,* far too often their need for total acceptance and validation as a person by even one person is not met – this is much the same as ego or confidence boosting suggestions in hypnotherapy, saying effectively, if only by implication,

'You *can* solve problem x.'

Those who visit readers with severe anxiety etc. should be directed to seek professional help. It may just be better to listen on such occasions, lest in their anxious state the client goes into negative trances or misinterprets innocuous remarks etc. This is especially true of those experiencing the trance we call 'depression'.

Don't, don't don't, don't: Don't believe the hype!

Some cold readers, amateurs and pros alike get so good at what they do that they start believing they DO have real psychic powers. They copy the client's pattern and start noticing only their 'hits'. Intuition, experience and instincts play a large role in any such 'successes'. Also any techniques eventually become unconscious habits. Over time you will notice similar 'types'; after all people ain't that original are they? This is not to say that genuine psychic ability does not exist. I once believed that all psychics were total frauds. This was until a murder occurred not far from where I live. A beautiful teenage girl had been stabbed to death, literally on her doorstep, after her ex-boyfriend had dropped her off after an evening out. Little did she know that a psychopath had been stalking her. After he killed her he had 'sex' with her bleeding, mutilated corpse. The case was so horrific that it became national news in the UK. The devastated mother of the girl believed in psychic ability and while waiting for news of the murderer's capture took part in a psychic reading. This reading was televised. The lady asked the male psychic what he could find out about the killer to help the police catch him. He gave her a specific name: Mark.

The killer was caught: he was an Australian immigrant working as a chef in a nearby pub. It transpired he had already come to police attention for masturbating in front of lone young women at night time. It turns out he was called Mark. I cannot just explain this away: can you?

It is well known that the US, Russia and China

have spent a great deal of money on investigating potential psychic abilities for intelligence purposes. The richest and most powerful - heads of corporations, senior bankers, Royalty, Hollywood celebrities frequently make use of such 'services' – if there is *nothing* in it, why go? If genuine psychic abilities do not exist why would they bother? These people do not waste time. Both Estabrooks and his mentor Catton investigated psychic abilities and believed them to exist; the former even penning a book on his findings. The truth is I don't know if such 'powers' do exist but I am not a 'coincidence theorist'. Decide for yourself.

Role playing and props?

Whether you are a TV mentalist, psychic, hypnotist etc. the audience wants someone paying a two-dimensional over the top role. They want an actor with a cheesy act. No matter how many young pretenders come along and pretend to do 'street' this or street that – it's the same old horseshit, it's just a got a different flag stuck in the top! People will relate to you as they would to an authority figure; someone who has taken the time to develop a kindly confident alter-ego or stage persona. Remember: your key audience will be women – no ifs or buts, just look at those TV psychic shows. In the UK we currently have a lady known as 'Psychic Sally' who is a cheeky, funny, 'mumsie' (US - matronly) lady who is wildly popular on TV. She has an endearing accessibility and sympathetic persona. Her packed-out theatre audiences are largely filled with women of all ages. Women's predisposition to this kind of things is beyond the confines of this book. In a low-key way you must act as if you have a 'special gift'. This will give you an aura of confidence.

Like hypnosis props which I covered in 'Forbidden hypnotic secrets' a cold reader's props are entirely surplus to requirements. You can do the readings without them. Whether your shtick is palm reading, hand writing analysis, magic tricks, tarot etc. they are just **plausible cultural rituals** which create/trigger a state of **heightened expectation and suggestion** in the susceptible. In many ways they are cues for the client to enter waking hypnosis especially with repeated visits or past experience. The props fixate the client's attention AND the psychics which facilitate **focus of attention** for *both*. This facilitates access of the reader's creativity and intuition. External reality is ignored. The client **fractionates** between

- **Expectation,**

- **Attention,**

- **And memory retrieval**

in response to readings: each time this cycle is repeated the client goes deeper into waking trance. Hypnotic fractionation is covered in my other books.

Props can be **utilised** as prompts for both reader and client. Using the 3 'psychic zones' which I identified earlier a 'palm reader' may use a **hypnotic double bind** and say,

*'Would you like to **focus** on the heart or wealth line as we begin?'*

Or if you feel 'health' is the issue...

'I feel we should start with the life line.' Geddit?

If you feel stuck while staring at your prop you can say in a **tone*** of mystery that may well evoke **hypnotic confusion** –

*'I **feel*** that this x is open to interpretation that requires your feedback to fully understand etc.'*

Cold reading clients are rarely passive but active co-creators in a reading. They will try to help you 'fill in the blanks' – their creative unconscious is using the occasion to problem solve. You are merely there to create the context in which this occurs. Readings create a trance that allows this to occur.

(*Those who have read my other books will understand the importance of tone and feelings in hypnotic communication.)

The strange rise of 'Fortune-telling' in the West.

So far we have only explored 'character readings' but psychics claim to be able to predict the future. What is fortune telling? Quite simply it's about predicting the course of a person's life. It is identical with 'divination' – but whereas the latter is part of a religious or pseudo religious rite and involves the invocation of 'spirits', 'deities' etc. - modern fortune telling involves suggestions, positive 'predictions', 'flattery' for 'spiritual' or practical reasons. Divination is much like the practise of ancient hypnosis in Egypt and Greece.

The history of fortune telling is odd and has an anti-Western bias. So called fortune-telling grew out of an acceptance by the common people of Renaissance magic, this was brought back into Western Europe by the Romani people (Romany Gypsies); this is also linked to the so-called 'Occult Revival' of the 1400's. Between the 19th and 20th century Oriental methods of divination such as the I-Ching became increasingly popular amongst influential circles in the West, which led to a cultural 'trickle down' to the lower orders. This neo-occultism is even stronger today: the Magic 8 Ball being just one example.

All the major Abrahamic religions advise their followers to avoid such practises as highly dangerous, with only mystical sects therein dissenting. As marijuana is generally recognised as a 'gateway' drug to harder ones, so too certain religious groups see fortune-telling as a gateway to darker and much more dangerous occult practises.

Palm reading and astrology are by far the most popular forms of modern fortune telling in all Western countries. It seems many just can't tolerate uncertainty one lil' bit!

Developing your own process: personality double binds.

Psychologists etc. 'reductionists' that they are, love to categorise people into neat little packages that they call 'types'. This predilection is ancient. Hippocrates in ancient Greece wrote about bullsh*t like 'phlegmatic' (laid back), 'choleric' (aggressive/angry), 'sanguine' (happy go lucky) and 'melancholic' (misery guts) personalities. Even Ivan Pavlov based his findings on dubbing his dribbling dogs in this manner.

Nutcase occultist Jung took this one step further and developed his 6 mythological apposition of opposites, double bind types; these were...

- **Thinking – Feeling.**

- **Intuition – Sensing.**

- **Extravert – Introvert.**

Note for the budding cold reader: surveys say around 75% of people are 'extroverts' – bear this in mind when dealing with folk. Countries have these tendencies too; the US culture produces a decidedly more outward focused, extravert person by and large.

Jung claimed these represented 'tendencies'.

By the early 60's a pair of Briggs's, mother and daughter team create – The Myers Briggs Indicator (MBTI for short). This was based on the 6 types of Jung and went as follows...

NOTE: The following relates to how you receive and interpret incoming data.

The E-I scale: E = Extroversion and I = Introversion. This was supposed to say how 'sociable' you were. Extroverts are broadly 'doers' - they engage with the external world and reality. Introverts are self-hypnotised, engaged in their own thoughts, ideas and reflections - 'thinkers', 'meditators' etc.

The S-N scale: S = Sensing and N = iNtuition. This supposedly relates to how you receive and interpret incoming data. Did you do it through the senses (evidence) or did you intuit stuff (gut instinct etc.).

The T-F scale: T = Thinking and F = Feeling. This was important with regard to how we reach and make decisions. Did you <u>think</u> (logic) or <u>feel</u> your way to them?

The J-P scale: J = Judgement and P = Perceiving. This was the Briggs' ladies own creation. Sort of. It combined two of the earlier scales.

- Judgement = Thinking and feeling.

- Perception = Sensation and intuition.

These supposedly measured how you interacted with reality. Whatever that means?! Note these are all either or. These are examples of hypnotic double binds, apposition of opposites as already pointed out. In fact no one is either or but depending on context one trait predominates over another; that is unless childhood conditioning has suppressed natural traits and created an imbalance. An example would be university professors who through operant conditioning have overvalued 'intellect' over all over features. People's professions tend to attract certain types and create them. The personality is lopsided. Parental preferences will also nonverbally 'suggest' preferred ways of being, through copying if nothing else. Children are little copying machines as any parent knows. We will stay with Myers Briggs for now but there is a better system of personality typing that I may cover in one of my upcoming books. If you are thinking, 'All very well but so what?' hang on, there's a method to my madness!

Another subgrouping?

Have you ever heard of 'identity seeking personalities'? Me neither. At least I hadn't till I started researching this odd subject. This comes under the Intuition-Feeling category (NF – apparently we can be any weird combo!) are said to be 30% of people who do online surveys, personality tests etc. These are the sorts into self-help, 'exploration' etc. - people looking to 'explore the self' in a multitude of weird and whacky ways. Complete selfish narcissists at the extreme end. Good types for cults to ensnare! The type that says, 'I want to find out who I am etc.' Good...grief!

Remember – 'identity seekers'.

<u>Conclusion</u> – people likely to be eager to try cold readings. Bear this in mind when generalising my padawans.

13% of those online tests tend to be Sensation-Perception ('SPs' – are you keeping up with all these abbreviations? Me neither!) These are people who you might call 'sensation seekers' – people looking to get physical thrills and excitement! Entertainment in other words. Think 'experience junkies'. Or...

Remember – 'sensation seekers'.

<u>Conclusion</u> – a small but sizeable percentage of people going for cold readings want to be entertained and excited. They are playful and have a higher than usual need for play; their unconscious ideology is the 'Fun Ethic'. Construct generalisations tailored to such folk when you meet them. These are all skills that can help you build rapport in many areas of life when seeking to influence. Not that you're interested...Riiii-ght.

These two categories represent a potential

whopping 40 plus percent of a cold reader's potential clients. You could bear this in mind when advertising etc.

Myers Briggs has four types of personality generalisations that you can use to boost your cold reading prowess.

The 4 M-B types.

The following will cover the largest % of folks and work down. I have added my own 21st century twists on the 'classical assessments'.

1. ***Sensation Judgement (SJ): 40-45% of the population.*** MB calls them – Security Seekers. These are that percentage who seek **security** above all else. Security is a basic human need but these people are basically non-risk taking stiffs on one level and the backbone of a civilised society on another. They like to **follow rules** AND importantly enforce them. The question arises, 'Whose rules'? They see themselves as **highly moral** and upstanding citizens etc. They like **order and routine** and seek work that facilitates this desire. These folk uphold **traditions** in a society and so may be called

'**conservative**' with a small c. They are generally **conformists** to any social system they find themselves in. Not great in critical thought and somewhat **accepting of authority** as a rule: no matter what that authority is. They like detail and are emotionally, financially, socially **stable** etc. They like facts, if they confirm their prejudices, and are definitely not highly creative or imaginative. They are like dogs: **loyal, hardworking,** they do not give up easily. They **keep an eye** on world events, the news, their local surroundings etc. – probably on the lookout for unwanted change. They are tools/observers of the system, not doers in the sense of being the originators of it. They are not loners and prefer the security of the group. They like acts to be **justified** to them. They bring up their kids to be little clones of themselves. They seek continuity and continuance. **Think: stability.** These people will be businessmen, police officers, the military, teachers, civil servants, local politicians, your neighbours, accountants etc. They can be manipulated when their sense of security is seen to be threatened. Slow to anger but a force to be reckoned with when roused! They can be methodical and systematic. <u>They fear change.</u> These people will not be very witty or funny or great personalities and tend to be emotional cold, at best lukewarm. They are good at keeping society's cogs going. We'll call them **'security junkies'** – key words for creating generalisations for cold readings: **security, rational, rules, order, old, routine, habit, traditions, morality, conservative, justice, right, experience, stability, hard work, determination, effort, earthy, responsible, aware.** As a hypnotist these are 'trance words' for such folk. Think good old reliable Watson of Sherlock Holmes fame.

2. ***Sensation Perception (SP): 35 to 40% (Actually probably closer to 70% these days) of the population.*** These people are the **hedonists** and probably are at a higher percentage now than since the fall of Rome! Especially since the 'social revolutions' of the 1960s. The 'Fun ethic' is their God. Their main

goals are **pleasure, joy, fun, play** etc. These are the **risks takers.** They would describe themselves as **'liberal', laid back, easy going, tolerant, spontaneous, adaptive, flexible.** They like **change**, any change. Usually they don't know why they believe in anything but it just **feels right.** They value **freedom, independence, spontaneity and impulsivity** – on their terms: they are **adventurous.** They seek the company of like-minded people (as do all types). They may be **daring** and **bold;** often for no good reason. They are doers, in that they like to 'do' not watch – they like to 'be in the thick of things'. They crave primary experience, to be **involved**. <u>They fear/hate boredom and stagnation.</u> Basically, in some ways, they are teenagers who never matured. They value 'youth'. They will often be attracted to 'left-wing' and 'radical' ideologies. They can **compromise** to achieve goals and are good with **technologies** and tools. They are hands on people. City life and **speed** attract them. They are more likely to be **creative.** In reality they are often as big a conformist as the security junkies but think otherwise. They will value **emotion** as much, if not more than thought. At an extreme polarity they may be **nomadic** and **unstable.** They are more likely to abuse drugs, go in for extreme sports etc. Ideally you will find them in sporty professions or pursuits, some artistic pursuits (acting, rock bands) etc. They are addicted to their own pleasure centres of the brain. As kids they focused on having fun first. Probably much better company than the security junkies but at an extreme they may create division in society almost for its own sake. Attracted to change for change's sake. In seeking 'progress' they may be destructive to security junkies' much loved stability. Security junkies will see them as 'layabouts', 'ner-do-wells', 'get a real job' etc. They tend to raise their kids in a **permissive** style. Classically they are called Sensation Seekers. We'll call them **'pleasure junkies'** – key words for cold reading influence are: **freedom, change, adventure, new, flexible, adaptive, expansion, consciousness, spontaneous, pleasure, joy, fun, just**

do it, if it feels good do it, thrills, feel/ings, bold, risk, emotional, radical, do you own thing, permissive, creative, freedom of expression, playful, hedonist, why not? On the 'left' think certain types of Hippy, liberal, Green Peace, 'Marxist' (of the useful idiot variety) types. There are 'right wing' varieties parodied in comedy – Homer Simpson and Ed Griffin from Family Guy leap to mind. Yuppies etc. fit the mould precisely – soulless materialists.

3. ***Intuition-feeling (NF): 8-10% of population.*** Who the hell am I? Identity seekers. I am reminded of a story about British Comedian Peter Cook. In an altercation with a very arrogant man, the latter self-importantly barked, 'Do you know who I am?' Cook being very quick-witted held out both hands as if to stop passers-by and cried out, 'Will somebody please call a psychiatrist! This man is having an identity crisis.' To put it bluntly this group are the **'philosophers'** – those looking for the **meaning** of life? Why are we here and does anyone care? They are often said to feel they are engaged in a

battle between good and evil – often in themselves. They believe that the good will prevail. So on some level they are 'spiritual warriors'. They seek to make the lives of all those they care for and beyond better than they currently are; especially with regards to boosting others self-esteem and self-acceptance. At worst this could lead to a form of **mystical** retreat from the harshness of reality. They are often deeply loving. As children they are said to have **vivid imaginations** and **fantasy** lives (highly hypnotic). They encourage their children to explore their fantasy life and play. They may be described as **opinionated, subjectivist, individualistic.** They will be more resistant to group pressure. Although they have a tendency to 'think for themselves' they may be attracted or side-tracked into religions and cults as a result of their 'spiritual yearnings'. They may in fact flit from religion to religion believing the 'answer' lies there; something I call 'religion shopping'. They are often very **insightful** and **intuitive** being born therapists/psychologists. They are more '**introvert**' than extravert. I have decided we'll call these people '**spiritual questers'.** They often feel there is more to this world than the material and seek to transcend (trance-end) it. They often speak slowly and thoughtfully. They want 'world peace' etc. Some become hermits, more often musicians, unconventional teachers, artists, priests/holy men, the more sociable - 'New Age' councillors etc. I think this type couldn't take the world of business, at least not for long, feeling they were 'prostituting' themselves. *They fear 'the death of the soul'.* Key words of influence – **spiritual, subjective, creative, intuition, beyond, meaning, philosophy, unconventional, holistic, gestalt, thoughtful, ponder, meditate, unconscious, dreams, non-linear** etc., etc. Think Moulder from the X Files; they can be brilliant, kooky and believe the 'truth is out there'. Agent Cooper from Twin Peaks is another example.

4. ***Intuition/thinkers (NT): 5-7% of the population.*** In a word **analytical** types. These people are attracted to 'science' – the myth that 'rational thought' can solve

all Man's problems. They, like the spiritual questers are introspective – this basically means that they think about stuff. Unlike group 1 and 2 who tend to be reactive. Think Scully from the X files. Brilliant but often emotionally colder than the other types and at worst 'socially autistic' and seeing themselves set aside as a more perfected type of man – 'the scientist'. The priest of the New Millennium. Good problem solvers. Intensely inquisitive BUT conventional by and large. Not given easily to controversy and the new, they make a religion of science called 'Scientism'. They seek a rational basis for all they do which tends to mean following their scientific indoctrination. In their favour they are curious about reality; want to know what it is and how it works. The problem is once they think they've found it, they stubbornly resist counter-evidence and merely forge new dogmas for old. Words used to describe such folk are **logical, thorough, precise.** They are attracted to 'systems'. They can be inventive IF their creativity hasn't been smashed by the school system or parents who poo-pooed unconscious processes as somehow being that bit less valid. They also worship the **conscious mind.** They are usually very **academic**ally gifted as children and were the only kids who liked school, often being teacher's pet. They can at worst tend towards an 'Ivory Tower' mentality which regards the common man as a kind of experimental guinea pig that doesn't know what is best for him. This can lead some to 'eugenical ideologies'. They are often reductionist and see things at face value not comprehending the 'politics of everyday life'. They have a poorly veiled contempt for 'anecdotes'; that is anyone but a scientist's *opinion* on anything. On the plus they often demand **proof.** Classically these boffin types are known as knowledge seekers. We shall call them –

'conventional rationalists'. They often share traits with the security junkies. Art is unfathomable to the worst of them. *Greatest fear – that they are wrong!* They will despise the idea of 'psychic powers' as being 'unmeasurable'. Tend toward atheism or are recovering Christians. They will want to know how cold reading 'really' works. If they undergo one, it is to discover the 'how' rather than the why. They undervalue the emotions, seeing them as some sort of evolutionary vestigial limb that needs removal. Professions? Sciences, doctors, teachers, technicians, computer programmers etc. Key words? **Analyse, think, rational, irrational, science, evidence, conscious, proof, tangible, bunkum!** Think Doctor Spock from Star Trek, Sherlock Holmes etc.!

5. ***'Total persons': 0.1% of the population of earth.*** MB does not acknowledge this category. These are the people who do not fit the illusion of 'type'. The have qualities of all types. Often renaissance men and women, some are geniuses: multi-talented, unpredictable, sane and possess high integrity. Can see through all bullshit, posing a danger to elites. You will meet one, once in a blue moon. Born leaders often nowhere near leadership positions. Other types find it hard to classify them or slot them into unconscious stereotypes – this unnerves them. To do otherwise would require thought. This is one of the Rogue

Hypnotist's classifications; do with it as you will. **Key words: genuine, special, talented, the 1%, clued-up, different, individual.**

What we are uncovering here are unconscious drives. The first two I will identify relate to the limbic system or primitive brain – psychoanalysis's 'Id'. The second relate to the higher functions, the part that makes Man man, the neo-cortex stuff. The 'ego'/'superego' of Freud. In reality all drives are interconnected.

- **The drive for security.**

- **The drive for pleasure.**

- **The drive for self-knowledge.**

- **The drive for knowledge of reality.**
  (These last two are related to 'truth seeking'.)

The first two drives and the last predominate in the West. The third in the East, which is why they are so God damn poor! The West has opened itself up to infiltration by oriental religions and fads due to the collapse of Western Christendom. In the West the 'spiritual drive' of Man cannot find completion: result? Misery!!! All unconscious drives open completion templates that seek satisfaction of drives in reality.

In many ways we are all a combination of all types depending on context. There may be an inbuilt genetic bias toward a 'type', it may be due to operant conditioning in childhood that fixes certain traits in their socially acceptable expression – at worst these are actual ego states which stifle the 'whole person' who is squished and dissatisfied beneath the surface. Now, how can we use this plausible sounding horseshit to be better cold readers?

Categorising your victim fast!

You need to think in clichés. You need to be reductionist. You need to use a lot of double binds and you need to think fast Kato! But how? Ask yourself a lot of either or questions. Get the first impressions ball rolling with...

1. **Are they introverts or extroverts?** Are they shy, a wall flower, very self-conscious etc.? Can they look you in the eye comfortably? Do they smile, cough, fidget nervously? Do they speak quickly, in a high,

strained voice? Do they act as if they hope people like them? They dress down – don't notice me. Their energy is drawn inward – shoulder's hunched. They are actually flitting/fractionating in and out of external/internal awareness – checking pictures in their heads, commenting on them internally, checking feelings, especially anxious ones. Their need for enough positive attention from others is often not met. Obviously tick the internal introvert box. Or are they overly talkative straight away (like that Irish girl in the pub last night who would not SHUT UP!)? Do they stand relatively close and look you in the eye? Are they externally focused on you and the room; such clients often look at how your house is laid out, notice ornaments etc. Mentalists say this and it's true -the extraverts do tend to wear 'bolder' clothes, 'brighter' colours, more jewellery. The worst ones will have vulgar painted nails, four inches long with no taste, whore's tattoos etc. They want and like attention! Women versions wear tarty/slutty makeup, so it's not all bad. They grab attention, are good socially but tend towards the shallow end of things. Tick the extravert box. Sticking to our human needs theme you might want to re-label these two sets of people - **inward-anxious and outward-attention.**

So what are the usual traits of these two types? What best guesses can we make to seemingly create some sh*t hot, obvious truisms about them? Remember if you make accurate truisms about someone it – makes them feel understood, makes them feel more rapport and connection with you, makes them relax, makes them establishes an unconscious 'yes set' (see books 1 and 2 in my series), and makes them more suggestible. Those you pace you can lead. Cold reading is a form of utilisation.

Anxious-inward or introverts.

Say crap like this...

'I feel you feel more comfortable alone than in a crowd.'

'Popularity isn't that important to someone like you. I feel you prefer a few close, long term friends to whom you are intensely loyal. Depth of relationship is more important to you than

quantity.'

'Do you find that when you find yourself in large groups of people, especially if they are new to you, that your energy levels **tend*** *to be sapped more quickly than usual?'*

(*If you talk about 'tendencies' you cover your butt. You are probing the surface before delving deeper.)

If they say yes – you scored a hit. If not say sh*t like…

'Exactly, I didn't feel you were like that at all. I was just checking to confirm my intuition.'

Plausible deniability.

Related to the above, if they answer yes –

'Do you find that after a period of socialising that you feel a real need to take a rest, to recharge? Do you like to go off on your own and spend what you might call some 'me time'?

If they say yes and smile you say nodding your head sagely.

'I felt that was true about you. I think we are

getting somewhere...etc.'

Use the word **feel** a lot, one it is suggestive of your subconscious and theirs and so bypasses resistance, two the word feel is just that, a 'feeler', you are testing things out, so it doesn't matter if your feeling take a bit of time to warm up. Remember clients want you to succeed, they will help you. Thirdly it is a 'softener', you are not stating arrogantly like some kind of Hannibal Lecter – 'This and that are true about you, deny it!' which evokes a challenge response. You are not an authoritarian communicator but rather using a sly form of conversational hypnosis. If you aren't sure if this is conversational hypnosis, notice all the trance words – I have said nothing solid once! Go check out 'How to hypnotise anyone' and 'Mastering hypnotic language' – both in paperback form now I hasten to add (shameless plug I know!).

Introverts like working on their own quite a bit. They like to experience intimate trance states of deep absorption in reading, using new technology, working on research, listening to music that totally absorbs them. They can go into external trance states in activities meaningful to themselves. Socialising does not necessarily/usually evoke such an intense social trance as it does with hedonist extroverts. There are always exceptions! So knowing this, how can we use it?

'Would it be fair to say that you feel absorbed in private activities that have meaning for you?'

'I feel you are the type of person who can lose themselves in a book/film/piece of music/an activity/hobby that engrosses you?'

Notice another tactic you can use are 'softener questions' – *'Would it be fair to say x ?'* (X being your educated guess.) Or, *'Do you find that y?'* (Y being what you guess they habitually experience.)

In the early phase think: probe, probe, probe – gently around the edges before going deeper. Seek as many yeses/hits as possible, take few risks. If they ever say no, say smilingly,

'I thought so...'

If they say yes, say smilingly,

'I thought so...'

Let's deal with the brash extroverts! How can we Billy Bullshit them effectively? Well what lame generalisations can you make?

'Your social life is so important to you. I actually feel it makes you feel more alive. Would I be right in that?'

'You are the life and soul of the party when you want to be, aren't you?'

'A wallflower you have never been!'

Extraverts need people like a drug! They are often very other-directed and herd like.

'The problem you have with parties is buying enough invitations!'

'You are a people person!'

'Would it be true to say you love having a wide circle of friends? I feel you are comfortable at gatherings.'

'If you want to meet someone new, that is just not a problem for you. You can relate to princes and paupers easily. You know how to talk to anyone. That's my impression of you.'

'My intuition is that you feel things aren't quite right if you are alone for too long...'

Extraverts are drained by loneliness, they hate it, it makes them deeply uncomfortable. They love yapping to any fucker! They just get off on talking.

'Peace and quiet, the countryside are not quite your thing. You would hate to be left alone on a desert island. Am I right?'

That would be a fair guess. Often men that are 'more successful' with women are just natural extroverts. Maybe this is why there are more of them! They breed more!

'For you meeting someone new is just an opportunity to connect...'

'You just adore socialising. I feel you actually depend on your energy and well-being to a great extent to your positive interaction with others. Am I headed in the right direction?'

If they say no, hit your head as though it's defunct technology and say,

'Wow, my intuition is a little bit rusty after those 6 scotches last night!'

I advise you don't go all intense, lighten up. It's bullshit after all! It's a game. A guessing game! You get better with practise, honest. Ok let's say you meet a whole person or someone who is a contrarian. It will happen – how to cover all bases?

'I feel that you like to socialise and spend time with others of course but there are some times where you feel - I need to chill out and just gather myself in some way to feel more comfy, correct?'

Or even more cheeky,

'You flip between introvert and extrovert, don't you my friend.'

All good cold readers assume instant familiarity. This let's someone relax, good readers are NEVER judgemental. This allows the victims to comfortably leak the truth through body language stripped of anxious interference. Ok people have a set of assumptions about themselves that they want to be true, that they want others to perceive as true for a whole host of reasons that you can ponder for yourself. What the heck are they? Your wait is over bozo!

People in general statements.

*'Your bright **intelligence**, your **capabilities**...perhaps you don't acknowledge them as you should...'* **The wisdom part. (Our need to use our intelligence.)**

*'I know there have been times when your inborn **independence** has had to assert itself. You have also discovered you are more **resourceful** that you knew at times. I mean we've all been there.'* **The independent part. (Our need for independence.)**

*'You can work in a team; you have a good ability to be **cooperative** when you think that's right.'* **The team work part. (Our need to work with others.)**

*'I just get the impression you are the **hard working** and **dependable** type!'* **The worker part. (Our need to expend meaningful energy.)**

*'A **friendly** person deep down. That's what you are!'* **The friendly part.**

*'I think many people have experienced your **honesty** and **loyalty** even if you were not rewarded for that on occasion.'* **The integrity**

part. (Our need to be good.)

*'One way or another it all comes down to family at the end of the day. You are **family-oriented**; you value family life very highly indeed.'* **The family part. (Our need for family.)**

*'Well what you need to face up to is your qualities, what you might call your capacity for being a **natural leader**.'* **The leader part. (Our need to lead.)**

*'Some things might p*ss you off, if you don't mind me talking that way but basically you are a **good natured** person. You may even like to think the best of people and that got you in trouble didn't it? Yeah we've all been there.'* **The naïve part. (The part that denies reality!)**

*'When you need to, you can sure **problem solve**. I really get that hunch about you. You've surprised yourself.'* **The problem solver part. (Our need to overcome challenges creatively.)**

'If you were honest with yourself and sure, we have all made mistakes and gotten in trouble

but and correct me if I am wrong...it's your **people skills** *that have really been outstanding at times. Got you out of hot water, the works, right? Fundamentally I think you understand people.'* **The communicator part. (Our need to interact successfully with others.)**

'I get a good feeling about you, right here (Point to solar plexus!)*! You are great* **fun** *to be around and the closest to you know it. They love that fun side of you! You can be playful. I feel...you know what? You need to connect to that you more often.'* **The playful part. (Our need for play.)**

'Even as a child I just get the impression that...you have shown a **kindness***, a* **compassion, a caring, nurturing** *side of you...that sense of* **consideration** *that is unique to you in fact. Please validate that you more.'* **The helper part. (Our need to help others.)**

'Situations have arisen that have shown your **flexibility***. Maybe you discovered things about yourself you didn't quite know were there? Things can and do change; boy don't we know how?! But you've* **adapted***.'* **The**

adaptive part. (Our need to be adaptable when needed.)

*'If you like the task it's easy but even if you don't, you see things through to the end, you **complete** stuff. You get it done.'* **The goal driven part. (Our need to achieve and be consistent.)**

Cold reading seems deceptively simple. In fact it is based on a fundamental set of assumptions about the true nature of man which are incredibly insightful and penetrating. No wonder it holds such a powerful effect on so many. Unlike many systems of therapy it understands our needs and appeals to them. It aims to get them satisfied. This is what Governments claim to do or what they promise they will do but never really do!!!

We all have these 'parts' – generate generalisations targeted to them! This is useful for the hypnotherapist in tailoring suggestions too. Good cold reading is a type of informal hypnotherapy. Hypnosis is EVERYWHERE!!!

Trancing out women with cold reading.

Women love this shit! If you are a man and do this stuff effectively a woman might let you sleep with her on the basis of it! Seduction gurus often advise their overcharged saps they call customers to start the seduction process with such props. So what do women believe to be true about them – by and large? These are just generalisations which are generally true. This reminds me, I have to write about 'conspiracy theories' in the next book: you see everyone's a conspiracy theorist! Anyway, the ladies...

Now in my experience as a therapist I almost always hear this from women, especially those who are mums/moms –

'I put other's needs ahead of my own.'

This is especially true of their family and close friends. Many not so well intentioned people exploit this caring side to women, including brothers who will ask sisters to look after their children etc. I once had to hypnotise a women to stop being taken advantage of. She started yelling and getting angry at all the people who had ever taken advantage of her (a good first step) but we had to do a second session to calm her responses down a bit: firm but calm. The anger was really resentment release. Cold reading questions etc....

'I bet you are the kind of lady who on occasion lets others take advantage of your good will and caring nature. Am I right?'

'I feel you need to take time to get your own needs satisfied. You wish to help others as a nurturing person but where is the time for you in that etc.?'

Women often get a great deal of satisfaction helping others. It is their nature. This is why they are attracted to professions like child care, nursing and teaching etc. It is their mothering instinct, which is tremendously strong. They have it as little girls when they 'play' at happy families and being mums/moms pretty much all day long as anyone with girls knows!!! Knowing this fact and admiring it, what can we say?

'From your earliest childhood you have liked to take care of things. Could have been a favourite doll and you pretended to fix its broken leg. You feel a great deal of deep joy

and satisfaction in helping others. That is, I feel, a very special quality you have. You can acknowledge that strength.'

Women need ego-boosting in therapy, every, and I mean *every* belief system on earth tells them they are somehow deficient; especially certain versions of so-called 'feminism' which should be called 'hermaphroditism' or 'masculinism'. Note: women are more than capable of 'success' without changing themselves to fit some other designed mould. Why can't ideologues just let women be? The Abrahamic religions blame her for ALL the world's ills. I mean for fuck's sake back off!

From when women are very young they start noticing other's moods. They scrutinise faces and can almost see through others from an early age. My niece could do it within a year of birth! If not sooner! So?

'You are very perceptive. You can read body language well. You can see when people are hiding things, when they are covering them up. What their real intentions are. You can almost 'read their thoughts' so to speak, as if you were psychic and it's all effortless isn't it?'

'You are intuitive.'

'Your intuition has gotten you out of some sticky situations in the past.'

'You are somewhat psychic... (if they grimace) *for want of a better word.'*

'I feel that you are a lady who is very sensitive to others. To their feelings primarily. You can sense their feelings: you are deeply empathetic.'

'You have intuitions and insights that pop into your head and often turn out right.'

'You care about a great many causes.'

Women are ruled by their emotions 'the heart' not the head. They have a rich emotional life. Don't kid yourself with any femo-nazi delusions.

'You often let your heart rule your head. It has gotten you in trouble and been a source of great joy for you.'

'You feel emotion is as important as logic in making good decisions. Your rich emotional life has helped you in many ways that others don't realise.'

Deep down women want security. Their deepest drives make them seek powerful, strong men. Unless they are on the pill which screws with their natural hormone cycles and 'fools' them into being attracted to girly boys.

'You crave a sense of security. In some way it guides all you do.'

Women love to be admired for their looks. This is why ignoring them is such a turn on for them. But women are not generally as 'superficial' as men when it comes to looks; women claim that they like a man's look. Bullshit! They don't give a crap about a man's looks. When a women spends time with a man with qualities she finds attractive the toad morphs into 'good looking' before her eyes; ask any women...

'You judge someone by more than just outward appearances. Many admire this quality in you. You can see past the surface.'

Women often feel they are undervalued, by friends, families, kids etc. Women respond to words. They like to be told how valued they are. Not all the time: once would be nice! Men are action oriented and hallucinate that women are too. Having said this, women do it back, the other way around. An appreciative word or two, a compliment or two may just lead her to let you lustfully ruin her in the bedroom if you are her boyfriend or spouse. Don't overdo the nicey-nice or she'll just go off you as though you bathe daily in cow dung. Now...

'I feel something's lacking that you want...A sense of appreciation. A sense of others not fully recognising all that you have done for them. Sometimes relationships have their thankless task moments don't they?'

If you say stuff like this and it's true she may well cry. You hit a nerve.

'You would like to be accepted totally for who you are, physically, emotionally, psychologically. I'm not sure that happens as much as you'd like...'

'Tell me if I'm wrong but could you do with some more word hugs from those around you? Even the closest?'

If she says what are 'word hugs' say:

'Compliments!'

'Do you feel others give you enough validation for the unique women you are?'

'You are a great communicator. You feel many problems can be solved by talking them through.' (If only!)

They do, this is why they are more prone to depression than men: they ruminate and don't take action to solve things.

'Although you are a modern women you like nothing more from time to time than going shopping, having a day out with the girls and relaxing together over a meal. It's one of your favourite ways that you have to have fun and recharge! You'd like to do it more often. You know you deserve it.'

No shit Sherlock! If you can infer or slyly implicate flattery with women, so much the better. With modern ladies think of 'you go girl' stuff to bullshit their pretty heads with. Most women started off as princesses until the world shat on them.

Women value and define themselves through husband and family first.

'I doubt very much if *anything is more*

important to you than nearest and dearest; you are very family oriented. You worry about your loved ones often.'

Women are capable of a cutting and brutal bluntness due to their perceptive powers should you cross them by the way. If they have to, they bide time before getting revenge at your lowest moment. The ones that worship this ability and allow this tendency to take over are the ones we call 'bitches'. Often bitches merely point out the blindingly obvious in undiplomatic ways.

*'**You are more than capable** of defending yourself if you have to; a few people have underestimated you and ended up paying a price.'*

(The 2 highlighted sections in the generalisations above are known as 'psychic softeners' – these are weasel phrases that appear otherworldly and have an aura of mystic languaging about them. Sprinkle your generalisations liberally with such fluff. This is psychic jargon. I will add more for you to use as we go along. With practise you'll start generating your own unconsciously. If the unconscious sees you are determined to learn something it helps.)

When women are very young they are aware that they want to be regarded as pretty, beautiful even. This is part of the appeal of princesses to them. So?

'I feel that you place a great deal of focus on how you are perceived by others. You often feel a yearning for other's approval and compliments. My genuine intuition is that you would like people to see beyond the surface and recognise the attractiveness of the woman beneath that.'

If a woman is very attractive, she will have been treated very differently from other girls from an early age. She will have noticed men looking at her from her early teens. A very good looking girl receives similar treatment to a celebrity; this makes the more shallow ones and yes the clever ones arrogant. So?

*'**You attract** the attention of lots of people and some of that you find very flattering but on other occasions you would like to be seen for who you are. I sense some of the attention you could really do without. You are used to, what's the phrase? Good treatment*

from men especially...'

And that's a good time, now, to consider the men...

Stroking the bruised male ego.

Pretty much all men, unless they are very creative and sensitive, think they are Billy Big Bollocks* (*English word meaning testicles). They think the sun shines out of their big hairy ass and they are the best at everything, blah, blah blah. At least that's the front alter. They are permanently engaging in little boy pissing competitions with other men, over nothing but proving to themselves how great and fucking gifted they truly are! If only the world knew their genius. They often have answers to ALL life's problems. They are armchair generals, leaders of countries, sporting coaches, you name it. Until the midlife crisis and beer belly come along that is. Men like you to kiss their ass in cold reading, anything else may lead to a fist fight!

Men think they are 'confident'. Men think 'women' find them hotly attractive. We may call this sexual vanity. I think 'rejection' to a man is just busted pride. He is mummy boy stunned when some woman finds someone else more attractive than him. She's crazy! By the way most men are privately scared shitless of women if you haven't worked that out yet. Women have an immense power of which they are completely unaware. At the least it is the power to charm. *At the most, it is the power to create all human life on earth!* Think about the significance of that.

Men believe they are 'logical' and great 'decision makers'. Riiiight! We may call this the rational myth of man. Most are actually an overweight dumb ox by forty.

Men believe they can achieve anything they set their mind out to achieve. The fact they generally achieve nothing they really wanted to achieve by forty is by the by. This is the 'superman' myth. As boys they all want to be superheroes, which is a noble aim and they mean it too. But by twenty, if they have any spirit left, it's generally in the drink's cabinet. Men's aims are unfocused, nebulous and in reality they are mainly too scared to try. Men lack almost any insight into themselves at all being so externally focused. This generally leads them to make dumb, half-informed (I'm being generous) decisions. Do I come over a tad cynical?

Men like to achieve respect through consistency, loyalty, a determination to attain goals, a host of commitments, relationships etc. All men want respect. Few have it. There is no conspiracy of men to oppress women. 99.9% of men on earth have zero real power. Men by and large adore the women in their lives. *They would die for them willingly.* Men have been oppressed by ruling elites through history. They are the ignorant, tough workhorse and occasional cannon fodder of the powerful and seen as disposable, replaceable - nothing more. Like women, men's needs cannot be met without effort and struggle in this diseased society. Their boyhood dreams are laughed at, pissed on and frittered away by working for 'the man': self-pity and drink overtake him somewhere along the way.

Most men also believe they are fair minded if competitive. Often this is self-flattering bullshit and some will shit on anyone to get what they want. Now what about some cold reading stuff based on the above?

'At your core you are self-confident. You just need the right outlets, circumstances if you like to let them shine.'

'When you are expressing your true talents your confidence is obvious. I feel you must find more opportunities to let these qualities predominate.'

'What you want is respect. Respect comes from expecting it. It also comes from deserving it. I am not sure you feel that you have been treated as respectfully as you deserved from time to time. Is that not so?'

'When you want to be, you are logical. You like facts. You want proof. You make decisions based on the evidence you have gathered through your own efforts.'

'You prefer calm deliberation over emotion.'

'You are earthy and grounded. People like this quality in you.'

'Would it be true to say that many women have found you attractive but that your own insecurities held you back from making an approach from time to time?'

'You believe that hard work is what makes anyone successful.'

Some of them actually do! The fact is the higher ups do less work than anyone!

'You still have many goals, many things you want to achieve. You feel you haven't yet reached your potential. All that is required is a little self-belief and a few changes here and there in attitude and you'd be surprised what is actually possible.'

'When you set your sights on a goal you are all or nothing. You go for it with all that you have to give.'

'You are fair-minded but firm. You like to help people but only if they take some responsibility in the process, correct?'

Now that is true!

Many men are secretly deeply 'insecure' about a whole host of things. If they weren't, they wouldn't be seeing therapists, cold readers etc. now would they?

'You have untapped powers and potentials that even those around you do not

recognise...'

'You do not often feel understood. You are seen as a good provider but you have other qualities you'd like acknowledged. You often feel you have much more to offer.'

'When you are focused and determined you have an almost heroic energy that you can call upon! It is one of your strengths!'

'You have a great sense of humour that you use to lighten the mood and make others feel better. Although you feel work defines you in many ways, you have a playful side too.'

Men prefer to joke away problems. Or brush them under a carpet. Not because they are insensitive but because they are _so_ sensitive. Emotional pain is felt intensely by them - studies have shown even more so than in women, they just don't show it or hide from it. Why do you think almost all great art and poetry is created by men?

'You are a doer. You talk about things only so far as they lead to active solutions.'

'Many women find differing qualities that you have more attractive than you have

acknowledged. You are more admired than you know.'

Flattery and ego-boosting goes a long way Padawan. Just think: what are people really like? What do they need? And craft suggestions accordingly. Cold reading statements are suggestions – they are directionalising the mind. Be careful where you send it. Be uplifting! Be hypnotic!

Let's analyse men in a bit more depth. Cold readers as you will see are no fools. They literally often have a statistician's knowledge of their fellow men: all the better to con you with!

Men focus on their work/careers to a far greater degree than women; even following the injection of 'feminist' ideas into wider society. Although I have met many male clients who have set aside their own ambitions, at least for a while, to allow a woman to 'succeed' – this always causes tension and problems in a relationship being an inversion of the natural order. It can push a man to the brink of depression. I know: I have seen it professionally. This is cultural hermaphroditism and it is making men and women ill as they fail to get their real needs met and express who they deeply are.

In modern Western society, despite extensive automation, men will broadly enter either a 'brawn or brain' job. Men who enter a more physical outdoors career tend to be much more masculine and earthy. They tend to have greater common sense and actually hate being 'locked indoors' unlike an admin office boy. Such life choices are very much imposed by...

- Family traditions and prejudices. (The perfect peasant etc. discussed above.)

- Social class/snobbery.

- Money – for education etc.

Let's take brawn first. In the US this man is known as the 'blue collar worker' (slaves wear collars?); in the UK he is called 'the working class' (what's left of it!). What generalisations can we make about the working man on both sides of the pond?

- He is a doer. He is a man of action. He makes things happen physically. Generalisations? *'I **believe** you are a doer* *rather than a watcher. When you know what has to be done, you take action.'*

- He is much easier to get along with than his pencil neck, paper pusher 'white collar' fellow. He is more laid back, egalitarian. He takes people as they come and is broadly speaking more tolerant. They have better social skills than the office boy. Try - **'You will** *take people as they are. You are easy to get along with as long as someone doesn't put on fake airs and graces.'*

- They highly value freedom; they like a high degree of control over their lives and are willing to take the initiative. They often like running a small business: this fulfils their ideal of autonomy. They want to be left alone. They are so independent minded (in the UK they are called 'independent traders') that they only make commitments if they absolutely have to. This is why builders/construction workers often have several jobs on the 'go' – they seek variety and hate the regimentation of the pencil neck's stifling reality. **'You are the kind of** *man who is highly independent minded. Ideally you would be* *your own boss. You are a no nonsense individual. You value your freedom: your freedom to choose your own course is vital to your well-being.'*

- They are grounded in the 'now' – the present. They are not interested in Utopian ideologies by and large. They are practical and real. They are not usually troubled by doubts and anxieties unless their work dries up which can have a catastrophic effect on their self-worth as was proven by the Great Depression. For them 'the future' is more of the same but better. They want solid things like 'security', a 'sound economy', good food and holidays. When prosperous they tend to get a little portly as if to display their success. '***I don't sense that*** *you are a person who is given to wild daydreams about the future. I feel you are a very grounded man* (use the word man for manly men, they like it). *You like to work, you put your all your energy into it once committed and it defines who you are and how you see yourself and your role in this world.'*

- They are brilliant at finding swift solutions to technical problems and taking actions to solve them. Women of all social classes find them very attractive. I designed a set for a play once and the carpenter came in, saw my drawings and converted a pile of wood into a village cottage in about twenty minutes – he took a plan and made it real. He was incredibly self-confident as a man and in doing so. By the way all the buildings around you, all the cars you drive, the planes you fly in – THEY built them. *'Once you have identified a problem* **you are** *the kind of man who can solve it fast. You just get on with it, no ifs or buts.'* Procrastinators tend to be 'nervy' sorts.

- They have a good sense of humour and enjoy the comradeship of their male friends. They like sports. They are sexually straight. The only exception to this and I have observed this and so did Quentin Crisp author of 'The naked Civil Servant', is that 'toughs' from this background are often closet gays and their violent streak enables them to be physical with other men. Why do you think there are so many rapes in male prisons? *'You like being a man. You are comfortable with your masculinity. You don't like the company of metrosexual men. You think they need to 'grow a pair' right? You like the natural pleasures of watching sports with beer; that makes you a happy man.'* (These types generally read tabloid papers.)

- They are highly technical minded. They are hands on, they learn best that way, they are the boys that took that toy apart to see how it worked, or took a spaceship and tried to turn it into a metal detector! They are easily capable of abstraction but do not engage it in for its own sake. They only do so when practical reasons demand it. As abstraction is related to hypnosis, they are more grounded in present realities than pencil necks. Tools, machines and such are a God send to them. **'As a child** *you used to enjoy breaking up your toys to see how it all worked. You liked playing with trucks and diggers in the sandpit. At school you liked the practical subjects, the tangible ones; you learn best hands on. You are great with tools. Your wife loves the fact you save money with your DIY skills. She likes the way you are* *good with your hands.'* This may get a laugh.

- They like risk: they want results and feedback for their efforts now. They want bread today not dreams tomorrow. They only set out on achieving a goal if its realisation appears 'doable'. *'**A lot of other men** are not risk takers. You are aware of this because you are one. But you tend to take calculated risks, although you might enjoy a bet on the gee-gees for fun now and gain. You don't gamble on important things, you focus on what can be realistically gained through taking risk. You want solid results from the actions you take in a reasonable time frame. You don't trust people who claim that so and so will be great in ten years' time etc.'*

- They are great soldiers, patriots and doggedly devoted once let loose on an enemy. They are the salt of the earth of any nation and despised by elites. Politically they tend toward 'conservatism' with a small C but economic instability and a natural desire for egalitarianism allows leftist provocateurs to hoodwink them.

Secretly the leaderships of both 'left' and 'right' hate them – seeing them as some type of barbarian. Slow to anger but woe-betide anyone when their wrath is roused. Such men toppled Rome. *'**Based upon your energy/vibe** I feel that you are a peaceful man but that you will stand up for what you believe in. You won't be shoved around. You aren't attracted to change for changes sake. But if something is worth fighting for you're willing to do what must be done. You love your country and its best traditions.'*

• As leaders they motivate by hands on example. They work in the building trade/construction industry, as mechanics of all sorts, in factories, as drivers of lorries/cabs etc., make good policeman, soldiers, small businessmen. They have a great capacity for loyalty.

Instead of blue colour man think **ACTION MAN!** Now let's take his tame and civilised counterpart – office boy! The 'white collar' worker. It's white but he's still collared. What generalisations can we make about them?

- They are what we call 'high achievers'.
  They often have spent more time in school
  and have lots of certificates that make
  them feel good. They look down on the
  action man. Once they have a degree they
  feel they are a 'made man', little knowing
  the purpose of University is to narrow
  thought and not broaden it. '*It wouldn't
  surprise me if* *even as a young man you
  knew you were aiming high. You knew
  that you could set your sights high and
  were determined you had what it took,
  even if only deep down at first, to achieve
  those dreams. Your status in life is
  important to you. You are rightly proud of
  what you've achieved and it wasn't all
  plain sailing was it? You like to overcome
  challenges, it makes you feel alive. You are
  driven.'*

- They tend more to group think and are
  what you might call 'team players'. They
  had better be to succeed in an office
  environment which is ant-like and highly
  hierarchical. Whether it's priests in a priest
  hood, office clerks shifting paper or
  inputting data they are the bureaucrats of
  the 21st century. *'You work well with*

others. You are comfortable with delegating responsibility if you have to. You like to be surrounded by competent people who pull their weight and contribute fully to a group effort. You are well aware of the power of an efficient team.'

- They are future oriented. They are self-improvers. The want to move up the totem pole. They must be capable of planning. They look ahead and can conceptualise how things could be different. They focus on their goals; outcomes etc. are more important than the how of getting there which they leave to the action men to enact. They see themselves as the brain and the workers as the obedient body, following their instructions. **'You have** *a great capacity to see possibilities where others can't.* **The key is** *you are a visionary in your way, and others don't always appreciate that do they?* **Your strongest asset/one of your strongest assets** *is to plan, to see how things could be made better. You can see the forest for the trees. This is one of the reasons that you have natural leadership qualities that* *others lack. All good leaders can see past present difficulties. But you are human, at times your role, your very real responsibilities can seem a burden.'*

- They are capable of high levels of efficiency and thoroughness in their field. They are capable of getting the action men to do anything often, even if it's not in their best interests, having a knowledge of oratory, rhetoric, human management, cybernetics, systems theories, 'psychology' etc. *'**My psychic sense is** that you are a – if a job is going to be done, it is going to be done properly kind of guy. Your know how to get the best out of a team, what their strengths and weakness are. Whether they are comfortable in a role or not. You have great insight that allows you to spot talent. Somehow - you just know what to say to motivate those around you.'*

- They are often physically weedy/weak and tend more toward 'effeminism' – the body is a mere appendage, a head on a stick. In therapy they often need to be told to exercise to correct this imbalance They are more likely to visit the theatre and opera and like to see themselves as 'cultured'. Often they are little more than nouveau riche vulgarians. They read 'broad sheet' newspapers and feel they are well informed about...'things'. They pride themselves on seeing 'the bigger picture'. **'People who notice you** *see that you are a man to be respected. You like to enjoy cultural events, you patronise the arts to whatever capacity you can. You see the importance of such activities in a way that others cannot.'*

- They value 'the intellect' and 'intelligence'. They often enjoy telling others what to do, even outside of work. They feel they are a 'cut above', the natural leaders. They are glib and 'well spoken' in a kind of acceptably conventional way. **'My first impression is** *that you are a great communicator. It's your intelligence, your ability to analyse a situation, work out what needs to be done and relate that to people in an effective way that sets you apart from others.'* (Flattery often nullifies cynicism if handled correctly.)

- They are terrified of a lack of order, structure and routine supplied by others – they often feel they could 'run a business' but never have. Left alone they often lack the discipline to work without prompts. *'I perceive you possess a preference for routine and order, especially with regards to work. Within a structured framework you feel most comfortable. You dislike chaotic situations and lack of discipline. You recognise anarchy leads nowhere. A chain of command is necessary for things to function well.'*

- You will find them as army officers, managers (within corporations, bureaucracies), teachers, professors, politicians at all levels etc. They tend to extraversion at the higher levels. At the lower levels a good introvert can hide safely. *'**Deep within you** there are leadership potentials. I sense even greater than you consciously acknowledge yet.'* (Best not said if they are already the head of Mitsubishi cars etc.)

- They are time conscious. Time is money, money, money: they obsess over 'efficient time use' etc. Their own and others who they hate being 'idle'. *'You see your time as precious asset.* **You are able to sense** *when others are slacking. Not pulling their full weight, not being optimally productive. This serves you well. I feel in this world that you are aware that time is finite and that we must all make the best use of it we can while we are here. You are a 'seize the day' kinda guy/gentlemen etc.'* (These sorts are generally NLP 'through time' types. This makes them time conscious and good planners. They can conceptualise the future well.)

- At worst in times of intrigue they lean toward extreme right or left ideologies depending on upbringing. Not given to idealism but rather they see a given system and seek to benefit materialistically from it. Never rebels. Go along to get along. **'Nobody is going to tell you** *that every new idea that pops up is worth trying. You are an experienced man, you can see through such wishful schemes. Your motto is 'why rock the boat', 'why change what is working' etc. People need to convince you of the rationality of* *change before you'll willingly accept an innovation.'*

We shall call them **MANAGER MAN.** A subsection, a large one too, of this group are narcissistic personalities – in the clinical sense. They have no peoples skills, are ruthless and obsessed with status and being 'admired'.

There is a third type, an offshoot of the MANGER MAN but lacking the essential will to power, who you might call – **THE LONE NERD!** These are computer programmer types, rarely (these days) writers. They tend to be more sensitive, rebellious and imaginative than the manager types and surpass them in intelligence. They can be more introverted as a rule but not necessarily so. What do we know of this 'misfit' minority?

- He often has better written than oral skills, though not always.

- They hate an imposed external structure preferring to keep their own.

- They do not keep 'factory time' well and prefer to 'organise' their own day in their own way. Hates deadlines.

- Fiercely independent. May be attracted to 'conspiracy theories'.

- Likes to work in a way in which they spend time alone or are able to control their social input.

- They tend to be more highly empathetic of others than other white colour types. In fact let's be blunt – as opposed to the others of their kind they have empathy!

- They are not so classically obsessed with 'status', the 'rat race' etc. Seeing it for the fraud it is.

- In modern times often attached to a computer and they trust internet sources more than the 'main stream media' etc. In many ways better adapted to the technological society than all the others put together.

- Values freedom as highly as the action man.

Generalistions for the lone nerd.

*'**I very much doubt if** you are a conformist. You go your own way. You are fiercely*

attached to your need for independence. You feel swamped in a crowd sometimes.'

'**You are capable** of working with others obviously, but you feel a better use of your time is to really focus in on things in your own time and own way.'

'**I am willing to bet that** you are the type of guy/bloke who can become totally absorbed in a hobby, something you love doing. So much so you can forget everything else and you love being in that zone don't you?'

'**In my mind** you go your own way. Unlike others you can see through the fakes and the frauds in ways others can't. You gather information and move forward based on proof. The changing opinions of the masses do not sway you.'

'**Why am I getting the word** 'technology' popping into my mind? Somehow technology is vital to you.'

If you draw a blank...

'No. It's more...'innovation'!'

'As a child you were comfortable playing on

your own. Quite happy to do so at times. As an adult this has served you well in many ways but I feel the social side of things is being left out a bit. Your needs to connect with others could be better fulfilled, would that be fair?'

Often these types are isolated, lonely and lack social skills. They are frequently anxious in social situations and around the opposite sex to the point of phobia! The other two male types are generally dumbfounded by nerd man.

Turn on your inner 'Sherlock Holmes'.

In book 3, 'Powerful hypnosis' I touched on the subject of cold reading. We are taking it up a level. The outward physical signs between the first two male subgroups are easy to spot...

1. **Check their hands -** does he have soft, squeaky clean ones? Or big fat callouses and hands that look like they could bend steel? Believe me a person's hands tell you so much on close inspection (palm reading stuff aside) – a person's life and personality can lay in a pair of hands. *Think: what can I deduce about*

this person from his hands?

2. **Get physical** - Are they in tip top shape or do they look like they are about to experience a flab-a-lanche!? Office boys tend to be less physically tough and fit than their outdoorsy brethren. With age the effect of a lack of physical effort shows in the office boy.

3. **Skin colouration** - Action men spend time outdoors in daylight. They are often tanned with darker skin even if they have dark skin. They take their tops off while working. With age they look more 'weather beaten' by the exposure to the elements. Office boys tend to be paler (if white especially), pasty-faced. Like Gollum they look a bit anaemic and vitamin D deficient; the artificial light is not good. Their skin is softer. Not that I've felt it!!!

4. **Do they wear glasses?** - Attention to close detail = you need to wear specs, contact lenses etc. I draw a lot, and did so all the time as a kid. Result by 14, I needed specs. I wear contacts now – my baby blues are clear for all to see! Office boys tend to wear glasses more frequently. Actually I have never met a man who worked with his hands who wore glasses.

5. **Clothes, jewellery etc.** - In my experience most blue collar men turn up to my sessions in their work clothes and boots, they're covered in dust, paint etc. If they have hair it's tousled. The office boys are neatly dressed, like good little mumma's boys, smart side parting hair or sensible hair. Nice shiny watch. Smart casual clothes – the younger ones are quite fashionable if 'cool'. The older ones look like they play golf – golf slacks etc.

6. **General attitude** - Office boy when young (yuppies) and especially when old has a cocksure, smug sense of being a 'success' (financially). They look comfy, like well looked after pets. The working man turns up physically tired. In a fist fight you want working man by your side. They give off an air of what can only be called - 'struggle'.

You can find out what type of husband/boyfriend a woman has by listening to her responses to prompts etc. Note his type – make generalisations about her from her cues based on his type. You can also generalise what kind of relationship they have etc. Note social classes tend to 'inbreed' – this makes it easier to make guesses. This is why in England the middle class tends to be uglier but covers it with fashion accessories, fancy hair: with a smaller gene pool to draw from they are more inbred!

So what do we generally hate?

Men and women hate: change for change's sake, illogical directives/orders – doing things that make no sense to them and most importantly – **BEING CONTROLLED OR MANIPULATED BY OTHERS!!!** This is one of the reasons that we have a conscious mind at all, to protect us from this.

Note for thinkers: In all Western countries we are in fact experiencing, on a daily basis, all 3 of the above mentioned human hates; this is why everyone around you is miserable. And that kind of misery can't be hypnotised away.

Some generalisations that make you seem so smart based on these realities are?

'*I believe you have no fear of change unless that change is unfounded and what we might call change for change's sake...*'

'*I feel a strong trait in you is that if a particular course of action makes sense to you*

– you can carry it out, you'll even go for it but if it seems senseless you are as stubborn as a mule in resisting.'

*'**You are able to sense** when someone is trying to manipulate you and you loathe anyone who tries to foist their ideas and wishes upon you without concern as to whether you like it or not. This ability has protected you many times.'*

I might conclude this topic in an appendix in an upcoming book. Stay tuned! You could write 10 books on cold reading alone.

Appendix 2: Hypnosis and sport.

WARNING: *Do not hypnotise the talentless to believe they can compete with people who outclass them; you will only install delusions!!!*

I have helped quite a few clients improve their 'mind game' using hypnosis. Other things being equal 75-90% of winning in sport is down to the asset that having a real mental edge gives you. The Soviets were known to have experimented with sporting hypnosis a great deal. Results with weightlifters showed a marked improvement in strength. I have read quite a few books on sporting hypnosis too; most are a complete waste of your time. I am most often asked to help with what is known as 'mental toughness' and getting in 'the zone'. I have crafted a kind of all in one script below that deals with both these things in one intertwined module; first let me explain what both are!

Mental toughness.

Mental toughness and the zone are really pretty much the same thing. You can't have one without the other – they feed off one another symbiotically. **First you have to want to win, then you have to be <u>able</u> to win (realistically you must have the ability), you must <u>enjoy</u> what you do and have a damn good <u>reason</u> for doing so; really your sport should be an <u>expression of who you are</u> as a person.** You should be able to play in front of thousands as you would when 'practising'. So-called 'mental toughness' comes from believing in yourself and having a laser beam focus on what you are doing now. You are not anxious about self, past, future – you are just enjoying doing what you are doing. And you need that killer instinct – the ability to crush your opponent when the point of victory arrives. You must be able to control your emotions unconsciously. You must not give a sh*t who your opponent is. If they are human they can be beaten. Once you turn up for a competitive event you must trust your unconscious to play the game for you. You must believe you deserve to win and most importantly YOU must make it happen now. The iron resolve to win is what separates the eternal runner up from the champion. You simply have unstoppable determination to bulldoze your opponents into submission.

The zone – accessing flow states.

This is simply a state of absorption in the present moment that is automatic and therefore unconscious in origin. Anyone who is above average in sport or the arts enters this state when performing at their best. When you see an actor or sportsman 'forcing' a performance it is because he is using his conscious mind to direct things; often he is well aware and frustrated by his or her failure to get into the 'flow state' and this frustration only makes it harder to 'just let it happen'. Distractions, worries, stresses and everyday patterns of thinking are not necessary in flow states. It is really a highly focused yet effortless state of waking hypnosis in which you are alert and functioning at your very best. If you have experienced it, and you have, it feels amazing – flow occurs when we become totally immersed or as I am so fond of saying we 'become absorbed' on external activities. For a full description of 'flow' read the book **'Flow' by Mihaly Csikszentmihalyi.** By the way just because the Rogue Hypnotist recommends a book doesn't mean he agrees with everything in it: agreement is not the purpose of reading – the stimulation of your own further thought is the goal. With these two factors in mind as being highly important in sporting success I created the...

Optimising sporting potential script.

(Deep hypnosis assumed)

Step 1: Accessing states.

'There have been times in your life when you knew **you're in flow** have there not? You can recall other occasions when **you feel unstoppable determination to win.** And the amazing thing was...that when you **enter this euphoric state of absorption automatically,** effortlessly, you **play your best without trying, now...**And you know what this state is like...**There are no distractions...You forget the irrelevant in this place...You perform optimally yet do not seek perfection...**Because you **let go consciously and trust your subconscious** to aid you in all your efforts, sporting or otherwise, now...You feel relaxed, focused, alert and have total mental clarity on the task at hand...This all manifests easily when you **sincerely believe at a very deep level that <u>you deserve to win...</u>**

Flow is similar to **going into deep hypnosis** but with your eyes open, your mind only vigilant to relevancies of what is going on around you...At such times nothing else matters...**You enter the zone/groove/flow state easily...**more and more and more...in a self-reinforcing cycle of only greater success...You define success for yourself...proving nothing to nobody...You take a break from worries and concerns to **fully focus with iron determination on what you are doing and the process of doing it...**It all just seems to happen...Of course **you want to win...**and the best way to do that is to **feel that power when you play at the top of your game...**that powerful energy that you call upon without trying...Because another part of you...that we might call 'talent' can just do what it does...When **you are fully absorbed on the task** at hand...your perception of time alters naturally in this state...**you feel great...playing well makes you feel good...**You are playing for your own reasons...motivations and goals...and you can **powerfully enhance these factors** in this place of learning and change...Changes in states...The way you process information...Your better emotional control...Your drive...The joy of **being in flow now,** and when you need to be...But when you have prepared...when you have learnt the skills...you just **let them happen** at just the right time and place because...yes, **you have supreme mental toughness** but you do not ever try to force what is...Just as you don't try to grow another foot...Two are enough...You have what you need to win...It will manifest powerfully when you play...You **play as well in competition** as you do at any other time when...**you naturally play well,** at your best...That's right.

Step 2: Future rehearsal.

Imagine now, a you over there, playing with total mental toughness **fully absorbed in an amazing flow state...**Particular old, unwanted emotional responses are recalibrated and rebalanced...Many unknown re-associations, re-organisations...soothing certain things away...Re-connections occurring to create this reality...A peace of mind results...See how **everything you do is easy...**See how you can **ignore any competing stimuli** to **focus intently** in on what you are doing...See the grace and power of your body doing what it does...**You are calm and certain, full of a certain poise, now...**You express your sporting talents, character...the essence of who you are, as you **make your mark...**in ways that delight you...Great artists are just that...They know what they can do...And when it comes to doing that, they just do what they do...In the same way that the cheetah knows it can run fast...The elephant knows its **power without needing to know** how that power is...The eagle soars above the ordinary world in flights of triumph...Whereas others are limited, he knows that up there he is relaxed and in his element...The lion knows his strengths and need not seek to prove what is just instinctive...When **you act instinctively** like a Jedi Knight who need not see in ordinary ways...What he senses...What he feels...What he intuits by **letting unconscious learnings take over** at just the right time and place...And when **you have all these**

qualities of mind locked in... And you do...Your ability to **play superbly,** consistently reinforces your faith in your real ability to do so, when needed, now...

And when you are ready...float into that you who possesses that total mental toughness that all great athletes down through the ages have possessed...and is **in flow now...**Feel how good that feels...See through those flow-full eyes...Hear through those flow-full ears...**Feel your easy power,** that effortless expression of will and talent, drive, joy and determination all intermingled with **a pure sense of total self-belief, now...**that lead you inevitably to **play optimally every time you do**...I'll be quiet for a while you do what needs to be done. That's it!

(Allow 30 seconds mental rehearsal time...)

So now, with all these new learnings and understandings, **you can access flow when you want...** Look forward with positive expectations that you will and do play well...You reach your potential...You **express your potency...**Your **focus and intent** are strong. And won't it be awesome to discover what things you can do now...without even attempting...because you just know how to breathe...you know how to speak...you know how to walk...you just forget about it. It is a habit...taken care of unconsciously, now...So playing well is an inevitability that you can **feel ever so comfortable** about...and you will, can you not? Can you not? Haven't you?...That's right. And who weren't you never anyway who truly is a good/ great sportsman/woman? In your own unique way...And that as they say is that.'

(You can help anyone 'steal' the talents of others using a process called **deep trance identification**; basically get the person to imagine floating into someone who does something brilliantly and learn how to do it via osmosis. They imagine being the other person as they do something well. Then re-associate the learnings and lock 'em in: easy. The brain learns to generate such behaviours and attitudes instinctively and there is some real evidence it lifts performance measurably in many people.)

Appendix 3: Creating erotic trance.

Creating erotic trance script.

(This is an option for erotic hypnosis; you can use any standard induction in any style but...)

'Close your eyes and just adjust yourself so that you begin to **feel very comfortable...**That's it...You only need to **focus** on your breathing...In and out...In and out...That's it...As you do, you'll notice that just the sound of my voice relaxes you deeply...Your body starts to **feel even more relaxed...**as you focus on your breathing and **listen...**don't change that breath...just notice it...In fact there is nothing much you need to do consciously...for a while...Take a deep breath and hold it! And **relax even more** as you let go of that past tension...There is no place you need be right now...No one to want anything from and the other way around...Scan your body and notice exactly how...**that feeling of pleasurable relaxation spreads** without any effort...All muscles letting go...Cosy images...sensual feelings...naughty thoughts might come inside your mind...That's fine...Enjoy them...

Soon I'll say 'enjoy' and when I do...that will be your cue to find a way to **relax and go deeper** in your own way...Not right now, in a moment ok? Ready. 'Enjoy!' Go deeper - 10 times deeper! Now! A part of you hears this voice so another need not...Imagine that every word I utter only allows you to **feel more and more comfortable...**more and more open to every kind of wondrously pleasant experience...that you deeply desire...I'll say 'enjoy' again soon...and when I do...it only intensifies your most wondrous feelings 10 times more...Ready? Ok. 'Enjoy!' That's right! Just like that. You like it that way don't you? Do you have sensual memories you'd like to re-experience here?

Because this is your experience and that is very doable...in this state...of **complete absorption on pleasant things, inside...**And in this frame of mind and body...you will be able to **feel things even more wonderfully...**than ever before...You can **feel things you didn't know you could feel intensely...**but you can and will...There are new ways for you to discover, uncover your own innate capacity to **feel exquisite pleasure of every amazing**

kind...here...Be playful here...A part of you wants, desires and would love, would it not to **experience that pleasure in ways you never dreamed possible...**but another part knows far better what is so and what will be real for you...And again...when I say 'enjoy'...find your own way deeper...to a state of joy that you know is there...find it now, on...'Enjoy!' 10 times deeper and deeper **into erotic trance...**Erotic dreams...and you could...**go into an erotic daze of heightened pleasure...**that you are re-connecting to now...wasn't it?

Do you **feel that you are floating into a hypnotic oblivion?** Does it feel light and floaty? Or does your body feel heavier and heavier? As if you just don't want to move either way...because this just feels too damn good!? Things that aren't needed fade and melt, ebb...away...gradually or quickly...Arms and legs **so relaxed** that movement seems too much effort...Noticing those feelings merely allows them to amplify...Facial muscles **letting go more...**as though gentle but strong hands...massage that old state all away...You are in there...my voice out here...guides you only in ways that **increase**

your pleasure threshold...unconsciously... Allows you to play some different roles...Discover different aspects of your true total self...and the only real question is how much pleasure can you stand?

- What are you most curious about? (Pause for about 5 secs after each point.)

- Where do you want this to go?

- What delectable consequences en(in)trance your naughtiness most?

- How much more erotic trance is there to be immersed in?

- What things would you like to try out, in, or on here?

- If something new and thrilling was to happen, what would you most like that to be?

- If **news ideas penetrate deeply** in this place...which ones are you going to experience most vividly...

...as you **respond powerfully to these suggestions...**Because I am communicating directly with other than conscious processes, now...and your fantastical imagination will only help you learn...more of what you desire **inside, now...**Find your own way to **relax and go deeper...**A soothing pleasure well-comes you almost as if **you are having a sexual dream unconsciously...**Dream it as I speak privately to your most intimate parts...that crave what you want...And the deeper you go...the more juicy pleasure you fucking feel...You know that pleasure that makes you moan...And the more pleasure you allow yourself to indulge in...the deeper you go and these words probe and penetrate the deepest part of who you truly are...and what you really want to connect with...That's it! You are doing perfectly! Indulge yourself now because this is your time! And you can take in all the time you need here...

Your secret garden deepener.

Now in a moment, not now but in a moment...I am going to kiss you on your beautiful mouth...And that will be your cue to go 50 times deeper than you are...Ok Here it comes... (Kiss her) 50 times deeper than before...That's it! And instantly you find yourself in a very special place...it is your secret garden...it is so **lovely and peaceful** there...wander around it as you like...notice the sights...sounds...all the sensuous delights of that place deep inside of you...This is the place set aside so that you can experience...all of the most profound sexual pleasures that exist and that you would long, love and adore indulging in when and with whom it is and would be appropriate...It's a place where you can **rehearse in the safety of your mind** things you'd like to do...to discover if you would like to do them in reality...It is also just a place from which you can simply **access deep pleasures...**

When I kiss you again...your can melt into this zone within...and **become absorbed** by the possibilities of what can be...certain changes can occur for you...Get a sense of really opening up to that place...your senses are heightened to the highest pitch here...Can you **feel the atmosphere** of this garden, your garden, on your skin? Can you feel temperatures? What other sensuous things does your skin detect that make you **feel amazing** there? Your skin is made from the same matter as your nervous system when you were forming in your mother's womb...that is why it is so sensitive too and reveals your emotions...You may feel the kiss of the summer's breeze there as I kiss you now... (Kiss her) Sexually surrender, melt into it...Your beautiful femininity is recharged and reconnected to here...being a woman is a gift that you deeply appreciate...What smells do you smell that excite you in this place of only pleasure? Perhaps you feel a certain tingling? An electric feeling somewhere? There may be rock pools? Water features of some kind...If so, can you **hear** the water babbling there? It is a **comforting, peaceful** background to your experience? Maybe you just like to sit and watch the water flow...seeing a leaf being carried downstream...as you may have done as child...when your innate curiosity was new...

In this delightfully intoxicating place...**deep inside your mind, now...**all your senses are vividly alive here...it feels amazing...how you love your life! There is so much beauty here...In fact one part of your secret place is filled with intoxicating flowers...Just the aroma makes you **feel more and more turned on...**They have an aphrodisiac affect upon you which you simply cannot control but only **respond to powerfully!** Now, amongst these gorgeous flowers you see a rose...A red rose that represents all of your capacity...for increased, heightened, amplified sensuous sexual pleasure of all kinds...at the right time and place with the appropriate person...You head toward it and feel its hard stem...You grip the shaft of that and pull the flame bright red bulb toward you...You inhale the aroma which only increases your sexual arousal...You **feel all your senses are increasing in sensitivity to their maximum pitch.** And it feels ok to **feel that amazing...**You squeeze the stem and a puff of erotic smelling pollen puffs out and permeates the air with **powerful sexual feelings that grow even more in you...**You feel the bright red bulb's petals...they feel soft and sensuous...Stroke that bulb's petals and really feel the soft, velvety texture on your skin...Bring that bulbous head close to you and rub it against the soft skin of your face...You might **feel an erotic thrill tingle through** you as you do...That's right! Are you having naughty thoughts as a result already?

Move **deeper inside** your garden of

delights...breathe in all the fragrances that fill your senses with such delightful feelings...You may take a flower...any flower...and sit somewhere...taking your time to caress your soft yielding skin with the softness of that flower...Wherever you stroke it...On your neck...Forehead...Leg...Calf...The top of your chest...Between the cleavage of your bosom...Anywhere that delights you and thrills you in a way you'd like...And as you do...All **your sense of erotic touch and response to erotic touch is correspondingly enhanced...**The ability to enjoyably role play is easy! Like you did, in more carefree, imaginative days/daze...Rub, caress, stroke your body with that flower as you wish...You can open up to wholly novel experiences here...and somehow you just know it...as if by magic...allow your entire mind and body...to prepare to **open up fully and let in and out all the exciting, wondrous, delicious, enchanting sensations, experiences, performances and pleasures that you ever desired or craved...**Some will just be more intense and amplified...Don't be too surprised if some still are new...in amazing ways that you can't wait to experience fully...Erotic fantasy and anticipation....perhaps from a memory...perhaps from your sexual imagination...your ability to **act convincingly...now...**I would like you to **become intensely fascinated...**by a time when you had or could have had...an experience of intense and powerful sexual desire and total lust...Maybe it was a time when you positively knew...you were going to be able to **experience more pleasure than you ever imagined was really possible...**A time where and when you knew...really knew...that you wanted this more than anything else in the whole world...at that time that was or could be...**Feel that excited expectation and anticipation...**Be there now in that fantasy or memory or a bit of both...fully there now with a lover...Me. I'll be quiet while you take time to **experience that fully with all available senses** while I pause...

(Give her 1 whole minute of silence to enjoy herself.)

Appendix 4: Eliciting the erotic symbol of intense lust.

Feelings can be elicited or changed through symbolic manipulation. Below is an example of how this can be used in erotic hypnosis. You can adapt it in principle to create pleasant feelings in pretty much anyone. Deep hypnosis is best but the results could be achieved in a light waking trance depending on your subject and her willingness. A deep rapport, connection is assumed, plus the lady having been in and out of light trances now and again; this is powerful - use only with caution and consent or not at all.

Lusty symbols script.

(Deep hypnosis of some kind assumed)

'I'm a hypnotist and this is just for fun so with your eyes closed just **imagine** a symbol that represents your own, personal feelings of **intense lust...**The most powerful, uncontrollable, insatiable urge to have wild, passionate sex with a man. Me...I think you know what I mean, deeply...Accept the subconscious symbol given without question...

That's it. Notice every detail that you can about it... (Pause for 10 seconds) Great! Now, that symbol represents feelings...your feelings of **intense lust, now...**Put that symbol in that part of your body where it deeply desires to go...the place that feels just right... (Pause to let it happen) Now, let these powerful feelings of intense lust spread out from that place...as that symbols gets bigger and bigger! Let them build and build and only intensify and amplify more and more and more...Let them radiate all through you getting stronger and stronger...**feeling that lust only grow** insatiably, so you **feel that lust so intensely.** It's almost as though you want to **act on these feelings soon** in an appropriate, life-enhancing and safe way...as they grow...getting better and better all the time...so that you **feel so fucking horny!** And actually be-**come so intense** that these amazingly powerful feelings of lust spread and radiate out beyond your body...they are that powerful! Let that feeling of lust build to a wonderful pleasurable climax! Now in a moment as I count from 1-3 you'll open your eyes, feeling awake, horny and amazing...Keeping those intensely lustful feelings. You'll look at me and **reward me appropriately.** In fact you'll say...'I want you to fuck me now big boy!' Only once your sexual desires are satisfied will these feelings find satisfactory release! 1-2-3! Open your eyes horny girl!'

Appendix 5: women's orgasms in their own words.

The language of female arousal: words that turn her on. 'Do I make you horny? Yeah baby! Yeah!' Remember the bucked-toothed Austin Powers and his incredible ability to seduce women 'way out of his league' (exterminate that idea now by the way: no one is out of anyone else's league; except mine! Ha-ha!)? There is a language to sexual arousal. It's funny but women have such mundane ways of describing a process like arousal. They are far less fascinated by themselves than men are in them.

Women's descriptions of their own orgasms.

Often they will say, *'Like a sneeze. A tingling that intensifies* (this is when she cries out 'ah-ah') *etc. A short sharp intense increase* (the point where the sneeze will happen regardless - this part feels amazing)*, then the climax - the* (chhoooooooooo!)*, a very intense pulsing which feels like my is clit trying to turn itself inside out - lasts only a few seconds, then a throb, throb, throb... then a small gush, maybe a tablespoon total, then all of a sudden the intense sensation washes away, leaving* *only a very sensitive sensation.'*

You will notice that women's orgasms are very subjective things. Each women seems to experience it differently on the subjective level. She represents it to herself in her own unique way. Being relaxed and being able to let go also seems to affect the description as does masturbation induced orgasm as opposed to being boinked senseless.

'An orgasm with my lover is a weird out of body thing. I'm almost paralyzed from it, I may stop breathing for a bit, and afterward I cannot move for a while. It's not scary, just completely and wonderfully overwhelming.'

This one is more in depth...so to speak.

'First I feel a slight tickle where I'm being touched regardless of if it's with fingers, tongue, or penis. I feel my nipples start to tingle and I can feel the wetness I make begin to multiply. That tickle may fade in and out depending on the pace things are happening at. As the tickle rolls like waves against the shore of me, each wave becomes a little stronger, reaches a little higher up through the centre of me. The waves send shots of

electricity straight up through the centre of me and eventually through my arms and legs almost as I'm shooting electricity out my fingers and toes. The waves of glorious, tickling, electrical pleasure speed up and become almost violent, sending heat and pleasure to every part of me. I can feel my clit throbbing happily, my vagina pulsing with pleasure, my nipples extend to increase the magical tingling sensation, my skin ripples with a warm buzz, and the very core of me vibrates and rumbles with so much pleasure I feel like I'm going to absolutely burst. My body spasms, cries of inexplicable joy escape my lips, my legs tremble, and I can barely manage my breath until there's one final rush of warmth, electricity, and pleasure beyond description immediately followed by a soothing sigh. As I breathe that final often staggered breath, it's as if a warm, comforting peace washes over me. I feel a calm like no other. My skin remains sensitive, and that rocking pleasure just trickles now through the centre of me slowing and calming. There are sometimes an occasional shot of electricity that hurries out almost like an aftershock, interrupting the quiet slowing for only a moment. That continues until my breathing has normalized, my skin has stilled, and I've regained my bearings. That's when I wonder why I ever want to do anything else besides cum.'

By Jove young lady I need a cold shower after that! Like poetry! A short, terse example...

'I usually end up screaming or crying. Your whole body tenses up and it feels like all of your nerves are on fire. And then just when you're about to say no, you have to stop, I can't breathe, everything hurts, it's too much, too intense...Relief. Body convulsing, spasming, cross eyed, breathless, nearly unconscious, relief.'

Oh dear God! And there's more!

'Sometimes, when I can feel it building, it feels warm and I start gasping. I begin to get more excited as I feel my muscles tighten around my lover's member. My insides get tight, my stomach muscles, my lower muscles, my arms, my chest. Then it's like... an outer body experience; like I'm being lifted – it's exhilarating. The world falls away and nothing is left but my lover and I and the pleasure

rippling through my body, branching off from my groin, down my legs, up my stomach, down my arms and through my head. It's ecstasy for that moment and I feel so emotionally connected to him as my body ripples with the orgasm.'

And finally 3 varieties of 'gasms.

'Three diff orgasms for me: clit and G-spot + clit (the third, just the G-spot, is pretty rare).

Clit orgasm: *Like a string being pulled tighter, and tighter, and then a quick, gasping release. Legs get twitchy. Not much emotionally during this. Definitely easy/quick for me with some sort of vibrator.* (RH: hoochie mama!) *If it's clit stimulation only with oral, it's the same kind of quick release, but the build-up is slower, softer. Very easy to get overstimulated.*

Clit + G-spot: *The same kind of building, tightening, where muscles and body get wound tighter and tighter. Usually the build-up is a bit slower, a bit more pleasant, and then, depending on the depth/power of the release, there's just tons of spasming and the muscles of my pussy clench and unclench and* *clench again, and there's waves of pleasure. I've definitely cried after a really big or deep clit/G-spot orgasm, it can be very emotional for me; I can keep spasming and shaking for minutes after.*

The G-spot only: *is pretty rare for me, I think it's only happened four or five times in my life. It's less...pronounced or explosion-y for me, and more throbby satisfying than big release.'*

Good grief madam! What can we learn from this without drooling too much? There is a pattern of description nes pas? For starters - be careful of being too specific: let her have her own experience but there are common themes you can use in descriptions in erotic hypnosis.

1. Tightening of muscles (sexual tension).

2. An unstoppable build-up of tension that needs release.

3. Waves of pleasure.

4. Tingling sensations.

5. Muscle spasms.

6. Release.

7. A build-up of warmth and heat.

8. Sensitivity.

9. A state of total absorption (hypnosis).

10. Out of body experience (dissociation – deep trance phenomenon).

11. Seeing colours.

12. Connection to lover, the universe etc.

13. Mindlessness, unconsciousness – temporarily.

14. Peaceful bliss and after 'shakes'.

Ok so you can use words like this in your description and even if she's never had a very intense orgasm, by describing it, with her *associated into* the experience in trance you can train her to let go more in reality. Remember: hypnosis creates hypnotic realities which seek completion in reality. Trance is a

3D training simulator/stimulator!

Priming orgasm: sexual words and phrases to increase arousal.

Use these types of wordage to get your lady in a very happy mood. Words access the related part of the mind-body system (neuroscience has proven this): they consciously and unconsciously direct attention to it. Sexual words - having to do the continuation of human life on earth - are given high priority unconsciously. Remember the unconscious is listening and decoding language whenever we speak – you don't have to think about it. A sexual priming word list follows; it is somewhat different from that found in my fourth book, 'Forbidden hypnotic secrets'. Those words can and could be used in non-sexual contexts in order to sexualise them, as the author of 50 shades of Grey knew only too well, or with erotic trance; they are inherently sexually ambiguous...You are idea seeding but not seedy which is creepy! Read women's erotic 'literature', should that be cliterature; it is chock a block with this filth? Common themes are the ***1. Idea of losing conscious control. 2. Sexual***

domination. 3. Descriptions of physical and emotional sensations. 4. Sensual immersion, absorption.

- **Struggle.**

- **Double fuck.**

- **Exhausting.**

- **Deep inside.**

- **Muscles clenching.**

- **Euphoric.**

- **Grip like steel.**

- **Leering over her.**

- **She could see his cock.**

- **Admire the instrument.**

- **Wrestling with the idea.**

- **Virgin territory.**

- **Every nook, every cranny.**

- **Pressed against the flesh of her neck.**

- **Get down on her knees.**

- **Captive, captured.**

- **Sheer silk.**

- **Begged for more.**

- **Slut.**

- **Exposed belly.**

- **Like an old lover.**

- **Pressed against her x (chest etc.)**

- **Rubbed ever so gently against her x (nipples etc.)**

- **Young.**

- **Gripping her, exploring her.**

- **She imagines them x (watch/ing etc.)**

- **Licked her lips.**

- **Strong muscled man.**

- **Tanned skin.**

- **Oiled muscles.**

- **She pressed her legs together.**

- **Feeling the hard x against her slit.**

- **Eyes drawn to x.**

- **Tiny droplets of sweat on his chest.**

- **Fuck! She thought!**

- **Deep inside.**

- **Face looking down on her.**

- **His entire body was over her now.**

- **She could see his big cock.**

- **Admire the instrument.**

- **The only thing between them was her tights.**

- **His hot long rod that would impale her sex and bring her the relief she desperately needed.**

- **The heat of a volcano.**

- **Bitch.**

- **Tempered by her desire.**

- **The thrusting abdomen.**

- **His member aimed squarely at her sex.**

- **My God he's not even going to bother with my clothes!**

- **He taunted me, his big dick hovering just above my skirt.**

- **I can smell your lust, your desire; I've never had a woman who begged for it as much as you.**

- **Your body, excited by the situation, and somehow, irresistibly by me is on fire.**

- **It takes all your willpower not to slip a hand under your tights and pleasure yourself right here and now.**

- **The tension, the arousal is getting stronger and stronger, you are getting closer and closer to an absolutely unbelievable orgasm. RAMP UP THAT AROUSAL, NOW!**

(NOTE: about 20% of men and women can experience orgasm due to high levels of adrenaline. This is why some women and men orgasm during a sexual assault. They will say, 'my body betrayed me.' This is one of the things therapists who help such people have to help them deal with. ***Just because someone orgasms during rape doesn't mean it wasn't rape.*** After such attacks victims may however deliberately seek out 'rougher' sexual experiences, even orgies etc. and prefer more aggressive sex. The facts are horrible but true I am afraid.)

Appendix 6: Count up to 10 exduction procedure.

This is an alternative counting up module for exductions. Remember the rule of exductions from book 1, 'How to hypnotise anyone,' is by and large is: 'long time in, longer out, quickly in, quickly out': I find this true only with new clients. After the first session or two the conscious and subconscious learns how to go 'in and out' almost instantly. Throw in some positive words and ideas for luck to seal the deal!

New awakening process.

(Adapt for erotic hypnosis unless she has agreed to keep certain behaviours, responses etc.)

'As I count from 1-10 all I've said in this successful session stays with you only growing stronger every second of each passing day. Just a habit now. You continue with your confident, happy, relaxed and calm mind-set, able to **achieve your goals...**

1 – The unconscious will act upon these words automatically when needed.

2 – Awakening with **a much more positive attitude** in general. Feeling good, almost as though **a burden has been lifted.** All of your best qualities seem enhanced.

3 – Pleased and proud that you've overcome the challenges you once had. More joy in life as a consequence. More **faith in yourself!**

4 – Every muscle had been cleansed and purified as if by magic, and that was hypnosis magic by the way!

5 – You will feel so very good upon awakening! You'll **feel fully healthy and well!** Life provides you with opportunities which you seize with relish! Full of energy and life force - more aware of your body and environment.

6 – Normal feelings moving through you pleasantly! More aware of noises and the room out here.

7 – Realising that when **you awaken soon** you can forget to remember what you can remember to forget!

8 – Feeling better than you have in weeks, lightening up about so many things!

9 – Almost **all the way out** reinforcing all the best things you ever thought about yourself! You **feel so amazing!**

10 – Everything returned to normal! All bodily functions back to normal! **Back to 100% normal waking consciousness with a wonderful clear and precise mind!** Totally refreshed and rested as if you had a great night's sleep! Delightfully re-energised! **Eyes open** as soon as you're ready – feeling good! That's it: you're done!'

(Obviously your voice gets more stimulating, wakeful and rousing as they return to waking alertness – your voice should be as it was when you spoke to them normally in the interview/pre-talk part of the session! They then associate your 'hypno-voice' only with trance; all you have to do is 'put it on again' to start to reactivate it!)

Appendix 7: The Hitler youth vow - programming the young through song and prayer etc.

As in all authoritarian societies the programming of youth to slavishly obey was paramount in Nazi Germany. When young German boys and girls entered the Hitler Junger/Hilter Youth they were *inducted* through a ritualised ceremony. The sacred vow of allegiance to Hitler, the 'holiest' act of the rite went like this...

(The following is simply an authoritarian, waking hypnosis programming induction procedure – see my 4th book 'Forbidden Hypnotic secrets' to learn about waking hypnosis. My analysis follows the hateful hymn: read the original without my additions first.)

<u>Vow.</u>

'You Hitler are our commander!

We stand in your name!

The Reich is the object of our struggle!

It is the beginning and the Amen!

Your word is the heartbeat of our deeds!

Your faith builds cathedrals for us!

And even when death reaps the last harvest

The crown of the Reich never falls!

We are ready, your silent spell

Welds our ranks like iron!

Like a chain, man beside man

Into a wall of loyalty around you!

You Fuhrer are our commander!

We stand in your name!

The Reich is the object of our struggle!

It is the beginning and the Amen!'

And now - with notes...

<u>Vow.</u>

'You Hitler are our commander!

(Immediate unthinking de-individuation of the child. Hypnotic command implied – 'Do what the God Fuhrer says without question' – the conscious mind is told to stop operating)

We stand in your name!

(Group hypnosis – we are not individuals merely a mob of happy slaves; the children are collectively programmed to identify themselves as mere appendages of Hitler's will)

The Reich is the object of our struggle!

(Unspecified noun 'Reich' – what is the 'Reich' specifically? Unspecified goal 'object' – what 'objectives' exactly? Unspecified verb 'struggle' – 'struggle' for or against what? And you thought 'NLP' and hypnotic psycho-linguistics were new? The question is how did the Nazis know about it? How did this group

come from nowhere with a fully working system ready to be implemented?)

It is the beginning and the Amen!

(Implied command – your sole existence child is to serve Hitler's will. The 'Amen' gives a pseudo Christian feel to the rite. Nazism was actually deeply anti-Christian. Amen is derived from Amon-Ra, ancient Egyptian mythology's 'Satan')

Your word is the heartbeat of our deeds!

(Commands of man - of Hitler connected to the unconscious process of the heartbeat. In other words Hitler's orders are followed automatically at an unconscious level. The heart = a metaphor for emotions. The emotional system and will of the child is hijacked to Hitlerism)

Your faith builds cathedrals for us!

(Again we see the use of a pseudo Christian front in terms of languaging - 'faith', 'cathedral' etc. But we know the most senior Nazis were Satanists; (by

the way it doesn't matter if you don't believe in 'Satan', 'God' etc.: plenty of others do) belonging to the occult Thule society. There is a suggestion of building something 'holy' – but what? The Christian values of the children are paced and then lead somewhere darker)

And even when death reaps the last harvest

(This is martyrdom programming – a child is programmed to lay down its life! You harvest vegetables – the child is a vegetable – geddit!?)

The crown of the Reich never falls!

(You may die as an individual but the Nazi system goes on...)

We are ready, your silent spell

('Ready' for what? Spell???! Clear occultic languaging! I know this book is called Crafting hypnotic spells but that's a marketing gimmick. Children often believe in magic – they are being programmed that Hitler has a magical power over them; if they believe it, it is so!)

Welds our ranks like iron!

(Autocracies love metallic imagery)

Like a chain, man beside man

(You have no individuality! Your lack of this makes you strong – verbal operant conditioning)

Into a wall of loyalty around you!

(Protect the oppressor – pure sado-masochism. The abused is conditioned to protect the abuser)

You Fuhrer are our commander!

(Repetition of 'servants of the Fuhrer's will' meme – repetition of themes = hypnotic programming; unspoken implication – do not listen to parents, religious values, conscience etc. Hitler's voice is installed as a hypnotic voice to be obeyed, as a religious person would obey the word of God)

We stand in your name!

The Reich is the object of our struggle!

It is the beginning and the Amen!'

(Repetition of earlier themes – loop programming, over and over etc.)

Modern youth culture owes a lot to the Nazis. In many ways the modern world has silently co-opted many Nazi practises including regular package holidays which the Nazis invented. Like the Nazis, the West places huge value on vague concepts like 'achievement'. See my next book for more shocking revelations!

In 'Wizards of trance' I outline some of Hitler's evil methods of swaying the subconscious. Let me give you a few final shocking secrets about how Hitler used persuasion etc. to mind fuck the Germans into catastrophe. He was an expert communicator; more so than you know. An examination of his speeches reveals several things...

- He used banal speech (man in the street speech) with 'exalted' poetic speech. I call this **mundane-poetic fractionation.**

- He littered his speeches with **metallic imagery** – steel, iron this or that.

- He used simple **violence verbs** – 'smash' etc.

- His speeches initially took his listeners from the depths of despair and hopelessness to heights of joyous optimism – *if* his plan was followed. The formula: **induce despair – offer way out of it – reward with future-pace of 'Utopia'.**

Interestingly several political organisations are using many of Hitler's slogan tactics in their propaganda today.

Bonus appendix 8: sexual arousal and the brain.

I was going to leave neuro-science until your next book but thought I'd throw in this added extra. Would you like to know which parts of the brain are activated during human sexual arousal? No of course you don't!

- **The supramarginal gyrus.*** Involved in **empathy and bonding**, **word tone** and the **choice of word sounds (phonetic ambiguity etc.)** in general.

- **The fusiform gyrus.** Involved in processing of **colour information, face and body recognition, word recognition** – linked to basic **visual shapes** and **pre-semantic symbols** (believed linked to the human ability to read and decode the 'alphabet') and 'within-category identification' (identifying pigeons from birds in general etc. This would help people focus on feelings and states). Linked to **synaesthesia** and **hallucinations.**

- **The angular gyrus.*** (* = part of Wernicke's area.) Involved in **reading**,

semantics, complex **language comprehension and interpretation**, **metaphors** (especially spatial – 'He stepped down from his post etc.'), detection of **habitual or unexpected memory retrieval**, maths/math ability, <u>**out of body experiences,**</u> **awareness/dissociation of body** and **intentional movements, goalless default states**, left-side grapheme phoneme conversion (whether the first part of a word/sentence should be stressed – linked to dyslexia).

- <u>**The frontopolar area.**</u> Involved in strategic **memory** retrieval processes and executive function (conscious mind processes). Little understood brain region linked to limbic ('primitive' **emotional** functions). Stores abilities until needed while doing other things.

- <u>**The ventral anterior cingulate cortex.**</u> Involved in **motivation** and **will** (desire!). Linked to **learning, reward, winning and losses, error correction, expectancy of events** etc., **free will, pain** intensity, perception and **empathy.**

- **The dorsal anterior cingulate cortex.** Involved in cognitive/rational functions such as **reward anticipation, decision-making, empathy, impulse control.**

The anterior cingulate cortex is highly involved in almost all if not all hypnotic processes and responses as you will see in book 7.

Tip – use your creative intelligence to access all these parts with your specifically tailored languaging! You can now access this part at will. You are quite welcome.

Now you have had quite a hodge-podge of varying stimulations to draw upon to craft your own hypnotic spells; if you give it your all, you will find great rewards from your efforts! Wishing you are the best in weaving your hypno-magic! Quite a word horde for your efforts!

OUT NOW!

Look out for my 7th book – **'_Escaping cultural hypnosis!_'** It's totally original and FASCINATING! Amongst a whole host of other goodies, we will also discuss what neuroscience can tell us about hypnosis, what 'snapping' and information disease is and...Well I can't give too much away. There's nothing out there like it trust me Tonto!!! Keep your eyes peeled and your powder dry! For those dear readers that have hung in thus far, your kind words and support are appreciated more than you know; I thank you sincerely: **it's only going to get *JUICIER!* I promise you...**

;)

Yours,

The Rogue Hypnotist. July 2014.

Postcript:

I would like to thank Leesa in the UK for letting me know she saved a child's life with the info she gleaned from my books. You are a star! You have used the knowledge in just the right way – well done! I smiled all day after reading your inspiring comments.

17311745R00452

Printed in Great Britain
by Amazon